Revelation
Lessons from the Last Lap Home

Gordon Rumble

authorHOUSE®

AuthorHouse™
1663 Liberty Drive
Bloomington, IN 47403
www.authorhouse.com
Phone: 1-800-839-8640

First published by AuthorHouse   5/20/2010

ISBN: 978-1-4520-0724-3 (e)
ISBN: 978-1-4520-0723-6 (sc)
ISBN: 978-1-4520-0722-9 (hc)

Library of Congress Control Number: 2010904358

Printed in the United States of America
Bloomington, Indiana

This book is printed on acid-free paper.

PREFACE:

One of the best ways to motivate and strengthen the faith of believers is to tell them what is going to happen in the future! And that is the very thing that our Lord does for us in the final book of the Bible.....the Book of the Revelation!

Revelation deals with the promised return of our Savior! The graphic pictures that the Apostle John paints as he writes this book is more than sufficient to strike terror in the thoughts of any person who has never settled Eternity in their hearts! These same pictures, offer great incentive for the faithful believer in Christ to press on even in the times of hardship and trials. John also shows us that there can be unparalleled joy and hope in knowing that the imminent return of the Lord could be "at any moment!"

As we embark on our journey through the book of Revelation, you will be blessed because this book alone has a unique promise attached to it....."You will receive a blessing by reading it!" **Revelation 1:3 "Blessed is he that reads and hears the words of this prophecy, and keeps the things that are written therein..."**

The book of Revelation has been an incredible blessing to preach from for two years. One of its many beauties is that it came with its own outline for us in Chapter One, verse nineteen. In this passage Jesus tells John to write: **"The things that thou *HAST* seen, the things which *ARE*, and the things that shall be *HEREAFTER!*"**

I do believe that the contextual emphasis of this wonderful book is this. Jesus Christ is on the throne, He is in total control, and He is coming soon! Every thing is on an exact schedule, everything is going according to His plan, and this Bridegroom can hardly wait to see His Bride! This is the message of Revelation. The King of Kings is in command. The Lion of the tribe of Judah has prevailed. And yes, oh yes, HE IS ON HIS WAY!!! Our prayer today and tomorrow will remain the same, "Even so, come Lord Jesus!"

"Look up, lift up your heads, for your redemption draws nigh!"

This Book is dedicated to:

*My lovely wife Heidi, my three wonderful children, and my
6 beautiful grandchildren*

Bibliography: Works Consulted: John Courson, David Jeremiah, John MacArthur, Phillips, Tozer, Warren Weirsbe, Preacher's Homiletic, Basic Stages in the Book of Ages, Notes from Grandpa Rumble, Charts from Grandpa King, Handfuls of Purpose, Pentecost, Uncle Roger Gish, www.markpetersphoto.net

Contents

REVELATION 1:1-6

What An Incredible Future!

Reading of Revelation 1:1-6

The Revelation of Jesus Christ, which God gave unto him, to show unto his servants things which must shortly come to past; and he sent and signified it by his angel unto his servant John: Who bare record of the Word of God, and the testimony of Jesus Christ, and of all things that he saw. Blessed is he that readeth, and they that hear the words of this prophecy, and keep those things, which are written therein: For the time is at hand. John, to the seven churches which are in Asia: Grace be unto you and peace from Him which is, and which was, and which is to come; and from the seven Spirits which are before His throne; and from Jesus Christ who is the faithful witness, and the first begotten of the dead, and the prince of the kings of the earth. Unto him that loved us and washed us from our sins in His own blood, and hath made us kings and priest unto God and His Father; to Him be glory and dominion forever and ever. Amen.

We are beginning on an incredible journey together that is going to take some time! I want to say up front that I am excited about this book. I have been reading through the book of Revelation for some time now. Thirty years to be exact! It takes exactly forty nine minutes to read this book and that is just casual reading. Yet, if you pause and get your pencil out, you can add many awesome hours and minutes to that. But it does not take very long to read the book of Revelation. It is fascinating to read through the book. It is just twenty two chapters, and it's the last book that God enabled a man to write being inspired by the spirit of God, and it is so exciting!

Now I am going to tell you that I am not going to make it through the first chapter today, so we are probably looking at the first six or seven verses. I would like to title each message and I am going to do that right now. If I would have a title to the first chapter, I would call it, "**What an Incredible Future!**"

This may not even sound like some of the things we are going to talk about today, because we are going to walk through an introduction. I can say though, **what an incredible future!** God is going to reveal some things that are going to happen yet in the future even to us from the book of Revelation! And the obvious question that came to me a couple weeks ago as I began to jot some notes down, was this, How does one ever introduce a book like Revelation? Do you read a portion of Daniel? Do you read Zechariah? Do you read Isaiah? Do you read the Olivet Discourse? Do you read portions of the Epistles? Do you read the different gospels? What do you read, what do you share, in the introduction to this book? The more I thought about that, I did come to one conclusion. I don't have to give an introduction to the book of Revelation! Why? Because the Holy Spirit through a man called John the Apostle gave us a perfect introduction in the first three verses in chapter One. So I would like to read the first three verses of the book of Revelation and this will be an introduction for this book.

John writes:

The Revelation of Jesus Christ, which God gave unto him, to show unto his servants things which must shortly come to past; and he sent and signified it by his angel unto his servant John: Who bare record of the Word of God, and the testimony of Jesus Christ, and of all things that he saw. Blessed is he that readeth, and they that hear the words of this prophecy, and keep those things which are written therein: For the time is at hand.

That is the introduction to the book of Revelation. And not only that, John gives us a wonderful outline of the whole book as you turn to verse 1:19.....

Write the things which thou hast seen, and the things which are, and the things which shall be hereafter.

This is an outline of the book of Revelation and we will expand on it as we walk through the book. So, today as we begin, we have been given the introduction. And I believe that everything we will share together for the next two, or possibly three years will be traced back to those verses. Yet, before the Lord comes, and maybe He will before we are done, I am very thrilled to walk with you through the book of Revelation.

It has been said that the book of Revelation is kind of a big riddle, wrapped in a mystery, inside of an enigma. I don't think that is a proper understanding of the book of Revelation. Some will say, "Well it is just a bunch of symbolism and imagery of beasts, conflicts, and scary things." Even though some frightening things do happen, it is because there is very explicit language in the book of Revelation. Yet, this is not a mystery and this is not an enigma! And it definitely not just a riddle wrapped in something!

I counted out in this book and there are 404 verses. You will find that 275-278 of the verses are going to be connections from what connects back to Old Testament prophecies. Yet, looking at them, there is not one of the 275 verses out of the 404 that is a direct quotation of anywhere in the Bible. We will find that out of the book of Daniel, Zechariah, and Isaiah that there are connections that we can make back to the prophecies of the book of Revelation.

I must begin with verse three, a part of this introduction that states, *"He that readeth and they that hear the words of the prophecy and those that keep those things, there is going to be a blessing for that."* But we must also suggest from this book, not only is there a blessing by reading and hearing and talking about this book, but there is a cursing that comes from anybody that tries to take away from it! That is what the Bible clearly states, it is not something we dreamed up!

This revelation of Jesus Christ in verse one shows us we are going to see a lot of visible uncovering and unveilings of our Savior! I jotted some down. Let's look at them! Faithful Witness, First Born of the dead, King of Kings, Lord of Lords, Alpha and Omega, First and the Last, Beginning and the End, the Living One, the Holy and True, the Son of God, the Amen, the Faithful Witness, the Word of God, the Root of David- and that just makes it up to the first two chapters. So as we look at the book of Revelation together there is going to be a lot of application for our daily life, but also a lot of things that point to the future.

Who is the author of the book of Revelation? Again, we don't have to try and guess who it is! Four times in the book he says who he is: he says, "I am John." So the same apostle who wrote the book of Revelation is the same disciple who wrote four other books in the New Testament. He wrote the Gospel of John, he wrote 1, 2, and 3 John, and he wrote the book of Revelation. He wrote it on an island called Patmos, in Asia Minor and it is about ten miles by six miles, and John came there as a prisoner. As he sat there on that island, possibly working in rock quarries, he had the Spirit come upon him and he wrote this fascinating book.

I would like to give you a quick hint of some of the major doctrines and themes that we will be unwrapping in this book. These are 12 that come to mind, and I will possibly add more as we go on. Some of the themes that we are going to be talking about in this book involve things from the Seven Churches. Even though John is writing to the seven churches of Asia, what he writes to those churches are things that can be applied to our daily walk. It is not to a specific man or a specific time or an era, but it is for me today in the year 2009. So thank you John, as you write to the churches! All of us are going to learn some lessons about and from the seven churches. Then we are going to talk about:

1. Christ's ultimate victory over Satan.
2. The World System (Politically, Militarily, Morally)
3. The man called the Anti-Christ
4. The Rapture of the Church
5. The Seven years of Tribulation
6. The Second Coming of Christ with 10,000 of His Saints
7. The Battle of Armageddon
8. The Second Coming of Jesus Christ
9. The Battle of Gog and Magog
10. The Great White Throne Judgment
11. The New Heaven and the New Earth
12. The Final Invitation from the Lord

These are going to be some of the highlights that we will share as we walk through this incredible book.

So as we take our journey through the book of Revelation we will try to stick as close as we can to a literal interpretation, respecting those who would look at these scriptures in a different way. Some will allegorically spiritualize sections of the text and that is their privilege. I will be taking the text verse by verse, a literal interpretation of John's writings.

So John gives us an introduction in verses 1-3, He gave us an outline in verse 19, and then I had to ask, "How do we start this journey in the right way?" So I went back into my childhood and I thought of my 8th grade teacher Mr. Illick. I learned more from Mr. Illick than I did from any of my instructors in grammar school. And what is different about Mr. Illick? Well, Mr. Illick always asked questions in class even though he was the teacher. And then he would answer them or give someone a chance to answer them. I am not going to ask you questions and say I want an answer, but I am going to ask questions by way of opening up the application in the text. So, thank you Mr. Illick, I don't know where he is today, but you were a fascinating teacher!

I am going to ask 6 questions as we begin the book of Revelation. The first one I am going to ask is this, **"What is the source of this message in Revelation?** We find that in verse one, *"the Revelation of Jesus Christ that God gave unto Him."* The source of the message was given by the Father to the Son, it was given by the Son to an angel (possibly Michael) and it was given by an angel to the apostle John on the Isle of Patmos. So the whole message is given by God the Father to the Son to an angel to John the revelator, and then on down it us the servants. *"To show unto his servants".* This is the source of the message and it is the revelation. I want to look at those two words for just a little bit. I think those two words, "the revelation" is very essential to understanding the whole book of the Revelation. There is no mistake that the Holy Spirit started this book "the revelation". The Revelation of what? The Revelation of Jesus Christ. The reason we say that is because 'the revelation' is not a hiding, it is not a covering up, not an obscuring of a book. He says this is a **revelation**, this is the **apokalupsis**, it does not say 'apokolupto' which means, "The covering", but the apokalupsis. This is not a hiding of any truth whatsoever! Christ is saying, "I am coming to give the last book of the Bible and some very basic understandings of the last DAYS of humanity. It is not a hiding at all! There is no obscuring here at all. He is going to reveal truth. I think it is absurd or ludicrous to say God would take all the Bible from Genesis to Jude and write in clarity and precision and then all of the sudden get down to the last book and he says, "okay, we are going to cover this one up, and no one will understand it, and no one will comprehend anything in it". He doesn't say that. He says this is "the revelation". I am going to uncover, I am going to give full disclosure, it is not vague. It is the Apokalupsis! And you know, I went back and I thought I want to find the first time this big word is used! And do you know where the first time that he uses the word 'revelation' is? He uses it for the first time when Jesus came. It took place near a temple, by a man called Simeon, as he lifted up this Christ child in Luke 2:32 and he says, *"A light of revelation to the Gentiles"*.

If you look in the Greek, it is the same thing. This is now an uncovering, we now see the visible Christ. And even though the gospels present Christ in all four gospels as a Christ that experienced humiliation, now we are going to see the revelation, the uncovering of this same Jesus in His exaltation. Just as this is a "Him Book", from the Genesis to the Revelation, it is also a **scarlet thread of redemption** about a man called Jesus! Even though he began back there as a Christ child he is now coming to the final book and it is the exaltation of Jesus! No obscuring, no hiding, it is all about Him. Yes, we find application to us His servants, but it is all **about Him.** It is not about a hiding. And I love this as old Simeon stood there, *"A light of revelation to the Gentiles."* He is now visible to man. And then He goes to Paul and Peter and uses this same word, Apokalupsis. You will see every time it refers to an individual it is always a time of total visibility. It is not a covering. And as we walk through this we are not trying to pull something back and say, "Well we can't figure this one out so lets go on to something else." We are just going to walk through it, read it, and see the revelation that God brings. It is the unveiling, the apokalupsis. Well, that is the answer to the first question, the **source of the message is from God the Father** Himself as He gives us the revelation of His Son.

The second question that I would like to ask, "**What is the promise of the message?** Well, the promise of the message is very simple. It says in verse three at the introduction, *"blessed is he that readeth and they that hear the words of this book or prophesy and keep those things which are written therein."* Now I find that very interesting. Every one of these things that it says here, he that readeth, he that heareth and he that keepeth these things, these are all in present tense for those who are reading it. So as I read the Book of Revelation it is all present tense. This is for me to look, to understand, to hear. And even though there will be prophetic utterances, it is for me today right now where I live. What an incredible future as you think about that!

Now we come to our first beatitude of the book and we are going to have seven of them. I went ahead and pulled those out and jotted them down. We have the first one here in the introduction:

"Blessed is he that readeth and they that hear the words of the prophecy and keep those things that are written therein."

Then we are going to see in *Rev. 14:13 "Blessed are the dead which die in the Lord."*

Rev. 16:15 "Blessed is he that watcheth."

Rev. 19:9 "Blessed are they which are called to the marriage supper of the lamb."

Rev. 26 "Blessed is he that hath part in the first resurrection."

Rev. 22:7 "Blessed is he that keepeth the sayings of this book."

Rev. 22:14 "Blessed are they that do his commandments."

Beatitudes of Revelation. That is the source of the message. That is the promise of the message. It is a blessing.

What is the reason for the message? I thought about different ways of answering this, but you have to come back to this simple verse. The reason for the message is simply, *"for the time is at hand." (verse 3)* I looked that word up, and we are not talking about Rolex time, we are not talking about clock time, we are not talking about a grandfather clock, but we are talking about an era or a season of time. Blessed is he that readeth. What is the reason for the message? **For the time is at hand.** He is telling all of us, he wants us to understand that there is urgency in this. The imminent return of the Savior is so near! The apostle Paul and Peter, they were all looking too! And as I looked through the word of God, I found it very incredible and fascinating when Paul says, *"the night is about gone."*

John, the revelator, before he finished third John he says, *"It is the last hour* **children."** Sit up, take notice, take watch, the day we are living in, we are living in the last hour. There is urgency to the message. He says in Hebrews, "For the day draweth near." He says in James, *"Be patient, for the coming of the Lord draweth near."* So he is saying, the time is at hand. The reason for the message is that we all might sit up, take notice, and wherever you are living right now, be ready for the return of Jesus. **The reason for the message:** The time is at hand. And I guess I would have to add with that, does he desire that the time is at hand? Does he have a desire to lift back this curtain for us to get a peek of what is going to happen? I say yes, he does. Again I pulled out four and I hope I am not doing injustice to the word of God here but here are the four I came up with.

Does God desire that I can look back, knowing that the time is at hand, and look behind the curtain, yes.

Listen, "Surely the Lord God will do nothing but reveal His secrets unto his servants". (Amos 3)

> *"But there is a God in heaven that revealeth all His secrets." (Daniel 2) "I thank thee O God the Lord of heaven and earth because thou hast hid things from the wise and prudent, but has revealed them unto the babes." (Matthew 11)*
>
> *"Unto you is given to know the mysteries of the Kingdom of God." (Luke 8)*

I might add here "Why is it that in Matthew 13 he all of a sudden started speaking in parables?" Because those that were not willing to discern spiritual things, God spoke to them in parables and they never caught on after that. I think you could even tie that into Revelation. There are people who study this book and understand this book, but a person who is not saved, the person couldn't care less about, they are always going to look at the book of Revelation as a mystery of something weird, of something evil, of something of nothing more than conflict. But God says, no, I want you to read the book because I will unveil truth.

What is the theme of the message? Well we ought to shout this one with a trumpet! The theme of the message we find in verse five, **"And from Jesus Christ who is the faithful witness." The theme of this message of this book is about Jesus Christ!**

It is not about some special church, it is not about men, it is about Jesus Christ! I guess if you wanted to break that down, it is about Jesus Christ, it says in verse five it is his past work that he did in redemption. What did he do? It says, *"The first begotten of the dead, the prince and kings of the earth, unto Him that loved us and washed us from our sins in His own blood."* Thank you Jesus today that you didn't first wash me and then love me. No, he loved me first and then he washed me. And this is a picture of the theme of the message of Jesus Christ, the past work of his redemption. But he doesn't leave us hanging there, he says in verse *six, "The present work and hath made us kings and priest unto God, to him be glory and dominion forever and ever."* He works in the life of the believer the present work of sanctification. And he doesn't leave us hanging there. The redemptive work, the sanctified work, verse seven, the glorified work, *"Behold he cometh with clouds and every eye shall see him."*

I guess that would bring us to the doxology, even though this is not the ending today. He actually gives us a doxology. **What is the doxology of the message?** Verse*six, "To him be glory and dominion forever and ever, Amen."* That is a prayer in itself. Old Elder John, the revelator. I kind of wondered as I tried to picture in my own mind this man sitting on a rock possibly trying to write down these things and God in the spirit said. " I am going to reveal some things to you, I am going to have you write a book here." And he gets into six verses and all of the sudden he says, Amen. You mean this is all there is? But he says Amen so many times through this book. **The doxology of the message.** What a proper response to what Christ has done and what he is doing and what he has promised to do with such an incredible future.

One of the last questions I want to ask today is this. Does this book, Revelation, is it really here at the end of the Bible for a reason? **And what is the circle of this message here?** The book of Revelation, the reason it is so fascinating and exciting, it completes the circle of all truths in the Bible. Now we happen to be going through Genesis, some of you are doing the same thing, and I think it is wonderful timing for me, I am blessed to be able to be looking in the book of Genesis and here we are studying the book of Revelation because everything that starts in the book of Genesis will find a circle of truth completion in the book of Revelation. That is not something that man concocted up. I am going to give you five or six of my favorite ones that we are going to look at as we go through the book. But this book of Revelation does complete the circle of Bible truths of God's message to man.

Here is the first one: Genesis shows humanity's beginning, where? In a very wonderful place called **the Garden of Eden or the Paradise.** What does the book of Revelation do as it completes the circle of truth it shows the wonderful paradise that is to come and even mentions the trees and the streams that surround it! What started back there in the book of Genesis is now going to be completed in the book of Revelation.

The second one we have: Genesis shows how human beings lost a chance to eat of the tree of life. We were reading this yesterday in our Bible study. And Revelation shows that human kind will eat of that tree in the future (Rev. 22) and will live forever. All manner of fruits at the same tree. What God started back there He never forgot about it. And all of the sudden we see it coming to life again in the book of Revelation.

Three: Genesis tells of humanity's first rebellion against God, but Revelation promises to end humanities rebellion against God. There is a promise there. God is going to step into the scene and he will end all rebellion.

Fourth: Genesis records the first murder, the first drunk, and the first rebel. But Revelation promises a city where nothing impure will ever enter in, no one who does what is shameful or deceitful, but only those whose names are written in the lambs book of life. (Rev. 21) There is not going to be the murder or the rebel or all these kind of things. The circle of truth has made its cycle and what began in perfect truth and understanding is going to find it's fulfillment in the book of Revelation.

Genesis reveals the tragic sorrow that resulted from sin, but Revelation promises that God will wipe away every tear from their eyes. (Rev. 21)

Genesis records the first death, and we all know who that was. Revelation promises that there will never ever be any more death throughout eternity. No more death, the circle of truth completed.

Genesis shows the beginning of the curse. (Genesis 3:15) Revelation shows that the curse will forever be lifted and ended.

Genesis introduces the devil for the first time as a tempter, you know where he was in the garden of Eden. (Gen. 3) Revelation shows the final doom of this man called Satan.

Genesis promises that Satan's head will be bruised, but Revelation shows that Satan's is bruised and defeated forever.

As I started thinking about those circle of truths, and we are going to bump into more later on in the book. I find that very fascinating. Every major doctrine that God started in the book of Genesis, every major doctrine will find its fulfillment and even some more explanation in the book of Revelation.

Now this is the seventh question, I just thought about this a couple days ago. **Why did God take John the Revelator?**

I think he is the only disciple that died a natural death, so why did he take this man to write the book of Revelation? Now this is strictly my opinion. As I thought about his five books that he wrote, who better to write the book of Revelation than the man that wrote the book that started the beginning? You mean John wrote Genesis? No, but he wrote a book that starts before Genesis, because he wrote **John 1:1. "In the beginning was the Word, and the Word was God and the Word was with God."**

That tells me he punched through Genesis 1, and he went on the other side of that screen and saw Jesus Christ himself *before the foundation of the world!* So John the Revelator, the same one who went through eternity on that side, is the same man that God took to the Isle of Patmos and says, "Okay, now I want you to reveal the truth, a prophecy of everything that is going to happen in the future." He continues: " The same Son that you wrote about in John 1:1, Jesus Christ on that side of creation and you saw Him exalted there, I want you to complete this book when he comes with 10,000 of his saints!"

So I find it very fitting this morning, the same man that wrote the Revelation of Jesus Christ is the same man who wrote about the beginning. This morning I say yes to the doxology of verse six. I think it is the only proper response that we can have as we think about the incredible future that waits all of us.

"And to God His Father, to Him be glory and dominion for ever and ever, Amen."

In the chapter that follows, we will be looking at the certainty of his COMING! And a vision of the glorified Christ as it gives a depiction there in the last part of chapter one. But we are looking forward to this walk together through the book, a fascinating time in the book of the Revelation of Jesus Christ!

He's Coming – Look at Him!

"Behold, He cometh with clouds; and every eye shall see Him, and they also which pierced Him: and all kindreds of the earth shall wail because of Him. Even so, Amen. I am Alpha and Omega, the beginning and the ending, saith the Lord, which is, and which was, and which is to come the Almighty. I John, who also am your brother, and companion in tribulation, and in the kingdom and patience of Jesus Christ, was in the isle that is called Patmos, for the Word of God and for the testimony of Jesus Christ. I was in the Spirit on the Lord's day, and heard behind me a great voice, as of a trumpet, Saying, I am Alpha and Omega, the first and the last: and what thou seest, write in a book, and send it unto the seven churches which are in Asia; unto Ephesus, and unto Smyrna, and unto Pergamos, and unto Thyatira, and unto Sardis, and unto Philadelphia, and unto Ladodiceia. And I turned to see the voice that spake with me. And being turned, I saw seven golden candlesticks; And in the midst of the seven candlesticks one like unto the Son of man, clothed with a garment down to the foot, and girt about the paps with a golden girdle. His head and His hairs were white like wool, as white as snow; and his eyes were as a flame of fire; and His feet like unto fine brass, as if they burned in a furnace; and his voice as the sound of many waters. And He had in His right hand seven stars: and out of His mouth went a sharp two-edged sword: and His countenance was as the sun shineth in His strength. And when I saw Him, I fell at His feet as dead. And He laid His right hand upon me, saying unto me, Fear not; I am the first and the last: I am He that liveth, and was dead; and behold, I am alive for evermore, Amen; and have the keys of hell and of death. Write the things which thou hast seen, and the things which are, and

the things which shall be hereafter; the mystery of the seven stars which thou sawest in my right hand, and the seven golden candlesticks. The seven stars are the angels of the seven churches: and the seven candlesticks which thou sawest are the seven churches." As we open up this section of the scripture, I would like to look through verses seven through twenty, probably spending most of the time on verse seven and verse eight. So don't panic, we will be on verse seven and verse eight for awhile and then I will quickly go through the description of Christ!

The first six verses that we talked about in the last chapter we mentioned **the promise**, the **purpose**, and **the theme** of the message! (Christ) It ended in a doxology in verse six where it says; *"to Him be glory and dominion forever and ever, Amen."* Now we pick up in verse seven.

"Behold He cometh with the clouds."

When an author in this country writes a best seller, you will always find that the author will write something with a climax that builds and builds. That it is not that way with our Father in heaven. He didn't take the book of Revelation and just try to build and build to get our excitement up! No, from the very first chapter he says the thrilling words, *"Behold He cometh in the clouds and every body is going to see my Son."* He said it up front and everything that takes place in the rest of the book is going to be talking about Christ and what happens when He does come. No, there is no waiting around for God the Father in heaven, for He shouts and says, *"Behold He cometh in clouds and every eye shall see Him and they which also pierced Him, and all kindreds of the earth shall wail because of Him, even so, Amen."*

I guess you could say this is a kind of preview of coming attractions in verse even and eight. Yes, the book of Revelation is about excitement and yes it is a book about joy. But the best part about it is, it is a book with a happy ending. *"Even so, come, Lord Jesus."* And we are going to find out as we continue to walk through the book that we will be reminded again and again that there is a happy ending of joy. And as we begin in 7 and 8, there is a tremendous confidence in these verses and tremendous excitement about Jesus Christ coming again!

Now notice in verse seven, it says, **"Behold"**. I looked that word up and "idio," if I am pronouncing it right, or "idio", it is used thirty times in this book of Revelation. And everytime we are going to see this word "Behold", it means we are going to stop and sit up straight, pay attention to what He is going to say. He tells John to write these things down, and He says this nine times following the "Behold". Behold sit up straight, call to attention, what I am going to say here is very important and He is going to say He is coming in the clouds. Now if you look at that in the Greek text in which this was written, that is a present tense verb, not past tense. He is saying here, He is coming! In other words, He is just about here. And as John wrote it, he was looking for him. As the Apostle Paul wrote his epistles, he was looking for him and 2000 years later it is still present tense, *"He is coming again."*

He is just about here, pay attention to this, this is the promise that he wrote in Daniel 7, *"The Son of Man is coming in the clouds."* **(Daniel 7:13) John writes right here in 1:7** *"Behold he is coming in the clouds."* And even making it more exciting to me as I was reading this, is when you just take that word out, *"He is coming."* That is a word in the Greek that is called "erkomaya". Erkomaya is the title for the messianic title of the coming Messiah, the coming one. And all the times that this is used in the book of Revelation, this is used 9 times, erkoymaya, erkomaya, erkomaya, **this is the coming one**. This is the Christ, this is the Messianic Jew that is coming again. **Erkomaya, Behold he is coming again**. All you got to do is go back to Matthew 11:2 and 3. John is standing there and they were wondering, is this really the Christ and he says, is this the coming one, is this the erkomaya? Or do we have to look for someone else and they said, "No this is the erkomaya, this is the coming one." And this same Jesus Christ that came in the incarnation is the same erkomaya that is going to be coming again in the clouds. So that is why he said, Behold, write it down John, we don't want any mistakes here, this same Jesus is coming again in the clouds with great glory. The promise is in Daniel, the promise is in Revelation. The erkomaya, he is coming again!

I want to share with you something that upset me back in February of 2002. One morning I went down and got the paper, sat down, and opened it to a very disturbing article! There were some pastors that gathered together in Stockton, California. In their meeting together it was decided that there was no significance to the second coming of Jesus Christ!! That upset me. I will tell you why that upset me. Because 1,530 verses in this Bible are all about Jesus Christ coming again! How can you have a group of men saying there is no significance in the Second Coming of Jesus Christ?

There forty six Old Testament prophets that talk about the Second Coming of Christ and only ten of them talk about His first coming! That tells me that God the Father in heaven wants every single one that reads the Bible to understand that one of the major themes in the doctrines of the Word of God is this: **"the same Christ that came to save your souls IS COMING BACK!!!"** And I don't care who meets where, and what they talk about, He is coming again! And I read the Hal Lindsey thing that came off the screen in the e-mail, and it says that the World Counsel of Churches met in Evensten, Illinois, and 90% of those pastors said He is not coming back! That is not a pastor. You want to take hope out of your life? Then you try to read through the Bible and say He is never coming again. What is the purpose of living? That is why he says in 1 Corinthians 15, ***"We would be as all men most miserable."*** If my Savior is not coming back, what is the purpose of being here? One verse out of every twenty-five verses in the New Testament signifies and talks about Jesus Christ, the Erkomaya coming back! I would say that is a lot of validity in the Bible, **He is coming back.** That is why you have to call this a HIM Book, it is all about Him. Then I got off the "mad podium,' and I thought, well that is really what the Bible says, isn't it? People doubting about His coming? And I found in 1 Peter that it does reference this! It says, in the last days, what is going to happen! In the last days, there are going to be people who meet in Stockton, California and Evensten, Illinois and they are going to stand up at their podiums and they are going to say, ***"Where is the promise of His coming***?" That is scripture. That is one of the signs that we are living in the last days, when people that profess to know God, to know Christ, are going to stand up and say, ***"come on, where is the promise of His coming***?" They just fulfilled Scripture at that statement! I say that is pretty sad when men can stand up and say He is not coming back!

You know you can talk about the major doctrines of the word of God, and you can talk about the resurrection, you can talk the incarnation, you can talk about the virgin birth, blood atonement, salvation by faith alone, but you have to add in there the **second coming.** Can you imagine, being saved and redeemed by the blood of the lamb and never interested in Him coming back?

I don't want to hurt anybody else's feelings, but Delbert Kinzie is a very good Contractor. Delbert has built very big buildings and very solid buildings. Yet, there would be no success in the building industry for Kinzie Construction if he wouldn't start with a very solid foundation. If there wasn't an undergirding, if there wasn't something there to have a solid foundation, the building would not stand! When it says he comes in the clouds with great glory, and He is coming back soon, I would say there are four things that demand the return of Jesus Christ! And if you take these four truths, it will be a solid foundation all the way through the book of Revelation.

The first thing that demands His coming is the **promise of God the Father**. He has been saying in book after book in the Bible.........He is coming back!! And the first mention of it, the promise out of God's Word Himself is in **Genesis 49:10** *"The sceptre shall not depart from Judah, nor a lawgiver between His feet until Shiloh comes."*

That is the cryptogram that is in the message, **Shiloh,** all the way through the Bible. Even though it was a place, **Shiloh** is speaking about Jesus Christ! Now why do we say that the promise of God demands that Jesus Christ comes again? Because this **Shiloh** has not returned as of yet. God says in Psalm 2,*"There is going to come a time when every knee shall bow…"* and everybody shall bow down before the king of glory someday. It hasn't happened yet. That means the promise of God says it will happen and that means it is going to happen! The Bible says in **Isaiah 9, "The government shall be upon His shoulders."** It hasn't happened yet on the planet and someday it will. That is the promise of God. And I say that this promise demands His coming. **Jeremiah 23 says, "He shall reign forever as a King."** It hasn't happened yet, but Jeremiah from the heart of God the Father said it will. It **demands** His coming.

The second pillar that demands the coming of Jesus Christ is **simply the testimony of God the Father Himself.** I would say that the words of Jesus Christ Himself demand that He comes again. Twelve hours before the death of Christ on an old Roman stick outside on a hill called Calvary, He said these words, *"I will come again."* It hasn't happened yet folks, so that means He will come again. And when Jesus says it, as far as I am concerned, that settles it. In Luke 19 He talked about a nobleman that went into a far country. Then he came back one day and there was accountability that was given to all! Jesus Christ is the one that says six times in this book, *"I come quickly."* I come quickly… I come quickly… **I come quickly…** He is not here yet, but He is coming back. **The words of Jesus Christ demands that He is coming back.**

Third pillar. **The guarantee of the Holy Spirit of God demands that He is coming back** and I read in John 16:13, *"He shall not speak of Himself,* *only glorify Jesus Christ and show you the things to come."* So that tells me that two-thirds of the New Testament that point towards the Second Coming of Jesus Christ. It is found in 1 Corinthians 1, James 1, James 5:8, Colossians 1, Colossians 3. You can walk right through the New Testament and the Holy Spirit is talking about the Second Coming of Jesus Christ. He demands that He comes again and the Holy Spirit is not going to be talking about things concerning Himself, but things concerning Jesus Christ. I find that very fascinating that as the Holy Spirit inspired writers to write, again and again and again, that He told them to write about the second coming! That is the three pillars. Before I mention the fourth one, I just want to say this: The credibility of the trinity is at stake if He doesn't come. That means He is coming! Because God the Father, and God the Son, and God the Holy Spirit has announced for thousands of years, He is coming again! He is coming again! He is coming again! And the credibility of the creator of the universe is at stake if he doesn't come! YES, He is coming!

Who is the fourth pillar? I only want to mention this because I think that it is a part of the Word of God. There is a fourth promise and I think that it demands the return of our Savior and it is **YOU!** You and I are the fourth pillar! And why do I say that? Because I think the Holy Spirit is in all of us, and He reigns in our life. The expectations and the confidence and the hope in my breast today demands the Second Coming of Jesus Christ. That is why He said in 1 Corinthians 15, *"**We would be of all men most miserable.**"* If we didn't have the hope and the promise of Jesus Christ. And so I think that the expectations of the saints today demand the coming of Christ!

I remember grandpa John King encouraged us to memorize Titus 2. And so some of us grandkids- we memorized Titus 2. And the reason we did that was because he said in Titus 2, **you will never be blue.** Yes, I realize you can memorize things but still get blue. But he said the reason is because you can camp on verse twelve or thirteen, and these verses bring great comfort to the believer! Notice the words of the text: ***"… for the grace of God that bringeth salvation hath appeared to all men teaching us that denying ungodliness and worldly lust we should live our lives righteously, soberly, and Godly in this present world looking for the blessed hope and the glorious appearing of the great God and Savior Jesus Christ who gave Himself for us that He might redeem us and purify unto Himself a peculiar people zealous of good works. These*** *things I speak and exhort and rebuke with all authority, let no man despise you."*

Go back to verse thirteen, where it says, "*the blessed hope, the rapture, and the glorious appearing of the great God and Savior Jesus Christ*", the Second Coming. Make no mistake about it, He is coming back! That is the hope that we have as saints in the body of Christ, He is coming again. I think that is a great text when we talk about the rapture and revelation. One is a hope and one is a revelation. The HOPE is the imminent return of Christ, the REVELATION is when every eye shall see Him!

As far as I am concerned verses seven and eight settles it. It is not what I think or what man's opinion is when he says, "*I am Alpha and Omega… I am coming back in the clouds,*" as far as I am concerned that settles it, He is coming again. I say Hallelujah to that. He is coming back. Well, how is He coming back? It says here in verse seven that he is going to come in the clouds. I think that is just saying that He is coming with the brilliant light as God's presence. And it is kind of interesting that it says that every eye shall see Him.

You see at the incarnation, the birth of Christ, who saw Him? The shepherds. And then at the transfiguration who saw Him? Peter, James, and John. But down here in Revelation chapter 1:7-8 who is going to see Him? Every eyeball on the planet. "*Every eye shall see Him.*" Not half, not two-thirds, EVERY EYE SHALL SEE HIM! Those who pierced Him, all kindreds of the earth shall wail because of Him. That is talking about every tribe, every nation, everybody who put Him to death, whoever it is. Every eye shall witness the return of our Savior. It is amazing! Some will wail because they will realize their sin and there is not going to be any repentance on their part. When He is done it is just like He is saying yes, yes, Yes! "*Even so, Amen.*"

Look for a moment at verse eight. I guess I would like to call this His **declaration**. In my Bible it is written in red, so that means that according to those who translated this Bible and put this together, everything in red is where Christ is speaking. He says, "*I am Alpha and Omega, the Beginning and the Ending, saith the Lord, which is, which was, and which is to come the Almighty.*" I had to think about that for awhile. What is He simply saying here? Just take verse eight by itself, what is He saying? He is simply saying, **Look, I am in charge. I am the Lord speaking here, I am Alpha and Omega, I am in charge. I have this thing in control.**" In fact if you want to dig a little deeper with me now, we will consider Christ's three great attributes. The first one he says, "*I am the Beginning and the Ending of the Alphabet.*" That is just saying He is omniscience, He is all knowledge. "*I am Alpha and Omega.*" That is the beginning and the ending of the Greek alphabet. All knowledge belongs to me. I understand everything. You can't find anything out of context of my knowledge as the Son of God. I am Alpha and Omega, I am the supreme sovereign alphabet. Nothing is outside of my scope of understanding. Now you think, how many letters are in our alphabet, yes, there are twenty-six. Do you know what you can do with twenty-six letters? I would say it is pretty amazing. You can take twenty-six simple letters and as you arrange them all around and get them all into the English language and think about the endless combination to convey all kind of knowledge. I would say that is pretty phenomenal. Twenty-six simple things, and then you go into the Chinese language and they have a bunch of sticks put together and then you go into another language and they have all these droopy things and yet God said, 'I am Alpha and Omega." I've got all that in a box, I understand all of that. I understand it all.

And then he also says, "*Is, was and is to come.*" What is He talking about there? It is the omnipresence of God. He is everywhere present. There is no place in the universe, outside the universe, inside the earth, He is everywhere present. He understands everything, He has all knowledge and control and He is open-ended. In other words He is everywhere at all time. That is just one of His attributes. It is a signature of the one who is coming again. But He doesn't leave us there. He says at the bottom, "*the almighty.*" The omnipotent, all three of them. And this is the one who is coming in the clouds. It says in the Bible that all power belongs unto God. In another place it says, "*Twice have I spoken or heard this, all power belongs unto God.*" He has all knowledge. He is everywhere present. And He is all-powerful. What a declaration!

And again I feel just like John there. It is just like he's getting his pen and just about breaking the lead here again. The Almighty, the one that Is, the one that Was, the one that Is to come and he breaks his lead and sharpens it again and He is… and he just goes on and on… I would have loved to have been there on the Isle of Patmos with this man John… and I… well, that is just my imagination, but I believe he had papers out there and he was breaking lead right and left. Yes! Yes! And he would write that down and make copies of it to make sure that nobody misunderstood it. Because

God the Father says to write it down and you write it down, and get it right. And here He is, all knowledge, everywhere present, the Almighty one!

I then really love the way he says in verse 9, **"I John, who am also your brother!** I am here on this island folks because the Word of God that I spread and the testimony that I stood up, is for Jesus Christ." That is why he was on the island. He wasn't there because it was secluded and he could write a little better. He was there because he stood up for the word of God and the testimony of Jesus Christ. And He said, **"I was in the spirit on the Lord's day (possibly Sunday) and heard behind me a great voice as of a trumpet."** Now this is kind of amazing as we think about the description here. Again, we have Christ speaking and we are going to open this up later in chapter's 2 and 3 so we will just read it here. Jesus is speaking and he says again, **"I am Alpha and Omega, the First and the Last, and what you see John, I want you to write in a book and send it to the seven churches which are in Asia, Ephesus, and unto Smyrna, and unto Pergamos, and unto Thyatira, and unto Sardis, and unto Philadelphia, and unto Ladodiceia."** I want you to send one letter to all the churches; it is all going to say the same thing. And they are going to get the message when they get this letter.

So John writes this down and he said, **"And I turned to see the voice that spoke with me. And being turned, I saw seven golden candlesticks; And in the midst of the seven candlesticks one like unto the Son of man, clothed with a garment down to the foot, and girt about the pap's with a golden girdle."** And when I read that, it doesn't sound that attractive. One that looked like the Son of Man, he is clothed with this long garment clear down to his feet, it just looks like a long dress or robe, and then he is gird about the pap's with a golden girdle and that doesn't sound that attractive. But if you look back in Ezekial and Exodus and Leviticus, I think it is telling us something here. What is he doing here? He is trying to describe in his own way as he looks up into the heavens what he sees! All of the sudden he turns around and he sees Christ in the midst of these churches. That is what he is saying here. He says, I turned and I seen this voice in the midst of the candlesticks, which would be the churches, and He looked like the Son of Man and this is what He looked like. So we have a picture of Christ standing in the midst of the seven churches. So what is he saying here? Number one, verse 13, I believe that he is saying, this same Jesus who you see in the midst of the churches is the Jesus that empowers the churches. Why do we say that? Because he says in the gospels, "*Where* *two or three are gathered together, there I am in the midst of them."* And this same Jesus, it says He is standing here in the midst of the churches. Doesn't that sound like Hebrews 13, *"Low I am with you always."* He is not outside the church. He is standing right in the midst of the seven churches, which is a depiction of the chosen children in the body of Christ.

And folks today, He is in the midst of all of us. He is empowering us today. He is empowering His church. We are not talking about worshiping some well-meaning martyr or well-meaning man who died as a hero. We are talking about the risen Christ. That is who is in the midst of the churches. But he doesn't leave it there. I believe the reason he wrote verse 13 also is because when he says that he is dressed with this robe and paps about the girdle and all that. I think he is saying, look, that same one who is empowering the church is the High Priest. That means He is interceding for us today. He is not only our advocate today, but he is interceding for us.

We live in Turlock, California. If my house is burning right now, my neighbors or somebody will call the Fire Department. What happens? The Fire Department will get the call and they will go to my house. As it is being burnt they are interceding for me, and I am not even there. And I don't even know it is happening. Because you know he is not only our advocate, which is when we call upon Him, but also today He is interceding on our behalf when we don't even call on Him. There are times when Christ is interceding on the right hand of the Father today and you may have problems and troubles in your life and the Lord Jesus Christ is interceding as the great High Priest on our behalf. Now I hope my house is not burning, but if it is, somebody is doing intercession for me on my behalf and I am not even there. He is interceding where ever you go in your life and your walk today, because he is the High Priest empowering His church. Activity on our behalf today and promised activity for the years to come!

Verse 14. *"His head and His hairs were white like wool, as white as snow; and his eyes were as a flame of fire; and His feet like unto fine brass,"* What is he saying here? He not only empowers His church, He not only intercedes for us, but He also what? He is purifying His church. White as wool. And everytime the Bible talks about it in the Old Testament or in the New Testament, it is always talking about the chastening and the purifying of His church. He wants us to have continued fellowship. We have the relationship because of Jesus Christ on the cross but He wants us to have the continued walk and the fellowship. And when I get out of focus and out of wack and I sin, I kind of lose that close communion with Him. So what does He do? He chastens me. Not because I am a bastard, but because the Bible says I am His son. He chastens those who He loves and He purifies. Why? Because He wants to present to His father a chase virgin, blameless, above reproach, without spot, without wrinkle. That is what He is doing in the midst of the churches and He is purifying His body. And as I looked at that a little closer, I thought, Wow! Like Father, like Son. Here we have a picture of Jesus Christ, this is talking about Him right here. And I went back in my Bible to Daniel 7:9 and I read these words, "*The ancient of days did sit, whose garment was white as snow, and the hairs of his head was pure like wool and his wheels where as a burning fire.*" That is talking about the ancient of days, God the Father. Like Father, like Son. Purifying His church, the attributes of my Savior.

And He doesn't leave us there. You can look in verses 15 and 16 and it says, " *and his voice as the sound of many waters. And He had in His right hand seven stars: and out of His mouth went* a sharp two-edged sword: and His countenance was as the sun shineth in His strength." What is He saying? He is saying, I not only empower you, I not only intercede for you everyday, I not only purify and chasten you because of my tremendous love for you, but He says I am also speaking the truth to the church and I want you to stay with the truth of the word of God. A sharp two-edged sword. You will find no place in the Bible that it ever says that the church or the body of Christ ever produces the Bible. In fact he says later on, you want to try it? You go ahead and try to add something to the Bible and I am going to take care of you really good! I will blot your name out! The church is not to produce the Bible. No! The church is to be subject to the word of God! He is saying this. **We are to be subject and to love the Word of God. He says, I am in charge here, I control the church and you only follow what the Word of God says. I say Hallelujah to that.**

Then He does something very interesting and John saw this when he looks at this picture of Christ. Verse 17. "*And when I saw Him, I fell at His feet as dead. And He laid His right hand upon me, saying unto me, Fear not; I am the first and the last: I am He that liveth, and was dead; and behold, I am alive for evermore, Amen; and have the keys of hell and of death. Write the things which thou hast seen, and the things which are*(chapter 2-3)*, and the things which shall* be *hereafter*(chapter 4-22)." Can you imagine? Here he is on the Isle of Patmos, he just wrote the declaration of what Christ looks like and when he saw Him, John just falls on his feet as if he was dead, and as he lays there he feels his right hand on his shoulder!

I say that is kind of a ditto of what happened to Him in Matthew 17. Isn't that what happened on the Mount of Transfiguration? They saw this glorified Christ and they fell down and they felt the right hand on their shoulders. And here we are on the Isle of Patmos in chapter 1 as he is beginning to write and he falls down as dead and the right hand of Christ comes down on his shoulder and he says, *"you don't have to fear."* I say that is rather amazing because the right hand of the Word of God is always a depiction of strength. Sometimes of judgement and also a picture of the comfort of the Savior. "John, you don't have to fear because I am the one that lives and I am the one who was dead, but I am now alive forever more. And all I am asking is to remember that I have the keys to hell and to death, and as you write this book, get that message out to the churches! And I can just see John wetting his pencil, sharpening it one more time and getting everything exact and probably praying at the same time. **"Oh God, thank you for this opportunity and make sure I get it all right!"**

One of the thrills that I got out of chapter one, is just the simple fact that this same Jesus that left heaven in humiliation, **this same Jesus is coming back someday in exaltation and every eye shall see Him.** This same Jesus that left heaven to be killed on a cross is the same Jesus that is going to come back someday and he is going to kill those who reject Him forever. This same Jesus that left heaven to serve in humiliation (Phil. 2) is the same Jesus who will come back someday in His exaltation and we will serve Him! This is the same Jesus that came from heaven to offer grace, free grace to fallen man, is the same Jesus that will come back someday in His exaltation and demand justice for those who reject Him. This same Jesus that came from heaven (Luke 19:10) to seek and save that which was lost. This same Jesus is going to come back and search and destroy those that don't like Him or love Him. And that is just the hint in chapter one.

So, already we have learned about the uncovering of Jesus Christ. Already in chapter 1, we have seen Jesus, the Christ, the Faithful Witness, the Alpha and Omega, the First and the Last, the Beginning and the Ending, the Almighty, the Son of Man, the one who comes in clouds, the one who loved us and washed us, is He that lives and was dead and is alive for evermore. This is just the beginning. Don't ever try to tell me this is not about Jesus, and don't tell me that He is not coming again you skeptics in Stockton, California! He is coming again and it may be really soon, and I say Hallelujah, even so come Lord Jesus!

REVELATION 2:1-7

Ephesus
Is the Honeymoon Over?

"To the angel of the church of Ephesus write; These things saith he that holdeth the seven stars in his right hand, who walketh in the midst of the seven golden candlesticks; I know thy works, and thy labor, and thy patience, and how thou canst not bear them which are evil: and thou hast tried them which say they are apostles, and are not, and hast found them liars: And hast borne, and hast patience, and for my name's sake hast labored, and hast not fainted. Nevertheless I have somewhat against thee, because thou hast left thy first love. Remember therefore from whence thou art fallen, and repent, and do the first works; or else I will come unto thee quickly, and will remove thy candlestick out of his place, except thou repent. But this thou hast, that thou hatest the deeds of the Nicolaitans, which I also hate. He that hath an ear, let him hear what the Spirit saith unto the churches; To him that overcometh will I give to eat the tree of life, which is in the midst of the paradise of God."

Revelation 2:1-7

We are continuing our walk through the book of Revelation. We will take the message today out of the second chapter verses one through seven. I would entitle this message: **Is the Honeymoon Over?**

I forgot to check with my father-in-law, but I remember when I was desperately pursuing a young lady, his daughter, by the name of Heidi. I would meet with Ed (dad) at the City Hall. Many times we would go out to get a bite of lunch together. And I remember him telling me one time that there was a couple at the City Hall that dated for seven years. They dated for seven years and then a year or so into the marriage things kind of fell apart and the whispers circulated in City Hall, **"Is the honeymoon over?"**

I am thinking about two giant corporations a few years back here in America that decided to pool their finances and their corporations together. They finally managed the merger. Even though there was a lot of concern about the merger, they did show a profit the first year! Yet, in the third year all of the sudden they declared bankruptcy and the Wall Street Journal asked**, "Is the honeymoon over?"**

I am thinking about a young man who was 23 years old who went into graduate school. He graduated at the top of his class with honors. He was rewarded with a job that was going to pay him $400,000 his very first year. Things went good for six months, but by the seventh month the job was over and he bailed out! The people in the office begin the whispers**, "Is the Honeymoon over?"**

I am thinking about a young man, an individual of 17 years old who gave his heart to Christ. He celebrated it in Christian baptism. He joined a church and began a walk with Christ full of enthusiasm, a passion, and a zeal for the Lord. Then all of the sudden because of some private sin and private problems, he bailed out. He told his close friends, "Christianity doesn't work for me anymore." And they asked,

"Is the honeymoon over?"

We are going to look at a church today that is going to give a lesson not only to this church but to us as individuals, a lesson to any married couple, and you can ask yourself the question,

"Is the honeymoon over?"

All seven churches that John writes to here get the letter and they get the message. All seven churches begin with this statement, *"I know your works."* Every single church is going to get this statement. All seven churches are going to get the promise, *"he that overcometh."* There is a reward for you. All seven churches are going to get a same conclusion, if you have an ear I want you to pay attention because what I am saying to you is for you! You as a church, you as an individual, and you as a family, this message is to you! All seven churches had a personal application that went right down into the heart of everyone that attended that church.

All seven churches represent a development of every age that we have lived in for 2000 years. All seven churches begin with an attribute that Christ had in the first chapter. He had seven attributes in the first chapter; every church gets one of them. The one here in Ephesus gets the one where it says, "*He is holding the seven stars in His right hand who walks in the midst of the seven churches or the seven golden candlesticks.*"

As I began to look at this church, there are three things that jumped out that need to be mentioned before we begin to look at the verses. Here is a church called Ephesus, a church that reminds us of a love that was so right that went so wrong. And when we say a love so right, here is a church if anyone had an advantage, it is the church at Ephesus. A love so right that went so wrong in 45 years time! The Apostle Paul himself was there for 3 years. He was the one who got it started! Timothy then took over as the pastor. Apollos preached there. Priscilla and Aquila was a part of the body of believers there. John himself was the old pastor there before he was chained and took to the Isle of Patmos and wrote this letter.

This church had a real advantage! They had tremendous leadership. But it is a church that reminds us of something that was so right and all of the sudden it turned so wrong. It is a church that reminds us of total faithfulness as far as the deeds being done in the church, but they had one fatal flaw that will undermine any church, **no love and passion any more for Christ!** A church that reminds us; okay, you have the activity, you have programs, you have things you are doing, fine…… But if you don't have a passion for Christ and you don't keep Him first, you have a weakness like a cancer that will destroy your church!

I would like to break these seven verses down into four areas. The first area that we are going to look at today is going to be the area which I call: **The wonderful compliment.** And as you look at these compliments in verses two and three it is going to be followed by a "nevertheless" in verse four. I am going to call that: **The terrible complaint.** You have a wonderful compliment followed by a terrible complaint, followed in verse five by a: **Listen to me command.** Then he ends with a **challenge.** So we would like to look at those four areas today. You have **a Compliment, a Complaint, a Command, and a Challenge. A challenge that will reach down to the year 2009.**

"*Unto the angel of the church of Ephesus write, these things that saith He that holdeth the seven stars.*" This is about the seven leaders or the seven people that are controlling the churches. I've got you in authority in my hand, Christ says. "*Who walketh in the midst of the seven golden candlesticks.*" And he tells us what the seven candlesticks are, "*they are the seven churches.*"

So here you have in verse one a picture of Christ walking in authority, keeping the men that are in charge of the church in His hand. He is walking amongst the seven churches and the seven golden candlesticks. Now this church at Ephesus was a literal church. You can say I don't need four walls and a pastor or preacher. Well we say, yes you do! Not maybe the pastor or preacher, but you need to worship. There is a movement today that says, well I can sit by my bed, and you can, but you will be called a "bed-side Baptist". You can do that and there are people who do. But there is something that is very rewarding as Christ talks to the churches and puts His sanction on it as He writes to churches. Hebrews even comes along and says, *"Not forsaking the assembling of yourselves together."* There is a reward for the fellowship and body of believers who come together in worship! It is not about the four walls and it is not about the preacher, it is about HIM. The reward for the body of Christ is to come together.

So the church of Ephesus was a literal church. I would like to say it was probably the biggest and the best thing in town! Because the church at Ephesus, who was once known in Ephesians 1:5, for its tremendous love for God, now all of the sudden it seems to be slipping away. That is the warning he is going to give. But it was a literal church. It was a church that was built in the city near Ephesus, a big city, and 400,000 people lived there, at the head waters of the Kyster River. It was not too far from the seventh wonder of the world, which is the temple of Diana. And here was a building that if you would have walked to it, it would be amazing to see a temple like this. It was a temple of prostitutes and criminals and a goddess of fertility. Here you have a building of pillars it says, as high as a power line ! (95 ft .high) 127 awesome pillars to support the building, a building consisting of 93,000 square feet. (That is over 2 acres under roof.) And people would come from all over the world to go there and visit the sight! A lot of them were just attracted to the prostitutes. A lot of them were just attracted to the activity that went on there. And all kinds of terrible things and deeds were done in this attractive cesspool! It was also considered the bank of Asia, so nobody was going to rob this **temple.** Thousands and millions of people would come to this center at Ephesus and located nearby was the church of Ephesus.

Now notice something here as we think about this **compliment.** Let's think about John for a moment. Here he is on the Isle of Patmos and he takes his pencil out and he is ready to write. And the Lord says, *"Okay now, I am standing here in the midst of all of these churches and I want you to write a letter to the church that you were pastoring. And John you were taken away from that church because of your testimony for me, but here you* *are on an island., Now write this compliment to the church that you were the Pastor of!."*

And I can see the smile that comes on the face of this man! WHY? Because think, when you get this kind of a compliment, that is the kind of church I would have liked to have been a part of. More so than any of the other seven churches. I don't know why this one was first. I think it is because they did begin with love. I also think this was the church that started the satellite churches of the other six. And here you have this compliment. Look at it in verse two, (now this is not some deacon or pastor saying this, this is Christ himself).

He says, **"I know your works, I know your labor, I know your patience, and how you can not bear them which are evil, I know that you have tried them that say they are apostles and are not". (In other words, there are people that come into your church who say, I am an apostle and you try them and you look right through and you see that they are not, they are fakes) "and have found them liars, and you have borne and have had patience for my sake, you have labored and you have never fainted."**

I would have to say that is a pretty phenomenal set of criteria for a rewarding, dynamic church! This is Jesus himself saying this. He is saying, *you are dynamic, you are doing everything, you are denouncing sin, you are alive, you are thriving and you are going out into the community, you are decerning, you have great things going on, and you are patient and persistent.*

How do you get any better than that? Now we have all heard of the good news, bad news comedies. And there is a new one out now called the **"Bad News, Worst News"**. I think David Jeremiah has this on one of his tapes about 'Laughter the Best Medicine." Look at the **Bad News and Worst News.**

A man called Bob comes up to an individual and says, "I've got some bad news and I've got worst news. " Bill says, "Oh I will take the bad news first." Bob says, "Well, the bad news is, we have looked here at your sheet from the doctor and you are going to die in three days." And Bill says, "How can anything be worst than that? What is the worst news?" And Bob says, "Well, the worst news is, we have been looking for you for three days." **Bad News, Worst News.**

Now here is a church that gets good news but it is also going to get bad news. But what a compliment this church gets! I would love to have that kind of thing said about this church. I think if the Lord looked down, I think He could say a lot of these things today in many churches. There are people here that persevere, they have patience, they resist sin, and they are disciplined when they are wrong. There are those here that try to critically examine things that are in error, and people here who do not faint. I can see people here that are fulfilling Galatians 6:9, they are not weary in well doing. And these are compliments. I also was mused, can you imagine having an annual report that would go something like this:

"Annual Report. New members. None. Baptisms. None. Sunday School Classes. None. Gift to the Missions and Outreach. None. Prayer meetings together. None."

And then at the end of this report it said it was signed by an elderly deacon that wrote these words. **"Brethren pray for us that we would remain faithful until the end."** I mean that is sick. You could never say this about the church at Ephesus. Because the church at Ephesus if you read verses 2 and 3, they are probably going to bring smiles and enthusiasm! YES, we are doing things right! And Jesus Christ himself is giving us this compliment. Yes, we do persevere. Yes there are members here that are very patient and never weary. Yes there are all kinds of programs that we have going in this church! This is Christ speaking this.

Then as you jump to verse six, he even gives them another compliment. He says, *Because you don't even like the things that are going on with the Nicalatians."* Then he says, *"by the way, I hate that stuff too."* **This is a compliment to the church at Ephesus.**

What is he saying? Now there are all kinds of things that you could read on this subject but I would like to narrow it down to this truth. In fact all three churches had some involvement with the Nicolaitans. The Ephesian church hears the words, **" You hate them just like I do!"** It is a compliment to them. But the church or the people of the Nicolaitans, if you break down the word itself, tells you what it means. Nico means "conqueror". Laos or latians means, "The people of the laity.

There was a deacon back in Acts 6 by the name of Nicholas that started this sect and he completely domineered and conquered these people like a bishop or a priest. He was in charge of them and he ruled them to the point that he said, "There is a difference between that which is spiritual and that which is physical." "We can do anything we want in the physical realm or sexual perversion" and they did. This is nothing more than blatant heresy! And the deeds of the Nicolatians were that. They had men that would come in and control a church, and they had to do exactly what they ordered! You can see that later on in Catholicism, Mormonism, and other Eastern Religions! Yet Christ steps in and tells this church, "You spotted that, you didn't allow that to happen. You didn't see a big break down between the clergy and you kept things on an even keel. And you hated that and I compliment you for that" Now if a person could just stop here at verses two, three, and verse six, you would say EVERTHING IS GREAT! We got everything right. Christ stood in our midst. He says we have great labor, we have great works, tremendous patience, we are resisting that which is evil, we don't allow people to creep in and lead us astray and we are doing it right! YES!

But when you come to verse four, you read this big word that says *"Nevertheless.".* And as John penned this word, **nevertheless**, I can see this pastor's heart begin to sink. Here is Christ giving everything they had worked for in this tremendous church at Ephesus and all of the sudden Jesus standing there, he says, "Okay John pen this word, it is called, **'nevertheless'**."

I have "Nevertheless something against you because you have left your first love." This is the complaint. The compliment was tremendous, but the complaint is severe. He didn't say you **lost** your first love here, he said you **'left'** your first love. This is not somebody, an outside group coming in and trying to survey! This is the x-ray vision of the Lord himself saying the fatal flaw in your forty years, **the honeymoon is over**! You don't have a passion for me anymore. You have lost your love for God, you have lost your love for me! Which comes down to this truth….. you really don't love each other like you should and obviously you are not going to love the people of the world!

The compliment was that at one time they did love Him! And then all of the sudden they had no passion or love for the Lord and everything changed! There is something we need to really think about as we think about this **complaint.** We need to think about it as it relates to this church. We need to think about it as it relates to our marriages. We need to think about it even in a business setting. We need to really think about it!

You can stand visibly and you can stand verbally and say everything and do everything right. And yet, if you don't have the passion of the Lord in your heart, then you are just playing games! You see, love is the motor in the individual that drives that individual in the right way! And if I take love and a passion out of my heart for Jesus Christ and I do not keep Him NUMBER 1, then I will just play church. He is saying here, " You don't have any love for me anymore!" And any time a human heart says no more Jesus, then that human heart will always grow cold. And anytime a human heart says, "Okay no more room for Jesus", then that human heart will always ache. Anytime a human heart says, "no more Jesus", then that human heart will always go dry. Because God himself through Christ will always be examining us, and if I lose my passion and love for Christ, I am still a furnace- but I don't have any fire, and that is **tragedy**. Can you imagine a perfect organization, thriving growth, skillful and dynamic activities, relentless energy of service, hated and rebuked sin, effective community penetration. They looked the part but they **had fallen out of love with Jesus Christ**.

Take a snapshot of the church. Take a snapshot of your life. Take a snapshot of your heart. If you take a snapshot of Ephesus, you can just see a church of purity. But if you get alittle closer and you zero in, there is no passion there anymore. If you take a snapshot of Ephesus you could just see a church of tremendous labor. But no more love. If you take a snapshot of Ephesus you would see duty and service, but you would see no more real devotion and no more real sacrifice or spirit for Christ. I think as he writes here, we should think about the complaint for all of us.

Because if the love of Jesus Christ begins to erode in my heart and my life, it will begin to decay! How do you share the gospel with somebody if you don't even love Him yourself? I will tell you exactly what may happen! You begin to talk about your thing, your program, your church, or whatever, and they never get the message. And I have had people come to my door and they want to tell me about their church and their programs and how they look at prophecy and all of these things, **but what about Jesus?** What about the trinity? What about this and what about that... but no, that is not what we are talking about. Slam the door... no don't do that... tell them... well never mind. You let the Lord say how you answer those questions. Here we have **the complaint.** They left their first love and that was the decision and choice of these people's hearts. I just tremble when I think about my life and my heart. I can look back in 1967 on the 23rd of August when thirty-two of us celebrated that a wonderful passion and love we had for Christ! And we celebrated that belief in Christian baptism....and we were walking on cloud nine! And if I don't go back to those moments and those times in my life, then there may come moments that I feel myself drifting or not having the same love or thrill that I once cherished! .

Now that brings us to verse five and I think that is why he gives **a command** to them. He says, "Nevertheless folks, I've got something against you, you have left your first passion and first love!" You don't stand in awe of me anymore. So in verse five He says, I want you to do something. He says, *"**Remember** therefore from whence thou aren't falling,* (Remember is the first one) *and **repent*** (that is the second) *and do the first works,* (And instead 'do' I am going to say **Repeat** the first works) *or else I will come unto you quickly and I will remove your candlestick out of his place except you repent."*

Now, what is he saying here? He is saying if you don't remember me, and if you don't repent, and if you don't repeat these works, he is going to come unto me quickly! Yes, that is what he is saying. Now this is not the Second Coming, but this is the local judgement to an individual, to a church, and he is going to remove the candlestick. Does that mean he is going to get a bulldozer at Modesto Sand and Gravel and level the four walls? That is not what He is saying. He is saying, if you don't do these things and if you don't get back to your first love for me, I am going to remove out of your heart and out of this church your usefulness and your testimony in this community. Look at it like this. If you don't have any love, then I am not going to give you any light. And it is the Lord who brings the joy in a person. And if you don't have a love for me and if you don't keep me first, I am not going to give you any light in this community. There will be no witness. And you can play church and you can do all of these **things**, and you can even add to your numbers, but there is no light there. The only time that the church has an effective light and witness in a community is when they first have a passion and a love for the Lord. Now why is he saying that? Now this is serious. Very serious! He said if you don't have a love for me, I am not going to give you a light because I don't want this world and I don't want this community to get the wrong impression of what Christianity is all about. And if you don't keep me first, FIRST, then the message is going to go out wrong. That is how serious it is. So He says, I want you to **remember.** I want you to go back to the place of your departure. I want you to go back to the place just like the prodigal son when he says what? He remembered father's house. I want you to go back to that place like it says in Ephesians 1:5 *"your thirst and your love for God and others."* Your church did have it. He says to just start remembering those things and the lesson is to all of us. I want you to remember your first love that you had for me. Not the four walls, not the preacher, not the programs, not what they are doing, but **the love for me**. Just remember that, because if you are a true believer born of God by the shed blood of Christ, you will remember that. Go back to that time. And as I say these three things, the same application is on a parallel track with a marriage.

I just want you to remember that. Create in your mind that day that you came to the Lord.

I had to think about my wife and I. Things get out of kilter, and we all know that it happens in marriages because nobody is perfect. Yes, there are times that we have disagreements. There are seasons in marriages that are tough. And I want you to go back and remember, remember the time that I consistently gave her flowers and she consistently made me doughnuts… please remember that! Oh! ☺ But remember the walks, the talks, even the intimacy. There are all kinds of things that can come into marriages to take that away, but remember that first love! Then He says, when you remember that, I want you to do a **matineo,** which is the Greek word for repent. You know, and you remember now, and I want you to repent and change and start loving again!

I had to think about Noah. When Noah stood, I can just see him going up the ramp and it is starting to rain! And Noah has a crowd of people probably still laughing at him as it begins to rain and Noah is just standing on the ramp. His message was not, **I am okay and you are okay, and everything is cool and everything will be all right**. His message was **repent!** That was his message. You are going to have to change, and you are going to have to repent!

That was the message of John the Baptist. He didn't get his head cut off from Herod because he wrote some book about how to win friends and influence people. His head was cut off because He said, "Repent!" People do not like to hear that message today, but when Jesus gives us that message, and if you have lost your first love, remember it and repent!

And then He says, **"do."** You know when a love begins to come back into an individuals heart for the Lord, there is a true repentance. One of the first responses that will always happen, you can not separate it, there will be the first works again. It always happens. He is saying, just do the things you did at first, you loved me, that is what brings revival. That is what brings revival in a marriage. I don't care if somebody is not doing it for me, do it for them. Because if your heart is right and the attitude is right, and you really do care and there is a love there, then do the first works! What a message that needs to stroll through our cities today**! REPENT!**

That brings us to our fourth thing, the **Challenge.** Verse seven, "*He that hath an ear let him hear what the Spirit saith unto the churches. To him that overcometh will I give to eat of the tree of which is in the midst of the paradise of God.*" What a challenge. He looked at the church, he says this is the compliment, and yes you folks have done a lot of things right. He then gives them a complaint and it is very severe, saying they left their first love. This is the area he wants them to go as a **command**, he says I want you to remember, I want you to repent, and I want you to repeat the first works.

And then he reveals the **challenge**. "*To him that overcomes.*" Now I think this is interesting. I could probably ask a lot of you here today, "What does it really mean, 'to him that overcomes?'" And you know one response, because I have asked people. They say it is when one just does more works for the Lord! That is not what he is saying. Do you know what a true **over comer** is? A true **over comer** is someone who just goes back and loves CHRIST! That is exactly what it says in 1 John, the book that this same apostle wrote.

He says there, "*Whoever is born of God overcomes the world.*" How are you born in God? It is when you love Jesus Christ and have placed your faith in Him! It goes on to say, "*the victory that overcomes the world is what? It is faith in love with Jesus.*" So he is saying here that the challenge will be, if you have an ear, I want you to hear what I am saying! And to him that really loves and pledges their faith in Christ, you are the one who is going to eat of the tree of life. He is just saying you know what is wrong in your heart, you know what is wrong in your life, and you know what has to change. He says I want you to stay close to the spring that will always refresh your heart. It will always refresh your marriage. It will always be refreshment in the church. It is when you just put your faith and love in me. Why is that hard for us to understand? Well one of the reasons, he says in Revelation, there is a tremendous battle going on in all of our lives. There is the flesh and the spirit and they are just struggling back and forth. When we make a decision in the morning, and at noon, and at night, to always keep our passion for Christ alive, then watch the JOY!

He is the reason that I am going home to be with him someday! Everything about life, my job, my marriage, my family is all incredible, but the number one thing is that I stand in awe of Him. How are you going to stay close to Him? It is not redundant to say this. You get into the Bible. Make it a part of your day, and every single day of your life! That is going to keep you close to the Savior.

I jotted some things down that are a thrill to me, when I think about the overcomers. They are the people that understand that Jesus Christ is their Salvation all alone. You are not going to add anything to Him and He is walking in the midst of all the churches, and He walks right through here. He walks right down the road to another church. He walks across

Modesto to another church. And the overcomers in that church are those who keep their faith and love strong for Jesus. You want to stay close to the spring today? You have to understand every day that you wake up, **He is the author and the finisher of my faith.** He is the beloved one, He is the balm of Gilead. It doesn't matter the problems or trials or the frustrations that I have, He is the balm of Gilead. Thank you Jesus, He is my Shepherd, He is the only Shepherd. He is the door to the sheep. He is everything, He is all.! He is not only the King of Kings and Lord of Lords, but He is the friend of sinners. And folks if Paul says he is the chief of sinners, why don't we join that and be honest, we are too. We are too. And yes you may do things right this week and next week, but when you wake up you have a capacity to do terrible things. Yet understand as you love Him, and stand in awe of Him, make sure your love for Him is Alive and Well!

And that brings us to the **Promise!.** You can eat of the tree of life. This is the picture of eternal life. A life so real that there is nothing fake! And all the service and the works are to the glory of the Father!!! So every one of us as we go about our work and life as believers, what is it for us? Is it real? Are you a part of a GREAT CHURCH that loves the Lord? A loving heart that pants for the Lord. That will make any church. It doesn't talk about numbers and programs, it is not interested in any of that. What makes a solid, dynamic church? A great church like Ephesus? A church where all the members make a commitment to have a love for God?

Then I read something that proved that. A poll was taken at 8,400 churches and they asked, "What is the main thing, the top of the list that you would want for your church?" And it just came back, **a church that loves!**

"By this shall all men know that you are my disciples if you have love one for another." Now that is a very clear message. More important than the preachers, more important than the activities, more important than the programs, more important than the Sunday schools, more important than the four walls, more important than the money in the bank, more important than the practices, more important than the vision, it is those who LOVE Jesus Christ! The church at Ephesus got a letter and God looks at each of us and the same letter is given to us today. If we have a problem in our church, if we have a problem in our marriages, if we have a problem in a relationship, go back to the basics, remember what it used to be like. **Repent** if there is wrong there. **Repeat** those first works and make sure you keep **Jesus Christ first!**

And just this morning as we were leaving Bible study, I had to think about what means so much to us as a minister. (I think you could find this at the Ephesian church) A CHURCH COMMITTED TO LOVE! A church of love is always going to have a maternity ward. And you say, "what do you mean by that?" Well obviously physically people still have babies, but there is something very special about a church that has babies and youth! No youth, then there is no promise of a future! That tells me something. That means there is no love somewhere. I am grateful when I see the maternity ward here and I know it is just a little body of believers here. You know what the '**maternity ward**' is? It is just young believers who love the Lord. When I see people coming to Christ, and when I see young people get out their Bibles at a Bible study, I see something there that reminds me of the passion that I need in my life. Maternity ward! Young believers! Because of their love for the Lord, it makes me want to continue my love for the Lord, and together we can be an effective witness in any community! Where there is love, there is light. Where there is light, God will always be honored! Amen!

Revelation 2:8-11

Symrna
A Church Under Fire

"And unto the angel of the church in Symrna write; These things saith the first and the last, which was dead, and is alive; I know thy works, and tribulation, and poverty, (but thou art rich) and I know the blasphemy of them which say they are Jews, and are not, but are the synagogue of Satan. Fear none of those things which thou shalt suffer: behold, the devil shall cast some of you into prison, and ye may be tried; and ye shall have tribulation ten days: be thou faithful unto death, and I will give thee a crown of life. He that hath an ear, let him hear what the Spirit saith unto the churches; He that overcometh shall not be hurt of the second death."

We talked about Ephesus last time and we talked about the strengths and the faults of the church there. We saw the tragedy of that church and how they lost their first love. And today we are going to be looking at the church of Symrna. They had strengths, but they didn't have any weaknesses. This church was located in Asia Minor, where the country of Turkey is today. So we are going to be looking at the church in Symrna, a church under fire. We have read just four verses today out of the book of Revelation, chapter 2, verses 8-11.

Symrna was a church under fire. A church that was full of fear and suffering. I want you to consider for a moment as we begin to look at the life of a young man. Notice was takes place in his life.

He was 3 years old when his dad died. His dad was a cheat and a murderer. He knew this at 3 years old. His mother took over and soon this boy's step-father was on the scene and the mother murdered the step-father of this young lad. She poisoned him with poison mushrooms that she collected in the forrest not too far away. As a teenager, this young man was in a group of young people. One afternoon he got upset because they were teasing him and making fun of him. So he took a knife out and killed the individual who was making fun of him! At 15 years old this young lad got married. He soon found out within a couple months that he didn't really care for his wife, so he had her killed. He paid to have her killed. 15 years old! This young man married again a year or so later and he killed this lady too. And by the time he was in his early 20's, his mother was so upset at the way he was living that she began to bug him too much, so he had his own mother killed. He does not sound like a very good individual. At age 31, because of some of the things that happened in the country that he was in, he was sentenced to die, yet he ran and hid in a basement out in the country! I am not sure how the story goes here… but that man at age 31 died in the basement. Anybody want to guess what his name was? His name was Nero. Now this was one of the Caesars, the Emperors of Rome.

Can you imagine a young man starting out at 3 years old, going through all the things that he did? Here he was, the ruler of one of the greatest powers this planet has ever known. **Nero.** Now with Nero as a Caesar, as an Emperor, he was one of the ones who really started this stamp of disapproval and persecution of the early church. But then Nero died. There was another Caesar, and his name was Domitian, and he was on the throne. And if you think Nero was bad, Domitian was even worse.

Domitian was the individual who was ruling at the time that Symrna came under intense pressure. In fact if you look at the Greek word there, it talks about tribulation, and that is the same word as "**supreme pressure**". It is like if you took El Capitan and gently started leaning it down on your body and never letting go, and letting the pressure mount and mount and mount until it never ends and you are crushed and dead. That is the kind of pressure that the church at Symrna went through. The Bible talks about ten days. Now that could be a literal ten days, but it may be a ten Emperor time period as the ten Emperors starting with Nero and ending with Diocletian. For nearly 300 years, intense El Capitan pressure was crushing on this early church. People were dying right and left. 5 million people died under the intense pressure of these Emperors at Rome. In fact, it was five million Christians. No let-up. And it was during this kind of persecution that these experiences were happening. Symrna was "under the Rock!"

In this wonderful city of Symrna, all of the sudden the church wasn't liked at all! They didn't want believers around and they hated the Christians. Then they had the stamp of approval from this man called Domitian that said, "**Kill them when you can. Slaughter them in the streets, boil them in the oil, crucify them on the hills, rack them and stretch them. I want them dead.**" How would you like to be in that church? Did you know that that is the kind of thing that is still going on today? Not here at the church in Modesto, or the Church in California, but you can find churches around the globe today where this same kind of pressure is going on.

So then, is the message really relevant for us today? Yes it is! Because you may not be going into the boiling oil, and you may not be getting on the rack today, and you may not be getting persecuted and shot at the wall today, but all of us have things that we are going through that are trials and suffering! So the application for the church at Symrna is the same application for us.

Symrna means myrrh. In fact, if you look back in Matthew chapter two at the birth of Christ, the Wise Men brought gold, frankincense and myrrh. Think about Jesus Christ on the cross in Mark 15. They gave him something to drink, didn't they? They gave him vinegar, but they also gave him Symrna, myrrh. You think about Jesus Christ in John 19 as they laid him in the tomb. They covered him with spices and Symrna, myrrh. Intense suffering and pain in the church at Symrna gave it the perfect name!

So the second round of persecution begins and John writes the letter. In fact, I think it was Domitian here who sent John to the Isle of Patmos. And as John wrote this letter and as he begins to write about Symrna, I know that in John's mind he is thinking: " I know these people. I know the bishop there. I know the elders. I know the leaders of the church, and this is what I am going to write." "*These things saith the first and the last, which was dead and is alive; I know thy works and tribulation and poverty.*"

So let's look at the city. That includes the church. Symrna was about 40 miles north of Ephesus. This is the people who lost their first love. Yes, the honeymoon was over for these people. So now we are going to go up here to the church in Symrna. If I would have to pick the favorite place to live as far as any of these churches, it wouldn't even be close, **It would be Symrna!** Symrna was the **Carmel by the Sea**, a place like Monterey that was right in a wonderful little harbor. It went right up to a mountain called Pagos. There were famous streets there. One they called the Street of Gold. It is probably like Lombard Street in San Francisco. People would come from all over to go to Symrna because they wanted to vacation there. Because of that it became a very fun spot for all the Senators and the people from Rome. They would come to Symrna and fall in love with Symrna, and then the people in Symrna fell in love with Rome. This prompted them to build statutes to the Caesars. Caesar worship really did begin in Symrna. You can see why the hatred for the believers was everywhere! If you did not bow your knee to the Caesars of Rome, they would haul you off and you would die a tragic death!

This is also the city that started the mass executions. Some of these things you hear about in the arenas at Rome, like feeding the lions; well, some of these things started in Symrna. So they set the example.

So lets look at verses eight and nine. *"I know thy works, and tribulation, and poverty, (but thou art rich) and I know the blasphemy of them which say they are Jews, and are not, but are the synagogue of Satan."*

The question I ask is, "Was there anything favorable going on here?" Yes. Do you know what Christ is telling this church? He says I know exactly where you people are in your life right now. I have been there, I know. I know every sob. I know every tear. I know every individual who has been shredded by the lions. I know the poverty you have gone through because some of you used to be wealthy. You were part of a building guild there in Symrna, and that was all taken away. And you are living in extreme poverty. I know what you are going through. It is kind of like a 'burning bush' of a church on fire. And Jesus is looking down here and He is saying, "Really this is one of your strengths."

What is it like when someone comes over to your house and they sit down with you and they look across the table from you say, "**I know what you are going through and I understand**." You know there is something about that that is very comforting and encouraging. I know the things that we have gone through, the little ups and downs, and someone will call at the right moment. And I know it has happened a lot of times in my life. But I distinctly remember one as it just comes to me now. I remember when we lived up there on Ladd Road years ago. It was probably eighteen or twenty years ago. I remember a man calling me in the middle of the night and giving me a scripture verse. It was the right verse for the right time! And Jesus is looking at this church and He says, "**I know what you are going through.**" This is a church scattered. In fact, you will never see anything else in the Bible about the church. We are a church scattered. We are not a church sheltered. There is no promise in the Bible that we are a church sheltered, that you are in a special compound and there is no suffering that is ever going to come to your life. We are a church scattered. By being a church scattered it does not matter if you are suffering here or China or wherever. What it does mean is that when you are a church scattered, the Gospel is going out. And that is one of the strengths here. This is a favorable response. He says I know what is going on.

Notice the word as it speaks to us in Hebrews 11, "**Quench the violence of fire, out of weakness we are made strong… they waxed valiant in fight… the women received their dead raised to life again… the others had trials of cruel mocking and scurgings… bonds and imprisoned… they were stoned and sawn asunder.** I guess that just means it was like taking a saw and cutting them in half. They were tempted and they were slain with the sword. They wandered about in sheep skins and goatskins, they were destitute and afflicted and tormented.' And it goes on and on there. Smyrna was realizing this first hand. This is the reality at the church at Smyrna. I know your works. I know your tribulation. I know the poverty you are going through, but you're rich. Now what does that mean? But you are rich. He is telling the church at Smyrna here, he is saying, I know that you are poor; but spiritually, because you are in me and you have kept your faith in me, you are rich. That doesn't sound like Laodicea, because later on you are going to see in this last church, he says, "I know you folks, you're rich, but you are really poor." You may have a lot of things and stuff but you are really poor spiritually. In fact, you are so lukewarm spiritually, I am just going to spew you out of my mouth. He is not saying that to Smyrna. He says you might be in extreme poverty, but you are rich and you are rich in me. He knew what they were going through and He knew their every need!

45

Now what is the meaning here when he says, *"I know the blasphemy of them which say they are Jews, and they are not, but they are of the synagogue of Satan?"* Some of the worst persecution that the early believers had was from people that said they were believers, and maybe even said they were professing Jews, but they really were not. They were like little detectives sneaking in. So he says they are nothing more than the synagogue of Satan. Now they may have been Jews but they were not converted over to Christianity. The synagogue of Satan was those that thought Judaism was the real way and Christianity was the wrong way! These people were doing everything they could to persecute Christianity. God says these guys are just like the synagogue of Satan. Judaism without Jesus Christ, and given recognition of Him as the Savior, is the same as Caesar worship! In fact, you could go and say that anything that does not recognize the gospel of Jesus Christ is a part of the synagogue of Satan. You can't add an ounce of 'strychnine' into a thousand gallon tank and say that is pure water.... it dilutes it. And that is what some of these folks are doing here. They are saying, 'Oh no no, wait a minute. We are the right ones. We have Judaism,. We have the real way. Christ is not the right way. Then they turn right around and turn these people in.! Sad to say the hostility of some of these things that were happening in Smyrna came from their own people, the Jews. And he says they are not real Jews.

Did you know the Bible proves that?

I flipped to the left in my Bible to Romans chapter **2:28**, *"For he is not a Jew, which is one outwardly.... But he is a Jew, which is one inwardly; a circumcision of the heart."* **That is the real Jew**. It is not one who comes along and says, "Hey, I am a Jew because look at me. I am a part of this group here. I was born a Jew. I am a Jew." That doesn't make you a Jew. A real Jew is a Jew inwardly, the circumcision of the heart. And the believer is a believer because of the circumcision of the heart. These Jews here in the synagogue of Satan were nothing more than spiritual pagans. They were the allies of the Roman Empire! These were some of the same people who would take their own relations and burn them at the stake, as well as put them in the boiling oil! They would stop at nothing to stamp out the Christian faith!

I want to make a couple comments about this. I would like to call it a **"bonfire of a trial"** that is going on in this church. Let's look at it in three ways. There was **MISERY**, there was **MYSTERY**, and there was **MINISTRY**!

The misery at the human level that was going on in this church was overwhelming! At the Satanic level, there was a strange mystery that was circling the church. People could not comprehend the confusion! But with that not only was there a misery, not only was there a mystery, but there was a ministry that God was working in their midst!

You can read in the Foxe's Book of Martyrs about this type of misery! I will pick out a few:

A 92-year-old man in the church of Smyrna chose death and starvation rather than recant his faith in his Lord and Savior.

An 18 year old girl that was abused by the soldiers, (you can imagine what I mean when I say 'abused by the soldiers'). Then her lifeless body was thrown in laughter to the lions and shredded to pieces!

I think about a 15-year-old lad who was flogged to death right in front of his family, rather than say Jesus is not Christ! What a Faith!

Would you be willing to do that today? We live in a wonderful country. Until the Lord comes maybe it will continue this way and maybe it won't. And I have to think as I was just looking at these three accounts of this supposition:

What if that door would open and some men came in here with Uzi machine guns and say, "Recant your faith in Jesus Christ or we will kill you and all your family!" It is all you have to say. It is that simple. Just verbally as you file past, say that you do not love Christ!"

What would you do? Would you say "FIRE"? Or would you try to make a deal? Or would you even say, "You know let's talk this thing out." We may not ever face that. And that doesn't make us better Christians because we are living in a land of freedom.

Then I thought about the Satanic level of **this bonfire of a trial**. The **mystery** of it. Don't tell me that these families that were getting together and were kneeling every night, that they were praying to the Lord and were confused because there was no CHANCE! They thought, what a mystery, Satan is having his way here! Not so!

Look at it like this. There are times in your life where you may go through a tribulation and a trial that was prepared for you! There are times in your life where you may go through a trial or tribulation for those around you. But there may be times in your life that you go through a trial and tribulation for Satan. Because God knows that you are strong in faith, He will pick you out just like He did Job and He will say **"Have you ever considered my servant Job?"** He didn't ask Job's permission. Have you ever considered my servant Job? Yeah, but you always have him protected. Well, I will lift this. And He did and Job lost everything. You talk about suffering! This man went through it and he never recanted his faith in the Lord! You also see it in the life of Peter and Paul! You see that is a mystery sometimes to us but not to God and His sovereignty. It may be for me, or for others, and the witness that I live out in my daily walk, it can be for the cause of the Kingdom!

I will mention this Man's name now. Does any one know who the head bishop was at Smyrna? It sounds like pollywog, but it was Polycarp! ☺ Polycarp was an individual who did meet John. He was the bishop, he was the leader at Smyrna, and he witnessed and watched the suffering of his church. He saw his people dying. And there came a day that he was approached by soldiers. They said to him, "Polycarp, we are going to give you the opportunity to say that Christ is nothing."

They told him, "Listen Polycarp. Swear by the fortune of Caesar and repent and say, 'away with Christians.'" But Polycarp, gazing with a stern countenance on all the multitude of the wicked heathen in the stadium that day, waving his hands towards all of them while with groan, he looked up to the heavens, and said, **"No, away with the atheist."** Then the proconsul urged him and said, "Swear and I will set thee at liberty. Just reproach Christ." And Polycarp answered and declared, **"Eighty and six years have I served Him and He never did me any injury, how then can I ever stand here and blaspheme my King, my Savior, and my Lord!"** And they went back and forth verbally like that for nearly an hour. They never got him to say no to Jesus. And they took him out and burnt him at a stake. The misery, the mystery, and the ministry of the bonfire at Smyrna.

Let's consider more of this ministry! This is actually a ministry in this sense, because the martyrs

and the blood of the martyrs was one of the greatest germinating seeds that Asia has ever seen. You try to stamp them out here and they show up over there. You try to persecute them here and they spring up over there! And as you read through the book of Acts, time and again, Satan tried at least seven different ways of trying to persecute and kill the church, and it just kept springing up! In fact, the Bible says that they turned the whole world upside down! And that happened because of the ongoing persecution! What a ministry!

If I would ask you to give me some of the side affects of persecution, could you give me one? What would be a side affect of persecution?

You say, what about **Victory and Patience**? That is good! Often People take off and they scatter. What about this on? Do you think there were any hypocrites in the church of Smyrna? I don't think so. Not in the true church of Smyrna. There is something about intense persecution, that in time hypocrites will run, and sinners flee! They don't like to live like that so they just say, "Okay, I will go the easy way." If there is a type of persecution that brings a choice between Christ or nothing, they run.! False faith crumbles under that kind of persecution. But one of the great side effects of this church, do you know what it was? It was the very thing that these people of Ephesus were accused of doing wrong. You see when you are under intense persecution, there is one thing that remains hot, and that is your **first love**. Your first love for Christ is always going to remain hot and He will continue to fan that flame when that persecution comes. **II Timothy 3:12** *"All those that live godly shall suffer persecution."*

And again I say it might not be boiling oil for us, or standing at the wall and getting shot at. It could be something very basic and simple like **ridicule.** It could be something like a broken down relationship, or a disappearing of finances. It could be something as simple as having to go to someone else to get your hair cut instead of Ron. ☺ But think about the things that happened to this church. The devil thought he had them right where he wanted them- just on the verge of being wiped out, and it turned into a ministry! He thought the same thing at the cross, didn't he? He thought he had him right where he wanted him and Jesus Christ voluntarily gave us his life and that was Satan's doom. Yes, Satan got his teeth kicked in at Calvary, and he has been "gumming it" ever since!!!

I just want to close this chapter as we think about the trial at Smyrna. Verses ten and eleven.. *" Fear none of those things which thou shalt suffer: behold, the devil shall cast some of you into prison, and ye may*

be tried; and ye shall have tribulation ten days: be thou faithful unto death, and I will give thee a crown of life. He that hath an ear, let him hear what the Spirit saith unto the churches; He that overcometh shall not be hurt of the second death."

I am going to confess something to you. I guess it probably happened first with my grandfather King. I remember going down there as a teenager and opening up to grandpa King about a situation that was troubling me! I remember grandpa answering something like this, "Well Gordon, just try to remain faithful and don't get so stirred up about it. Fear Not!" I remember being a little disappointed because that isn't what I expected or wanted to hear! I wanted it mapped out. I wanted a way out. I wanted this situation to go away! But you know, that is exactly what Jesus says here. And sometimes you may have people come to you wanting a "quick fix." This is a great start, "Be faithful and fear not! In fact there is 365 of them in the Bible, one for every day of the year. Fear not! And he goes on to say, I just want you to remain faithful. That is what the text is saying here. Be faithful unto death. Jesus Christ is saying, "If you are going through something, I want you to understand that when you share in my cross, that you will share of my crown."

If you endure this kind of persecution and suffering, there will be a crown of life. There may be times for the rest of your life that you will have to suffer under the cross of Christ. Yet He said if you do, that you will share in my crown! When God picks this family or an individual to suffer a certain trial or tribulation, that is taking up the cross of Christ! The promise is that you then receive his crown. That is a ministry. These people at Smyrna, as you look at the pages of these saints, they were taking up the cross of Christ because they knew that this was ministry!

These folks at Smyrna loyally stood and confessed Jesus Christ before men, even to the point of death. That sounds like a guarantee in the Bible, because my Bible says in Matthew 10:33 *"If you confess me before men, I will confess you before the Father."* So you look at those people who were being racked, who were being killed. They were confessing the Lord Jesus before men. So what was the ministry of these people?

The ministry at Smyrna would teach us three things!

1. They cared more about the reputation of Jesus Christ than they did about the reputation of a Domitian or Nero or any Caesar of Rome.

2. They cared more about the recognition of Jesus Christ than any Roman man or any man in the Senate.

3. And they cared more about Jesus Christ than the recognition from Rome.

I would like to look more into that "builder's guild" and exactly what that meant. Some very wealthy Christians had everything taken away, yet they cared more about the riches of Jesus Christ than the riches of Rome. These were the kind of people living there and this was the kind of message that they were saying. "We are not going to fear, we will fret not because of evil-doers, and we will always stand for the cross of Christ. That would be our prayer for all of us. We are at the church in California. We may be going through some things in the near future or right now. But if you would get in your mind the suffering that you may be going through along with the sovereignty of God, you can live a steadfast life. For you see suffering and God's sovereignty can in His time produce steadfastness. It did at Smyrna and it can here today 2,000 years later.

I am reminded of a poet. His name is Aramdo Valldares, a Cuban poet. He became famous,yet he is dead now. In 1960 he was taken by Castro, because he was writing these poems and was making fun of Castro and the regime in Cuba. So he was taken to a prison, where Aramdo was beaten and ridiculed! He was forced to take showers with human urine, forced to do terrible acts, and he was nearly whipped to the point of death. He hated it down there in captivity, and he hated even the thought of writing another poem. (everything written got him in trouble) And during this time Aramdo says, "I want to tell you what changed my life. " He said I was near death, my body was in complete pain. I then started noticing through the bars people going by with a big grin on their faces! These people were being taken out to the firing squads to be shot! He says all of the sudden I remember hearing, "**Long live Christ our King**." Then he said a few moments later I would hear the explosion, "BANG, BANG, BANG!" And a few days later someone else would go by my cell and I would look out and I would see rapture on their faces. Instead of wretched woe, they would get out there and say, "**Long live Christ our King**." And the guns would go off. The ministry of Christians suffering in a Cuban prison brought Aramdo to consider Jesus Christ. He not only considered Him, he became a believer before he died!

I don't know what you are experiencing folks. Sometimes we probably need to share more of the heartaches we have. But don't forget that it may be a ministry for you personally, it may be a ministry for those around you, and it may be a ministry to prove that the Lord still has faithful believers. But whatever it is, persecution can be a ministry and ultimately it can bring glory to the one who saved us! Thank you Smyrna!

REVELATION 2:12-17

Pergamos
A Drifting Church

"And to the angel of the church of Pergamos write; These things saith he which hath the sharp sword with two edges; I know thy works, and where thou dwellest, even where Satan's seat is: and thou holdest fast my name, and hast not denied my faith, even in those days wherein Antipas was my faithful martyr, who was slain among you, where Satan dwelleth. But I have a few things against thee, because thou hast there them that hold the doctrine of Balaam, who taught Balac to cast a stumbling block before the children of Israel, to eat things sacrificed unto idols, and to commit fornication. So hast thou also them that hold the doctrine of the Nicolaitans, which thing I hate. Repent; or else I will come unto thee quickly, and will fight against them with the sword of my mouth. He that hath an ear, let him hear what the Spirit saith unto the churches; To him that overcometh will I give to eat of the hidden manna, and will give him a white stone, and in the stone a new name written, which no man knoweth saving he that receiveth it."

The title of our message today is "Pergamos – A Faltering, Drifting Church". One of the exciting things about going through Revelation is that we know what is coming next. It has been an incredible journey just thinking about these churches. One advantage of studying the churches for me is, I can look at the churches as a whole, and I can map them all out and know what is coming next.

Pergamos was a church that was having a real problem. And yes, you look at all the churches and they were all having problems. In fact, when this letter was written in AD 96, there were only 100 churches on the entire planet as far as Christian churches. One hundred possible churches on the planet. Now that is not very many. But even then there were people beginning to ask the question: Which one is really the best one? Or which is the right church or which church really has it going better for the cause of Christ? And this was even some of the greatest of New Testament saints.

So the Lord came along and gave John the inspiration to write this. He picks out seven literal churches, and he writes a letter to each one of them. There is not only a commendation for them, but there was also a warning- a warning that comes down through the centuries to us today in our communities. So every letter that he wrote to every church is a letter to this congregation. Maybe in one aspect a little more 'fever pitch' with this warning or maybe a better commendation in this area or that area, but we can all get a lesson from every church. And we can get a lesson from the church of Pergamos.

These letters were written to all churches of all ages. There is not just a hundred churches on the planet anymore, there are millions! I think the largest denomination in American is 47,500 churches, and then there are a lot of other groups and callings. So there are hundreds and hundreds of thousands of churches just in the United States.

There are people meeting right now in all three time zones in America and they are worshiping Jesus Christ. There are hymns of Zion being sung in all kinds of churches. You can't hardly even find a little town in America without some church somewhere trying as hard as they can to worship the Savior. They were trying it at Pergamos and they had a lot of good things going there, but they had a lot of wrong things too. You know, it doesn't matter where people worship, there good things there and sometimes there are some faults we need to be aware of! There is no perfect church, but there is a perfect body of Christ. That body is those who are in Him by faith .

We looked at the church at Smyrna which means myrrh, the persecuted church. There are churches today on the earth that are experiencing the exact same things that Smyrna had. You go to Indonesia today! There are Christians being slaughtered there for the cause of Christ! That is persecution. So you can see that as they read this letter to the church at Smyrna, we can understand in a measure of what they experienced.

We are at Pergamos today, and it means "marriage." What happens in marriages? So many times there is compromise, to the point that people begin to drift, and that is why we are going to call this the drifting church. They needed to get back together.

We will look next at Thyatira, which means "continual sacrifice". Thyatira was in the same time frame and era when the Catholic Church started. That is where the clergy took control.

Then we will look at the church of Sardis which means, "The remnant church". The reformation.

Next will be the church of Philadelphia, which means "brotherly love."

And the last one we will look at is Laodicea, which means "people's rights" or the " Worldly Church. "

So there will be a lot of lessons from these churches and we are excited to visit each one! I am going to break down this message on the church at Pergamos in three ways: We are going to look at the **faithful men** in verses twelve and thirteen. We are going to look in verses fourteen and fifteen, **the false creeds** that were actually creeping into this church at Pergamos. And we are going to end up with verses sixteen and seventeen, a **very fearful crisis** and warning that Christ gave the church at Pergamos. Again we say as we look at this faltering, drifting church, there are relevant lessons and applications even for us today!

"And to the angel of the church of Pergamos write; These things saith he which hath the sharp sword with two edges."

This is a picture of Christ standing right there in the middle of Pergamos. He is saying, *"I have got a sword here with two edges and if there is not going to be repentance here, this sword is going to be yielded and there is going to be judgment!* We can see back in chapter one, this is one of the pictures of Christ. He begins a movement here of judgement. This is not a happy **welcome** introduction to the church at Pergamos. Immediately He says to the church at Pergamos, I have a sharp sword with two edges, and I know exactly what is going on here. This is the same One who looked at Ephesus and Smyrna, and He is now zeroing in on Pergamos. There are three good things, but there is one thing that is really bad and it is fatal. You are going to receive some severe correction!

"I know thy works, and where thou dwellest, even where Satan's seat is: and thou holdest fast my name, and hast not denied my faith, even in those days wherein Antipas was my faithful martyr, who was slain among you, where Satan dwelleth."

What is He saying here? He is saying,

" Pergamos look, I am Christ, and I am the head of the church here. I know what you are going through. You are in the midst of a society from where the headquarters of Satan functions! The headquarters

of Satan used to be down in the Babylonian Empire and once that place failed, it came back and set up its seed here at Pergamos. Some of you are living faithful in the midst of all of this idolatry, this snake worship, this scapal worship, this Zeus worship, yet you have remained faithful to my Name, and you have never denied the faith!"

And their leader, Anthepus, he went the ultimate sacrifice! They took him into one of these strange temples. They put Anthepus, the leader of the Pergamos church, in this large brass bowl. They lit a fire and roasted him alive to the cheering crowds of the idol worshipers.

And the Lord is looking down at this church and He says, "I know it is trying. I know what you are going through and I want you to know that I am right here with you. I commend you believers for life of faith that you are living!"

But then we come down to verses fourteen and fifteen. And He gives this compliment, thank you to those who are holding fast to my Name. Thank you for those who are not denying the faith. Thank you, all of you, who are faithful witnesses or martyrs! (that is what martyrs means, "faithful witness").

But then he comes with this conjunction in verse 14.

"But I have a few things against thee, because thou hast there them that hold the doctrine of Balaam, who taught Balac to cast a stumbling block before the children of Israel, to eat things sacrificed unto idols, and to commit fornication."

What is he saying now? In professing Christianity, there are some people who are getting sucked up into false creeds. And he says, I can not stand what is going on here. This is the doctrine of Balaam and this is the doctrine of the Nicolatans. Satan will try everything to get you folks away from me. Any kind of design, any kind of denying, he will do it and it is happening right here at Pergamos. The doctrine of Balaam and the doctrine of the Nicolaitans are false teachings!

If you go back in Numbers chapters twenty two to twenty five, you will see where Balaam was really caught up in two things, wealth and women. As a prophet, Balak was scared of the Israelites, so he made a monetary deal with Balaam. If you just go out and curse the Israelites ,things will work out great for you! Well he tried it three times and it didn't work, so he went to plan B. And he thought to himself, well cursing them didn't work. It just seems like every time it came out as a blessing, so lets go to plan B. I still need the money. I will do everything I can to get the Israelites going in the wrong area. But he said, if you can't confuse these people, then you have to corrupt them. And the only way we are going to do this is to get your people together and have your women seduce the Israelite men! Get them to intermingle; and as they do that by sexual perversion, then they will start sacrificing to idols! That is exactly what happened! This is the doctrine of Balaam. They got on the wrong page and they allowed this perversion of immorality to come in and all now they were saying, "Well, let's make a truce with them! But you can't make a truce with sin!

That is the lesson for us today. You can't make a truce with sin! Sin and Faith will never sit on the same bench. If you love the Lord, you are going to have enmity with the world. You can't have them mixing. Balaam mixed them and there was disaster. That can happen in the churches today. You try to bring in a little paganism and a little bit of sexual immorality and a little bit of homosexuality and you will have disaster!!! What communion hath light with darkness? It doesn't. I even thought about the analogy of the Israelis and the Palestinians today. God loves the Palestinians and God loves the Israelis. But you know what folks? There will never be any peace there until one of them is completely gone, or the love of Christ comes into their hearts! All the little truces and all the covenants they are trying to put in place will never work! Until Christ comes and brings real peace, there will always be conflict in the Middle East. You have 756,000,000 Arabs and 5,000,000 Jews. It would seem like one would wipe out the other.... but God has a plan and it will happen according to Him!

It is no different in the area of sin. Unless there is the mortification of sin in our bodies, it will make a truce and it will keep backing up. And before you know it, there is corruption in our lives! That is why the church at Pergamos has sometimes been called the worldly church. Ah, that is a quaint word, worldliness. No, worldliness is just any time there is a preoccupation with anything other than Christ. It happened to be with these folks, bent in the direction of idols. They would worship these idols and then they would allow prostitutes to come in, and before you know it they were completely gone. He was saying, you know if you allow these false priest to come in, you are following after the doctrine of the Nicolaitans!

Let's examine this Nicolaitans teaching a little closer. Nico, means "to conquer." Laos or Lao means laity. You are allowing the priest or clergy to take over! . It started back in the Middle Ages, in those times where they had complete control, and they would go out and slaughter people. Look at the evil during the terrible inquisitions. And he is saying, Pergamos you have both of these things going on and if you don't watch it, if you don't refuse to control this error, it is going to crop up in your church and it will be a deadly disaster! Even though there are the faithful few who really do care, there is an evil trying to creep in and destroy the Church! Anytime there is a preoccupation with anything other than Christ, anything that is temporal, that is worldliness. In time it will erode holiness and all things Godly!

"So hast thou also them that hold the doctrine of the Nicolaitans, which thing I hate. Repent; or else I will come unto thee quickly, and will fight against them with the sword of my mouth. He that hath an ear, let him hear what the Spirit saith unto the churches; To him that overcometh will I give to eat of the hidden manna, and will give him a white stone, and in the stone a new name written, which no man knoweth saving he that receiveth it."

We live in a society today where there is a flavor of everything. I want us to remember something. I want us to be confident. Yes, we are worshiping here, but we need to have the confidence that we have brothers and sisters in Christ everywhere in this city. They are everywhere out there. You who are involved in the Gideons, you have gone a lot of places. You know what we are talking about. There are good people everywhere. And we need to be praying for the saints everywhere. And this church at Pergamos, they too were relying on the sister churches around them! They relied on the brothers and sisters at Ephesus, at Smyrna, and all the surrounding churches. And as they worked together, they built each other up. There are good things you are going to learn from the people you work with who are in other churches. You need to have the conviction to thank the Lord for these brothers and sisters in the body of Christ wherever they worship. I think that there may come a time in the near future that we will not survive without the support of others in the body of Christ!

I am a minister of the Gospel. I love to present the gospel. I know what the gospel is, it is all about the Lord Jesus Christ! But you know what, I had a man who was dying in a hospital bed last week and I couldn't reach him! And the reason that I couldn't reach him is because I can't speak the language. Mario, who is one of the men working for me, ten days ago went to the hospital because he was going to die unless he gets a kidney transplant! He was on dialysis. So this is what I did, I called my son-in-law, who is involved with a man named Bill from a local church in the area. Bill knew a man that speaks fluent Spanish! He hooked me up with a man named Bob. He is a Christian and he has taught Spanish for thirty seven years at a high school. So I had a three minute conversation on the phone that went something like this, " Bob I have a gentleman in Room 320 at Doctor's Hospital. I do not know if he is saved. I do not know if he is going to live. Can you come and share with him?" His response was, "I would love to!"

Well, the very next day I get a call as I was driving the tractor through the Almond orchard. I shut the tractor off and I heard Bob say, " Well, I have great news! I went in and talked to Mario and his family, and he gave his heart to Christ! Not only that, but he had an aunt from Mexico City there and she did too! Thank the Lord for the Body of Christ and believers everywhere that has a willing heart to help in time of need!

Folks, we are not going to have everything right and perfect. Whether it be language or even the knowledge, we may have to rely on other people in the Body of Christ to set a course. And these people at Pergamos, they needed that kind of direction too. And I like to think that there were saints down there at Ephesus who had a hot love for Jesus Christ after they got that warning! They knew these idols were wrong. And as they worked together they shared back and forth among the churches. We can do the same thing today! I can learn from you and I can learn from my neighbor.

I will be eternally grateful for Bob. I thanked him and I asked him if I could call again sometime. He kind of chuckled and he said, "Hey this is what cranks me up! Yes, anytime!"

That is a vision we can all have. You have people that you work with. And pray to God. If you don't know the language, pray to God to find a person that does! Eternity may be in the balance for that life! Because things that are not temporal are the soul of man and the Word of God. And as you put that together, someday Mario is going to thank Bob throughout eternity because he came into a hospital room and he shared Christ. That is awesome!

"Repent; or else I will come unto thee quickly, and will fight against them with the sword of my mouth. He that hath an ear, let him hear what the Spirit saith unto the churches; To him that overcometh will I give to eat of the hidden manna, and will give him a white stone, and in the stone a new name written, which no man knoweth saving he that receiveth it."

Look at verse sixteen. **Repent.** You know there is only one remedy for sinful behavior and it is right here. **Repent.** He is not saying, well let's just cut a deal here and let's move over in this direction because we don't want to hurt anybody's feelings. He is saying look! **Repent!** There is wrong here.

I want you **to repent**. And the Lord is standing right here in the midst of Pergamos with His sword. And he says, ***"Look, I will come to thee (or you) and I will fight against them."*** He is saying, I will come to you who practice this sin and I will fight anyone who even tolerates it.

And that is the message to us too. He doesn't like the practice of sin and he doesn't like the priest or clergy in charge who even tolerate it. He says to repent from all of that. He is not saying, "Okay, you folks blew it and you are not my church anymore." That is not what he is saying. He is saying, "It is still my church." That is why He is speaking to them. But he is saying, "To those who are defiling my name, I am going to bring judgement."

I don't want that to happen here. Sin is a stalker. Sin has a tendency to kind of "hang around". We think we have things going rather well, and all of the sudden there is the temptation, " Let's make a little truce here." And the minute you make a truce and you sit on the same bench with sin, the next time it is a little bit easier to cave! Sin is always going to be a stalker. You can't make peace with sin. Without Christ you are hopeless against the power of the evil one! There must be a mortification to sin. And the wages of SIN is DEATH!

"He that hath an ear, let him hear!"

On one side of that sword, Christ is saying, "Please, I want you to repent because I know what it is doing to your life!" And then He is saying in a wooing way, "I want you to open your ears up and I want you to listen to me. You have idolatry, immorality, and infidelity in you midst! Stop it!" It is in the church at Pergamos.

"You have idolatry, but guess what? You can refuse to eat those meats that are sacrificed to idols and I will replace that with hidden manna." What is he saying? You don't have to eat that meat that was sacrificed to idols; you can have the hidden manna, which is the recognition of the daily intake of the Lord Jesus Christ. That is exactly what He said in **Philippians 4:19** *"I shall supply all of your needs according to His riches in glory in Christ Jesus."*

That is the hidden manna. That is the wooing of the Spirit. He says, "Look Pergamos, you don't have to do that. This you can have. The hidden manna." And he doesn't leave it there. He says, "I don't want you to have anymore problems with this sexual immorality and the debauchery of this sin. Instead you can have this **white stone**." What is he saying? He is saying, everytime a victor comes back from the Roman Empire and they walk in, victorious over anything they conquered, they were presented **a**

white stone. And when you refuse to have that sexual perversion, I will give you the **white stone** of purity, knowing that you can have a walk, a close walk, with the righteousness and **white robes** of the Lord.

And then look at infidelity. He is saying, "if you refuse to worship any other person or idol, I will give to give you a saving faith with **a new name!**" You can have confidence every day you wake up in Pergamos. You don't have to do the idols and you don't have to do the sexual debauchery and you don't have to defile my Name to be accepted by me! You don't have to bow down to anything except me. Why? Because you have the **hidden manna**, you have the promise of the **white stone**, and you have eternity with **your new name** written forever in heaven!

"Please," he says, " keep living for me! Honor me and I will honor you and I will give you the hidden manna! I will give you the promise of the white stone! I will give you the promise of your name forever written in heaven!"

So where does that leave us today? I am going to use myself as an example. Any time that my life is too preoccupied with anything other than Jesus Christ, then I am bowing my knee, in a sense, to an idol. And you can call that idol just about anything. You know what your life is like. I know what I am attracted too. But anything that elevates itself above my love for my Savior, my God, then I'm bowing my knee to it! And Jesus is saying, "Please, for my sake, don't do that! I want you to repent of that! And turn back and just put me first." And the church at Pergamos gives us that lesson. **Repent and enjoy the abundant Christian life.** If we refuse to repent, you will continue to not only receive disfavor, but God has a very special mechanism that He has built in all of us. It is called, UNREST! And He will never allow you to receive the peace which passes all understanding and the joy unspeakable until there is repentance and change!

Thanks Lord, for the message from the Church at Pergamos. Because even though it has been 2000 years, the message is still applicable for us in America. It is still applicable for those in Africa, those in Asia, wherever the church is located. Any one who gets their focus off of Him and bows their knee to an idol will bring correction and unrest!

I would like to close with a story. Something I have remembered for many years. In the late 60's, early 70's my job was to drive a 40-foot van and take melon loads to San Fransisco and San Jose. I really enjoyed those trips to the bay area. But there is one thing as we look back at those days of driving to the coast-the filth in the life of a "Lumper." A Lumper is someone you would hire to unload the melons if you needed extra help due to a time schedule. They cursed and swore, told filthy jokes, and threatened to slash your tires if you didn't hire them! You don't mess with a Lumpur. And I look back to a very hot day at Banana King Louies. A man was sitting all by himself on a crate of corn, with his lunch pail open, reading a Bible. You know, that was a lesson for me. In the midst of the evil and filth and ridicule…..he just kept reading the Bible! Sure, I might go back to my truck, hide, and pray for a meal, but this man was just like a Christian in Pergamos! There were people running everywhere in degradation and sin, yet right in the midst of that, this man sits on a crate of lettuce, opens the Word of God, and cared less about the life around him! They might have laughed at him and joked about him later on, but they never bothered him. He was partaking of the **hidden manna,** and there was the promise of the **white stone,** and he knew without question **that his name was written there**.

And this man and others that we would see do that from time to time, they had the confidence of who they were in Christ Jesus. The same thing was alive in Pergamos, and the same way can be true in all of you today. You who are involved in construction work, you know what we are talking about. You will see all kinds of people and every once in awhile someone will go away and sit down and open their Bible and pray in the midst of all manner of conversation……and you know that is faith, that is righteousness. What makes this happen? How can it happen? When there is a complete unashamed dependence upon the Lord Jesus Christ! .

So I would like to encourage all of us in our walk with our Savior this week. Do everything you can to remember that you have the promise of the **white stone**. You have the **hidden manna**. Everything that you need in life is right here. It is the one thing that will keep you separate from everything that is wrong. And it is right here, with the promise, knowing that **your name is written there**. A letter was written to Pergamos, the drifting church, that was being swept out into the sea of carnality. And Christ said to repent, and so many of them did, and they came back into fellowship with the Lord. And that is the lesson for us today.

Thyatira
A False Church

"*And unto the angel of the church in Tyatira write; These things saith the Son of God, who hath his eyes like unto a flame of fire, and his feet are like fine brass;*

I know thy works, and charity, and service, and faith and patience, and thy works; and the last to be more than the first. Notwithstanding I have a few things against thee, because thou sufferest that woman Jezebel, which calleth herself a prophetess, to teach and to seduce my servants to commit fornication, and to eat things sacrificed unto idols.

And I gave her space to repent of her fornication; and she repented not. Behold, I will cast her into a bed, and them that commit adultery with her into great tribulation, except they repent of their deeds. And I will kill her children with death; and all the churches shall know that I am He which searcheth the reins and hearts: and I will give unto every one of you according to your works. But unto you I say, and to the rest in Tyatira, as many as have not this doctrine, and which have not known the depths of Satan, as they speak; I will put upon you none other burden. But that which ye have already hold fast till I come.

And he that overcometh, and keepeth my works unto the end, to him will I give power over the nations: And he shall rule them with a rod of iron; as the vessels of a potter shall they be broken to shivers: even as I received of my Father.

And I will give him the morning star.

He that hath an ear, let him hear what the Spirit saith unto the churches.

I was thinking the other day when I was studying this passage, that Revelation is kind of like riding a horse. I am just trying to hold back on the reigns because I see the current events that are happening in the world, I would like to jump into some things in later chapters, yet we will get there. But it is just like I am holding back and I am in a slow trot at the present!

On May 18, 1980, a few hundred miles north of here, there was a mountain that danced and belched and finally blew. Mount Saint Helens. We have heard about it and read about it, and we even saw pictures of it. Some of you have even been there and seen the destruction of Mt. Saint Helens. Just prior to that, a couple days before that infamous day, there were all kinds of radioactivity going on and people giving warning signals: DO NOT GO NEAR MT. SAINT HELENS! There are a lot of earthquakes. People said there is going to be something very tragic getting ready to happen in the near future, so do whatever you can to get away from the mountain. By citizen bands and radio and media, they got the people off the mountain because they said it would blow. All except for one man, Harry Truman. Harry Truman was interviewed by NBC there at Spirit Lake about five miles from the mountain, with a great big grin on his face. Harry looked into the camera and said, "Don't warn me. There is nobody that knows Mt. Saint Helens like I do and she ain't gonna blow on me." Well, two days later Harry Truman and sixteen of his cats were vaporized in that tragic eruption. In some ways he is a infamous old man now. You read about him. But Mt. Saint Helens did erupt and Harry did die because "She did blow!"

You know, with all of those warnings, there wasn't anything that was going to change his mind. And in some ways that is tragic. But I find it parallel as we go through Revelation. Revelation is a very exciting book. The Bible calls it "the Revelation". That is the "apocolupsis," the unveiling. The first time that we walk into the book we see the uncovering or the unveiling and the warnings that Christ gives to His creation. As He looks at every one of the seven churches He gives a warning each one of them. And these warnings reach out for 2,000 years even to where we are today. So we can take things from Ephesus and Pergamos and Thyatira and Laodicea and all of these are warnings for us- as individuals, as communities, as churches, and as eras of time. As we look at the book of Thyatira, yes there is a condemnation even of this church.

. In Daniel 12:4, the Lord is telling Daniel that He has given him all this prophetic evidence here and "I want you to seal up the book. I want you to seal up the book until the end of time." So Daniel sealed up the book and nobody has ever really understood Daniel until that prophetic verse that says, **"And in the last days men shall run to and fro and knowledge shall be increased."**

And now all of the sudden here we are in Revelation 22:10. It says for John to open the book now, I don't want you to seal this anymore! I want you to open the book of Revelation and I want people to understand what we are living in and what they are going to deal with. And so all the way 2,000 or 3,000 years ago from the sealing up of the book until now in Revelation 22:10, there is the unveiling of the book. It is not a hidden mystery anymore. As we walk through the book of Revelation, this is a message to us and to all nations. .

This is the smallest of the seven churches, but it gets the longest letter. I really don't know why, but there must be a reason. I would suppose as I studied this section that maybe they have the longest letter because these people were way off base, allowing the tolerance of sin. Thyatira was a small berg about thirty five miles south of Pergamos.

Christ is not calling Himself the Son of Man anymore. He says he is the Son of God. And He says He has eyes like a flame of fire and can come down and look at your communities and your lives. He is saying that you folks down here are tolerating sin and "my eyes they see it and I can bring judgement at any moment." This is a warning to the church at Thyatira. He says that "my eyes see everything like x-ray vision. My feet are ready to stamp on it in judgment!"

Yet he gives them a commendation in verse 19. **"I know thy works, and charity, and service, and faith and patience, and thy works; and the last to be more than the first."**

He repeats "thy works" again and I've wondered why. But he says, "and the last to be more than the first". Now this may have meant one of two things. He may be saying here that you are finally starting to mature even though you are tolerating these things going on. I do appreciate that. I see patience, charity. I see your love. Ephesus didn't really have that love for me, but you have a little bit there. You have a caring for the community. Then He says the last may be more than the first. He may be saying, "now watch it, because maybe now your service and your works are starting to mean more than the charity." At least it is a commendation. He has given this little group of believers some good compliments for them. He said He sees it with His eyes. You have charity, patience, faith, service and works and I don't want to forget that. I want to remember that because now he comes in with both feet and lands on this church with a condemnation.

"Notwithstanding I have a few things against thee, because thou sufferest that woman Jezebel, which calleth herself a prophetess, to teach and to seduce my servants to commit fornication, and to eat things sacrificed unto idols.

And I gave her space to repent of her fornication; and she repented not. Behold, I will cast her into a bed, and them that commit adultery with her into great tribulation, except they repent of their deeds."

Now the apostle John says that he wants to tell them what is going on here. I see it all with my eyes. Now we are not sure if this women's name really was "Jezebel". But someone in that congregation had all the characteristics of that I Kings 16, Jezebel. One of the most wicked women in the Bible. In fact, you look at her and Judas and you do not see anyone calling their children "Judas" or "Jezebel". I don't even think her name was Jezebel. But she had all the characteristics of that wicked women, the wife of Ahab. Christ says this prophetess was named Jezebel. If you look at history, she was the wife of one of the church leaders at Thyratira. And as history says, she was so good-looking and eloquent and so intelligent and smart and so gifted in communications that she literally took over and was leading the church at Thyratira into a literal spiritual hell. And you say, "well, how can someone do that?" Well, I don't know, but it was happening.

It is one thing to think about vicious wolves coming into a community from the outside. But it is a completely different thing when you think about the compromise and the unrest of that sin that starts on the inside and then spreads out into the community. This is what happened with Jezebel. Allowing this big objective of this women to take over a church and nearly ruin it. We see later on that she doesn't completely ruin it. But if you would go into the church of Thyratira today and you would go back 2000 years ago, you would wonder what is going on here! You would say we would never tolerate that. But it starts very subtly. I will tell you what is happening there. Thyratira was possibly started by a women named Lydia. Lydia was converted by Paul in Philipi. She was the seller of purple and she sold it from Thyratira because that is where she lived. Thyratira was noted for this selling of purple. In fact, Thyratira was the beginning of unions and building guild. Tanning, wool, dye…. Thyratira was a business section and this seller of purple, Lydia was the woman who came back because of the influence of Apostle Paul and helped start the church there. She was not Jezebel. Jezebel was a different woman completely.

Let's talk about some of the things that she was encouraging. First of all, the sin that was creeping into this church was when she took over and was teaching and controlling the men. Now we are equal in the sight of the Lord as far as Christians; but there is a place in the Word of God, it says in Timothy 2, about how the authority of the churches should rest primarily upon the leadership and under the leadership of men. Now women have the ability to teach the Bible, and it says that in Titus 2 "Let the aged women likewise teach the younger women." And in that setting and capacity there are times where women have a place for teaching. But not in the authority or leadership of a church. Jezebel comes in and she was so good that she even convinced all the men.

Now in my background and the heritage where I come from, this happened in the 1700's or 1800's. I do not remember the lady's name, but she would go and take over these churches. She would preach in some of those churches and convince the men that they were all wrong! And then others would go down and try to council her and some of these men and they would say, "Well, she is a better communicator of the word than we are." And they couldn't do anything about it. Sarah Majors was her name!

So this woman Jezebel comes in and she not only has control over the men, but they like it because she is so good at it. Here is what she is doing there. She was teaching immorality as a part of the Christian community. She was saying, "There is nothing wrong. We are Christians in this community; and if we are really going to reach out to these lost people, you must be a part of these union guilds." At the end of the weekly meetings and feasting, they would have their times of sexual perversion. She says that if you want to really get down there and reach people, just kind of slide into that lifestyle. And as you can contact them they became a part of us! And Christ comes and says, "**You have seduced my servants to commit fornication and to eat things sacrificed to idols.**" That is where she had them. And not only that, there was also the teaching of the idolatry with it and to be totally unrepentant about it. People would come in from other areas, possibly from the church of Ephesus and Pergamos and they hated this sin, but they wouldn't repent

There should be a red flag when a group of men would try to come in and take the preeminence of any community of believers away! Because if it is not founded on the truth of God's Word, red flag! You can look in Acts and see this same thing happening! Look at Diotrephese. Look at Hymenaeus. They came in and the Bible says they loved to have the preeminence, and they came and wrecked churches. That is a shame! They could care less about the people who fell out by the way. They ruined these churches because they wanted to be the leader. So they took over and it was " my way or the highway!" Red flag!

The lesson today in the year 2009, if anyone comes in like a Jezebel, and gets away from the foundational truths, there should be a red flag of concern!

I will mention about six of these cardinal truths that should always stand! Resurrection.

Virgin birth. Deity of Christ. Trinity. Second Coming. Salvation by Grace through Faith Alone. Authority of God's Word Alone. If anyone comes and starts to tamper with one of these truths, watch out! They may say, "You know, resurrection isn't that big of a deal. You know, He is not really coming back. That is just a way He wanted to spiritualize it. If we live good enough, then someday we will just go on into eternity and maybe see God. Christ is not coming back, and if He did, it would be in a million years! You know, salvation through grace by faith is the way to get it started; but really, if you look at the Greek text there, when He says it is finished on the cross, what He was really saying is this is just the beginning. I want you to finish your salvation by your works. THAT IS ALL WRONG!

When somebody tries to creep in and start something so subtle to get away from those truths, that is what Jezebel was doing. I think if you would go back and look at that little community at Thyratira you would say, "You know, this is kind of a different looking group, but they look happy and Jezebel is such a wonderful lady. She is so hospitable in her home. Surely she can't be that wrong." Well, what Jezebel was doing in essence, and you see it at Pergamos and at Sardis, was that Jezebel started her own wicked culture. That is what she did and that was what they had! And people came in and they fell prey to this. Oh yes, they would say the right words and they would read from the Old Testament, and they had a church,; but when they were there long enough, they would seduce them to commit these kind of acts. That is an extremely wicked culture and a culture of gross sin!

I was fascinated by something the other day. I do not know if someone shared it with me. But you just take the word 'culture'. There is nothing wrong with that. I think cultures are interesting. But you take culture to the point like Jezebel did and notice what happens. Spell culture. CULT and URE. And this gentlemen says, "If you take URE, E standing for expanding or extracting from the Word of God, then you have the first four letters all made up for you, and you are ready to go." If I would come into this church and say, "I love this little community of believers, but there are some things like the resurrection. Hey, he never rose again. He was a good man but he never rose again." You would be taking and expanding things apart from what the Word of God says. You are extracting, you are expanding. And this is what Jezebel was doing and she took it into a religious cult. And she is judged for it. Look at her punishment in verse twenty one and verse twenty two.

"And I gave her space to repent of her fornication; and she repented not. Behold, I will cast her into a bed, and them that commit adultery with her into great tribulation, except they repent of their deeds."

So now you have a warning from the Lord. He is looking down here with x-ray vision. He has His brass feet ready to bring judgement and He says, "I have warned Jezebel about this." And it is no longer they and them, the personal pronoun is starting to change here. He says, "I will give you according to your works." You are going to fall prey to this wrong teaching and sinful habits. Then you will become a follower of this false church like Jezebel. You will experience this second death.

Now we know and we are familiar with the fact that we can all fall into sin. And we can fall into all kinds of sins; but to lead knowingly others into sin like Jezebel was doing, I think there is a stronger condemnation with that. You look at Matthew 18 and you can see that. Jezebel couldn't care less and she was not going to repent. So the Lord said He would bring this swift punishment to them.

As we said before, these churches can represent eras or they can represent specific happenings. I went back in my studies and found what was brought in during the era of Thyratira.

- Boniface III made first pope
- Kissing the Pope's foot
- Worshiping the images and relics
- Use of "holy water" begun
- Canonization of dead saints
- Fasting on Fridays and during lent
- Celibacy of the priesthood
- Prayer beads used
- The inquisition

- Sales of indulgences
- Transubstantiation
- Adoration of the wafer (Host)
- Bible forbidden to laypeople
- Cup forbidden to people at Communion
- Doctrine of purgatory decreed
- Doctrine of seven sacraments affirmed
- Jesuit order founded
- Tradition granted equal authority with Bible
- Apocryphal books put into the Bible
- Immaculate conception of Mary
- *Syllabus of Errors* proclaimed
- Infallibility of the Pope declared
- Public schools condemned
- Assumption of the Virgin Mary
- Mary proclaimed the mother of the church

This is over a period of years. But this is the warning that this will happen if you allow this to continue under the setting of a church like Thyratira. And we see how some of these things have become. It took over people's lives.

"Behold, I will cast her into a bed, and them that commit adultery with her into great tribulation, except they repent of their deeds." What He is saying here is, if they don't repent, they will experience the second death because they never even had a relationship with me. They will see death, hell and the grave! You can't have a worst judgement than that. It's an opportunity to repent.

He says, *"And I will kill her children with death"*. He is talking about any body who follows the teaching or counsel of that kind of an attitude of a Jezebel. I will wipe them out and forever they will be apart from me. But God says He has given an opportunity to repent.

"But unto you I say, and to the rest in Tyatira, as many as have not this doctrine, and which have not known the depths of Satan, as they speak; I will put upon you none other burden."

What is He saying? He is making it very simple. I went back in Acts 15 and I thought it sounded identical to when they met there. And notice how they gave the decree of how they were going to handle the idols and the blood. Do you know what they said? They said, "We are not going to put any more burden on you. Just follow the Lord." That is exactly what is going on at Thyratira. He is saying He knows there are some of you who have not fallen prey to this doctrine. And He says, "I am not going to place any other burden on you. All I am saying is, Don't follow Jezebel." Do not follow the doctrine or the Satanic things that she is involved with. Do not go down to those orgies. Do not eat the meat that is sacrificed to idols. And do not explore the depths of Satan.

Did you know there are people today who actually think that if they are going to reach someone in some area of sin, they have to go join them? Christ was with the sinners, but he did not partake of their sin. That is what He is saying here. You are in Thyratira, but you do not have to be a part of that cultist doctrine. And you do not have to know the depths of Satan. You do not have to go out and shoot up with crack, cocaine or heroin so you can reach some biker that you know. You do not have to do that. You can take the Word of God, the Light and Truth, and go anywhere you want to with it. But you do not have to be involved in their sin. He tells us not to get involved in their activities.

There is a lesson in this. There is a great danger today when churches try to integrate non-Biblical ideas into their faith. This is a part of the new Emergent Church! That is a danger. All of the sudden you are saying, "Well the Bible doesn't really say anything about this so I am going to come up with something that sounds good and let others decide!"

The Bible has the answer for everything! The Bible has the answer to everything that is about sin. Even though there may be a practice that people can look at differently, that doesn't make them a non-believer. I look at prophecy differently than some people. But there is a real danger in what happened to Jezebel. They said, "Well there is no Bible on this and that. You show me where it says I can't go down and be a part of a guild party, so I will just go join it." In time, they quit looking at what the Word of God said about homosexuality and incest and they became involved in the sin. There is a danger today when a church tries to integrate non-Biblical ideas into their faith. And it can happen. It did back years ago, and it can today!

"But that which ye have already hold fast till I come.

And he that overcometh, and keepeth my works unto the end, to him will I give power over the nations:" Now this could be a prophetic time when rewards are given out. It could be a part of the mellennial kingdom that we will look at later in Revelations 20 –22. I think there will be rewards given out for deeds done in the body.

"And he shall rule them with a rod of iron; as the vessels of a potter shall they be broken to shivers: even as I received of my Father.

And I will give him the morning star.

He that hath an ear, let him hear what the Spirit saith unto the churches."

"He shall rule them with a rod of iron" is talking about Christ. *"And I will give him the morning star."* In other words, everything about Christ is going to be indwelling in these people. Just like in Ecclesiastes, "their face shall be made to shine!" Why? Because Christ, the Morning Star, is in them and eternity is set in their hearts and their faces will literally shine.

I like to think that if you went back to Thyratira and could see the people who did not fall under the seducing hand of Jezebel, their faces would be shining because Christ was still the main factor of their lives. If you would ask one of them, "How is the Lord?" they would say, "Oh He is the joy factor of my life." You may talk to a person on the bench next to them and they look like wretchedness. Maybe they fell prey to this sin. Sin marks people.

Go down to the post office and look for the FBI wanted list. You can't even tell the age of those people. Sin wrecks the countenance of an individual. For the joy of the Lord brings light to the eye and a face that will shine. That is what He is saying here. *"I will also give you the Morning Star."* - A reflection of a risen Christ.

I love the way He says, *"He that hath an ear let him hear what the Spirit saith unto the churches."* He says this to nearly every church. He is saying that he wants them to sit up, pay attention, and listen to what He is saying. If you look back at this letter to this church, He is saying, "There is serious judgement when people openly tolerate and practice sin in the church." Thyratira, you have the warning. I want to see a pattern of obedience like some of you had. I want to see it continue." In spite of the sin that may be around you, you can still experience the joy of Christ in your walk no matter the church that you are in.

Every church has problems, but there is always a remnant of believers in every circumstance who love Christ.

In my mind I reviewed the churches this week. There are possible dangers that we experience in our lifetime, in our churches. But like Ephesus, you can get so caught up in your zealous good works that all of the sudden your "hot pant" after Christ is gone. That is a lesson for us. We need to keep the fervency when we wake up. The best thing in our life is the salvation of the Lord our God. He is the one who is preeminent in our lives and He is the one who leads and guides us. He is the one who gives us the Holy Spirit. He is supreme. And if we get away from that and we start looking at what we do each day, the flavor is gone. That is Ephesus.

Same thing can happen at Thyatira. Loving and allowing sin then caring less about discipline. There was no discipline in the church at Thyatira.

"Hey! Are you guys going to a party?"

"Yeah, just a minute. I'll get my Bible and come along!!!"

No discipline. They tolerated it.

Pergamos tolerated idols and evil and even invited the judgement of God. And if you will remember Smyrna, there was not really any condemnation to them because they were under such persecution. The Lord gave them encouragement to hold fast. But we have had a warning with Smyrna, don't cave in. When someone tries to influence you away from Christ, don't cave in.

And that is thrilling to me. That is why He starts the book of Revelation in this manner. The unveiling is because He is warning every single era and every single church that this is a possibility for your life. Don't let it happen. "Take my blessing. Take my commendation and run with it because the Christian life is thrilling and exciting and there is nothing like it! But if you allow yourself to get burdened down with the Jezebels of life and the persecutions of life and the sin of life, you will break." Every single time the Lord Jesus Christ is looking at the churches with love in His eyes, he is looking right at you!

It is so exciting to me. I have read through the book of Revelations a few times now. And we are going to get through the churches. But one of these days we are going to get to chapter 4 and we are going to get up to heaven. And we will be in heaven a long time. And we are going to look at a lot of tragedy that will happen on this planet. But you know, the book of Revelation is so exciting because it ends with a bunch of "Hallelujahs" and "Amens" and a bunch of "choruses" and a bunch of people singing. This is the way the book ends!

When He puts the final dot on the history of man, it is in GLORY! We will be giving praise throughout eternity to our King!

REVELATIONS 3:1-6
Sardis
A Dead Church

"And unto the angel of the church of Sardis write; These things saith he that hath the seven Spirits of God, and the seven stars; I know thy works, that thou hast a name that thou livest and art dead. "And unto the angel of the church of Sardis write; These things saith he that hath the seven Spirits of God, and the seven stars; I know thy works, that thou hast a name that thou livest and art dead. that are ready to die: For I have not found thy works perfect before God. Remember therefore how thou hast received and heard, and hold fast, and repent. If therefore thou shalt not watch, I will come on thee as a thief, and thou shalt not know what hour I will come upon thee. Thou hast a few names even in Sardis which have not defiled their garments; and they shall walk with me in white: for they are worthy. He that overcometh, the same shall be clothed in white raiment; and I will not blot out his name out of the book of life, but I will confess his name before my Father, before his angels. He that hath an ear, let him hear what the Spirit saith unto the churches."

Today we will talk about one of the most tragic churches that are mentioned in Revelations. Everything that Christ said to the Pharisees and Scribes is the same thing that he could have been saying to the church at Sardis. He could have been saying the same thing to them, "Woe unto you! Woe unto you! Woe unto you! You are nothing but a bunch of white sepulchers! You are dead inside! You are full of iniquity! Woe! "

Today will be talking about the church at Sardis as we continue our march through Revelation. Every one of these churches seems to have a little bit of good with them, but not the Church at Sardis. That is why

I call it 'tragic'. If there is any hint of life here, it is the verse that says, *"Some of you, I want you to strengthen what you have left here."* We are going to talk about that today. The church at Sardis is a **'dead'** church. I thought about calling it the **'black-line'** church or the **'brown rock'** church because I am a farmer. If you were a banker, you could call it a **'bankrupt'** church. If you were a doctor, you may call it the **'flat-line'** church. Anything that talks of death would be a great description! So we will call it the **'dead' church.**

I have really been enjoying this study because of the lessons for today! But what does a 'dead' church have to do with churches today? Just what are the lessons? Well we will walk into the text and see!

Sardis, **"Woe unto you. You are a dead church**!"

You mean we have to read this in our congregation? They take the letter to this city in Sardis and the leader, Milito, reads this letter to the church. **"I know your works, you have a little bit of a reputation here, but you are dead."** What would go through your mind if this letter was read to your church?

Astronomers tell us that the light from the polar star takes thirty three years to get to planet earth. Now if this star would all of the sudden be extinguished or banished, we wouldn't know about it for thirty three years. Something happened in the town of Sardis. Maybe it was just living on the light of its brilliant past! I can walk out into a walnut orchard and I can look at a tree. And sometimes at the first glance I can't tell if it has **black line** disease. Yet if it has black line disease, it is finished. It is dead! It is not going anywhere because there is no life. There may be leaves for awhile; but after a period of time it is dead. This is a picture of Sardis. They were playing church. And as we read in some of the history books, they played church for a couple of centuries. They went to church but they were dead. They had a name, but they were dead. They had programs, but they were dead. They read from the Bible but they were dead. They had functions, but they were dead. They had services and songs, but they were dead. Wow, that sounds pretty conclusive!

Well, what is the definition of a dead church? Is it everybody sleeping on the benches? That is not a dead church. A dead church is when there is no Spirit of the Lord in the midst! Isn't that the same way it is with your physical body? If there is no sign of life, if there is no spirit there, you are dead! And that was the way it was at Sardis. It was a dead church. "Ichabod", the Spirit of the Lord had departed.

He is giving them a warning. He says for them to look up. "You have a sad reputation, yet there are still some believers here. There is a remnant and I do not want you to go the way like all the rest of them." I had to wonder how many people he was talking about. You can read many accounts, but there is not a lot said about Sardis. There may have been 2,000 to 3,000 people there who professed to be believers at the writing of the letter. Did you know that the majority of those people were probably not born-again people? And many were in some positions of leadership. Maybe some of them were involved in things they thought were right but they were a dead church. When the Spirit leaves the body it is dead. I call that tragic. Colossians 1:18 *"Jesus Christ is the head of the body."* And when the head of the body looks down and looks at a church and says, You are dead! Wouldn't that be the ultimate shame? I would think so. Because the definition of a healthy church is: **'Where Christ dwells'. Where Christ is. Where the Holy Spirit is vibrant. Where there is life among the believers.**

I would like to break down these six verses. I want to look at the **reputation** of Sardis in verses one and two. Then I want to look at the **reformation**. This change that desperately needed to be seen here in Sardis in verses three and four. Then I came to a conclusion last night as I was studying that there was a bright promise that was given to **the remnant** in the Church at Sardis.

"And unto the angel of the church of Sardis write; These things saith he that hath the seven Spirits of God, and the seven stars; I know thy works, that thou hast a name that thou livest and art dead."

Now this is the reputation that He is talking about as He looks at this church Sardis. It's weighing in time! When boxers get together and get ready to fight in the ring, they have a time called, **"weighing in time"**. They weigh in and then they go into the ring. Now our God in heaven has a very special balance and measure that He weighs individuals and churches and nations and families. He weighs them in the balances. It is weighing in time for this church. God is the judge of this church. He says, "Get on the scales Sardis, I am going to judge your works." Now can you imagine the picture of these people? They look right, they look clean and respectable, and maybe they looked in order. (Matt. 23) They climb on these scales and they do not even come close to measuring up. The verdict comes and the Lord says, "Yes you have a name, a reputation that you are a great church, but you are DEAD!" There is no life in this church. And here you stand on the scales and what are you going to say? "Oops." What are you going to say? This is the Lord speaking here. A church fully weighed by the Lord and found wanting!

I can't imagine a group of believers getting to the point in their walk with the Lord that they completely forgot their heavenly calling. This church had forgotten their heavenly calling. This church had forgotten what it was all about. This church might as well put a sign out on the door, "Out of Business." As I studied this church at Sardis, this name Milito kept coming up. Milito was one of the godly men, possibly one of the founders of the church at Sardis. So there was a remnant of godly people there.

I want you to notice as we think of a 'flat line' church, how this can quickly happen. It can happen in the year 2009. You have a man who is moved by God. He has **the movement** of the Spirit, and people are with him. Then all of the sudden it changes into **a machine**. Then it ends up in **a monument**. That is death. It can take one year or it can take one hundred years. But when a man forgets his heavenly calling and the people working together forget about Jesus Christ, it will die a tragic death!

Do you know what was happening at Sardis? They had the rags out and they spent all their time polishing the monument of the church. They thought they had a reputation. They may have had a nice building and looked good. It was a wealthy town, but all they had was a **monument**. God looks down right through all of that. He says, "I don't care about the man, the machinery, the methods, or the monument! It is dead and I am not going to have my presence there anymore!" Have you ever been to a church like that?

I am so grateful for my grandfather Rumble. As a Pastor in a Baptist Church in Modesto, sometimes he would load us grandsons in the car and go to different churches in our area! Some we really enjoyed. But I can distinctly remember one in Stockton and one in south Modesto that really got out of hand! Finally grandpa loaded us up and got us away from the strange worship services that we witnessed. Then he would explain what happened and why. These were learning experiences for all of us as young children.

There are Sardis churches on the planet today- people so hung up on the monument or the sign or what they stand for that they forget about the Holy Spirit. Can you imagine bringing someone into your home or church and drilling them about how you must live or else? That is death.

I look back and see why there was not life in some of those buildings and Churches!

He is saying the same thing to Sardis. He says, "I know you. You have a name. You stand for something. You think you are living, but you are dead." I say that is pretty direct and powerful.

*Verse two: "**Be watchful and strengthen the things which remain**."* Now He is talking in verse two but referring to verse four. He is saying that He knows there is a remnant here in Sardis, a dead church. "But I know there is a remnant of you who are alive. And I want you to be watchful and strengthen the things which remain or they will die." He is telling the remnant that in the body where they worship there is death, but you are alive. So strengthen the things that do remain!

What things is He talking about here? As I studied the word 'things', it is really a neuter noun in Greek, and it is not talking just about objects. It is talking about truths, spiritual realities, and doctrines. He is not talking about a billboard sign or a principal of exactly how you wash feet or a practice that you may have. He is talking about **spiritual truths**. Do not let the truths of the Word die. Salvation, Sanctification, a Loving of the Lord, Resurrection, Virgin Birth, Second Coming, Trinity, Authority of the Bible- do not let those things get away from you. Strengthen those things which remain. **Wake up or you will end up being a club**. Your **movement** at some point will be a **monument**. Your **conviction** will be a **culture**. He is telling them to wake up. Go back to the basics because that is where I am at.

Did you know Peter was written at this time? They could have gone back to 1 Peter. Strengthen that. They could have read Peter and went back to those basic truths. He is telling them to strengthen these things or they will become a marble monument. And you can get your polish out and wax away all you want, but you are dead. And many didn't even know that God was gone.

Do you know who that reminds me of? It reminds me of Samson. Samson had it together when he was following the Lord. He had all kinds of strength. His strength was in his long hair and God was working in his life until he got caught up with Delilah. She cut off his hair and all of the sudden he went out to do battle and his strength left him! Then he became blind and then he was out there grinding grain. That was the picture at Sardis. There was no more strength of the Holy Spirit working in their lives. **It is so tragic when a church gets to the point of being a monument where nothing is left but a culture**. They are bound up in themselves. There is death there with just dusty symbols and weirdness.

That is a warning for my private life. I can look like a Christian. I can quote Scripture. I can present the Gospel to you. But I am dead inside if I do not have the Holy Spirit and a life that is a testimony of Christ. If there isn't excitement in my life about the Lord, then there is something wrong! You can get great actors out of Hollywood. There are actors and they can put on a façade or a mask......but they are still dead with the Holy Spirit of God in them! And the proof of that was Symrna. We looked at Symrna and there was not anything going right on the outside, but they had the Spirit of God in their life.

"Remember therefore how thou hast received and heard, and hold fast, and repent. If therefore thou shalt not watch, I will come on thee as a thief, and thou shalt not know what hour I will come upon thee. Thou hast a few names even in Sardis which have not defiled their garments; and they shall walk with me in white: for they are worthy."

There are three things we want you to consider. He is telling them here to remember **the past**, to recognize exactly where you are in **the present** and to strongly be ready for **the future**. Now, that is very applicable for us. We are a remnant of God's people. The Lord has His remnant of believers everywhere. There can be a remnant of believers in every denomination, in every church, even in a cult. God knows the heart. So He is saying here that He wants them to remember the past. What is He saying? Look what he says in verse three, *"Remember therefore how thou hast received and heard"*. I want you to remember the time when you had the Holy Spirit-not only presented to you but you accepted Him in your life! Every church is born at a time when there is a moving of the Spirit. I think what has happened here, this moving of the Spirit, has now taken on slabs and slabs of man's traditions-Ritualistic traditions, everyone slouching into complacency, holiness not "fun" anymore! He is telling them to remember what it was like in the past.

He says to *hold fast*. Now He is talking about the present. "Sardis, I want you to hold fast. All the dynamic things you have heard in the past, I want you to remember that. And by way of self-examination and introspection, look at your life, Judge your church. Judge your own heart and look to me." I believe the remnant was doing this. He says to remember the past, recognize the present. How hard is it to just judge yourself? You know, when someone comes up to me in a right way to show me my "blind" spots, I appreciate it. And they say, Gordon, you should consider this and that. Sometimes you kind of get a little ticked off, but that person loves you and really does care!. I would like to encourage you believers in the body of Christ. When you see things that are going wrong, and you love that individual, go talk to them. Because you both win and you both mend! If you have a problem, I want you to deal with it. And then use self-examination to judge your own heart.

I love this story about two small boys. Their dad and mom decided they were old enough to stay at home alone when the parents went out to dinner together. They were seven years old. The parents left these two seven year-old boys at home alone. When the father and mother were pulling back into the driveway on their way home that evening, there was not a light on in the house. They panicked and they wondered what happened. They went in and turned on the light, walked into the kitchen, and there on the table was the most expensive vase the mother had and it laid in a shattered mess. Nothing but a broken pile of many broken pieces. At the bottom of this pile was a note that was stuck under the pieces. They picked up the note and it said, "Dad and mom, we knocked over your vase, we are so sorry and we went to bed without any supper." Do you think that father and mother went upstairs and got them out of bed and spanked them? No. The boys had judged themselves, made the confession, and had hopes for the future!

We do not know the end of Sardis and the Church there, but maybe this remnant kept this church alive for many years. Then He continues with another message.

He wants them to be ready for the future. He says, "If you do not pay attention to what I am trying to tell you here, I am going to bring judgment to this congregation. If you read about Turkey and Asia Minor, and if you went there today, you would find very few Christian chrches. Most have been wiped out and there are reasons for that. You read in Acts, the world was turned upside down because of persecution. I like to think that the remnant of believers were persecuted so heavily that they did flee and kept their faith alive as they relocated in other areas. He tells them he wants them to be ready for the future.

"Thou hast a few names even in Sardis which have not defiled their garments;"

And this brings up a promise that I want to leave with you. So many times when people get to this section in Revelation, they take it as a threat. It is not a threat. It is a promise. It was a bright promise to the remnant in Sardis. ***"He that over cometh, the same shall be clothed in white raiment; and I will not blot out his name out of the book of life, but I will confess his name before my Father, before his angels. He that hath an ear, let him hear what the Spirit saith unto the churches."***

There is something you need to consider here. It says *He that ove rcometh.* Who is an over comer? It is not somebody who is living better than somebody else or doing better deeds. An over comer by definition in the Word of God, 1 John 5:5 ***"Him who believes and has faith in Jesus Christ the Son of God."* That is an over comer.**

He says He is going to clothe them in white, which is the righteousness of the saints! You are going to have a continued name in the **book,** and I will confess your name before the Father.

Now what He is not saying here is this: some people assume that this verse teaches that a Christian's name can be erased from the Book of Life. But that is not what He is saying here. Contrary to that He is saying, "Look, this is a positive thing! I am not making a promise into a threat!" This is not Exodus 32:32. He is talking about the Book of Life here. He is saying that if you are an overcomer your name is not going to be blotted out. That is a promise. That is positive. Some people think that, well, if I do not live right, I am not an overcomer. Yes, if you are not an overcomer, your name is not going to be in the Book of the Living! No one will ever be in that book unless their faith is placed in the shed blood of Jesus Christ! Period.

I like to think that this is a very good promise, because you can tie that in with Romans 8, **there is nothing that is going to separate you from the love of Christ. Not height, not depth, not principalities, nothing.** That is the security you have as an overcomer. Your faith is in Christ. Your name is not going to be wiped out. There will be a continuation of your name forever! I think the remnant of these people, as it was read to them, it was a very positive thing. That is the beauty of the incorruptible seed of God! It will abide forever!

"He that hath an ear let him hear what the Spirit saith unto the churches." What is he saying? He is saying, if you are a zombie out there, you better pay attention. "If you are letting things slip away in your life, I will remove your candlestick." (your usefulness) I believe even some of these people who even professed Christ, their candlestick was removed. What am I saying? The effectiveness of the Christian testimony was completely gone. But to the remnant, if they sat up, were obedient and listened, there was a promise to them and a tremendous blessing in the future for ministry!

I read an account in 1750 where the Catholic Church made a statement. If you didn't adhere to certain things and follow them, the Pope came up with an edict that you would not only be struck from the role call of the churches, but you would be struck from the roll call of heaven. That shattered the lives of hundreds of thousands of millions of people. People gave up hope. People knew it was signed by the Pope, and since they did not follow their dogmas, their names were scratched from the roll call of Heaven! And finally a man by the name of Savana Rola walked up, took one look at the edict, and before ending his life he said, "I do not care if you have struck me from the roll call of what you call the 'church militant', but you will never strike my name from the church triumphant." That was the message that was going to Sardis.

Now I would like to close by giving **an autopsy** of the church of Sardis. I would like to give them a definitive autopsy report. And maybe it would go something like this. How did this church ever die? How did this church ever die to the things of the Lord? As we stand there looking at this dead church and we speak into this tape recorder, we can ask questions and make some statements. We know they didn't die from an enemy on the outside, because a church can't die from an enemy on the outside. And if you want proof of that, you can look at Symrna again. They were still thriving under severe persecution. A church is not going to die because somebody pounds on the door. Contrary to that, the church probably spread the most under intense persecution. The Bible says their whole world was turned upside down. As we look at Sardis, we know they didn't die because of the enemy from without.

Let's look at it a little bit closer. Did they die because all of the sudden the congregation at Sardis stood up in unison and said, "Lets quit". No, they did not die because of that. That is not the way a church dies. They don't vote on it. They didn't die because they didn't have the right kind of finances, or the proper programs in place. That isn't what kills a church. "Well if we would have just had a better singing program, and if we would have allowed Eternal Praise to come, then maybe we would have lasted another 200 years." That is not what kills a church. Now there can be frustrations in a church because of the song services, yes, but it isn't what kills a church.

Well maybe they died because God just walked away from them. You can't stack that up with the Word of God. I have never seen God walk away from anybody. God is the most merciful, forgiving, and longsuffering God. He is the only one. He loves this church so much that He gave them this letter. He talks and pleads with the remnant. He doesn't walk away.

Then what killed the church? I will tell you. They died because somewhere at some time people became completely indifferent to their Savior. What about the Second Coming? Forget about that, we have things to do. We are taking a field trip. And somewhere and at some point in the life at that church there was no more panting after the Lord,. There was no more recognition that without Him we are nothing. There was no more caring, and you can see the prayers disintegrating and they came together for fun or for the monument. "Look what we have! Look at our stain glass windows! Look at the money we have in the bank!" They got away from their thirst for God in heaven. And because of that indifference and carelessness, this church died. There was still movement, there were still people, and there were still programs, but God had departed!

Result. They died because they were willing to go to sleep in the present as they dreamed about the past.

I confess today that there are times in my life when I have been in conversation with people and have referred to something that was exciting in my life three years ago. But, what about yesterday? Has there been a long "gap" since I shared Christ? When you share the Gospel with others, make sure it has been recent, because that will mean more to the individual and it will mean more to you. That means God is currently alive in your life. Not because of something that happened seventeen years ago, but because yesterday Jesus answered this prayer or whatever it is. Christianity is relevant to our communities today! Yes, we can dream about the past and be thankful for things that have happened 200 years ago, but it is what happened yesterday and today that will make the difference in someone seeing your excitement about JESUS!

Sardis, was a dead church. Started with **a man**, had a **little movement**, looked like a **machine** and ended up **a monument**. And they polished it for hundreds of years. Let that not be said of your life and my life and the church.

Revelation 3:7-13

Philadelphia
A Feeble, Yet Faithful Church

"And the angel of the church at Philadelphia write; These things saith he that is holy, he that is true, he that hath the key of David, he that openeth, and no man shutteth; and shutteth and no man openeth; I know thy works: Behold, I have set before thee an open door, and no man can shut it: for thou hast a little strength, and hast kept my word, and hast not denied my name. Behold, I will make them of the synagogue of Satan, which say they are Jews, and are not, but do lie; behold, I will make them to come and worship before thy feet, and to know that I have loved thee. Because thou hast kept the word of patience, I also will keep thee from the hour of temptation, which shall come upon all the world, to try them that dwell upon the earth. Behold, I come quickly: hold that fast which thou hast, that no man take thy crown. Him that overcometh will I make a pillar in the temple of my God, and he shall go no more out: and I will write upon him the name of God, and the name of the city of my God, which is new Jerusalem, which cometh down out of heaven from my God: and I will write upon him my new name. He that hath an ear, let him hear what the Spirit saith unto the churches."

The church of Philadelphia is the feeble, yet faithful church. If I would have another title for it, I would just say, Philadelphia the **true missionary church**. If I was an individual who could sit in any of these seven churches, and I knew there was going to be an individual walk in and read a letter to me, this is the church I would like to be sitting in. The church at Philadelphia has no condemnation whatsoever. There are only good things the Lord has to say to this church. A feeble church, yet a faithful church. When I say feeble I am not talking about a lack of strength and power. It is just that they were the smallest of the churches. He says in one place, "little strength". He means "little power," because there is just a little group of them. And yet they were a faithful and obedient church. I had to think about that. These are real churches, with real people, in a real place, in a real time period, and they were actually in buildings worshiping together. Only two churches out of the seven does the Lord give any real confirmation by saying that these churches are doing anything right. I am not sure how you are with percentages, but that does not sound too good, does it? Two out of seven.

When Craig and I went to Australia, we woke up on a Sunday morning and looked in that huge Melbourne book that had 475 churches. Which one do we go to? Well, we finally agreed on one and we went to it and we enjoyed it. But I had to think that out of 475 churches , only 150 were decent places of worship? I don't know. But I know one thing, 2 out of 7 were the only ones where Christ had no condemnation whatsoever to say. Smyrna and Philadelphia. One was persecuted church and one was a very small, obedient, faithful church.

As we have studied these churches, we have seen a whole array of believers. I think there is a purpose for this. In all seven churches we will find application for churches today. There are good things from these churches about this congregation, and one down the road, and one across the block, and in the next community, and the next state, and the next continent. But the same warnings that have gone out to the seven churches are things that we should think about for ourselves.

All of these churches fit into time periods. One thing I like about Philadelphia is that we are living in the Philadelphia time age today. The missionary age. And even though there is application from Laodicia, because they do kind of over-lap, I like to think that the Laodicean church age is the church age that will go on into the tribulation. I will say more about that later.

"And the angel of the church at Philadelphia write; These things saith he that is holy, he that is true, he that hath the key of David, he that openeth, and no man shutteth; and shutteth and no man openeth; I know thy works: Behold, I have set before thee an open door, and no

man can shut it: for thou hast a little strength, and hast kept my word, and hast not denied my name."

Everything the Lord is saying here is positive. "You have a little bit of power here, but you have not denied my Name. You are a good church." What is He saying about this key? He is talking about Christ. He is the one who is holy. The Bible is very clear. He was holy at His birth, Luke 1:35. In fact it even says, *"and this thing which is holy."* He was not only holy at His birth, but He was holy at His death, Acts 2:27, *"He will not suffer His soul to see corruption."* And He is also holy in His priestly office today as he is praying and interceding for his body, the church. Holy, harmless and undefiled, Hebrews 7. So He was holy at His birth, holy at His death, He is holy as He is seated at the right hand of the Father today. And this same one who is holy is also true. In other words, He is genuine. There is nothing false about Him.

This same one who is holy and true is the same one who has the key. What is the key? Anyone in the Bible who has a hold of a key is the person who is in the position of authority and control. So Christ is saying, I am holy and I am true and I have the key. I am going to open the door and when I open it, no man will shut it. The application: When Christ is walking in the midst of the churches as in this incident with the church at Philadelphia, He is saying, "I am looking at this church. I have the key. I am walking in and opening the door now and you have the greatest opportunity for missionary effort that has ever been seen. Walk through the door and I will honor it through you." This explosion of this church age of Philadelphia is awesome. The great revival has taken place in the Philadelphian church age. The greatest things that have ever been started in Christianity has taken place in this church age.

I was thinking about the Salvation Army, the Gideons, the Hudson Taylors, and all these godly people. It is all during this time period, because someone was willing to walk through a door, that no one was going to be able to shut. That is why He is saying there just might be a handful of people here and there ---- you people are walking through because you are faithful and obedient. That is a compliment to the church at Philadelphia. Three times the Lord calls on this church to behold. "Behold! Listen! Be quiet and pay attention. Take notice. I am taking the key and I am opening the door and it will not be shut. Walk through it." Even though He saw their weakness and their smallness, He saw their willingness.

As He looks down here in 2010, is He seeing the same thing? You may think you have no strength in you. But if you do, great. That is exactly what the Apostle Paul thought. My strength is made perfect in weakness. What He wants to see is a willingness to walk through the door. And if God calls you to walk through the door for Him, then do it!

I like to think that is why they were placed 30 miles south of Sardis in the trade route because everybody who knew Greek had to go through Philadelphia. What an opportunity. And all of the sudden they see someone new in town and they share with them. Open door. They walked through. No one is going to shut it. What a unique opportunity for them.

I had to think of the Apostle Paul. 1 Corinthians 16:8-9, "*There is a great door open unto me.*" The Apostle Paul was excited about that. He said that. There is another place in 2 Corinthians 2 "*A door is open unto me.*" That excitement continued in Colossians 4, "*A door of utterance is open unto me.*" What is he saying? Everywhere I am at in my missionary journeys it just seems like the Lord is opening up a door of utterance that I can share and speak the gospel of Christ. And that is exactly why he wrote in Romans 1, "*I am not ashamed of the gospel of Christ.*" It is the power of God unto salvation to everyone who believeth. And Bob Monroe understands that. He told me that anytime I want to call him with any of your friends that you can't speak with, "you call me and I will go."

Can you do that? If someone has a troubled friend and they call you on the phone, are you going to drop everything you are doing? That is an opportunity. It may not be sharing the gospel. It may be a kind deed or helping hand or just to pray with them. That is the door open unto me, the spreading of God's Word. That is so incredibly awesome!

I think about this **key**. A lot of times when I see something like **key**, I will jump back and get my concordance out and look up everything that has **key**. So I find it very interesting. Did you know that you can have a verse that sounds just like this one in Revelation 3. It is all the way back in Isaiah 22:22. And there it talks about Eliakim, who was like the Prime Minister under King David. Eliakim had a **key** to the palace. The Bible says in Isaiah, "*only Eliakim can open the door and no one can open it and no one can shut it except for Eliakim.*" Eliakim opens the door and he shuts it. And here we have a picture of Jesus Christ not only opening the door for the opportunity of salvation, but He also has the key on into the millennial kingdom that He, as He reigns as a Messianic King, He is the only one who can open that door and no one can shut it. I say Hallelujah! This is our Savior speaking.

So I would like to say that verses seven and eight is proof that all saints are under the control of the heavenly king. He has the key. He has the authority. He has the love and he has the ability to look down into our hearts. And He can say the door is open for you. I want you to walk through it. All saints are under the control of the King.

"Behold, I will make them of the synagogue of Satan, which say they are Jews, and are not, but do lie; behold, I will make them to come and worship before thy feet, and to know that I have loved thee."

What is He saying? In verses seven and eight He said that all saints are under my control! Now He is just saying in verse nine that all unbelievers and sinners are under His control. This sounds negative when He says that some of them are saying they are Jews and are not. What He is saying is that "they are rejecting me and rebelling against me, but there will come a time when they will bow down." I think it is a picture of what the Apostle Paul went through. Wasn't there a day when he claimed to be the greatest of all the Jews? And he was the one who was following God and he did everything right. Then all of the sudden after the Damascus road experience and a complete about face, he is bowing his knee with the name of Jesus- Right along with the other Christians. He is saying that here. "If you have a willingness to follow me there will come a time when some of these folks who are unbelievers will bow their knee along with you, because I know these people and some of them, in their hearts, are not really Jews. They will get saved just like you." I call that very positive. He is in complete control of the sinners.

Some of them were out to kill and destroy. Then all of the sudden things changed. The rest of his life he was worshiping the Savior. The same thing could happen in the town of Philadelphia, a change because of Christ.

"Because thou hast kept the word of patience, I also will keep thee from the hour of temptation, which shall come upon all the world, to try them that dwell upon the earth. Behold, I come quickly:" This is exciting, I would title this '**All situations and circumstances are under His control**.' Why am I excited about that? This is the first open hint that

Christ is going to come quickly and He is going to save His people out of this terrible time of tribulation. I am going to give you a little run down of how people may look at this and what I believe the Scripture says. I am not trying to diminish other peoples beliefs.

Sometime Christ is coming back. I think all Christians understand that. He is coming again because He said He was. But when He comes and how He comes… this is the way I look at it, pre-tribulation rapture. Christ could come right now. If He blows the trumpet, He could come right now. And I like to believe that. There is nothing that could exempt Him from coming right now. Nothing has to happen. That is called 'pre-tribulation' rapture. Others would believe that they will go 3 ½ years into the tribulation and that is called 'mid-tribulation' rapture. Others believe that Christ will not come until the end of the 7 years of tribulation and that is called, 'post-tribulation' rapture. There are some that believe that there will not be any tribulation and we are in it now and that He will just come again. That is fine because He IS coming again. I would never break fellowship with anyone who wants to believe that. But I believe that He could come at anytime for one simple fact, but I will share some others with you.

Anything that takes away from watchfulness to me is in error. If you place the coming of Christ in any other time period, you are looking for something else. Because once we start in chapter 6 of Revelation, we know exactly every day and every month what is going to happen in the tribulation period. It says what is going to happen. We will see all of that and we know what is coming next. I believe that the Apostle Paul thought that the imminent return of Christ could come in his time.

I am not looking for signs. I am looking for the sound of the trumpet. I Thessalonians 4, says that He is coming. If you do not believe that way, it does not mean that you are not a Christian. It does not mean that you are not saved. It doesn't mean that you are an immature Christian. In fact I would encourage you to study Revelation on your own. Do a complete inductive study of this book alone. But as I present the book of Revelation, to me it opens it up here when He is saying to the church in Philadelphia, "Because they have kept my Word of my patience, I am going to keep you from the hour of temptation which will come." The Bible says in Daniel 9 that there will be a 70th week and this is going to be a literal 7 years. You will see that in the book of Revelation. This terrible time of Jacobs's trouble will come upon this planet. But I believe that the church will be called out of that when it says, ***"kept from this hour of temptation."***

I dug a little deeper. I like to do that. When it says to 'keep from the hour of temptation' the Greek word is *teloek*. Everywhere else in the Bible it is *teloen*. There is a big different here. When he says to keep from the hour of temptation, the other places in the Bible mean 'to keep you through it' or 'keep you around it' or 'keep you in it but from the hurt'. But *teloek* is different, *teloek* is 'I want you to take them out or completely away from' this hour of tribulation. I think that is very significant when He says he is going to keep you from this tribulation completely. I find it very interesting in chapters 1, 2, and 3, when God gives a vision of Himself, and when He talks to the seven churches. Nineteen times he uses the word 'church'. We are going to find from the 4th to the 19th chapters that there is no mention of the church at all. Not once. Why? Because it is not here. We are going to see John and go up with him. We are going to look down in a panoramic view of what is going to take place on planet earth for seven years. Then all of the sudden the church is going to show up again.

There will be people saved during the tribulation. They are called the tribulation saints. I like to think that when He says He will keep us from the hour of this temptation. Why would He come in chapters 6 & 10, 7 & 14 and 9 and then break His promise. To those people who are dying there, everything is reduced to martyrdom. Everything is reduced to "if you do not accept the mark, then you are finally saved". That is not the call of the church. I want to keep this very basic. Jesus Christ could come right now. You say, "Well I see signs happening all around on the planet." Hallelujah.

Luke 22 says, *"When you see these things begin to come to past, then look up your redemption draweth nigh".* I think we are that close. As I get close to San Francisco, I begin to see signs of advertisements for San Francisco. We are living on the last page of the final chapter of mankind. And we are seeing the blessings of the signs of his imminent return.

Romans 5:29, *"We shall be saved from the wrath to come."* I Thessalonians 1:10, *"We wait for the son from heaven who will deliver us from the wrath to come."* This is the same promise he made in Revelation 3:10. He will deliver us from the hour or wrath of temptation. You can also find other places in Scripture that will support this.

I do want to mention one more thing that bears our consideration. When we talk about a clear distinction between the church and the nation of Israel and God's chosen, there has to remain a clear distinction. I know some people will say that they blew it in AD 70, so now all the blessings go to the Church. I do not really think that is right. That is called "Replacement Theology and I do believe it is a serious error! The church and Israel are two separate things. I think there is a clear distinction between Israel and the church. That is why you have a clear distinction in Revelation, of the first 3 chapters concerning only the church. Chapters 4-19 are written to the nation of Israel (the Jews) and to unbelievers, regarding what happens on the planet.

So we are looking for His coming and not for events. I like the flow of Revelation as He encourages the Philadelphia church to remain faithful. As He says this in verse ten, notice it is very future. He said this hour of temptation will come to pass. It hasn't happened yet and it is not happening now. It is in the future. Not only is it future, but it is limited… an hour of testing. And not only limited… all of the sudden we notice it is worldwide and not just this church. Why does He specifically talk to the other churches, and then he comes to Philadelphia and says, *"This hour of temptation that is going to come upon all of the World"*. Because it is worldwide.

Then He says it is to the unbeliever. Why do we say that? Because the saints are removed and it will come upon the earth. That is when he uses the words, *"Behold I come quickly."*

As a young child we had worship with my dad and mom in our home and when we would go to my grandparents also. So many times, even as a teenager, when we would jump in the car to go do something, dad and mom would say, "Now remember, Son, the Lord could come!" "The Lord bless you. We might not see you for a week or two, but live for the Lord. He could come!" And I remember as a child there were times when I didn't want Him to come! We would get ready to go on a trip somewhere and I didn't want Him to come before that exciting trip! I wanted to go on a trip! Or we would get ready for a little league game and we would play for the championship, and I didn't want the Lord to come. It would mess up the game. But that is immaturity.

I want to ask you a question? **Do you really want Him to come**? Or is there something else that you would rather see happen in your life before He comes. I know it is good on all of our hearts, I would love to see some of my close friends come to the Lord. We pray for that. But there is nothing that has to happen before He comes. I will confess that even as a teenager, I really wanted to get married before He came. Then all of the sudden I was married, and that was really great, but then I really wanted a child before He came. Then that happened and that was neat then all of the sudden I wanted a grandchild before He came, and then that happened, and that is neat… and now I'm ready! ☺ We all have things like that. We would like to see Him come, but maybe in our time period. As we wake up every morning we should be looking for His coming. I love the songs about His coming again because it is going to happen.

I called Levi Bowman one afternoon, a student of end-times, with a question on this Laodicean church. I asked why, if we are living in the Philadelphia time period, why would Laodicea be mentioned later if they are the church that is at the end of the age? He told me to go back and read what He said to the Laodicean church. He is standing on the outside knocking, trying to get in. He says that he really believes that even though those overlap, from the rapture to Laodicea, there will be a church during the tribulation period, but it will be a false one. There will be people so caught up in themselves and Christ will be on the outside knocking and trying to get in. He is sitting in the midst of the first six churches and he is working in the lives of the believers. I like that thought. On the outside trying to get in. What a picture of what could be happening during the tribulation period.

"Him that overcometh will I make a pillar in the temple of my God, and he shall go no more out: and I will write upon him the name of God, and the name of the city of my God, which is new Jerusalem, which cometh down out of heaven from my God: and I will write upon him my new name."

I would like to call this verse the divine promise of our Savior. He has three 'I wills' here. He says, "I will make them a pillar in the midst of God. I will write on him the name of my God. I will write upon him my new name." Now this is the Lord, the one who has the key, the one who is in control and the one who has all authority. He is looking at this little church and he says, "you who are overcomers', you who believe in Christ."

And he says, " I will make you a pillar in the temple of God." What is he saying? I am going to promise you an eternal place in the heavens. And even though you think you are weak and undone and feeble, I will make you stable, solid and strong. I will even make you a part of your heart that can give you the confidence to endure to the end." He also says he will write on him the name of my God. In other words He will place a mark for all of eternity. "I am going to identify you with my grace and my mercy and my love." The song says, "Now I belong to Jesus". That is what He is saying. That is the promise to the overcomer. Those who live and are looking for that time when He takes them home to be with Him.

He said he will write upon him my new name. What is He saying? You know, not one of us can really describe our Savior. We love him. We know he died for us and rose again. We know that in faith believing we can have this eternal salvation. We can have the confidence to know we are sons of God, but we have not yet seen Him. Someday when that trumpet sounds and we stand face to face with our redeemer we will be able to call him a new name. Because as we stand and behold and stand in His presence, the fullness of His person and just seeing Him for who He is, face to face, we will be able to say this new name.

I thought about that little statement, **"my new name."** How passionate are we to want to stand in the presence of our redeemer? If you had the opportunity to walk outside with no one around and you knew that Jesus Christ in His fullness will stand there and He is going to talk to you face to face, would you have any apprehension whatsoever? I think that is our humanity. To prove that, you can look at every human in the Bible who faced God, They fell on their face and said, "Woe unto me." Paul! Everybody! I think we will be the same way. But the Bible says we do not have to be ashamed of His coming. If you love Him this morning, make sure that your supreme motivating passionate desire is to know Him and know more about Him and to love Him and live like Him. In fact if I would reduce these verses 7-13, I would just say, "Behold the King. Behave like the King." And if you do that, you are going to live with the King.

And he closes here, ***"You who hath an ear let him hear what the Spirit saith unto the churches."***

There was a story that took place in the battle of Britain during World War II. The spitfires and the hurricanes were really getting shredded. As the story goes, these men would come in from these flights trying to stave off the German bombers. These men would come down onto these dirt runways and crawl out of their planes and go to sleep immediately. They were exhausted and hadn't eaten or drank in days. They were at the end of their ropes. As the story goes, there were forty men out in this field and their planes parked in all different manner. They had all been refueled and everything, ready to go! But the men were sleeping from exhaustion and the man who controlled the radio said words like this, "**Bandits at 15,000 feet over your section P25 over.**"

And when that word came across to those men who flew these spitfires and hurricanes and they heard that, every man, EVERY man out in the grass or laying in the dirt, every man who heard this call, they stood to attention and said, "**message received and completely understood.**"

Now folks, there are times like this in our lives. Admit it! We get so caught up in this world. We are lying out there in the arena of life and we are tired and weary. We are going through things and all of the sudden we read a passage in scripture and the Lord says, "Wake up. Pay attention. Listen to what I am saying." **And I am asking you, can you say, "message heard, message received and message understood"?**

This is the call that Christ has for every one of us as we live in this age. The return of Christ is right around the corner. Not only be ready, but make sure when this door of opportunity is opening and that you are there in a position of willingness just like the church at Philadelphia. Listen, we have the textbook. We have the Bible. We have the Savior.We have prayer warriors everywhere. If you are getting ready to walk through a door, call someone and they will pray for you. The opportunities are ripe for the harvest. Walk through the door!

There was an old man in South Carolina. He was a pastor and he said this to his congregation and I love it. He said, "**Folks, this may be the time to wake up, sing up, preach up, pray up, never give up, never back up, always lift up, build up, so that when the trumpet sounds we can go up!**"

Laodicea
The Apostate Church

"And unto the angel of the church of the Laodiceans write; These things saith the Amen, the faithful and the true witness, the beginning of the creation of God; I know thy works, that thou art neither cold nor hot: I would thou wert cold or hot. So then because thou art lukewarm, and neither cold nor hot, I will spew thee out of my mouth. Because thou sayest, I am rich and increased with goods, and have need of nothing; and knowest not that thou art wretched, and miserable, and poor, and blind, and naked: I counsel thee, to buy of me gold tried in the fire, that thou mayest be rich; and white raiment, that thou mayest be clothed, and that the shame of thy nakedness do not appear; and anoint thine eyes with eyesalve, that thou mayest see. As many as I love, I rebuke and chasten: be zealous therefore, and repent. Behold, I stand at the door and knock: if any man hear my voice, and open the door, I will come in to him, and will sup with him and he with me. To him that overcometh will I grant to sit with me in my throne, even as I also overcame, and am set down with my Father in His throne. He that hath an ear, let him hear what the Spirit saith unto the churches."

Laodicea, the apostate church. It is the last of the seven churches. All of the churches here in Revelation were actually real churches in Asia Minor, and all within a radius of 150 miles from each other. Some of the churches were big and some were small. Laodicea happens to be one of the bigger churches. Laodicea was also a very wealthy church. They were so wealthy in fact that Rome would try to send funds to them. But they refused them because they didn't need financial help. They had that reputation for having wealth everywhere in the church.

The Laodicean church was kind of like a cosmopolitan church - real fancy and fashionable church. But it was an unregenerate church. It is a very sad picture when God says at the end of this chapter that He is on the outside knocking, try to get into this church. He said, "You have my name but you don't have me. Just let me in." As we think about the Laodicean church today, maybe it can wake us up in some areas of our lives!

I want you to imagine a scene with me as we begin this chapter. I want you to imagine that when you get up tomorrow morning, you do not feel very well. I mean you really feel bad. You feel so bad that you tell your family that you have to go to the doctor because there is something wrong. There is something inside of your body that is so wrong that it feels like the life is being sucked out of you! So they take you to the doctor. And you go in and the doctor takes you in a special room. He takes blood samples and your temperature and he runs all kinds of tests. They get the tests results back and the doctor says words like this, "Thanks for coming. Just go down the hall on your way out and pay $40 to the receptionist. I do appreciate your visit."

And you say, "Wait a minute doctor. I don't feel very good. I did all of these tests. And you know because I heard you making all these sounds and motions while I was going through these tests! You are telling me to go down here and pay my $40.00 and leave? Doctor, there is something wrong with me!"

And he says, "Well yes, in fact there is something wrong with you. You have the final week of the swine-flu plague. You are going to die and it will be soon!"

You say, "Well doctor, can't you do something? If I have the swine-flue plague I may have contaminated someone. Can't you put me in the hospital? Can't you give me some kind of pain medicine, a shot, or at least try something?"

And then the doctor says, "Now wait a minute. Don't get all riled up here. Everybody dies, and we all have to die sometime. This is just your week to die." So deal with it and pay the $40.00!

Now can you imagine a doctor saying something like that to you? You have an incurable disease and he just kind of sluffs you off and says thanks for coming. Now I cannot imagine a good MD caring less about disease and contamination and hurt in the body. I can't imagine that. And likewise we should not be able to comprehend a church that is lukewarm about Jesus Christ. Yet there are churches around the globe today that are entering this apostate feeling. They could not care less about Jesus Christ. I can't imagine a church that could not care less about Christ! And yet we can't imagine a doctor not caring about disease. There are people today that do not care about the Lord of Glory, the King of Kings and the Lord of Lords! And they are playing church, and they are going to church. They may be wealthy like the Laodiceans, but Christ is not there! I can't imagine that! And yet as time goes on, it will get worse and worse and worse! When Christ is knocking on the door, He is trying to get into the church. Even this passage is used as an evangelistic message trying to knock on the human heart and that is applicable too. The context of the scripture is "Let me into your church." That is a pretty sad picture.

"And unto the angel of the church of the Laodiceans write; These things saith the Amen, the faithful and the true witness, the beginning of the creation of God;"

As we think about Israel and how they turned away from the Lord in unbelief and was turning to idols, they forfeited so much blessing because of it. This is parallel to a church doing the same thing with Christ. They are walking away from Him. They do not want to listen to Him. Before you know it, you have people in the church role who have unregenerate hearts. There are people like that today who have no light, no life and they are walking in and joining churches and they Do Not Care!

If we would go back in time and go into the church at Laodicea about 1700 years ago, we would probably see a great building. And when we walked in, people would be smiling and doing a lot of things right. Their liturgy may have been right, but it would probably have been more of a social gospel and not much said about Christ. He was outside knocking, trying to get in.

As I look at this church, I think He is talking about a church where almost no one is saved. Because as you look at the context of these nine verses when He is on the outside knocking and trying to get in, if there were even two people there, then there is church. All He is asking is for somebody to answer. I think as we see people going on into the tribulation period, there will be a church somewhere, but Christ will not be present!

He is saying, "I am the Amen, the Faithful and True Witness." What is He saying? He is giving His resume! And as the elder reads this letter to this church, He is saying, **"I am the Amen of Isaiah 65:16,** *"I am the God of True. I am the God of Truth."* It is the same Hebrew word for Amen. I am the God of Amen. I am the first Amen in the Bible and the last Amen in the Bible. I am the Alpha and Omega. I am the one who is writing this letter to you! Pay attention! Hopefully some of them were thinking they should listen.

He is not only the all-conquering Christ, He is also the Faithful and True Witness. He is saying that there is no one who has ever come down from heaven- not anybody, anywhere, equal to Him! It is in human nature for us to sometime distort the truth. Not this one. He is saying that He does not dilute the truth or distort it, but He says, *"I am the way, the truth and the life."* Listen to me as I am knocking. I am the all-conquering one, the all-convicting one, and the all-controlling one. That is why he says, *"the beginning of the creation of God."* Not that He was created first, but He is the author of all creation. He is the one who created.

I got up this morning and I went outside. I looked at our lawn and there was dew everywhere! I thought, there is not one blade of grass springing up this morning without the permission of Christ! And there is not a speck of dust floating around in the room you are sitting in without the permission of Christ. And He is the one who is writing this letter. He is saying, **"I am the First and Last, I am the Amen, I am the Final One, I am Beginning One, I created everything, I am all-powerful, I am all-conquering, I am all-convicting. So please listen!**

You know, if a person creates something, does he not control it? There is a special contest of mechanical objects where they are in a room and they have go beat the other mechanical object up. I am not sure what it is called, but it was humorous. They stand behind a cage and they have their joystick and they bang at each other's machine and they clobber each other until one machine "dies! But those objects out there are controlled only by the person who invented them. And everything that is happening, everything that is in motion, every soul that has ever been created is in the hands of a loving, controlling God. And the same one who has this control is writing to the church at Laodicea and saying, "**Please listen to me**."

And then he begins to speak in a very direct and revealing manner! *"I know thy works, that thou art neither cold nor hot: I would thou wert cold or hot. So then because thou art lukewarm, and neither cold nor hot, I will spew thee out of my mouth. Because thou sayest, I am rich and increased with goods, and have need of nothing; and knowest not that thou art wretched, and miserable, and poor, and blind, and naked:"* Here is a church who believes that they have it all together and they have do not need Him. Yet these people are blind and poor and naked. And you can't get anymore more blind, poor, or naked than being outside of Christ.

I know my imagination runs sometimes; but I think that the elder of this church gets this letter and he stands up in the congregation and he begins to read this letter with great passion! There were probably people there starting to get mad. "Who is this person telling us that we are lukewarm? Look at this building we are in, and look at our programs and our projects. Look at the community service that we are helping with."

"Sorry, I do not really care about your goodies and projects. You do not have anything inside. And you really need me." I think the Lord does this all through the Scripture, and He does it here in Laodicea. Metaphorically speaking, He will mention things that have something to do with the church.

Laodicea was the church furthest south on a plateau. It was in the tri-cities. Well, Laodicea did not have much of a water supply, so five miles outside of town on another little plateau was a cold water spring that came down to supply their needs. By the time it got to Laodicea, it was dirty and foul smelling. They had to do things with the water before they could use it. So the Lord is using this example that they are so lukewarm that He will just spew them out of His mouth! Like drinking water or ice tea in Indiana, their water stinks, even in the showers. The Lord is saying that this same tepid, foul-smelling, disease filled water that is flowing into your city, you have to take care of it! You are living in a way that you are foul-smelling and lukewarm. The Lord hates this warm and tepid life!

There are three kinds of hearts in the Bible. You have the heart that was walking down the road to Emmaus, hearts that **were burning** within them!

Then in Matthew 24 it talks about the **cold, icy** heart - no love of Christ. Then you have the **lukewarm heart**. And Jesus says that He wishes they were at least cold or hot. I can deal with that, but not lukewarmness.

In fact, it is a picture of Lot. I was thinking that a church similar to Laodicea was the church at Lot's house. That is kind of a picture of Lot's house or church. This man had totally compromised. The Bible says in one place that he was a saved man, but he lost his family. He lost his convictions. He lost the testimony of his own children! And he almost lost his faith.

It's like the little girl who came home from Sunday school and her mother asked what she studied this morning. She told her mother they studied a very famous verse. **"Many are called and a few are *frozen*."** And really, the Laodiceans were like that. They thought they were on the Lord's roll but they were **frozen**. You might even call them the **First Church of the Frigid Air**!

We are living in a time where we are walking into an apostate society and church. We see them everywhere, in every town, in every country. I say that an apostate church is a church where they deviate from the Word and they get caught up in **'isms'**. Any time you get caught up in any kind of 'ism', you are walking away from the Lord. Now think with me. Aren't people so much more concerned today with their version of **godliness** than they are about God! A red flag should go up! It is God first! And then as He works in your life and sanctifies you, then there will be godliness. But it is not godliness first. If a man walks in that direction then he will smother out the Lord. Look at your own life. People are escaping into all kinds of 'isms' today.

Take "Cultism". We will all agree that that is a bad one. You may say, "Well that is the New-Age Movement. I don't have anything to do with that one." Well, that same New-Age Movement, that same cultism, that same "whatever" can start breathing into people that causes them to drift away from Christ! Even the Missional Church movements and the Emergent Church doctrines are classic areas where churches are departing from sound doctrine and the pure Gospel!

What about "fundamentalism?". Everything has to be our way, doing everything exactly right, but this reveals an ice-cold heart that exposes itself in tremendous judging of others. It's People calling themselves Christians and thinking they are the only ones doing it right and no one else follows Christ the way we do! That becomes such a judgmental spirit that there is no love left. It can happen in a life and in any Church. I have sat down with bikers at a Revival Meeting and I have to admit, when you see their enthusiasm for the Lord, you know that what comes from the heart is what really counts!

What about "exclusivism?" People who escape into that are of the thinking that they are the only people of the truth. There is no one else like us. We are the people of the truth. And if you do not worship like me and you don't understand the way I am, then you are not the people of the truth (until you get on my team or look at things my way). You have no hope of being accepted by God until you do. When I sat down with that pastor in Wasco, that man believed passionately, that he was the man of truth. Yet He wouldn't pray with me. I even had to leave his home because he said I didn't have the right words on our Church sign out in front!

What about "ritualism?". There are churches today that are so caught up in their liturgy and their functions and practices that it is all focused on the procedures. And if you are not doing all of 'that' then you are really not a part of God's church.

What about "materialism?". Like the Laodiceans, they had it so put together doing everything right, that they refused any kind of gift from anybody else. That is a problem. There are people who believe that if you are not living financially secure and have everything right, healthy and wealthy, then you are probably not living a very good Christian life.

Try telling that to the widow with only two mites. Try telling that to the people in Foxe's Book of Martyrs. Try sharing that with the Christians in Smyrna when their businesses were being taken from them because of the cause of Christ. Materialism is something that can creep into a life. It can come in and get a little foothold and become so believable. But life is not about material things. Life is about our Savior.

I thought of a three-letter word, YUK! Yuk. Because 'yuk' means that I am about ready to vomit myself and spew all of this sick religion and get rid of it. And as the Lord looks down with His vision into these hearts, He is saying something like, "Yuk! You are going to have to do something here. You are proud, you are popular, you are polished and prosperous, but you are powerless because I am not there!" There are people today who are proud, popular, and prosperous- but they are powerless because there is no indwelling of the Spirit!

I read somewhere that a man walked into a very popular church. He was so amazed that he said to the Pastor, "This is awesome. I have never seen a building like this and I understand you have 6,500 people coming here." And he went on and on. Then the pastor sadly replied, "But guess what? I have never seen a person in the last few years care or come to the Lord! I haven't seen a spiritual healing for years. There are none of us who can walk on the water and we have a lot of problems." But the man said, "Well wait a minute, look at all of this!" But the pastor said, "No, I am sad to say that people are excluding the Lord and caring more about us, our building, and our church involvements, and it grieves my heart." There is a pastor who understands.

"I counsel thee, to buy of me gold tried in the fire, that thou mayest be rich; and white raiment, that thou mayest be clothed, and that the shame of thy nakedness do not appear; and anoint thine eyes with eyesalve, that thou mayest see. As many as I love, I rebuke and chasten: be zealous therefore, and repent."

Christ looks at this church and says He will give them **a choice** and **a challenge**. He says, "I know my Father and we deal in grace. But there comes a time when God will be dealing in judgement and if you do not repent and if you do not change, there will be judgement." So He is making a plea here. This is the love of God making a plea with a church. He wants them to restore their spiritual values, spiritual virtues, and their spiritual vision. Because if you do not have a vision, you will walk in darkness and not light.

Did you know that ungodly living will always cloud your spiritual vision? When people say they do not really have a vision in the Lord anymore maybe they better check their life and have an acute self-examination. There are times when we need to have introspection. Instead of blaming people and having all of these contingencies why things are not going right, just look in the mirror! What about my life, my heart, my secret areas. Yes I better check myself out. Because if I want a continued vision of the Lord, I need to check my daily walk in the Lord! Ungodly living will always cloud your spiritual vision. That is the way the Spirit of God works.

Have you ever thanked God for that little mechanism he has placed inside you called **guilt?** We should be thankful for that placement by the Father! Because when we do things that are disobedient to the cause of Christ, that guilt is triggered. And you are never going to have that sweet communion and fellowship until that is dealt with in confession. You are still saved but you will walk like David did for two years in a lot of misery, with absolutely no fellowship!

How do we repent? He says He will tell them how to repent. "I want you to purchase some gold which is a representation of the priceless gift of salvation." You will never receive anything greater in your life than the gift of salvation. Christ went to the cross and purchased that salvation. And then He says, "I want you to have this white garment. That is a symbol of righteous deeds that will always accompany your great salvation." And remember all of these purchases are done by faith. The gold is purchased by faith. The white garment is purchased by faith. And then He says, "Here is some "eye salve." He said, "You are going to need this eye salve because you are going to be blind without my life in you." People are walking in darkness who are clueless that they are walking in darkness, because God has blinded them. He is not going to let you walk in enjoyment without keeping Him NUMBER ONE, because our God is a jealous God.

I would like to boil this down and say that there is only one cure for a lukewarm heart. There is only one cure for a lukewarm church- when there is a re-admission on your part of an **excluded Christ.** That is the answer for a lukewarm heart and a lukewarm church. When there is an honest re-admission of **an excluded Christ**. And when I exclude Him out of my life and out of my thoughts and out of my prayers, I am not going to go anywhere in joy. Paul says, "I die daily." When I want to know more about Him and the power of His resurrection, that is just a re-admission daily of that Christ that we need. We are in a battle. That is what the Bible says. It is the flesh against the spirit and the spirit against the flesh. And if we yield to the flesh, we will exclude Him. That is the course and the nature of the human heart. Without Him you will never do anything. And He knows what He is talking about, He is our God!

He brings a dual challenge in the final two verses. *. Behold, I stand at the door and knock: if any man hear my voice, and open the door, I will come in to him, and will sup with him and he with me. To him that overcometh will I grant to sit with me in my throne, even as I also*

overcame, and am set down with my Father in His throne. He that hath an ear, let him hear what the Spirit saith unto the churches."

I want to say something about verse 19. He says, **"as many as I love I rebuke and chasten. Be zealous therefore and repent."** I will tell you why I think this is a sad verse. Because when I went to the original text in Greek, it is not *agape* love that He is talking about here, it is not *agapao* that He is talking about here. He is standing outside of the church knocking and He tells them as many as he has affection for, *phileo* love, or friendship love. God has a desperate love for mankind. He says so in John 3:16. But the love He is talking about here is *phileo* love. I want to come in and I will rebuke and chasten you. But He wants them to repent. That is a need when you come to the Lord Jesus Christ, a need for repentance. I am standing here with a love for you. But I want to have that intimacy, that closeness with you which is that *agapao* love. I want to come in. PLEASE LET ME IN!

He makes three promises here. He says, *"I stand at the door and knock if you will hear my voice, I will come into him."* That is one of the promises he makes to the Laodiceans. And He makes it to all of the ages. Promise #1, **I will come in.** That is about as personal as you can get. If someone would come up to you and tell you that salvation is collective, that it is only when 105 people get together and agree on it, then you have salvation. No. Salvation is very personal. The Bible says in Romans 14, *"So then every one of us will give an account of himself."* You and I will stand before our Savior someday and give account of ourselves. If you open the door, He will come into you.

Promise #2, *"and I will sup with you."* You are not going to get any better fellowship and intimacy than that, when Christ comes into a relationship and now He sits down and fellowships with you.

Promise #3, *"and He with me."* What is He saying? He is saying that He will not only come into your heart. I will not only sup with you. But sometime this same supper that I am having with you will change into a life of eternal blessing!

A few hours before Douglas Hess passed away, I had the privilege of calling him on the phone. Patrick (my son-in-law)laid the phone up to his ear. I chatted with him and he only made groaning responses. But in Douglas

Hess' life, he is now realizing all three promises! I remember hanging up that phone and Heidi and I talked about it for a few minutes. We get so caught up in this life! But in light of eternity, the things that we do and the things we are involved in, even the good things we do, in light of eternity, it is pretty insignificant, isn't it? In the light of eternity it is like picking up a dandelion and blowing….it goes to nothing so quickly!

Here is the Lord, the love of all the ages, standing and knocking at the door. He is looking inside of people who He loves and He is giving them three promises. I want to come into you, and sup with you, and live in eternity with you.

Have you seen the picture of Christ standing at the door knocking? It is a famous painting by a famous artist, Homan Hunt. There is the Lord standing at the wooden door with trees around. As the story goes, the painting was displayed in St. Paul's Cathedral in London. A lot of artists would come in and look at it in amazement. And then all of the sudden the critics started saying that Hunt made a mistake in the painting. And he kind of smiled, but they wouldn't drop it. They kept telling him that he made a major mistake in the painting. He smiled and asked them, "What mistake?" They said, "The colors and perspectives are so perfect, but you forgot the handle on the door!" And he said, "No, I didn't forget that. The handle is on the inside."

We make the choice. The wooing of the Spirit as He knocks on your heart is your choice. It is my choice and my response. He is not going to beat a man over the head until he comes to the Lord, but that is not the way our Father works. There has got to be a response on the part of man! The goodness of God leads men to repentance. There is not a better God. He is the only God. And He loves everyone! It is not God's will that anyone should perish. He is knocking and knocking and knocking. Some churches open the door and there are some churches that do not!.

Quote from a pamphlet: **"Perhaps none of the seven letters is more appropriate to the 20th century church than this. It describes vividly the respectable, sentimental, nominal, skin-deep religiosity, which is so wide spread and in so many churches today. Christianity in America is flabby and anemic. We appear to have taken a lukewarm bath in all kinds of religion. Wake up church!"**

That is the message to the Laodiceans. *"He that hath an ear let him hear what the Spirit saith unto the churches."* The challenge today is like it has always been. It is something we need to take to heart for our own lives, especially as His return approaches!

REVELATION 4

A Visit to the Throne Room

"After this I looked, and behold, a door was opened in heaven: and the first voice which I heard was as it were a trumpet talking with me; which said, 'come up hither, and I will shew thee things which must be hereafter.' And immediately I was in the Spirit: and, behold, a throne was set in heaven, and one sat on the throne. And he that sat was to look upon like a jasper and a sardine stone: and there was a rainbow round the throne, in sight like unto an emerald. And round about the throne were four and twenty seats: and upon the seats I saw four and twenty elders sitting, clothed in white raiment; and they had on their heads crowns of gold. And out of the throne proceeded lightning's and thunderings and voices: and there were seven lamps of fire burning before the throne, which are the seven Spirits of God. And before the throne there was a sea of glass like unto crystal: and in the midst of the throne, and round about the throne, were four beasts full of eyes before and behind. And the first beast was like a lion, and the second beast was like a calf, and the third beast had a face as a man, and the fourth beast was like a flying eagle. And the four beasts had each of them six wings about him; and they were full of eyes within: and they rest not day and night, saying Holy, Holy, Holy, Lord God Almighty, which was, and is, and is to come. And when those beasts give glory and honor and thanks to him that sat on the throne, who liveth for ever and ever. The four and twenty elders fall down before Him that sat on the throne, and worship Him that liveth for ever and ever, and cast their crowns before the throne saying, Thou art worthy, O Lord,

to receive glory and honor and power: for thou hast created all things, and for thy pleasure they are and were created."

A visit to the throne room. People have always been fascinated with the afterlife. Heaven is mentioned over 500 times in the Bible. You can read so many opinions and beliefs about heaven. People believe they have had visions of heaven. But there have only been two people who have really been there and seen it as it really is: the apostle Paul when he was caught up in the third heaven, and then here when John the Revelator was caught up in the Spirit to the throne room. This is a very fascinating chapter. I will be telling you how I look at Revelation chapter four today. I am convinced as I study the balance of scriptures that this is the way I understand it. So exercise a little charity if you must.

We will walk into the fourth chapter with a very convincing statement: This is the separation that begins, what I call, **the rapture chapter.** I say that for this reason. Revelation is broke up into a very convincing outline which John gives to us in **Revelation 1:19,** *"I want you to talk about the things which are, the things you have seen and the things which shall be hereafter."*

We are entering a section of Scripture which is the largest portion of this outline. Revelation 4 through Revelation 19 and even into 21 is the largest section of Scripture in the book. The rapture will introduce this large section. Revelation chapter 1 is the glorified Christ. Revelation chapter 2 and 3 are about the seven churches which stand in an era of 2000 years. We just ended that and we are now starting Revelation 4. I am convinced that the big change here is the rapture of the church! The church is taken up into heaven. John is a part of that when he hears the words, *"come up hither and I will show you the things which must be hereafter."*

Now there are some very obvious things that take place here to me. I will share those. The sequence of this outline **demands** a change. In chapter 1 John wrote, *"the things that you have seen."* What did he see? He saw the glorified Christ. The end of that chapter ended that portion of the outline. Chapters 2 and 3 is the second part of the outline. And we span all seven churches, real churches, and a time period of nearly 2000 years now. That is why he said, *"the things which are."*

And now in Revelation 4:1 he says, *"Now I want to show you the things which must be hereafter."* That is a Greek phrase which says "metata" which means hereafter. This starts the final phase in the outline of the book of Revelation. Can you imagine a man like you and I caught up into heaven, standing there in the throne room, talking to the Savior who is sitting on the throne, and He says, "John, you are going to see everything now that will take place in the future." And from Revelation 4 to 19 we will see the "metata", everything of the hereafter.

What are the things hereafter after? It is after the calling away of the Bride of Christ. Why do we say that? Because you will never see the mention of the church, in chapters 4 to 19. Why? I do not think the church is present. It is in heaven. How do I know this? Because as we walk in the door we see the church sitting there in the throne room of God! The church will show up again in Revelation 19, when the church comes back with 10,000 of his saints.

Question. What is the relationship that we as the body of Christ, believers, have with God the Father? It is when we have that special relationship through Christ that we can openly cry out to Him and cry, "Abba Father," Our Father, which art in heaven. There is no mention of any of the Tribulation Saints or Gentiles, or the Jews saved during that time who will ever call him Father. Why? Because the church is not here. You will always see God and Lord and one time mention of the Father when he is taking about the relationship with the Son.

Here is another thing that I thought was very convincing-the phrase in chapter 2 and 3. Every time He talks to the churches, specifically to the churches, He says, '**he that hath an ear let him hear what I have to say to the churches.**' He says that seven times. In fact the word church is mentioned about 19 times in those chapters. But from Revelation 4 through 19 you will never hear that again. There is one comment in Revelation 13:9 where he says, *"He that hath an ear let him hear."* (period). Why doesn't He say 'churches'? **Because they are not there, they are in heaven!**

In this panorama of events that will take place, this time period that we read about in Matthew 24, Luke 17:21, Mark 13, this is written to the Jew. He says in Daniel 9 (this is what I call the balance of scripture), *"Seventy weeks are determined upon my people."* Who are His people? It is the Jew, the Israelis of the seventy weeks, sixty-nine of them have already taken place. That sixty-ninth week was cut off at the crucifixion. There is one more week to go. God will start His stopwatch with the signing of the covenant. One more literal week, seven years, yet to take place. And that time is called "Jacob's Trouble." We will see all about that in Revelation 5-19.

There is something else to consider. In II Thessalonians 2 it talks about *"the wicked one that shall be revealed."* Before it mentions that it says this restrainer shall be taken out of the way. The Holy Spirit is indwelling in us today. When the rapture takes place, at any time, the Holy Spirit will be taken out of the way. Then the Bible says in Thessalonians, **"the man of sin shall be revealed."**

Now the most conclusive proof to me that this is the **rapture chapter** is balanced in three scriptures. And it comes in the element of three words. Revelation 4:1, I Thessalonians 4:16, and I Corinthians 15. (Read them on your own). To me this takes verses and places them together as proof that this is the time of the rapture. Now what are those words? The three words are simple. "There is a voice which I heard…There is the sound of a trumpet…I was in the spirit in immediate change." In every one of these books you will see the same thing. In Corinthians it says that we are changed in a moment of a twinkling of an eye. In Thessalonians it says that there is the sound of the voice of an archangel, the trump of God. And you shall be changed in the moment of a twinkling of an eye. This is the rapture. Look at the balance of this. There is a difference between the rapture and the revelation of Jesus Christ. The rapture could come at any moment, at any time that there is the sound of the trumpet of Jesus Christ calling His children home and it happens like this. But not so with the revelation. The revelation of Jesus Christ will take place in chapter 19, **"Every eye shall see Him, He shall come with 10,000 of His saints, the whole heavens are filled with His glory."** That is not the rapture. That is the revelation.

Right now we are going to look at the *rapture*. The church is those who are saved through Christ, both Jew and Gentile alike. But God has a plan for His people and those who rejected Him will experience the *Great Tribulation*. The rapture could happen right now. There are things that have to happen before the revelation. We will see the events.

"After this I looked, and behold, a door was opened in heaven: and the first voice which I heard was as it were a trumpet talking with me;

which said, 'come up hither, and I will shew thee things which must be hereafter.' And immediately I was in the Spirit:"

Now here is the Apostle John taken from the Isle of Patmos walking into the throne room of heaven. If I were a George Lucus who can put something together on a screen, this is what I would try to do. Can you imagine trying to put together something like what we are going to see here, and putting it on an IMAX?! Now there is something very exciting going on here. It said a door was open. Again I think this supports the rapture. Because when it says the door is open in Revelation 4:1, John is caught up and he walks in through this door. There is no mention of a door open in heaven again until Revelation chapter 19 when Christ comes back to the earth with all of his saints. The church is ushered in, for seven years it will be with the Lord and it will come back and rule and reign for 1000 years.

We are in the throne room of God the Father. Everything we are going to see will happen from the throne room. We are going to be in the throne room in chapter 4 and 5 and we will look back to the earth on Revelation 6 –19, of everything that will take place on this earth. It is going to happen some time and it will happen like the Word of God says.

I counted about twelve things that are going on around this throne. We see people about the throne bowing before the throne, amidst the throne, around the throne, before the throne, behind the throne. We will see all of this in these eleven verses.

"And immediately I was in the Spirit: and, behold, a throne was set in heaven, and one sat on the throne. And he that sat was to look upon like a jasper and a sardine stone: and there was a rainbow round the throne, in sight like unto an emerald."

Does that sound very exciting? But here you have a man like you and I caught up into the third heaven standing in the throne room. How is he supposed to give a description? "It has not entered into heart of man" to be able to describe heaven yet. If I was caught up into heaven today and God allowed me to walk into paradise and I got to see the gardens and fountains, I would probably come back and say something like this (I would have to show you a comparison), "It was wonderful! It was like Yosemite!" So immediately you would think of Yosemite. Or it is like Castle Rock in KS… not really! ☺

But the best thing that you can think of here is the way you would try to describe it. So John comes back and looks at God on the throne and he tries to describe it as a jasper stone and sardine stone, and crystal like a diamond. It is clear that you can see right through it, it is ruby red, it is beautiful and it is a rainbow. That sounds ugly to me. But he says a green rainbow. What is he saying? He is saying that there is completeness and this fullness of our God sitting on the throne! I find it very interesting that on the breastplate of all the priests, they would always wear the 12 stones on it. The first stone on it was jasper. It was clear like a diamond. The first stone was Rueben meaning "behold a son". What is the last stone mentioned here? Sardis or Sardine stone. It is Benjamin. What does Benjamin mean? It means the son of my right hand. From the beginning to the end, everything you see on the throne is the tri-Godhead, a complete circle of the rainbow. There you have it. God the Father, God the Son and God the Holy Spirit. A promise of another rainbow, not only mercy but there will be impending judgement to come!

John is trying to write all of this down. I can't imagine standing there and witnessing what this man saw and then trying to get my pen out and writing it all down.

"and there was a rainbow round the throne, in sight like unto an emerald. And round about the throne were four and twenty seats: and upon the seats I saw four and twenty elders sitting, clothed in white raiment; and they had on their heads crowns of gold."

Who are the four and twenty elders? You can read all kinds of commentaries on this. Some people will say the four and twenty elders are Jews. I would not look at it that way because their national judgement and national salvation will not happen until later on in the book. Some say they are twenty-four representations of angels, and I would again say not so for the balance of Scriptures, because there has never been an angel with a crown on his head and there has never been an angel seated in front of the Father. So who are they?

As I look at the Scripture, it would be my understanding that the four and twenty elders are guess who? You! It is you. The four and twenty elders is a picture of the 'called out' and 'chosen' bride of Christ. I think the representation is great because He has twelve, which represent the twelve tribes and the twelve disciples. It is a description of everyone who has come by faith, but is called the Bride of Christ. As John walks in the door, there you are! Now what do you think was going through John's mind when he saw some of these saints from the first church there and he is looking at them?

Why do I say that I believe that the four and twenty elders represent the church? Three reasons:

- The praise on their tongues
- The clothes on their backs
- The crowns on their heads

What is on their lips is not what Jews sing. And what is on their lips an angel can't sing. What is coming out of their mouth is the song of redemption. (chapter 8) They are thanking the one who was slain for them and they are singing for the redemption that they have through Christ Jesus. There is only one person who can sing that song, and it is you! And it is every nation, every kindred, every tribe, and every tongue. **That is the Body of Christ seated around the throne.**

The second reason is because of the clothes on their backs, white raiment. The only time it is ever mentioned in the Bible besides this and Revelation 19, the only one who can ever wear the righteousness is the righteousness of the called out chosen. Angels do not wear it. Jews do not wear it, (unless they are saved) but you do.

The third reason is that they have crowns on their heads. Who wears crowns on their heads in the Bible? Who has the promise of a reward in the Bible called a crown? Only one people and they are those who come by salvation, by grace through faith at the foot of the cross. That is called the church of God. They are the only ones who have crowns. If God would call you home today, you would go to the judgement seat and you would have a crown placed on your head for the deeds that you did in the body. Not for your salvation but because of the reward for your life lived. There are two mentions of crowns in the Bible. One is called the 'diadem'. The only one who wears the diadem is the King. We are not king. He is. The Greek word here is 'Stephonous' which means the victors crown. We are overcomers. This is you!

This is why the twenty four elders represent the church:

The praise of your tongues, the clothes on your back, and the crowns on your head. Some will have more than one crown!

"And out of the throne proceeded lightning's and thunderings and voices: and there were seven lamps of fire burning before the throne, which are the seven Spirits of God."

There is a lot of conjecture on this. We will let the Bible be our commentary once again. If you want to look up lightnings and thunderings, the last time it was written in the Bible was back on Mount Sinai (Exodus 19) when there was impending judgement that was going to come if people did not receive the Word of the Lord. This lightning and thundering is going to happen again.

These seven spirits are the Holy Spirit in His fullness. He is the one that John says in chapter 16, who will reprove the world of sin.

So John is standing before the throne and he is seeing a prelude of things that are going to come on the planet. This lightning and thundering and wrath is to come. It is going to be a marvelous display of wrath. We can not imagine it.

"And before the throne there was a sea of glass like unto crystal: and in the midst of the throne, and round about the throne, were four beasts full of eyes before and behind And the first beast was like a lion, and the second beast was like a calf, and the third beast had a face as a man, and the fourth beast was like a flying eagle. And the four beasts had each of them six wings about him; and they were full of eyes within: and they rest not day and night, saying Holy, Holy, Holy, Lord God Almighty, which was, and is, and is to come. And when those beasts give glory and honor and thanks to him that sat on the throne, who liveth for ever and ever."

This is a more difficult verse to understand. I read many different commentaries, and the more I read, the more confused I became. Then I remembered that someone once told me that if I want a better understanding of the Word, then just use the Word. The best commentary you will every use is the Bible. An inductive bible study is the best way to see the Word of God revealed!

Who are the beasts? Well I like to draw, but if someone would ask me to draw these four beasts, it wouldn't look good. The translation of the word beast comes from 'Zo on' and means "a living marvelous creature." So who or what are these four living creatures and what are they doing in this passage? What is the speculation of them? Why does God allow these creatures to come around the throne? Well, I would suggest to you that they were marvelous creatures. Because in the presence of God, He does not do things halfway. So the Bible answers who these creatures are.

Ezekiel 10: *"This is what I saw, I saw every one of these four faces and they had the face of a cherub and the second face was the face of a man, and the third had the face of a lion, and the fourth was the face of an eagle and the cherubim's were lifted up and this is the living creature that I saw by the river of _____."* **And he goes on to describe about exactly what we read in Revelation 4. Now notice this in verse twenty,** *"And this is the living creature that I saw under the God of Israel by the river of shebar and I knew that they were cherubim's."*

That just answered who they were. **Angels.** These are the angelic created beings of God that will hover around the throne throughout eternity. And not only that, if you look up 'cherubim's' it is a created angel. They are an exalted order of angel and they have specific things that they do, not only around the throne. They are the ones who are going to bring this judgement out in a panoramic display of this tribulation period.

They guard the throne, they lead in worship around the throne, and they proclaim God's holiness at the throne. These are the angelic beings, a chosen order of angels that are hovering around the throne. You now have a divine war machine in motion which God will unleash down here on earth. These divine cherubims will be a part of that activity.

"And when those beasts give glory and honor and thanks to him that sat on the throne, who liveth for ever and ever. The four and twenty elders fall down before Him that sat on the throne, and worship Him that liveth for ever and ever, and cast their crowns before the throne saying, Thou art worthy, O Lord, to receive glory and honor and power: for thou hast created all things, and for thy pleasure they are and were created."

This is what is taking place here. It is phenomenal to me. You have John caught up in the third heaven. He is stunned when he walks in and he looks at the throne room. He looks around and he sees the saints. Then he looks at the exalted cherubims and he is overwhelmed. But what happens in these verses probably brought him to his knees. I will tell you why. How many people do you think he saw there in heaven? Again we will go to the Bible because you will not find this in a commentary. I do not know how many people will be in heaven. They estimate that there have been 60 billion created people since the beginning of time. How many of them will be in heaven. I have no idea. But I do know this. In Revelation 5 and Daniel 7, the Bible gives a close picture of who is around the throne. My Bible says 10,000 times 10,000 and thousands of thousands and that is a minimum of 110 million. Now here you have John standing in the throne room and a minimum of 110 million people. This is the sequence of events that begins to take place. There is a quartet of angelic beings and this is what they begin to sing,

"Holy Holy Holy."

And here they are about the throne, these marvelous creatures singing and looking to God. And you are so caught up in it that this is what you begin to do. The choir breaks out in an anthem of songs and you begin to sing a new song. (Rev. 5) And you break out as a choir and you begin to sing to the top of your lungs to the Lord. And it doesn't end there. The Bible says that you get so caught up in it that you begin to pick up your harp and play your harp with your singing. Can you picture that? A quartet of angels, hundreds of millions of people playing their harps and their instruments giving praise to the one on the throne. To me that is overwhelming. We join in with an anthem and song of redemption. And there we are before the throne.

I say that this is pretty incredible, marvelous, too awesome to grasp! If you do not know where you are going, you need to make that decision now! There are only two ways that man will die, either in your sins or in the Lord. If you die in the Lord you will be in the throne room some day! If you die in your sins, we will see what happens in Revelation 20 and 21 at the throne of judgment. This is your choice.

In 1967 I showed some animals at the cow palace. At the end of showing the animals, there was an announcement made that the greatest auctioneer know to man at that time was going to be down in the sheep barn. When we were finished showing our animals, we headed off to the sheep barn.

This guy was good! He had a voice that could speak as fast as some women! (ouch) This guy could click it off and yet every word he said was very clear. He was up there just a rattling off words and I would never forget the comment he would make when he would slow way down at the end of a sale. He would say slowly, "going, going, gone!" And every time he sold a sheep he would say those haunting words.......".going, going, gone!"

I do not know where you are at today, but the Bible says that His spirit will not always strive with man. (Gen 3) Time marches on and time is going and going and some day it will be gone!

I asked my son-in-law Patrick what he was doing tonight. He said he was going back down to the fair to witness to the crowds that walk through the exhibits. Patrick stays down at the fair every night until midnight in a booth sharing the gospel. I had to think about how many people will walk by and how many people will go in… Going, going, gone! It may be the last opportunity for someone today at the Turlock Fair in Sunny California! But it may be their first opportunity to know Him!

Going, Going, Gone!

Revelation 5

Can You Open the Book?

"And I saw in the right hand of him that sat on the throne a book written within and on the backside, sealed with seven seals. And I saw a strong angel proclaiming with a loud voice, Who is worthy to open the book, and to loose the seals thereof? And no man in heaven, nor in earth, neither under the earth, was able to open the book, neither to look thereon. And I wept much, because no man was found worthy to open and to read the book, neither to look thereon. And one of the elders saith unto me, Weep not: behold, the lion of the tribe of Judah, the Root of David, hath prevailed to open the book, and to loose the seven seals thereof. And I beheld, and, lo, in the midst of the throne and of the four beasts, and in the midst of the elders, stood a Lamb as it had been slain, having seven horns and seven eyes, which are the seven Spirits of God sent forth into all the earth. And he came and took the book out of the right hand of him that sat upon the throne. And when he had taken the book, the four beasts and four and twenty elders fell down before the Lamb, having every one of them harps, and golden vials full of odours, which are the prayers of the saints. And they sung a new song, saying, Thou art worthy to take the book, and to open the seals thereof: for thou wast slain, and hast redeemed us to God by thy blood out of every kindred, and tongue, and people, and nation; And hast made us unto our God kings and priests: and we shall reign on the earth. And I beheld, and I heard the voice of many angels round about the throne and the beasts and the elders: and the number of them was ten thousand times ten thousand, and thousands of thousands; Saying

with a loud voice, Worthy is the Lamb that was slain to receive power, and riches, and wisdom, and strength, and honour, and glory, and blessing. And every creature which is in heaven, and on the earth and under the earth, and such as are in the sea, and all that are in them, heard I saying, Blessing, and honor, and glory, and power, be unto him that sitteth upon the throne, and unto the Lamb for ever and ever. And the four beasts said, Amen. And the four and twenty elders fell down and worshipped him that liveth for ever and ever."

Throughout recorded history there have always been pretenders. In the Garden of Eden Satan came and he wanted to take over the planet. That is why he deceived Adam and Eve. He did every thing he could to take over. In Ezekiel and Isaiah he said he was going to be like the Most High God, and he was going to do things above God! And he fell as lightning from heaven. For the last recorded 6,000 years he has tried to inspire certain men to be the ruler of the throne of this planet. He has tried that and he has failed every single time. He will continue to try. Even when the Anti-Christ comes on the scene, the Bible says that the whole world will wander after the beast. Throughout recorded history man has tried to take over the throne of the earth and failed. You can go back to the time of Nebuchadnezzar, Genghis Khan, Stalin, Lenin, Hitler, and Sadaam Hussein. You can put anyone in the blank, yet nobody made it and nobody will.

We will now see in chapter 5, that for the first time somebody who will be willing to step forth and open the title deed to the throne of this planet. They will open this scroll and open the book. We are going to ask ourselves the question, "**Can you open the book?**" We will see what the answer is.

There is a very significant change going to take place here. I am going to try and verbally draw a picture of what we are seeing. Imagine that I am John. I am in heaven and I am overwhelmed because I am in the throne room and there is the throne with God in the midst! Around the throne are the cherubim or living creatures, the mighty angels of God. Around the throne are the four and twenty elders. It's you, the church. Along with that is a myriad of angels and believers, a minimum of 110 million.

"Ten thousand times ten thousand and thousands of thousands."

Now how can you get that many people in a throne room? Do not try to imagine any building you have ever been in. Try to imagine a great amphitheater if you can, where you can see a sea of glass, and millions and possibly billions of people. This is where John is at in Revelation chapter 5. He is standing there. There is God and the church of all ages. There are the angels everywhere, and they all have crowns and harps. It is a wonderful scene.

But something else begins to slowly change the picture. The attention is going to turn from the throne and the attention will turn to the One who comes out of the throne.

"And I saw in the right hand of him that sat on the throne a book written within and on the backside, sealed with seven seals. And I saw a strong angel proclaiming with a loud voice, Who is worthy to open the book, and to loose the seals thereof?"

That is the question. Can you open the book? Who is the one with the right hand? That is God sitting on the throne. And in the hand of God as He sits on the throne there is a scroll in His hand, this is a book. It is written on the backside and the front. There are a lot of commentaries on the scrolls in the Roman times but the one I appreciate the most is that the scrolls would roll out and open up to thirty feet. So here you have a scroll that is possibly thirty feet long and here you have someone who wrote and sealed it and then wrote some more and sealed and he wrote some more and sealed it until he had this scroll with seven seals. And as he begins to unfold those, he will take one apart at a time.

Seated on the throne with all the sights and the sounds is God the Father with the scroll in His hand and we ask the question, "What is in the scroll?" I believe this scroll is a title deed to the earth of everything that is going to happen with a culmination of the final redemption, not only of the planet, but of God's chosen. That is all recorded in the scroll. We will see it unveiled as we continue to study Revelation.

Who is the angel? I suggest to you that this angel is the same angel that went and gave the message to Mary. I would suggest it is the same angel that gave the message to Daniel and Ezekial. I would suggest this angel is Gabriel. Although there is no proof of that, it does fit the text here. So, here you have Gabriel standing at the throne and saying in a loud voice, **"Who is worthy to open this book?"**

125

Who is worthy? I want you to notice the question. The question is not, "Who is **willing** to open the book?" The question is, "Who **is worthy** to open the book?" Because if you would have had the question, "Who is willing to open the book?", there would be a lot of humanity who would have raised their hands just out of curiosity. I would love to open the book and see what is inside. I would love to know what is going to happen in the future. But that is not the question. The question from the strong angel is, **'Who is worthy to open the book?"**

"And no man in heaven, nor in earth, neither under the earth, was able to open the book, neither to look thereon. And I wept much, because no man was found worthy to open and to read the book, neither to look thereon."

That is the answer. Can you open the book? No, because you are not worthy. If you follow the search of the angels with me, you will know why. In the search of the angels, he goes and scopes the whole universe. He may start with the angel first. Not one angel who has ever been created is worthy to come up to the hand of the Lord and take the scroll out of His hand. He can't take it. He can't look on it, and He can't look inside it. The Bible says that no one in heaven or in earth. That means that no one who has ever been created is worthy to stand in the presence of God, walk up to the throne, and take the book. No one. And there have been a lot of good ones. Adam probably had the title deed if any one did to the earth at one time but sin entered and he was expelled from the garden. You can take all of the heroes out of the hall of fame in the book of Hebrews. Abraham, Isaac, Jacob, Noah, Moses, the Apostle Paul.. no one is worthy to open the book.

I find it interesting as this scroll is in the hand of God (and no doubt John is looking at it and the elders are looking at it, and the angels have always been looking at it), because inside of it is everything that is going to be unleashed.

But he says something interesting. He says no one is worthy to open this book that is written on the inside and the outside. That tells me that this has to be only from God himself. Even Jesus does not know the day or the hour that He is going to come back. Some day God will look over at His Son, at His right hand and say, "Go get my people."

It is all in the book. It is written on the front and the backside. Do you find it interesting that the only other time that a book is recorded in the Bible as being written by God is on Mt. Sinai (Exodus 32) and it says, *"**God wrote on the front and the backside of the tablets.**"* And in Revelation God writes on the front and the backside of this scroll and he seals it all up. You will find this same scroll mentioned in Ezekial and in Daniel.

"And I wept much, because no man was found worthy to open and to read the book, neither to look thereon."

Why is John crying? I wondered about that. Maybe because he knew that if someone would not be able to open this book and see the future of what will take place on the planet then that means man will be continually locked in his depravity and there is no hope for the future of man and everything will remain as it is. Maybe that is why he is crying. Or maybe because he knew that no one is without sin. And even though the church in a sense is sitting there and they are watching John begin to cry, maybe that is why. Because we are all worthy of eternal punishment; but because of Someone who was worthy, we are going to be able to go home someday.

This is the last time in recorded Scripture that humans cry. Later it says that tears will be wiped away but this is the last time that tears are shed. This is the apostle John crushed because no one was worthy to open the book.

"And one of the elders saith unto me, Weep not: behold, the lion of the tribe of Judah, the Root of David, hath prevailed to open the book, and to loose the seven seals thereof. And I beheld, and, lo, in the midst of the throne and of the four beasts, and in the midst of the elders, stood a Lamb as it had been slain, having seven horns and seven eyes, which are the seven Spirits of God sent forth into all the earth."

I want you to get this picture: the sights and the sounds and the green rainbow, and God on His throne, and the scroll in His hand, and a church member walking up to John as he stands there weeping because no one was worthy. He then places his hand on him and tells him that he doesn't have to weep. And so John quit crying and he turns around and looks up at the throne and he doesn't see a lion. He sees a Lamb standing as if slain from the foundation of the world. Amazing! Here you have a man saying that the Lion of the Tribe of Judah is going to be the one who is worthy and he turns around and looks and he sees a Lamb. That is the picture of Jesus Christ. He says He is not only a lion of Judah, the Root of David, but He has prevailed to open the book and to loose the seals thereof. And in the midst is a Lamb as it had been slain. And I add, "as from the foundation of the world." **That is what the Bible says. He heard it to be a lion and then he turns around and sees the Lamb**.

I would like to introduce to you the One who comes out of the midst of the throne. How do we know that this is Jesus Christ? Because we have irrefutable proof right here in these verses. No one except our Savior fits the description other than our Savior.

There are four distinct things that prove the identity of our Savior. Number one, He is the Lion of the Tribe of Judah. **Genesis 49, *"Judah your brother shall praise you, your hand shall be on the neck of your enemies, your fathers sons shall bow down to you. Judah is a lions whelp and from the prey my son you have gone up. He couches, he lies down as a lion and as a lion who dares rise him up. The scepter shall not depart from Judah nor the rulers staff from between his feet until shadow come and to him shall be the obedience of the peoples."***

There is only one who fits the description of the Lion of the Tribe of Judah. It is Jesus. He is the scepter. He is the one out of Shiloh. He is the one who is going to reign. Psalm 2 and Isaiah 11, he is the one who will reign for a thousand years. He is the Lion from the Tribe of Judah.

He is also the Root of David. He will rule the earth. The Bible talks about the Root of Jesse. Jesse is the father of David. And it is out of this line of humanity will come the deity. This is Jesus Christ.

It also says that He has prevailed to open the book. The Greek word is "overcomer". He is the overcomer. There is only one person who is the overcomer and it is Christ. And the only reason we are ever called overcomers in the Bible or encouraged to be overcomers is because we go to the one who overcame with his blood shed on Calvary. That places us in the same camp with an overcomer, when we place our faith in the blood of the One who overcame at Calvary.

He is also the Lamb slain. If you would see a slain lamb they are usually laying down, not walking around. But here we have a picture in the Bible in Revelation chapter 5 of a Lamb standing in the midst of this throne as if he were slain. It says, He was slain. I think we have a picture of Chirst.

Not only a Lion of the Tribe of Judah, not only the Root of the stem of David, not only the overcomer, but the lamb that was crucified is now standing ready to execute judgement on those who do not believe in Him. And not only ready to execute judgement (Rev.6-19), but the one ready to come back to bring redemption to this planet. No question, this is not an angel. This is not some great man. This is Jesus Christ.

There are two times in the Old Testament that you ever hear the metaphor of Christ being called a Lamb. **Isaiah 53:7,** *"a lamb led to the slaughter."* **Jeremiah 11:19,** *"A lamb as being slaughtered."* There are only four times in the New Testament that the word Lamb is used for Christ besides Revelation. From now on in Revelation, we are going to see twenty nine times this revelation of Jesus Christ called the Lamb! He is the only one who fit the description in the Old Testament and New Testament, and He is the only one who will ever fit it. This is the Lamb. This is Christ. He stands ready to move out.

I find that very thrilling. A lot can be said about the eyes and horns but I will just mention this one thing. Horns are always a depiction of power and authority. The eyes and the spirits are always a depiction of the fullness of God as He moves in the Spirit. We will see that happen in Revelation as He moves His messengers out to accomplish His will on the earth.

"And he came and took the book out of the right hand of him that sat upon the throne."

Here you have all this movement that is going on. And Jesus walks out from the midst of the throne and He walks up to His Father and He takes the scroll from the hand of the Father. I had to think about that for awhile. I used my imagination. I do not believe this violates Scripture. But as Jesus takes the scroll from the hand, He takes it into His hand. What if God would have asked His son, "From what basis is your claim for being able to take this book?" I believe that the Lord could have looked up into the eyes of His Father and He could have said, "the world is mine by creation, because I created this world."

Colossians says, *"He created all things, whether visible or invisible."*

"So Father, by way of creation, this is all mine. And not only that Father, but by way of redemption, this is all mine, and not only because I went to Calvary but because Father I am going to redeem it back to myself during the millennial reign to show them what it would have been like without sin. And not only that, but by way of conquest this world is mine and I am going to claim it to fulfill what you said in the Word of God."

Psalm 22, 23, 24 is a great trilogy of the cross, the crook and the crown. Psalm 22 is Christ on the cross, *"my God my God, why?"* Psalm 23, *"The Lord is my Shepherd."* Psalm 24, *"There is the King of Glory! Who is the King of Glory? Let Him come in!"* This is the Lord. I can just see Him standing there quoting Scripture after Scripture... I am going back to reclaim them!

He will and I can't wait. Romans 8 says this old world is groaning and awaiting the redemption. The redemption not only of our own bodies. The Bible says this world will real to and fro like a drunkard. And Jesus is coming back to redeem the order of natural things.

What is the immediate reaction of what takes place here? ***"And he came and took the book out of the right hand of him that sat upon the throne. And when he had taken the book, the four beasts and four and twenty elders fell down before the Lamb, having every one of them harps, and golden vials full of odours, which are the prayers of the saints. And they sung a new song"***

You can back this up with Scripture. The Bible says we are going to be seated around the throne. And the reaction when Jesus takes this book, the reaction of the saints is that we will fall down before Him like we did in Revelation 4. We are before Him with the praise of a new song. Now if you have ever wanted to play an instrument (Rev 5:8), here it says that every one has a harp. Now you are not going to carry a harp around unless you can play it. So if you have ever wanted to play an instrument, here is proof. Every instrument is going to be in the eternal praise of our Father. The two instruments in Revelation that are always talking about praise are the **harp and trumpet**. I do not know why, but it is always those two.

Here we are, every one of us has a harp. Psalm 33 says that we are all going to have a harp and it is all going to be a ten-stringed instrument. It is also called a lyre in the Bible. *"And you shall skillfully play it."* You are not going to go to heaven and tinker around trying to play it. You will play the harp. And it will be only in praise and worship to Him. There we will be playing the harp and singing praise. You will be able to sing! We will have wonderful harmony in heaven.

As I thought about singing this new song, in a measure this whole universe is kind of out of skelter. I am going to show you four things that in a measure are out of place in the universe right now.

Number one, **we are out of place. The church.** I do not see the bridegroom anywhere. The bride and the bridegroom are supposed to be together. So we are waiting for the marriage supper and that time to be with Him. So in a measure, the church is kind of out of place here. We are living for Him and loving Him, but we are not with Him.

Second, **Israel is out of place.** The Bible says that His chosen people are supposed to be back in the land and living in peace. That is the promise in the covenant. They are not.

The third thing that is out of place is **Satan.** Satan is supposed to be bound up and in the Lake of Fire because of the rejection of the Savior and because of his choice. He is not there. Where is he at? He is walking to and fro upon the earth. (Job 1) He is doing everything he can, seeking whom he can devour. (2 Peter 5:8)

The fourth thing out of place is that **Christ should be reigning**. Right now, the Prince and Power of the Air, the one who has control of the planet, is the devil. He is out of place.

But when this scroll is taken out of the right hand of the Father, everything from that moment is going to change. Everything that I said is "out-of-place" will be taken back into His control and everything will be set right when He comes. We will be with Him. Christ will rule and reign for 1,000 years. Israel will be back in their homeland. And all of this will be set right.

There are nine times in the Bible where it talks about the 'new song'. Every single time it is talking about the song of redemption or salvation. So why is it called a new song? There are two Greek words for new song. It is not new like a brand new car. This new song is a different Greek word. It means new in the sense of freshness and quality. It is the same song, but it is newness in the sense of quality and freshness. In other words, we will be singing it better or playing it better or louder, but it is the same song of redemption.

"What can wash away my sins, nothing but the blood of Jesus."

It is new because we will have new bodies around the throne-new in the quality of freshness of being in His presence.

"And they sung a new song, saying, Thou art worthy to take the book, and to open the seals thereof: for thou wast slain, and hast redeemed us to God by thy blood out of every kindred, and tongue, and people, and nation; And hast made us unto our God kings and priests: and we shall reign on the earth."

What do you think was going through John's mind as he stood here for the first time? I think it was overwhelming to him. Here he is looking at all of those saints and they are singing a new song. All colors of people from every nation, every tribe, every kindred, every tongue and John is witnessing it. Every harp and every tongue were all singing the same thing. It would be overwhelming.

"And I beheld, and I heard the voice of many angels round about the throne and the beasts and the elders: and the number of them was ten thousand times ten thousand, and thousands of thousands; Saying with a loud voice, Worthy is the Lamb that was slain to receive power, and riches, and wisdom, and strength, and honor, and glory, and blessing."

The first word, *myriad's*, is a Greek word for 'ten thousand'. It was the highest number in the Greek text. Ten thousand is as high as they went. But when it says myriads of myriads. That is plural plural. That means it is innumerable. The angels are saying, not singing. They are always saying. I think that God has allowed the singing for those who place their faith in Him. The song of the heart is able to worship Him. Angels say and believers sing.

"And every creature which is in heaven, and on the earth and under the earth, and such as are in the sea, and all that are in them, heard I saying, Blessing, and honor, and glory, and power, be unto him that sitteth upon the throne, and unto the Lamb for ever and ever."

If there is any picture of Philippians 2, it is right here. *"Every knee shall bow and every tongue shall confess that Jesus Christ is the Lord."* And there will come a time when every tongue will confess and every knee will bow and confess that this lamb is Jesus. Can you imagine standing there with John? You are caught up in that scene and overwhelmed by the sights and sounds as you stand there in front of Christ. The picture of the One who stands there is not the same as the One who walked in the hot Judean countryside in the land of Palestine. But it is the same person. All of His deity and all of His humanity is present as He stands there. John is overwhelmed by the sights and the praises and everything that is going on.

"And the four beasts said, Amen. And the four and twenty elders fell down and worshipped him that liveth for ever and ever."

He writes down that the angels were saying, "Amen and Amen." They are saying, "Let it be and let it happen." I like to think that maybe he was handed a harp and he joined in and sang, "Amen and Amen." Let it be and let it happen. And it will. Everything is going to happen just as God recorded it.

What does that have to do with me in the year 2009? Revelation chapter 5, has practical application. We know as believers that history is going in the wrong direction. If you do not have that confidence, then you need to get on your knees or meet with some saints or read your Bible, because as a believer you should have the confidence of the direction you are going. You know what direction history is taking and what will happen in the end. The application in this chapter is: I need to be committed to everything that these saints were doing in this chapter as a priority in my life tomorrow. What was it? It was worshipping Him as the priority in every one of these saints' lives.

Revelation 6:1-8

Here come the Horses!

"And I saw when the Lamb opened one of the seals, and I heard, as it were the noise of thunder, one of the four beasts saying, Come and see. And I saw, and behold a white horse: and he that sat on him had a bow; and a crown was given unto him: and he went forth conquering and to conquer. And when he had opened the second seal, I heard the second beast say, Come and see. And there went out another horse that was red: and power was given to him that sat thereon to take peace from the earth, and that they should kill one another: and there was given unto him a great sword. And when he had opened the third seal, I heard the third beast say, come and see. And I beheld, and lo a black horse; and he that sat on him had a pair of balances in his hand. And I heard a voice in the midst of the four beasts say, A measure of wheat for a penny, and three measures of barley for a penny; and see thou hurt not the oil and wine. And when he had opened the fourth seal, I heard the voice of the fourth beast say, Come and see. And I looked, and behold a pale horse: and his name that sat on him was Death, and Hell followed with him. And power was given unto them over the fourth part of the earth, to kill with sword, and with hunger, and with death, and with the beasts of the earth."

Here come the horses! As you study the Old Testament in looking at horses, they are galloping all through the book. Horses always have to do with authority and power. And here we are going to see the same thing in the 6th chapter of Revelation.

We have come to a time in the book where the action really begins. We are going to see the wrath of God revealed. Michael Buffer, a couple decades ago, made a name for himself because of five words. "**Let's get ready to rumble**". That is all he says. And in a measure this cherubim stands forth and he looks at the seal as God breaks it and he says, "Let's get ready to rumble, bring on the horses!"

There is no question in my mind that this world has yet to see Matthew 24 and Revelation 6. This planet hasn't seen these events yet. Some will say that this took place in A.D. 70. One million people died in A.D. 70, yet in this chapter alone, 1.5 billion people die. Some people say this really transpired during the 14th century when 9 million people might have died from those bubonic plagues. Some people say, really this took place right after World War I and World War II when not only with the wars, but also with the events that were happening. It was considered that forty to fifty million people died. I would suggest today that this hasn't happened yet. I would like to conclude that this is a parallel chapter with Matthew 24.

Remember that when God opens a seal, He is talking about a literal thing happening on earth. And he says, "I am going to open the seals now. And when he opens the seal judgements, we are going to see all the things of how this world can be ruined with the hand of man. That is the seal judgements. When you take the last of the seal judgements, out of that will come the trumpet judgements. And you will see how the wrath will be revealed in the onslaught of Satan. So you have the world being ruled by man, the world being ruined and ruled by the beast, Satan. And then out of the last trumpet judgement is going to come, the time of the vile judgment, and how the world is finally rescued by God.

I would have to suggest that even though this is going to be traumatic and terrible when the four horses ride, with this is also a message of the grace of God. Because even during this time period, millions will be saved because of the grace of God. That is incredible. This is a time of severe trouble. And it is also a time of terrible tribulation. It is also referred to as 'Jacob's Trouble' or the seventy weeks mentioned in Daniel. In 2 Timothy 3 it is called a time of terrible rage and perilous times!

"And I saw when the Lamb opened one of the seals, and I heard, as it were the noise of thunder, one of the four beasts saying, Come and see."

He is not talking to John and telling him to come over and look at what is going to happen. He is actually saying to each one of these horses, come! The seal is open. Do your thing now.

"And I saw, and behold a white horse: and he that sat on him had a bow; and a crown was given unto him: and he went forth conquering and to conquer."

The riding of the white horse is a picture of the blasphemous philosophies that are going to take place right before the Second Coming of the Son of Man. The reason I say this is because here we have a promise and a cry of peace around the planet. And a man will come, even though the horses do not have a literal individual riding them. Behind the horses is someone who is in control and I would suggest that it is the greatest counterfeit of all time, the **Antichrist**. Even though this first horse looks nice and some would say it is Christ, I would suggest that it is not Christ for this reason. This personification of peace is riding in on a white horse with a *stephanos* on his head. We understand in the Greek that it is nothing more than the *victors crown*. But when Christ rides in on the white horse in Revelation 19, He is wearing the *diadema*. It is the crown of the king of Kings. He is the Lord of Lords. I would suggest that this white horse is the greatest counterfeit of all evil that there ever has been and this is what we call the Beast. Welcome the prince and power of darkness, the **ANTICHRIST HIMSELF**!

The Bible says in Jeremiah that there will come a time when everyone will be saying, "Peace. Peace. Peace." And the Bible says that there is no peace. I would suggest that the time period of these four horses will take place within 3 to 3 ½ years. The Bible talks about 1260 days, that is 3 ½ years, a total of seven then, when counting the last 31/2 years after the desecration of the temple by the Antichrist. In this time period of the four horses we are looking at the beginning of the week of this tribulation period of 31/2 years.

The first horse is peace. *"And I saw, and behold a white horse: and he that sat on him had a bow; and a crown was given unto him: and he went forth conquering and to conquer."*

It doesn't say anything about arrows because this man with his philosophies will be crowning the world with nothing more than promised peace, promises that everything will go right. It is diplomacy and we see this happening today.

Quote from leader of Belgium: **"The methods of international peace have all failed, the United Nations, the ECU, the INF treaties, the "Salt" talks, the Camp David meeting- they have all come for not, and I would call them "frauds". This world, what it needs, is one man to give us the answers. Let him come and let him come soon."**

Now this is the president of the Council of Belgium. I do not understand what his connection is with all of this, but here is a world leader standing on the stage saying that we need someone to come and set the stage. And when he comes, we will follow after him because that is what we need.

We are seeing the beginning of these things. There is someone who will come on the scene some day who has the charm of a Kennedy and a Clinton. They will have the brilliance of a Napoleon. They will have the steel of Alexander the Great. They will have the persuasive powers of a Hitler and men are going to follow him to the ends of the earth. The Bible says this will take place. Think with me. Are we on the threshold of that right now? People are flying all over the planet to try to bring peace to the world. We are trying to do everything we can for peace, to get this planet unified. Someday a man will step forward. But it is all fake, it is counterfeit.

In one of our studies, I pulled out an old humanistic manifesto. I think it was started back in 1936, ratified in 1972, and later brought together in the 80's. I would like to suggest that this is just a shadow of what will come to pass on this planet. When this beast takes over, all of the sudden this globe will experience this human manifesto in its height. It says:

"Evolution is the key here. There is real evidence that God never has existed. And the universe is just the result of chance and the life forms that we know of gradually have emerged over billions of years. Believe it."

That will be the word preached at the end of time. The second teaching of their manifesto is situation ethics.

"Man is the final authority for all of his own actions. There are no absolute rules, especially no rules from a fundamental Christian."

Do we hear of this being talked about today? Of course we do. It's really permeating the schools today.

"Moral freedom; everyone, including children of any age should be exposed to all the viewpoints that are realistic, including profanity, immorality and perversion. These are all acceptable methods of great self-expression. The Christian gospel is not realistic and it has no place in our system whatsoever."

"Self sufficiency; man is not accountable to any higher power. He is just responsible to himself and to himself alone. Sexual permissiveness; all forms of sexual expressions are very acceptable and should be taught in all schools free from biblical bias."

This is not something we are talking about happening in 100 years. It is here today!

"Anti-Religious Bias; Religion is harmful, it is either meaningless or irrelevant to the question of survival of our human race." What a shame!

"Socialism; government ownership or control of the economy should replace any private enterprise, there should be an all persuasive, welfare pervasive, welfare state for man. One world government; global citizenship should replace national self-determination. There should be a system of world law, enforced by an international police force transcending any special government of its own.

Death Education; there is no life beyond the grave. Euphensia should be employed and suicide endorsed as acceptable ways to terminate human life.

Human Destiny; man should take charge of his own future and realize that he has within himself the power to achieve the world of his dreams and maybe become a god."

Everything that is mentioned here is happening today. As we think about this personification of peace and everything that will look great on this planet realize that it is all false.

Isn't it amazing that people want peace, but with it is always the word 'conquer'. I would like to suggest that as the rider of the white horse comes on the scene there will be someone standing up and claiming to be great ---- and he is going to have the answers. And everybody will be so down and out that they will do everything they can to get him up in power. It will only last for a little bit.

" And when he had opened the second seal, I heard the second beast say, Come and see. And there went out another horse that was red: and power was given to him that sat thereon to take peace from the earth, and that they should kill one another: and there was given unto him a great sword."

The rider of the red horse will be one of war and conflict, deadly bloodshed. Do you realize that from the beginning of recorded time there have been 15,500 recorded wars? There is a time period when everyone is promised peace and then all of the sudden there is no peace, like Jeremiah says. And now when the red horse comes, there is nothing but conflict and bloodshed.

I like following the chronicle, 'World Review'. They still have it every Saturday. It talks about everything that is happening on the planet. Do you know how many wars are going on right now? There are 18 wars going on right now. Isn't that what the Bible said would happen at the end of time. Matthew 24 says, *"there will be wars and rumors of wars."* There have been 35 major assassinations since World War II of people in leadership of governments? There are 75 rebellions since World War II where hundreds of thousands of people have died. There have been coups and coup-d'etat that have happened every other month on the planet since World War II. A 'coup' and 'coup-d'etat' is when somebody comes in and tries to de-throne the present ruler.

And it is getting worse. It is escalating. We say that we do not believe that it can happen. We think that there are enough minds today that there is going to be peace. How can we say that when that is exactly what they were saying before World War I? And then it happened.

Jeremiah 4:7 *"Times will come when people will lie in ruins and cities will lie in ruins with no inhabitants whatsoever."* There will come a time of terrible bloodshed.

It says at the end of the verse that he will come with a great sword. If you look in the Greek, the soldiers that carried swords in those days had two types. They had the *"Rom fy ya"* sword which is the sword that they carried into battle. Everyone had one of those. But there was an elite group in the Roman army, we would probably call them "Navy Seals" today, and they carried a different type of sword called *"M Kyra"*. *"M Kyra"* means that there will not only going to be wars and people dying by the sword but there will be assassinations and groups of people murdering other groups of people. This is the riding of the red horse. People are not laughing anymore at all.

You have heard about the Big Five. They are the United States, Great Britian, Russia, France, and China. If these five countries would bring all of their nuclear armament together, they could destroy the world twenty five times over. For some reason, God allows men to use against themselves the very thing that He invents. And they have all of this stuff stockpiled somewhere over the globe and at some time all of this will be unleashed when the riding of the red horse comes along.

People will see the man with the smooth tongue. He will convince the world for a time. But all of the sudden he is in control; and when this planet becomes involved in bloodshed and war, he will be a part of all of that too. In fact he will be the proponent behind it. Truly a great sword!

The black horse is a time of consumption, blighted prosperity, and famine. Does that not go hand in hand with war? When there is war on the planet, a time of famine quickly follows. Not only have places been obliterated, but everything has been focused on the wrong thing. All of the sudden people are hungry and there is no food. There will be starvation of immense proportion across the globe at the riding of this black horse.

I did some calculations on this and it is interesting. 550,000,000 people will go to bed tonight right near the edge of starvation. Do you realize that is twice the population of the United States? It just doesn't seem to bother us at all, does it? 550,000,000 will go to bed on the edge of starvation tonight and we live in a country where there is one nurse for every 190 people. But you go to other countries and the equation changes and there is 1 nurse for every 2,700 people. When this time of malnutrition and this starvation comes on and this lack of immunity sets in, all kinds of diseases take over again. It will be terrible. People are going to be dying right and left. Then I did more calculations from the World Health Organization. Did you know that every morning, including this morning, there will be 205,000 more mouths to feed on the planet? According to W.H.O. there is a 75,000,000 net gain of births over deaths this year alone. We are at a world population of 6.7 billion today. That is amazing. The rider of the black horse is where we see a devastation of blighted prosperity.

Why does he say words like; ***A measure of wheat for a penny, and three measures of barley for a penny?*** This is talking about a 'denarius' which is a daily wage. This means that a man will barely make enough in one day just to feed himself and not a family of three, or four, or five. There will be malnutrition and there will be rampant famine when this rider rides in. Lamentations 5:10 says, *"Their skin will be black because of famine."*

"And when he had opened the fourth seal, I heard the voice of the fourth beast say, Come and see. And I looked, and behold a pale horse: and his name that sat on him was Death, and Hell followed with him. And power was given unto them over the fourth part of the earth, to kill with sword, and with hunger, and with death, and with the beasts of the earth."

The Greek word for 'pale' is *'cloros'.* We get our word 'chlorophyll' from which is the color of a sickly pale green. Here you have this pale 'chlorophyll' horse riding on the scene. It says that according to this planet right now, that a billion and a half of the people will die. This will be the greatest devastation of human life that the planet has ever known. Notice the companion here, Death and Hell. Doesn't that make sense? It is kind of like the gravedigger following the one who is dying. They are just like companions going along here. People are dying right and left and they are being buried.

So you have war, famine, and now you have pestilences. I find it amazing that man crowned with all the inanities that he may have invented like nuclear weapons, that now he has crowned them with something else that makes the bombs just seem insignificant. That is what he is talking about here. This may be the unleashing of this bacterial germ warfare that man has stockpiles today. Just as we have bombs to destroy the world twenty five times over, statistics say that we now have stockpiled germ warfare to do the same thing. Maybe God will allow man to unleash these kind of things on himself.

A fourth of the world will be destroyed by war, famine and pestilence. There is a fourth thing that is added here. I do not think the National Geographic is the Bible or anything, but I like looking through it. It kind of helped me in this verse in this sense, and this is my opinion. In this verse I was thinking about lions and bears, but what are the beasts that have destroyed more human life than any other from the beginning of time? The rat. In fact, it is not even close. During the 14th century, for four centuries, 200,000,000 million people were destroyed from the plague that was carried by the rat. Did you know how prolific a rat is? I looked back in some of the studies. Did you know that you can take 2 rats and in five generations you will have 350,000,000 RATS!. It happens very quickly. You can take a country that has rats and destroy the entire population of rats except for four or five of them, and within one year, they are back to where they were. Did you know that rats are the only beasts that have lived where humans lived? It may be these little beasts, rats, could come in very easily and they add to the elimination of a fourth of the planet. This is the riding of the **pale horse**.

The same God of grace is the same God of judgement tomorrow. And I had to ask myself if this is how God really looks at sin. Man will scoff at sin, but when you look in the Bible and look at the death of His Son on the cross, that is how He looked at sin. He does not wink at it. When men reject His Son and they turn from Him, there will be a time of judgement on the planet.

Man says that sin is a little accident that I had. But God says, "No, it is an abomination to my heart." Man comes along and says that sin is just a blunder, but God says "No, it is blindness"

Man says sin is just a chance I took and I got it wrong, but God says "It is a choice you made." Man says that sin is nothing more than a defect in my life, and God says "It is a disaster of your heart."

Man says sin is an error and God says "It is enmity against me."

Man says sin is just an infirmity of my flesh, but God says "It is an iniquity in your heart. "

Man says I just made a mistake, but God says "Sin is madness and rebellion." That is how God deals with sin. He brings judgement!

What is my attitude towards the four horses in Revelation?

Matthew 24:2-8

"And Jesus said unto them, 'See ye not all these things? Verily I say unto you, There shall not be left here one stone upon another, that shall not be thrown down.' And as he sat upon the Mount of Olives, the disciples came unto Him privately, saying, 'Tell us, when shall these things be? And what shall be the sign of thy coming, and of the end of the world?' And Jesus answered and said unto them, 'Take heed that no man deceive you. For many shall come in my name, saying, I am Christ; and shall deceive many. And ye shall hear of wars and rumors of wars: see that you be not troubled: for all these things must come to pass, but the end is not yet. For nation shall rise against nation, and kingdom against kingdom: and there shall be famines, and pestilence's, and earthquakes, in divers places. All these are the beginning of sorrows."

This is a parallel of everything that we just saw in Revelation 6:1-8. Look at verse 8. *"And all of these are just the beginning of sorrows."* This is the beginning of the tribulation period. It gets worse. What is my attitude in regards to this? What should be the believer's attitude when you know what should take place?

I would like to suggest three things that will challenge you. **Keep Praising Him! Keep a passion for the lost! Have a personal examination of your own life and your own heart!**

We can get so involved and so busy with everything around us, but we need to look at our own heart. What is our joy factor? What are our interests? We need to occupy until He comes again! Because the horses are getting ready to ride!

REVELATIONS 6:9-17

Great Persecution and Panic
In the Last Days

"And when he had opened the fifth seal, I saw under the alter the souls of them that were slain for the Word of God, and for the testimony which they held: And they cried with a loud voice, saying, How long, O Lord, holy and true, dost thou not judge and avenge our blood on them that dwell on the earth? And white robes were given unto every one of them; and it was said unto them, that they should rest yet for a little season, until their brethren, that should be killed as they were, should be fulfilled. And I beheld when he had opened the sixth seal, and, lo, there was a great earthquake; and the sun became black as sackcloth of hair, and the moon became as blood; And the stars of heaven fell unto the earth, even as a fig tree casteth her untimely figs, when she is shaken of a mighty wind. And the heaven departed as a scroll when it is rolled together; and every mountain and island moved out of their places. And the kings of the earth, and the great men, and the rich men, and the chief captains, and the mighty men, and every bondman, and every free man, hid themselves in the dens and in the rocks of the mountains; And said to the mountains and rocks, Fall on us, and hide us from the face of him that sitteth on the throne, and from the wrath of the Lamb: For the great day of his wrath is come: and who shall be able to stand?"

This great panic and persecution will be unmatched from what this planet has ever experienced.

Some time ago I had the question asked me, "Why is prophecy so important?" That is a legitimate question, because prophecy is not talked about very much any more. And I have asked myself that same question. When people started setting dates for the Lord's return, people became upset and they started arguing about prophecy. In my younger days, the largest section in a Bible bookstore was the section about prophecy. It is about the smallest section today. I was in a Bible bookstore a couple weeks ago and noticed that there are rows of 'self-helps'. Well, that kind of fulfills prophecy, because one of the prophetic statements in Peter says, "**People will say, come on, where is the promise of your coming. I want my needs met. What is in it for me?**"

Some of the great theologians of California met together in Napa several years ago, and they came up with a conclusion that maybe He really is not going to come. These men are religious leaders. So again the question, why is prophecy so important?

Number one: knowing God's plan for tomorrow is a very excellent sign of comfort for the human heart. As we study, we know He is coming again. We know when we see the signs come to pass. That is very comforting for the believer. It will not take us by surprise. We see what is happening on the planet today. It seems like the last stages of humankind are ready to be rolled up. That is very comforting to me to know that the immanent return of Jesus Christ is right around the corner. Prophecy then encourages us to stand and be courageous for Him. Yes, we are living in America and we are not going through what some countries are today. But the courage in some of these places is awesome to see. They are standing for Christ, knowing that He is in control and He will be coming back soon.

Prophecy not only tells us to take comfort and courage, but prophecy also tells us to stand for our convictions. Luke 21:28, *"Look up, lift up your head because your redemption is just around the corner."* It is important that we stand and remember and study the Second Coming of Christ. He is coming back. What a comfort and what an excitement. He has all of this in control and He is coming back.

I believe that just as literal as He said He would come as a baby to the town of Bethlehem and then die on a cross for our sins, that He fulfilled that prophecy in a very literal way. I believe that prophecy in the book of Revelation is very literal. This is my interpretation as I read the book of Revelation, it is a literal unfolding of what is going to take place right before He comes at the Second Coming.

The Bible says in the book of Daniel that there is a tribulation period, a 70th week of Daniel, It says, "These weeks have I determined upon my people." This is a time of tribulation for the Jew or unbelieving Gentile. Again, the reason I place the rapture of the Church in Revelation 4 is because there is no mention of the Church from Revelation 4 to Revelation 20.

John is standing there like he is watching an OmniMax theatre. And he begins to watch the panoramic view of everything that is going to take place, verse by verse chronologically in the 70th week of Daniel. I like to think of John, even though he is caught up in the spirit, standing and watching all of these things that will take place on earth. He had to gasp once in a while. I believe that he gasped in this chapter, Revelation 6.

In the book of Daniel, the 70th week of Daniel, it is weeks of years. It is seven years and all of these seven's are going on here in the book of Revelation, seven being the number of completion. God is now completing the end of the age for humanity. So, you have seven seals. We looked at the four horses and we will see the seven trumpets. We will have the seven vials at the end of the tribulation. We will have the seven dooms of Babylon. We will have the seven new things that will take place in the future in heaven. What a time of excitement!

"And when he had opened the fifth seal, I saw under the alter the souls of them that were slain for the Word of God, and for the testimony which they held: And they cried with a loud voice, saying, How long, O Lord, holy and true, dost thou not judge and avenge our blood on them that dwell on the earth? And white robes were given unto every one of them; and it was said unto them, that they should rest yet for a little season, until their brethren, that should be killed as they were, should be fulfilled."

The immanent return of Christ is brought out here. You might wonder how I get 'rapture' out of these verses. Well, simply this: Are you commanded in this dispensation of grace, the Church age, are you commanded anywhere in the New Testament to pray for vengeance? In fact, the first martyr set the stage, Stephen in Acts 7:60. He asked the Lord not to put this to their account. He was saying that he was not going to pray for vengeance upon his enemy here. This is a time of judgement. This is no different from what was happening here in this seven-year period as David was living in the Old Testament. I think that is why it resorts back to an Old Testament type of living. In the precatory psalms, what is David doing? He is crying out for vengeance on his enemies. He is calling for the judgement of God. Not so during the Church Age. You will not go home today because someone scared you and cry for vengeance to those who brought panic to you. We love our enemies and pray for those who persecute us. But not so during this time. I do not think it is any different than John the Baptist before Pentecost. They were preaching the gospel of the kingdom. What is the gospel of the kingdom? The Messiah has come. That is why in the "Olivet discourse" (Matthew 24), He was answering that question. If they would have accepted Him that gospel of the kingdom would have been set up right then. They didn't. What is going to be preached in the seven years? The gospel of the kingdom. What is the gospel of the kingdom? He is coming again! That is where it separates the two phases of His coming. The Rapture and the Revelation.

The Bible says in Titus 2, *"Looking for the blessed hope and the glorious appearing of the great God and Savior Jesus Christ who gave Himself for us that He might redeem us and purify in Himself a peculiar people, zealous of good works."*

I believe the souls that were persecuted, their lives were taken right here. There will be many dead people. The Bible says there will be a billion and a half. How many of them are Christians? We do not know. That just shows God's great mercy. He could have just pulled all of that restraining back with the Holy Spirit absent. He could have just unleashed and let Satan have his say and no one would be alive. But He does not do that. In His longsuffering mercy, He always has someone out there preaching the gospel.

Why? I believe for those who were left behind and their families who knew but who never came to Christ. It is their opportunity, and they are given that choice. All of Revelation is reduced to martyrdom. I do not believe the Church is to be reduced to 'martyrdom'. But everyone who dies in Revelation, if you do not accept the mark, you die. If you do not follow the Antichrist, you die. If you are persecuted you will die for your faith. If you do not recant your faith in Christ, you die. And these souls who are under the altar are saved people.

Now I am going to go way out on a limb here. I really believe one of the great things that is happening in the last days,(it says in Mark), is that he Word shall be published in all nations. One of the thrilling things that is in the hand of God, He is controlling all of this. He has allowed the American Bible Society and Gideons to produce more Bibles than ever before. I think they said that the Gideons have produced a billion now. These Bibles will all still be around when the Church is raptured. The Bibles will not be raptured. There will be Bibles everywhere and I thank the Lord that they will be around. And some of these people who see friends and then all of the sudden they are gone, I believe they will be opening these Bibles more than they ever had and saying, "They were right." And then God brings His messengers of the Jew who preach to the Jews. These are the souls who did not recant their faith and they die as martyrs for Christ.

We are not living in that kind of a country right now, are we? But if someone would come into the room right now and lock the doors and they have machine guns and they went up and down every bench and said to each of you, "You either recant your faith or a bullet is going in your head." You do not have ten seconds or five minutes. What would you do? Would you try to make a deal or would you say, "Fire"? It may happen here, yet I like to think it won't. I think that we still live in a very blessed nation where we can worship God. But try that in Indonesia. Did you know that there are 13 million on the planet right now being persecuted? Thirteen million people! There has always been persecutions.

You may think that Hitler set the stage for persecution. He killed 6 million Jews. That was nothing compared to Stalin. He killed 40 million. That was nothing compared to the events of the ruler in China who killed 72,500,00. There has always been persecution. It happened in the Old Testament when Hamen tried to kill all the Jews. 'Antiochus Epiphanes' came along and desecrates the temple and tries to kill all the Jews. And down through time, Herod, Polycarp, all of these things, men have always been persecuted. But not like here! It is just like a big ratchet and all of the sudden it is just pulled up another notch and this planet is going to go through intense persecution. Families pulled apart, people dying in the streets, and it will happen. Mass murder.

One leader in the European Common Market Community says this about mass murder; "It will become, unless there are controls on nations, it will become a state industry for many nations."

Let's take a country like Bosnia, or Iraq, or Indonesia. There is state industry of mass murders going on right there. You have leaders like the Kurds a couple years ago who annihilated thousands of their own people. Traumatic. And it is happening. We are commanded to pray for them who are in those situations, because it will get worse.

So these souls under the altar, and the reason it talks about *'under the alter'*, is when the Old Testament sacrifices were given the blood always flowed at the base of the altar. So these souls here are the lives and they are a very special aroma to God because they cried to the Lord with a loud voice saying, *"Oh Lord how long?"* Why were they crying? In other words, why were they killed? They were not under the altar because the Antichrist and his cronies decided to go out one day and do some mass murders. They are under the altar because of the word of their testimony. They were slain for the Word of God and the testimony, which they held. That is why they died. The reason they died was not because they had to get rid of some people. They died because of the Word of God and the Testimony of His Son Jesus Christ. When they cry out, "How long?" I do not believe that is going to be a prayer prayed in this dispensation. How did they die? The Bible does not say. I believe in these intense killings, some of them died because of the first four horsemen here, the famine, and pestilences. They were persecuted because of the Word of God.

Remember this: between the rapture and the revelation, persecutions will increase all the way up to the time Jesus Christ comes. It will get so intense. The Bible says if it wasn't for Him shortening that season, many more people would have their lives taken.

The question has been asked; why **white robes**? I do not know. I like to think that the white robes that were given to these martyrs was simply for their recognition and honor, because they stood for the Word.

"And I beheld when he had opened the sixth seal, and, lo, there was a great earthquake; and the sun became black as sackcloth of hair, and the moon became as blood; And the stars of heaven fell unto the earth, even as a fig tree casteth her untimely figs, when she is shaken of a mighty wind."

I read some different commentaries on this and it is interesting. You get to something like this and it does not seem like it is even possible, so many people will run in and spiritualize it. But I believe this will be a very literal happening on the planet. There is going to be an earthquake. This is a picture of a planet that is blindly out of control and every one is scared. Everybody is in this thing together. Later on it says the kings of the earth and everyone, it does not matter, they are in this together. And here you have a picture and a cause of great panic. We live near the San Andreas Fault. Everyone talks about California sliding off into the ocean. But really the biggest fault in America is in Missouri and it is called the "New Madrid Fault". They said if that same earthquake would happen on the New Madrid fault today, 15 to 20 million people would die alone-not even considering what it would do to the economic collapse. If God would decide to shake the planet through the faults on the planet, there would be catastrophic changes at that point. And that is just one earthquake. The blind panic of these earthquakes was going on. It effects everyone. Just because someone lives in a castle or is a president does not mean that they escape this panic. Men's hearts are like a parallel of Matthew 24. They will be to the point that they will actually die.

There are two things that fear can do to the heart. It can increase the heart rate or you can actually die. In this case I believe there will be people who actually die. Like back in the Old Testament when Abigail was sitting across the table from Nabal, her husband, and he asked if she talked to David. She told him that she had talked to David. He got so mad that it says his heart turned to stone and he died immediately. There is a man who became so angry that he died on the spot.

Not only earthquakes, but the Bible says that the stars of heaven fell onto the earth. The mediorites, maybe the asteroids, some of these things will slam into the planet. It will bring fear into the heart. In one of Zola Levitt's publications last week, he said that in June 2002, over the Mediterranean Ocean, there was a small asteroid that came to about a mile above the Mediterranean Sea. There was an enormous explosion like an atom bomb. They said if that would have happened over a city, there would have been people destroyed. Many people heard it. They didn't release this information until this week.

If you are looking up into the heavens and you are seeing things happen and then all of the sudden the earth is moving because of the forest fires and gas and clouds, all of the sudden the moon is changing color, it will create panic. The earth, sun, stars, moon, skies, mountains, everything is affected. I take the sun for granted. I will wake up tomorrow and see the sun come up and it goes down at night. It has always been that way. I look out at night and see the stars in heaven and there is the moon. It has always been that way. I go through harvest and I know what is coming next. It is fall, it has always **been** that way. But it will not always **be** that way in Revelation 6.

Look at the reaction of men:

"And the kings of the earth, and the great men, and the rich men, and the chief captains, and the mighty men, and every bondman, and every free man, hid themselves in the dens and in the rocks of the mountains; And said to the mountains and rocks, Fall on us, and hide us from the face of him that sitteth on the throne, and from the wrath of the Lamb: For the great day of his wrath is come: and who shall be able to stand?"

I do not mean to be funny, here but what just took place with the catastrophic changes on the earth just brought together the biggest prayer meeting of all time. I would say this is not a good prayer meeting. Again, this is my opinion. If you want to look at this a different way, that is fine. But when they start *staying to the mountains*, that is telling me that their god is Mother Nature. They are not repenting and crying out to God here. They are crying out to the mountains to hide them. Not one person will be able to stand apart from the grace of God in His presence. Here towards the middle of the week now we have this human response. In essence, they are blaming God. Their outrage is coming out. They are mad and crying for nature to cover them up. That is a real shame. Instead of crying out to Him they cry out to the rocks to fall on them. This whole seen closes with a very rhetorical question, *"Who then is able to stand?"* Five times in the book of the Bible a very similar question is asked.

Nahum 1:6 *"Who can stand before the anger of God?"* **No one.**

The conclusion of chapter six sounds like it is all over. I suggest to you that we are just at the beginning. Matthew 24 is a companion chapter to this chapter here. This is just the beginning of the troubles and this is terrible. How do you end this when you think about wrath? Wrath is nothing more than God's response to rebellion and evil. In essence, it is a compliment to His love. This is how God looks at sin and rebellion and those who reject His Son. Wrath and judgement will come. So man will always be faced with a choice concerning the love of God and the wrath of God. Man either accepts His Son or he will experience the wrath to come.

A very hard question came to me and I ask myself. What is the application for us today? How do I apply this into my life? Why don't we look at it like this. To me it shows the broadness of His love and mercy. We should be in an attitude of thankfulness to our Father in heaven that He has set boundaries and limits on war and famine and death, because there are still people who have an opportunity in this time period to come to the foot of the cross. We need to be grateful for that.

How does Revelation apply to me? Pray for the ones who are facing the martyrdom and persecution even as we read here today. There are people who will die this week because they stood for Christ. Pray for them in the hour of temptation. That is a commandment in the Word of God. Be faithful unto your death, any kind of death. You may die of cancer, in an accident, you may die of persecution. But be faithful unto death, whatever the death is. We are all going to die. Remain faithful.

With your life tomorrow help someone to catch a glimpse of the 'real love' of your life. A word spoken, sharing of the gospel, whatever it is. Help someone catch a glimpse of the real love of your life.

Read: "Whenever people turn away from God unspeakable horror will always result. More than a century ago a man by the name of James spoke at a gathering where Christianity were being made fun of and being questioned. He responded this way. 'I challenge any skeptic today to find one square mile spot on this planet where they can live their lives in peace and safety, where womanhood is honored, where infancy and old age are revered, where they can educate their children, where the gospel of Jesus Christ has not gone out first to prepare the way. If they find such a place then I would encourage them to migrate there and to proclaim their unbelief and atheistic attitudes.'"

Jesus Christ is in control. There is no question that He is coming back. We are living in momentous times where it is very exciting! We see these things begin to come to pass. Whether it is the nation of Israel or the debauchery and degeneration of man, whether it is the stains on the church steeples that are getting away from Christ. Whatever it is, it is a sign that He is right at the door. Keep looking for His return. Keep living a life of love for Him. Be ready when the trumpet sounds!

The Great Tribulation Revival

"And after these things I saw four angels standing on the four corners of the earth, holding the four winds of the earth, that the wind should not blow on the earth, nor on the sea, nor on any tree. And I saw another angel ascending from the east, having the seal of the living God: and he cried with a loud voice to the four angels, to whom it was given to hurt the earth and the sea, Saying, Hurt not the earth, neither the Sea, nor the trees, till we have sealed the servants of our God in their foreheads. And I heard the number of them which were sealed: and there were sealed a hundred and forty and four thousand of all the tribes of the children of Israel. Of the tribe of Juda were sealed twelve thousand. Of the tribe of Reuben were sealed twelve thousand. Of the tribe of Gad were sealed twelve thousand. Of the tribe of Aser were sealed twelve thousand. Of the tribe of Nepthalim were sealed twelve thousand. Of the tribe of Manasses were sealed twelve thousand. Of the tribe of Simeon were sealed twelve thousand. Of the tribe of Levi were sealed twelve thousand. Of the tribe of Issachar were sealed twelve thousand. Of the tribe of Zabulon were sealed twelve thousand. Of the tribe of Joseph were sealed twelve thousand. Of the tribe of Benjamin were sealed twelve thousand."

What we are going to witness in this passage, is the preaching of the 144,000 that will preach during the tribulation period. There will be 144,000 "Billy Grahams" if you please, who are going to preach during the tribulation period, the gospel of the Kingdom. (Answer to a question:

The gospel of the Kingdom is the same as we preach now, but the only difference is it is the same kind of a gospel that John the Baptist was preaching because they were saying, "Jesus Christ is coming." If they would have accepted Him, He would have established His millennial reign at that point. They rejected Him and so He is going to come again. This is His Second Coming. So the gospel of the Kingdom is, "Christ is coming back, repent and receive Him." There will be a multitude of people saved.)

This chapter is a very controversial chapter as you look at the Jews. I will try to explain that as we go along. I get very excited when I talk about God's people, the Jews. I want to spend a little time talking about God's people in this chapter.

In the early 1940's there was a man by the name of Adolph Hitler who stood up and made a proclamation in Germany and he said, "I want my best speakers to go into every state church in Germany and give this edict." This is what they did. They walked into church after church in Germany and the first question they asked is: "If there is any man in this congregation who has Jewish blood or is a Jew? I want you to stand." Men would stand up and they would ask them to come out the exit. Once the men had left, the second question that Adolph Hitler had them ask is, "Are there any women here who are Jews, would you please stand?" And the Jewish women would stand and they were asked to go out the exit as well. The next question they asked: "Are there any people here who have maternal or paternal grandparents who are Jews?" And they would stand and go out the exit. The next question they would ask: "Does anyone here have any Jewish ancestry?" And they would stand and go out the exit. And we all know the sad commentary of what happened 60 years ago. Six million Jews were killed because of the hatred that took place in the heart of one man.

Is God through with the Jews? Absolutely not! The Bible says so in Romans 11:1. Is God going to forget the Jew? No, God has a plan yet for His people. "God forbid." He loves His people. Has God cast away the Jew? God forbid. Even though they have rejected the Messiah and even though they are forfeiting tremendous blessing to the amount that they are going to be persecuted, God does not reject them to the point of total annihilation. Even though there are people who say that from A.D. 70 God has nothing to do with the Jews, God forbid. I would plead with you as you study the Bible, that if you start to mix the church and the Jews and Israel and the

Gentiles together, you will go down a road of mass confusion. You will find that when you read the book of Revelation, you are going to be trying to make it spiritual, allegorical, or metaphorical here and there and... it doesn't fit! You will have to take two thirds of the Old Testament and say all those blessings go to me now because I am a Christian. God forbid! There are Jews in the church of God today, Messianic Jews, and we praise the Lord for that. But there is a difference when God makes a covenant with the Jew and the Gentile. There is a blessing for those who support the Jews today. There is a blessing for countries who support the Jews.

I believe strongly that the Lord God of Israel has NEVER forsaken his people Israel and the formation of that nation in 1948 was a fulfillment of Bible prophecy! Sadly, some of the greatest crimes against the Jews have been done in the name of Christianity! Why? Because many of the Church Fathers in their allegorical approach to interpretation, ignored the teaching of the Bible concerning the Nation of Israel! Even the early Crusaders were promised eternal life and debt exemption for killing the hated Jews! There are some important truths to remember here:

1. God's Covenant with Israel is Unconditional! Gen 12:1-3 Gen.. 15:18
2. It is not cancelled by sin or disobedience from Israel
3. Its provisions do not go into effect immediately
4. It is to be interpreted literally.
5. It is irrevocable as seen in Psalm 105:8-11
6. Of the 77 references to Israel in the New Testament, they all refer to ethnic, national Israel, NOT THE CHURCH! The phrase, "the church is the Israel of God" is referring to Messianic believers and the first phase of the Gentile believers.

No, we are not "Preterists;" believing that everything in Matt 24 and Luke 21 has already past. It is yet to come and we will see it unfold in this book!

If we say God will annihilate them, we say God is an adulterer. Hosea 3 says, "*They are without a king, they are without a prince, they are without --- and there is no divine revelation given to the Jew anymore.*" But guess what, He loves them and He will bring them back. He says that. They are the apple of His eye. Ezekial 37:36, "God is pulling back the Jews to the nation of Israel in unbelief." I believe it is one of the greatest signs of the times. They do not believe the Messiah has come yet. And yet in His love and grace and mercy He is pulling them back. There was not even a country for 2,570 years and there was still a Jew, and He brings them back in unbelief.

He brings them through this time of intense fire. He says two-thirds of them will be annihilated, one-third will be saved, and at the end before they go into the millennial reign, they will believe the Messiah. I call that grace. Marvelous grace. A people who have rejected Him for thousands of years and He loves them so much that He brings them back. We get to witness that and we have the privilege of being the Gentiles who come to know Him in a special way.

You can call it all kinds of things, but there is an anti-Semitism that is cropping up in Christian churches today. Yet our God still has a blessing for His people. We have a blessing of the grace of God in our lives and the sealing of the Holy Spirit. But do not mix the Jew and the Church. When God makes a covenant with someone, He never backs up. He is not an adulterer.

"And after these things I saw four angels standing on the four corners of the earth, holding the four winds of the earth, that the wind should not blow on the earth, nor on the sea, nor on any tree."

This is not saying that the earth is flat and square. The Four Corners of the earth are representing the four quadrants, north, south, east, west. God has allowed some very powerful angels to step in on the scene and say, "Wait a minute here. I want you to hold something back." There is always judgement when God talks about winds. He has these angels come forth to hold back these judgements that are coming. I do not want to confuse you but there are three things that will happen in the book of Revelation and we are seeing them for the first time in chapter seven. I am going to call it a 'window' to make it easier to understand. A window is a parenthetical pause or phrase, John stands there looking at this little pause. God is saying, "Hold everything". I find it interesting that all the windows are right before the end of the judgements. For example: We ended the sixth seal and there was a parenthetical pause, chapter seven, hold the judgements, and we will see the same thing happen again. There is a reason. A practical reason for today is simple this. It is an on-going evidence of the marvelous grace of God at the time of severe impending judgement. We are seeing that happen here. John is witnessing these things and suddenly there is a time out as

God wants to seal some very special people, 144,000 of them. He wants them to preach the gospel of the Kingdom because the judgments that will come on this planet are so severe that if people do not hear the gospel of the Kingdom, they may never have an opportunity to see God. I call that God's grace at a time of impending judgement.

Here we have a parenthetical window. We are pausing before the blowing of the seven trumpets. Right before the last vial and bowl judgement, a time out. He is doing this so that He may seal 144,000 people.

I like to read many commentaries. But one thing I desire to do is follow the Bible literally. I most definitely believe in the literal birth of Jesus Christ to a virgin, and I believe He literally did come to Bethlehem and was born there. I believe He literally grew up in Nazareth. I believe in His literal resurrection from the grave. If I believe that, then I must believe that all of these things have to be literal. To all of a sudden take these things and try to spiritualize them, or say it is some fog bank out there, it does not make sense. Some of the things that are going to happen sound terrible. There is going to be a Kingdom coming. There will be twelve tribes ushered into the Kingdom, to see the land like it has never been seen by men. We are going to rule and reign with Him for a thousand years! It is going to be a time of excitement to be with Him!

"And I saw another angel ascending from the east, having the seal of the living God: and he cried with a loud voice to the four angels, to whom it was given to hurt the earth and the sea, Saying, Hurt not the earth, neither the Sea, nor the trees, till we have sealed the servants of our God in their foreheads."

Let's start asking questions. What is the seal? It says it is a seal of God. What is it? I do not know, but somehow whether it is a glow on the face like Moses when he came down from the mountain, or whatever it is, this seal is from God. I would like to tell you what it isn't. I do not believe this seal is a big **J** stamped on your forehead. There are cults that have started from this chapter.

I want to tell you a little story. In 1983, I was given the opportunity to go to Grace Davis High School where I graduated. I was in the ministry at the time and I was invited to come and talk on a panel. I went into the speech classroom for a "panel discussion" on religion. There were seven of us on the stage, each of us behind a microphone, each representing a World Faith.

I was to represent the Christian faith. I was the first in line to give a 3 minute speech of "What I believe." There was a Quaker, a Mormon, a Jehovah's Witness, a Rabbi, a Shintoess, and a Catholic priest. When we went in there, we had a hundred students come in at a time. We were there for about eight hours. It was fascinating. We each had three minutes at the beginning of every class to tell the students what we believed was the right "way." What would you say if you were told you had three minutes to tell someone what you believe? Where would you start? You had better start with the essentials. There is a difference between essentials and non-essentials. In essentials we better have unity, in nonessentials we will probably have disagreements- but we better cover it with love. I was astounded that not one person on that panel agreed with me. (except perhaps the Quaker and the Rabbl on some comments about the Jew) But every one of them, when speaking about what they believed, spoke of the nonessentials. I forget exactly how I worded it that day, but I did start by saying that the Bible is the divine inspired Word of God. I believe that salvation is by grace through faith alone in the risen Christ, that we have the Holy Spirit living within us, that we believe that the Bible is the divine authority without error, and the resurrection, and the virgin birth.

This is the sad, but also the silly part. I do not think that in eight hours that day, that I ever had more than five questions ever asked of me. I heard comments from Christians saying they believed like Mr. Rumble, but they all wanted to ask nonessential questions to the other religions. I will never forget what happened. The Jehovah's Witness referred to the seventh chapter of the book of Revelation. He said they have the stamp of the **J** on their foreheads, 144,000 of them, and they are God's chosen. The man said, " We are going to spread the gospel and that is why we go door to door because we want to warn people about the coming judgment." A young teenage man from the audience said to him, "Sir, I find that very interesting because you have 1.5 million in your church. Are you one of the 144,000? And his answer was, "Just like all churches we have a lot of black sheep in the family." The classroom erupted in laughter! That was not a very smart answer. It was actually sad. This chapter is not talking about the Jehovah Witnesses. It is talking about God's witnesses from Jehovah, but it is not them. So you have the fifth angel, and he is holding back the judgement. What is he holding back?

"And the seven angels which had the seven trumpets prepared themselves to sound. The first angel sounded, and there followed hail and fire mingled with blood, and they were cast upon the earth: and the third part of trees was burnt up, and all green grass was burnt up. And the second angel sounded, and as it were a great mountain burning with fire was cast into the sea: and the third part of the sea became blood; And the third part of the creatures which were in the sea, and had life, died; and the third part of the ships were destroyed. And the third angel sounded, and there fell a great star from heaven, burning as it were a lamp, and it fell upon the third part of the rivers, and upon the fountains of waters;"

Revelation 8:6

"And it was commanded them that they should not hurt the grass of the earth, neither any green thing, neither any tree; but only those men which have not the seal of God in their foreheads."

Revelation 9:4

If God did not hold back these angels and hold back the judgement, from what we just read here, everybody would be killed. So God holds back the judgement and brings on His chosen, seals their foreheads and they go out and minister the gospel of the kingdom. God in His divine sovereignty knew that there were people here and there. They came to the foot of the cross and died for their faith.

There are two divisions here and that is why I am stopping at the eighth verse. The first starts in the first verse where it says, *"After these things I saw."* Then verse nine says, *"And after this I beheld and low."* In the Greek that is the same phrase. What is He saying? "John, I have stopped everything for a moment. Everything is on hold. I want you to see an earthly vision. I want you witness 144,000 people on the planet getting ready to preach." Then in verse nine. "Now John, I want you to see a heavenly vision of the great multitudes that were saved here because of that preaching." We will see that in the next chapter.

What is the seal? It is God's divine seal. I like to think it might be a 'Godly glow'. When you have the Word of God in you, you are going to shine. There will be people in every one of these countries preaching, like at

Pentecost, in their own language and their own tongue. God is reaching out in His marvelous grace in a time of impending judgement.

You will have to agree with me that God does seal, doesn't He? Did God seal up Noah in the ark before impending judgement? Yes. Did God seal up Lot and his family and take them away from Sodom and Gomorrah? Yes. Did God seal Rahab and her household from impending judgement? Yes. Did God seal you? Yes. Do you have God's seal?

You are sealed with the Holy Spirit. (Ephesians 4:30) You have the divine seal of God. You are sealed and protected and when you die, you will never experience the condemnation of eternal hell. You will never get a better seal than that. You are sealed with that earnest expectation. Some day you will be at the marriage in heaven and you will go on your 1,000-year honeymoon with the Savior and God the Father, and then you will go to heaven, the new heaven and new earth. We have a GREAT future ahead of us!

"Now I belong to Jesus and Jesus belongs to me".

Who are the 144,000? Again, why don't we let the Bible answer it? What does the Bible say? The Bible says that there are twelve tribes, twelve thousand from each. That is pretty clear. Why do we have to make anything out of that other than what it says?

"And I heard the number of them which were sealed: and there were sealed a hundred and forty and four thousand of all the tribes of the children of Israel."

There is our answer. That tells me that they are not verse nine. They are not the Church because the Church is in heaven. They are not some special witnesses from the Gentiles because they are the twelve tribes. They are preserved in the tribulation but the ones they preach to are not. They die as martyrs. We can't mix the two. They are the tribes of Israel, they are the Jew. I believe that is very plain. They are not rewarded, so they are not the Church. The Bible says that the Church is rewarded. We are given different crowns to place at His feet. There is a difference between them and the Church. The proof is in chapter 14, where it talks about the twenty-four elders and 144,000, two different sets of people. They still worship the Lamb together, but they are the Jews.

In this time of intense persecution, even in times of judgement, God will always show His mercy. Think with me. Even in times of judgement, God is a merciful God. Even in Sodom and Gomorrah, there were people saved. Even in Jericho and even in this dispensation which we call 'Grace'. You see, even if we go down through every dispensation starting with Eden, then Noah, then Abraham, and all these covenants, there was responsibility, there was failure, and there was judgement. But in every one there is the mercy of God.

Habakkuk 3:2, *"Revive thy work in the midst of the years, but in wrath remember your mercy."*

Here, in a marvelous way we will see, even in judgement, God is merciful.

There was something that I thought about as I looked at this evangelistic team. My mind probably wandered, but I want to share it with you. Twenty-nine times in the Bible, God is very specific. He talks about the tribes of Israel. Twenty-nine times. Then all of the sudden in Revelation 7, there is a man missing out of here. Now, why would God who is so exact, mention the twelve tribes of Israel and come to one of the last books of prophetic statement and forget about the tribe of Dan? Dan is not mentioned here. If you dig just a little bit deeper, I believe there is a reason. If you think about it long enough, it will make you cry with joy. Dan is not mentioned and placed on the evangelistic team who are going to preach the gospel, because the tribe of Dan was the one who started and promoted and lead idolatry worship. It was a terrible time. In fact, one place in the Bible says that the tribe of Dan is like a serpent. God does not want the tribe of Dan on this team to preach during the tribulation.

Then why should I cry with joy? For this reason. In Ezekiel 47 and 48, when you get ready to go into the millennial reign and the twelve tribes get all of their kingdom back and all the land, then Dan is mentioned again. Now you talk about the grace of God! That's Love! That is Grace!

I think about my own life and the times that I forfeit blessings. I am not allowed to see things, do things, or understand things because of sin in my life. But I know the end result. I know I may be disciplined as a child; but the end result, just like Dan, is that I am saved and I will live with Him. God is merciful. Dan will not be here in the tribulation period, but Dan will be here in the millennial reign experiencing the wonderful blessings. What a Savior!

Why are they sealed? They are sealed so they would be protected. They are not going to die. They will preach all the way through the tribulation period. People may try to kill them, but they will not die, because they are sealed with the divine protection of God. They are sealed with the power of the Holy Spirit that they might send revival on the planet. They will go to every nation and preach with great power. They will send out a promise, the Messiah is coming again; and if you receive Him, then you are going to enjoy the blessings of the Kingdom. At that point they will fulfill the New Testament prophecies.

I love to hear about Pentecost. The twelve disciples stood out there and people were converted. They had such boldness and the Bible says that they turned the whole world upside down. Do you know what Peter preached on Pentecost? I think he quoted out of Joel 2, *"Give heed to the word, I will pour out my Spirit on all mankind and your sons and your daughters will prophesy."* What began at Pentecost will be fulfilled in the tribulation. If you read in that same chapter, the things are mentioned in Joel 2. Who are the sons and the daughters? Israel. Peter brings it back into focus. The twelve tribes will be the ones who minister during the tribulation period. When is it going to happen? At the end of time.

We are standing on the last page of the final chapter of humanity, if you please, because we have seen the fulfillment of the beginning of the signs of the times. The greatest sign today is the rebirth of the nation of Israel,(May 14, 1948) when the leadership of that region stood up and declared that Israel is now a nation. They are flocking back to their homeland in unbelief. The Bible says in Psalms, *"And when you see Zion begin to build up, the King shall appear in His glory!"*

The King is coming!

He will give you a divine power today no matter where your ministry is. He will give you a divine power and the right words at the right time. He will give you how much you need when you need it. He will protect you, maybe not your life, but 'big deal'. Paul says, *"Whether I live or die I am in the Lord."* But He will fulfill a promise in your life. That is where the good feeling comes, when you are living in the will of the Lord. You are the

144,000 in that sense today. You have the same promise. You are protected by the Holy Spirit. You have the power to go out!

I realized this in a very physical way when I was about 15 years old. I was scared to death of water. (My family are like a bunch of fish – they love to swim) But for some reason, I was afraid of water at the age of twelve and thirteen. You couldn't get me in a canal. So my mom took me to Ceres, CA to take swimming lessons. I began to learn to swim. I would dog paddle, hold my breath, and go under water. Then one day I got really brave. They had a high dive board that stretched about 12 ft. above the earth! I thought I was going to show them that I could not only swim now, but I could jump off the high dive too! I want to tell you something. When you climb up onto a high dive, it seems to be about 800 feet up! It is so far up there that I thought I could see the Altamont Pass. But I began to tremble in my 90 lb. body. Then I learned that there are only two ways off of a high dive. You either go back down the ladder or you can dive off. I remember standing there scared to death. I almost turned back many times. But finally something made me jump... (it wasn't a swan dive) and they had to drag me out of the pool because of my pathetic "belly-flop." But I know one thing that I was aware of that afternoon...... there was a victory, even in a "belly-flop." I DOVE...I didn't sneak back down the ladder in shame!

No matter where you are, there will always be temptation to take a step backwards, go the easy way, and don't say something at the proper time. But to dive and dive and dive and dive in faith will bring you tremendous joy in your heart. You may blow it all the time. But with the diving, God begins to help and you are going to have a marvelous experience of Him living in your life.

As we live today until we meet Him in the air, keep standing for the truth of God's Word! Continue to live in the light of His coming! How? With expectation and participation in your walk. That is how you live in the light of His coming!

REVELATION 7:9-17

The White Robe Harvest

"After this I beheld, and, lo, a great multitude, which no man could number, of all nations, and kindreds, and people, and tongues, stood before the throne, and before the Lamb, clothed in white robes, and palms in their hands; And cried with a loud voice, saying, Salvation to our God which sitteth upon the throne, and unto the Lamb. And all the angels stood around about the throne, and about the elders and the four beasts, and fell before the throne on their faces, and worshipped God, saying, Amen: Blessing, and glory, and wisdom, and thanksgiving, and honor, and power, and might, be unto our God for ever and ever. Amen. And one of the elders answered, saying unto me, What are these which are arrayed in white robes? And whence came they? And I said unto him, Sir, thou knowest. And he said to me, These are they which came out of great tribulation, and have washed their robes, and made them white in the blood of the Lamb. Therefore are they before the throne of God, and serve him day and night in his temple: and he that sitteth on the throne shall dwell among them. They shall hunger no more, neither thirst any more; neither shall the sun light on them, nor any heat. For the Lamb which is in the midst of the throne shall feed them, and shall lead them unto living fountains of waters: and God shall wipe away all tears from their eyes."

The white robe harvest of souls! This great revival is because God is going to unleash 144,000 of his great witnesses. They are going to preach for seven years during this tribulation, they will be like the apostle Paul or

Billy Graham, and they will go around and they will preach the gospel of the Kingdom, and possibly millions will come to the Lord.

Notice the effects of the rapture of the Church. It would be my understanding that Jesus could come back for his bride any time. The effects of the rapture could be kind of unnerving to people who are left. If you will recall in 1976, 500,000 people died in an earthquake in China, and in one week it wasn't on the pages of the newspaper any more. If you have hundreds of millions leave the planet via the rapture, I will guarantee you, because of the lies and the deception of the Antichrist, in time there will be a reason and people will forget about it The effects of the rapture of the church plus the 144,000 witnesses that God has brought will be incredible!

There are only 22,000 missionaries in the world right now. But then there will be 144,000 coming on the scene, plus the movement of the Holy Spirit as on the day of Pentecost (Joel 2). Remember when Peter said that in Acts 2? This is the fulfillment of that. What he said there in Joel 2 is like this 'clothed in tongues like fire' plus everything that is happening in the tribulation period. If you read Joel chapter 2, you will see what is happening, plus the chaotic conditions by God to shake man's false sense of security. All of the things going on during this tribulation period plus the world's largest population growth equals confusion! From Adam to 1930, there were 1.2 billion on the planet. In the last sixty years one billion more have been added. So the population of this world even with all the people dying, it will be a tremendous population. This is largely my opinion. But if you have the rapture, the 144,000 witnesses, the Holy Spirit of God like on the day of Pentecost, the conditions of the planet, plus the world's large population equals possibly more people converted than in the entire Christian era.

I got excited about this. When we talk about a white robe harvest, we are not talking about the Church here, and I will explain that. When we are talking about a white robe harvest during the tribulation period, it is the fulfillment of the love and the grace of God when Satan is unleashing his fury. You think surely he is going to win now during the tribulation period. No he doesn't! Because when God unleashes His Spirit and his people in that chaotic terrible time, even though these people will die as martyrs for Christ, I believe there may possibly be more people saved in that period than from Pentecost until now. There may not be. But as I read this and made the comparisons from chapters 4,5 and 7, I found that this may be true!

I need to ask another Question. Does a person ever have a second chance? I will close this chapter with that troubling question.

"After this I beheld, and, lo, a great multitude, which no man could number, of all nations, and kindreds, and people, and tongues, stood before the throne, and before the Lamb, clothed in white robes, and palms in their hands; And cried with a loud voice, saying, Salvation to our God which sitteth upon the throne, and unto the Lamb."

Throughout all the church age, from Pentecost until now, God has allowed us to have the wonderful scriptures in the Bible to comfort people who are going through severe trials and tribulations. Example:

"...Let not your heart be troubled...in my Father's house are many mansions..."

Ps. 23 "The Lord is my Shepherd, I shall not want..."

Is. 41 "Fear not if you are dismayed."

"I will never leave you or forsake you."

I find this passage in Revelation right in there with these comforting scriptures above. Why? Because you have a terrible time on the planet, and all of the sudden you have a great multitude standing before the throne who gave their hearts to Christ amidst all that suffering and they are singing this song: *"Salvation to our God who sitteth upon the throne and unto the Lamb."* It is a picture of the blessed dead who died for their faith in the Lord. I do not know how that will happen. But I know as we go on through Revelation 8-22, we will see the most chaotic conditions of what the wrath of God allows to happen. In the midst of all of that, you have a great multitude, a result of the 144,000 spreading the Word. They are going to die for their faith, and here they stand before the throne of God. That is so awesome!

Who are they?

What does it say in Revelation chapter 7:14? It says, *"These are they which came out of the great tribulation."* It is not the church. They are still saints. They still died for the Lord. They still put their faith in the shed blood of Christ, but it is not the church. The other difference is the church was dressed in Revelation 4 in white raiment. Here they are dressed in white robes. Revelation chapter 4 says they wore crowns on their heads. Here in Revelation chapter 7, there are no crowns on their heads. Revelation chapter 4 says they had instruments and harps and they were singing a new song. In Revelation chapter 7 it says they were crying with a loud voice and they had palm fronds in their hands. That is a sign of victory at last. This is the difference between Revelation 4 and 7. One is the Church of God and the others are martyred for their faith, but they are still around the throne. Revelation 4 says the church is seated around the throne. Revelation chapter 7 says they are standing before the throne. One of the elders, one of the church there, looks over at John who he recognized and wondered who these people were. And John says, (the idiom in Greek is "sir thou knowest") in other words, "I have no clue. I don't know who they are." The reason he didn't know is because they are not a part of the church. They are still saved, but they are the ones who came through the tribulation and died for Christ and now they are caught up to heaven.

What really helps it make sense to me is in Revelation chapter 6. The martyrs that died there are the prayers they were praying at the throne. They come and join the same ones here in Revelation 7. It even hints in Revelation 6 that other brethren are going to come on later. They knew there would be other people dying just like them.

So here we have a great multitude in heaven. There is a difference here, but basically it is Gentiles and Jews who are saved and martyred during this time of great tribulation on the earth. The great thing here is that they are together. In that sense, they are all saved. Some are seated, some are standing, but they are all together. They are with the Savior.

I would like to take a moment to mention this about the rapture. In view of the rapture, I do not think you will find any place in the gospel that the condition for the rapture is that there has to be some final person saved on the planet. That is not the condition for the rapture. The rapture can happen at any moment. The condition for the Second Coming of Christ, which will be at the end of the tribulation, there will be someone finally saved. There are multitudes who will be saved. There will be a final soul saved before the Second Coming of Christ, but as far as the rapture, it could come at any moment.

Let's look at these people for a little bit. They are standing before the throne. You can try to dig deep into that, but there is really not a lot of meaning other than, when those who have already been to the Bema Seat of Christ, (which would be the church age), they may be getting ready. There will not be a lot of opportunity for these people to have lived and do the good deeds in the body and that is why they are not wearing crowns. I believe that the majority of them did not receive the mark of the beast and they were told to recant their faith in Christ and they can live, but they say no. There will not be much opportunity to live for Christ during the tribulation. So they are standing here and that is their status, one of prominence before the throne. They are just glad they are there.

"And all the angels stood around about the throne, and about the elders and the four beasts, and fell before the throne on their faces, and worshipped God"

I believe we are witnessing, with John, the same thing that happened when you were saved. For every soul that comes to Christ, the angels in heaven rejoice. I think we are seeing that here. These white robed people who died for their faith, they are standing before the throne as the numbers are being added to, and the angels are rejoicing for every one who comes to repentance. They are witnessing this here in heaven.

" Amen: Blessing, and glory, and wisdom, and thanksgiving, and honor, and power, and might, be unto our God for ever and ever."

These people were willing to stand for you even in that limited amount of time. They are not going to recant or turn their backs on you. They heard the Word of God and came to the cross. And that caused the angels to rejoice. The angels in heaven are rejoicing for every sinner who comes to the Lord. Maybe this is just a peak for John to see what was happening when he came to Christ.

"Amen. And one of the elders answered, saying unto me, What are these which are arrayed in white robes? And whence came they? And I said unto him, Sir, thou knowest. And he said to me, These are they which came out of great tribulation, and have washed their robes, and made them white in the blood of the Lamb. Therefore are they before the throne of God, and serve him day and night in his temple: and he that sitteth on the throne shall dwell among them."

They are saved and in white robes. This is a depiction of this inward and outward righteousness that God gives them. This is called a white stoll. I do not know the difference. But it does specifically say that the church is dressed in white raiment and these martyred Christians in Revelation 6 and 7 are dressed in white robes. There is a difference.

What do they have in their hands? They do not have harps. They are not playing an instrument. They are not singing a new song. They are waving palm fronds in their hands. Why are they doing this? In John 12, when the Messiah road into Jerusalem, the crowds were saying, "Hosanna". Why? Because they knew that this was their Messiah. They are waving these palms as a part of the Jewish celebration. The saved people are the Jews and the Gentiles during this tribulation period. They wave it as they stand before the throne because they have deliverance at last. They have salvation and victory through the Lord.

You can look in Nehemiah 8 where they actually set up "Palm Booths," where they distributed things like this. I think they had opportunity there in John too to get these things and show that celebration of our Messiah. They stand before God and the Lamb, Jesus.

It says they are crying with a loud voice, "Salvation to our God." Not one of these people are standing there saying, "Well, now, I did pretty good." "Now why am I not wearing a crown like some of the others over there?" "I did a good job. I was three years during that tribulation period and boy, I stood for the Lord!" That is not what is coming out of their mouths. What is coming out of their mouths? All they are thinking about is Him!

Some of us have had the opportunity to be Christians for many years; but when we get to heaven and stand before the throne, we aren't going to be talking about what we did. We are going to be crying out like they were, saying thank you to our God.

I found a very interesting poem written in 1862.

Hark, the sound of Holy Voices
Chanting by the Crystal Sea
Hallelujah, Hallelujah, Hallelujah
Lord to Thee!

Multitudes which no man can number

Like the stars in Glory stand
Clothed in white apparel
Waving palms in each hand

They have come from the tribulation
They are washed in the robes of blood
Washed by the blood of our Jesus Christ
Tried, firm and brave they stood

Now they reign in heavenly glory
Now they walk in golden light
Now they drink in a special river
Holy bliss, never night

The Bible says they stand before the throne and in the midst of the throne He shall feed them, and He shall lead them into living foundations

"They shall hunger no more, neither thirst any more; neither shall the sun light on them, nor any heat. For the Lamb which is in the midst of the throne shall feed them, and shall lead them unto living fountains of waters: and God shall wipe away all tears from their eyes."

Just as the Bible says in Hebrews, I believe there are saints standing up there now, just like they are cheering us on. I believe we will be singing with them.

It says day and night here. Now wait a minute, I thought there was no night in heaven. So why does it say day and night? It uses day and night meaning there is no regard to time at that point. So when it talks about them serving Him day and night in His temple, that means there is no day and night in relation to eternity.

It says God shall wipe away the tears from their eyes. (mention my favorite song, "No Tears In Heaven" as not good theology) There are two times where He says He will wipe away their tears from their eyes. I find both times are at the judgement. That is interesting. When He wipes them away that means there will be no tears in all eternity. In this sense there is still the Bema Judgment, the Great White Throne Judgment, these are the times when the tears will be wiped from their eyes.

The Apostle Paul said, "Don't be ashamed at His coming." If I would walk away today and just not care about reading my Bible and live however I want. I may still have salvation but I would be very ashamed at His Coming. At that point, when I stand at the judgment seat of Christ, He will have to wipe away the tears from my eyes. Likewise at the Great White Throne Judgment, there will be weeping and gnashing of teeth.

Conclusion: This was an interesting study for me because I see a great multitude who will come to Christ in the Tribulation. That is exciting to me.

There is something very disturbing to me. I do not want to say this is final. Some of it may be my opinion. You need to study it. Now I want to rob a thought from you. If you are not 'in Him' today and the trumpet sounds and the rapture comes, do you have a second chance? **I say no.** But I will soften it a little by saying, maybe. In this sense. As I was studying Revelation, I thought how can God comes along and have millions of people leave by the way of 'rapture.'. Does that mean that it is over for those who have just heard the Word? But there is no second chance in this sense, if there is a continual rejection of someone who has heard the Gospel and they know what the truth is. I have heard people say that when they see people disappear, then "I will get my act together and I will get saved"– no you will not! I will share with you a scripture that yanks the rug out from underneath your thought if you really believe that.

II Thes. 2:10-12, (This is talking about the antichrist who comes on the scene after the rapture of the Church) *"And he comes with all deceivableness and unrighteousness in them that perish because they receive not the truth that they could be saved. And for this cause God shall send them strong delusions that they should believe a lie, that they might be damned that believe not the truth."*

If an individual resists the truth now, they will believe the lie then. I say that is very serious. If people can go on in life figuring they can just do their own thing and when they see their friends disappear, then they will step forward. No they will not, because if you reject the truth now, you will believe the lie then. God the Father says that He will send a strong delusion that you will believe the lie. "Because if you reject My Son and you have no regard for the Gospel, then this is what will happen."

You may be just now hearing the Word and you know what you should do. He knows that. In that sense, I believe many of those in the first part of the Tribulation may be in the number to die for Christ. There is no second chance in that sense. God will send a delusion that they will believe a lie.

Our Father in Heaven in so full of mercy. God has no delight in judging people to Hell. But God is a faithful God, and if you reject His Son, there will be eternal consequence.

Final thought. The purpose of Bible prophecy is not about setting dates and getting your calendar out. That is not the purpose of Bible prophecy. The purpose of Bible prophecy and knowing that He is coming back is to build character in believers. Every date-setter has become upset. They cave in. Bible prophecy is not about calendars. It is about building character.

How do we do that? We believe the truth, we guard the truth, we practice the truth, and we share the truth. Included in that truth and Bible prophecy, is that He coming again?

Even so come Lord Jesus!!!

Revelation 8

Here Come the Trumpets

"And when he had opened the seventh seal, there was silence in heaven about the space of half an hour. And I saw the seven angels, which stood before God; and to them were given seven trumpets. And another angel came and stood at the alter, having a golden censer; and there was given to him much incense, that he should offer it with the prayers of all saints upon the golden altar which was before the throne. And the smoke of the incense, which came with the prayers of the saints, ascended up before God out of the angel's hand. And the angel took the censer, and filled it with fire of the altar, and cast it into the earth: And there were voices, and thunderings, and lightenings, and an earthquake. And the seven angels which had the seven trumpets prepared themselves to sound. The first angel sounded, and there followed hail and fire mingled with blood, and they were cast upon the earth: and the third part of trees was burnt up, and all the green grass was burnt up. And the second angel sounded, and as it were a great mountain burning with fire was cast into the sea: and the third part of the sea became blood; And the third part of the creatures which are in the sea, and had life, died; and the third part of the ships were destroyed. And the third angel sounded, and there fell a great star from heaven, burning as it were a lamp, and it fell upon the third part of the rivers, and upon the fountains of waters; and the name of the star is called wormwood: and the third part of the waters became wormwood; and many men died of the waters, because they were made bitter. And

the fourth angel sounded, and the third part of the sun was smitten, and the third part of the moon, and the third part of the stars; so as the third part of them was darkened, and the day shone not for a third part of it, and the night likewise. And I beheld, and heard an angel flying through the midst of heaven, saying with a loud voice, Woe, woe, woe, to the inhabitants of the earth by reason of the other voices of the trumpet of the three angels, which are yet to sound!"

When he opened the seventh seal, it opened up all the trumpets. We are going to look at four of those trumpets in this chapter. As these trumpets blow, they will take place for nearly 3 ½ to 4 years and take place during this time in the tribulation picture. We are at the middle of the week right now. The time period of the seven trumpets may take 3 to 4 years. The blowing of the seventh trumpet will open the viles or the bowl judgements. It gets worse and worse. This is God pouring out His wrath on a Christ-rejecting world and Christ-rejecting Jews.

I would like to break down Revelation Chapter 8 in a very simple way.

1) We will talk about silence
2) We will talk about prayers
3) We will talk about the first four trumpets

I was studying prophecy in the Old Testament yesterday when I received a call from an individual who also loves to study prophecy. It just so happened that the questions that he had were exactly where I had my books opened to. We spoke for about 40 minutes. We talked about what Christ says in Daniel and its relation to Luke 21 and Matthew 24, *"when you see these things begin to come to pass, you better be looking up for your redemption draws nigh."* But when we got to the end of our discussion… it made us both think about the nearness of His return!

In reality, what is the application of Revelation 8 for me? I will try to share that with you at the end of the chapter.

This is the unveiling of Christ. This is going to happen sometime in the future. We are living in the last days right now. This generation shall not pass. What generation? It would be my understanding that that generation would be from May 11, 1948. What is a generation? If you take the 400 years in Egypt and follow the scriptures there, a generation is probably 100 years. If you take Matthew where it says that there are forty two generations from the time of Abraham to the time of Christ, then a generation is approximately fifty two years. Then do you place it from the time of the return of the Jew:(1948) or the time when they had both the land and the city of Jerusalem? (1967) I would suggest the latter, because the city of Zion is always connected to the land!

I know one thing-when we see all of these things beginning to come to pass, and we see the world as it is, the moral decay, the uprising of the European common dollar, we see the stains on the steeples, then we see the biggest sign and that is the rebirth of the nation of Israel. If you would have talked this way 100 years ago, people would scratch their heads. There was not a nation called Israel. It was an insignificant plot of land controlled by Arabs, an Ottoman, or whatever. But not today! You can't pick up a newspaper on this planet without the nation of Israel or Jerusalem being in it. Why? Because 2,507 years ago it was prophesied that this country would come back. It is here and it is here to stay(Amos 9). No one will pull them out. That is the biggest sign that we are living in the last phase of the final chapter of human kind; Jews in Israel. You mean to say that the Jews in Israel love the Messiah? No. The Bible says four or five places in the Old Testament that He will gather them in unbelief. They do not believe in Him. He will send the messengers to spread the gospel of the kingdom that they might be gathered in unbelief.

"And when he had opened the seventh seal, there was silence in heaven about the space of half an hour."

In the late 1970's, when I started in the ministry, my friends and I went to Capitola, California to hear Dr. J Vernon McGee. As we went up the church steps, everyone was coming out. At first I was upset because we wanted to hear Dr. McGee. The people coming out told us that he had spoken at 6:00 p. m. so we had missed him. I went immediately up to the pastor and I explained our situation and told him that we would like to go see him. I went back to a little room and there was J. Vernon McGee, lying on a leather couch and we spent 10 minutes with him. One of his great excitements in life was prophecy. He is gone now but he loved the word and he loved prophetic truth. But there is a story that happened to him and that brings us to this 8th chapter.

Jay Vernon McGee loved to be around young people. He said one of his favorite things was to go to camp. So he would go to youth camps and speak to them and enter their games and do things with them. But he said one time when he was at a youth camp, "I was going around a bin and I saw this young boy standing on a rock speaking to about 40 teenage girls. And he was waving his arms and they were waving their fist back at him. They were upset at him. He was upset at them too." And he said he walked right up into the middle of this mess and asked what was going on. The girls immediately told him that this guy is saying there are no teenage girls in heaven. And the boy told him there is not any teenage girls in heaven according to the Word of God. So McGee asked him to share with them what the Word of God said that would prove there are no teenage girls in heaven. So he said, 'Revelation chapter 8 verse 1, "There shall be silence in heaven for the space of a half hour."

I want you to think about silence for a moment. (told the story about being in Ohio before the tornado hit) There is a silence before a storm. Can you imagine five hundred million or a billion, (whatever you want), all of these angels and us singing to God the Creator, this song: *"Salvation to our God which sitteth upon the throne and unto the Lamb."* This wonderful noise of choir and music and all of a sudden God says, 'Stop'. And there is a silence for one half of an hour. Why? Why would there be silence in heaven for the space of one half of an hour. When God begins to sound the trumpets, it will be like nothing ever before. God knew there needed to be a silence for a couple reasons. One, there is now going to be a storm on this planet that God's creation has no idea what is going to happen. Nothing has ever been this bad. Not only that, but I believe He paused for reasons in verses 3 –5.

And I saw the seven angels which stood before God; and to them were given seven trumpets. And another angel came and stood at the alter, having a golden censer; and there was given to him much incense, that he should offer it with the prayers of all saints upon the golden altar which was before the throne. And the smoke of the incense, which came with the prayers of the saints, ascended up before God out of the angel's hand. And the angel took the censer, and filled it with fire of the altar, and cast it into the earth: And there were voices, and thunderings, and lightenings, and an earthquake."

What is happening here? There is a silence in heaven for half an hour. I like to think that God the Father, knowing what is going to happen now, has finally taken all the prayers of the saints. And all of those saints who died and did not recant their faith and did not accept the mark of the beast but accepted the Gospel, he has taken those prayers and is going to answer the prayers. Some commentaries say that all those prayers offered in the Old Testament which we call the 'imprecation' or the imprecatory Psalms, that God is now going to answer in Revelation chapter 8. That is not a prayer we prayed in the dispensation of grace. There are none of us who are taught to pray to kill our enemies. But in the Old Testament times and in the tribulation period, those saints are crying for the blood of those who took their lives. For some reason God says, okay, let there be silence in heaven.

I find no pleasure trying to describe the terror of not only the prayers that they prayed but the terror that is getting ready to be answered by God the Father. But the Bible says it is getting ready to happen. It is a test. It is a reality that those who do not receive Christ will face this on the planet. So He takes these prayers and answers them together in a very potent force that will take place the rest of the period of the Revelation. Trumpets will sound, bowls will be emptied, woes will pass, a war in heaven will come, and the dragon will be unleashed to add to that force.

There will be silence in heaven and God the Father answering these prayers in a special way and then the trumpets sound.

You will always find in the Bible that trumpets are used mainly for four reasons. Trumpets were blown when there was a call to war. You can see that in Nehemiah chapter 4. Nehemiah himself said he had the trumpet bearer right by his side. "When I get ready for war I have him blow the trumpet."

A trumpet was also blown for a call to worship. 1 Samuel 13, they blow the trumpet to call the assembly to worship.

A trumpet was also a call of warning, to announce things that are going to take place.

Now, when these trumpets sound, it is not a call to warning. It is a final call of judgement. There is no dealing here. There is no, "Hey, can you wait a moment?" There is no praising going on here. There are no announcements. It just happens. The trumpet judgements are strictly judgement. When the trumpets sound by these angels, this is going to happen.

When the seventh trumpet sounds, it says that the Second Coming of Christ is just about here. (we will see that in the ninth chapter).

"The first angel sounded, and there followed hail and fire mingled with blood, and they were cast upon the earth: and the third part of trees was burnt up, and all the green grass was burnt up."

If you would just go to Revelation 9:4, *"And it was commanded them that should not hurt the grass of the earth, neither any green thing, neither any tree."* How do you reconcile Revelation 8 where it says all the green grass was burnt up with Revelation 9 where it says not to harm the grass? Well, that is called 'time'. It may be a year or so and believe it or not, grass grows again. So I think when the fifth trumpet sounds, there will be grass again. But on this first trumpet the grass will be burnt up. Is this symbolic? There are Christians would believe that all the trumpets are symbolic and there are commentaries who would agree. Some would say it is all-spiritual. I believe the trumpets are literal. Why do I say that? It is easier to take the Bible literally for what it says. He said that Jesus would be born in Bethlehem, born of a virgin, literal. He said He is coming again… literal. The plagues in Egypt… literal. The plagues in Egypt are almost identical of what the trumpets will be on the whole planet. We have the advantage by looking at the plagues in Egypt, and we do not call that symbolic, do we? We say we believe the plagues did happen. I believe the water parted. I believe the frogs came. I believe that the firstborn died. There were plagues in a concentrated area but they were literal. I believe the same thing is going to happen in Revelation when the trumpet sounds and the bowl judgements come. It is going to happen! Do I understand it? No. Do I fathom it? No. Can I comprehend it? Hardly. I can't comprehend in my mind that kind of catastrophic thing happening. Look at trumpet #1. How do you ever imagine something like that? You talk about an ecological disaster. That is it.

Today we hear about the ozone layer. We hear about Global Warming. We hear about the spotted owl and other endangered species. We hear about the rain Forrest and pollution. It will not even be compared to what happens when the first trumpet sounds. When the Bible says that a third part of the trees and all the green grass will be burnt up, for a moment in time, that will be a reality on this planet. A tragic time.

"And the second angel sounded, and as it were a great mountain burning with fire was cast into the sea: and the third part of the sea became blood; And the third part of the creatures which are in the sea, and had life, died; and the third part of the ships were destroyed."

Some of the commentaries get way out there trying to make this symbolic. But just take it for what it says. (What is he talking about here? Does he mean Mt. Shasta will lift up like Mt. Saint Helen and jump into the sea? It seems more logical to me that some asteroid or star comes splashing down and does this kind of damage to the sea. The balance of life will be radically changed. It will affect people-not to mention the stench of the salt water and dead animals or fish. It will be a big upheaval for mankind to cope with.

So you have the second trumpet destroying a large part of the ocean. Three-fourths of the planet is water. That is quite a bit of water being destroyed. But notice how God is doing this in thirds. It is going to get even worst.

In 1980 there were 24,860 large ships on the ocean. In the year 2000 there were over 40,000 large ships on the oceans. Not little boats, but big ships. Can you imagine one third of 40,000? Approximately 12,000 immediately being destroyed, and the life along with them. There will be a man who comes along (the Anti-Christ) who will try to cope with these problems. There will be all kinds of sessions, things like the United Nations getting together and the European Common Market. Someone has to have the answers here and he will have them. He is going to somehow deal with these things, and they will stand in awe of this man and they will worship him. He is a diabolical creature who Satan enters, this man of sin, the Ant-Christ. But through all of the trumpets he is gathering people who will worship him through these terrible times.

"And the third angel sounded, and there fell a great star from heaven, burning as it were a lamp, and it fell upon the third part of the rivers, and upon the fountains of waters; and the name of the star is called wormwood: and the third part of the waters became wormwood; and many men died of the waters, because they were made bitter."

Notice the progression going on here. Here you have a third of the vegetation destroyed, a third of the salt water destroyed, and now you have a third of the fresh water supply destroyed with the coming of Wormwood.

Rivers. The Bible says in Job 9 that God names all the stars. He pulls one out, Wormwood, and it slams into the earth. Wormwood means poison or bitter. It destroys the water, killing many people. Do you see how it is just getting worse? Here we have all these people looking around frantically, watching people they know die. Vegetation is destroyed, salt water destroyed, and rivers destroyed. The Amazon, the Mississippi, a third of all of them are being destroyed. What are men doing? They are looking horizontally. How do we cope with this ecological thing?

"And the fourth angel sounded, and the third part of the sun was smitten, and the third part of the moon, and the third part of the stars; so as the third part of them was darkened, and the day shone not for a third part of it, and the night likewise."

Everyone is looking around at everything that is going on horizontally. Then all of the sudden the fourth one sounds and they all look up. You want to talk about the uniformity of day and night being destroyed. That will scare many people. A twenty-four hour day will be very different. The growing cycles will change. But the Bible says a third part of the sun, moon and the stars will be smitten. I find it very interesting that Jesus Christ, before He went to Calvary, met with His disciples one night. They asked when these things would come to pass. And He mentions in Luke 21and Matthew 24 that the sun, the moon, and the stars are going to be darkened. He tells them that when that happens, then He will come at the Second Coming. That is just a picture of what is going to happen.

When Wormwood slams into the planet, things will radically change the earth's environment for a season. Anyone who understands Science knows that the temperature does effect everything. I can't fathom how man will cope with these kinds of things. The sad thing is, as we get closer to the end of the seventieth week, men are going to turn from following the Lamb to following the Beast, because the Beast will give answers on how to cope. Instead of looking up and having redemption, the Bible says that the world will wander after the Beast. That is a tragic commentary on the heart of a man who is not willing to recognize God.

"And I beheld, and heard an angel flying through the midst of heaven, saying with a loud voice, Woe, woe, woe, to the inhabitants of the earth by reason of the other voices of the trumpet of the three angels, which are yet to sound!"

The Greek word here for angel is 'a flying eagle'. What this eagle is saying in our terminology is "You think those four were bad – woe, woe, woe – it gets worse". And so it does. And it is very tragic. In answering these prayers, God is allowing things to be unleashed on this planet that will be so catastrophic that it will overwhelm us.

Silence. Prayers of the saints. Four trumpets. I want to pause here as we think about this 8th chapter and jump into the reality of 2003. This is where we are at today. January 5th, 2003. We are not witnessing the trumpets. No one here today is in the millennium. I believe these things are getting closer because of the signs that we see. What is the message to me? Salvation is FOREVER. But a decision for Jesus Christ takes place in but a moment. So what does that tell me? If I know these things from prophetic truth will happen some time and I know that salvation is forever with Him, and I know that a decision for Christ is but for the moment, as I walk through the rest of 2003, it should encourage me as a believer to do everything I can to let others know that they do not have to experience the wrath to come! You have the truth and you know what is going to happen! You know that the salvation you have through Christ is forever! And if you know that and you know 'the building is burning' then we should be doing everything we can to let others know about Christ. You do not flee these things unless you are in Him! Or you go through it and die as a martyr. But in the opportunities that we have living in the last pages on the final chapter of humankind, the year 2003 may be the greatest opportunity we have to share the truth with those who do not know Him.

I have no clue what will happen in my life this year. I have no clue what will happen in your life. And you don't know either. I have understanding from the Bible that I am a saved individual and I will spend eternity with Him forever. That is settled. But I have no clue in 10 minutes from right now what will happen.

This year may bring a 'swerving car' and your life will radically change. 2009 may just start with a pain in the chest and your life is over. There may be a tragic event or a silent thing, but we do not know what our lives hold this year. But for the moment we do.

Philippians 3:13, Paul says (and he knew he was getting close to death) *"This one thing I do, I press towards the mark and for the prize of the high calling of God in Christ Jesus."*

What is he saying? He says he knows he is doing all these things for the Lord, but in the midst of all that there is, one thing he does; I am following after Christ. He also says, *"that I might know more of Him and the power of His resurrection."*

We may not know what will happen next, but we do know that we can be knowing more of Him. We can be living more of Him and sharing more of Him, that others can flee the wrath to come. It is one thing to believe and understand prophetic truth. Big deal. I like it and I believe there is a blessing in it, but it is one thing to stand and believe this and it is another thing to take it into your life and share it with others. There are people who speak everything right. They can quote Scripture. They can say the right things but they do not really care about someone going to hell. That is tragic!

Keep encouraging each other. We are going to be in eternity with them. We are going to live forever together with Jesus. The best is still yet to come!!!

REVELATION 9

An Evil Brewed From the Pit of Hell

"And the fifth angel sounded, and I saw a star fall from heaven unto the earth: and to him was given the key of the bottomless pit. And he opened the bottomless pit; and there arose a smoke out of the pit, as the smoke of a great furnace; and the sun and air were darkened by reason of the smoke of the pit. And there came out of the smoke locusts upon the earth: and unto them was given power, as the scorpions of the earth have power. And it was commanded them that they should not hurt the grass of the earth, neither any green thing, neither any tree; but only those men which have not the seal of God in their foreheads. And to them it was given that they should not kill them, but that they should be tormented five month: and their torment was as the torment of the scorpion, when he striketh a man. And in those days shall man seek death, and shall not find it; and shall desire to die, and death shall flee from them. And the shapes of the locusts were like unto horses prepared for battle; and on their heads were as it were crowns like gold, and their faces were faces of men. And they had hair as the hair of women, and their teeth were was the teeth of lions. And they had breastplates, as it were breastplates of iron; and the sound of their wings was as the sound of chariots of many horses running to battle. And they had tails like unto scorpions, and there were stings in their tails: and their power was to hurt men five months. And they had a king over them, which is the angel of the bottomless pit, whose name in the Hebrew tongue is Abaddon, but in the Greek tongue hath his name Apollyon. One woe is past; and, behold, there come two woes more hereafter. And

the sixth angel sounded, and I heard a voice from the four horns of the golden altar which is before God, Saying to the sixth angel which had the trumpet, Loose the four angels which are bound in the great river Euphrates. And the four angels were loosed, which were prepared for an hour, and a day, and a month, and a year, for to slay the third part of men. And the number of the army of the horsemen were two hundred thousand thousand: and I heard the number of them. And thus I saw the horses in the vision, and them that sat on them, having breastplates of fire, and of jacinth, and brimstone: and the heads of the horses were as the heads of lions; and out of their mouths issued fire and smoke and brimstone. By these three was the third part of men killed, by the fire, and by the smoke, and by the brimstone, which issued out of their mouths. For their power is in their mouth, and in their tails: for their tails were like unto serpants, and had heads, and with them they do hurt. And the rest of the men which were not killed by these plagues yet repented not of the works of their hands, that they should not worship devils, and idols of gold, and silver, and brass, and stone, and of wood: which neither can see, nor hear, nor walk; Neither repented they of their murders, nor of their sorceries, nor of their fornication, nor of their thefts."

An Evil Brew from the Pit of Hell!

It is not exciting to study this chapter. In fact, it is these few chapters here that are the least preached on chapters in the New Testament. The reason being, there is so much darkness, death, and destruction. I will start by asking a question that I have heard many times:

What is the purpose of this tribulation? Why? There are multiple reasons. I will give you four quick ones.

1) He is going to punish the Jews and also save the Jews.

2) He is going to punish the Gentile who rejects Christ and also provides an opportunity to save the Gentile.

3) It will be God's way of letting sin run its final course on the planet. Satan will have his final push and then God will clamp down and say "enough!" at the end.

4) It is to show how much God really does hate sin. We can see this as we walk through this book. God hates sin so much that He will bring judgement.

Everyone studies the word of God in different ways. My way of organizing messages and writings about the word of God is by using different versions, re-reading the text multiple times, comparing scripture with scripture, and reading at least 4-5 other commentaries on the passage. This works for me and I will do it in this chapter as I break it into 4 critical areas.

They are very basic. We are going to look at the Devil (verse 1), Dungeons (verses 2 and 3), Demons (verses 4-11), and Death. So that is the breakdown of the chapter. If you remember in Revelations chapter 8, an angel flew through heaven saying, "If you think this is bad, it is only going to get worse." And it does. We are also going to look at the next two trumpets.

I think it is universally agreed upon that there is a Devil! Some would scoff at that. Some people say that he is a myth or a principal of evil. But there is a devil and there are demons and they are alive. I also believe there are ranks of demons, just as we see in Revelation 6, 7, and 8 where it says there are ranks of angels. There are archangels, cherubims, guardian angels, and transporting angels. Lucifer has the same thing in the demonic world. Some are worse than the others. Some are so bad that God says He has chained them to everlasting darkness and they are never coming out of the pit. God will allow some of them to come out of the pit here for just five months.

There was a news article that came out recently. I am going to quote this Psychiatrist from this article. He says, "We are living in a time of intense trouble. Doomsday is around the corner." And he gives six reasons that support his thesis. This is the 'doomsday' that he says America is facing in the near future.

1. "Because of the wrath and rage of people today.
2. Because of pollution or economic collapse.
3. The numbing of the conscience of people (They do not care about right and wrong)
4. No capacity for joy.
5. Then there is the decay of morals. (Lack of family value and traditions)

6. There is the manipulation of the media." And he goes on to say that if you take these six things and mix them all around, we are all in trouble. This man is not even a Christian and he is so close to being right.

"And the fifth angel sounded, and I saw a star fall from heaven unto the earth: and to him was given the key of the bottomless pit, and he opened the bottomless pit."

This is Lucifer. The Bible says in Isaiah 14:12, *"How thou art fallen Lucifer, son of the morning, you were perfect in all of your ways."* He was created better than anybody, but all of the sudden he said that he would be like the most High God. "I will rise above the clouds, I will be like the most Holy!" And God cast him out. This is Lucifer, the star that fell from heaven. And now God will give him the authority to unleash this demonic world for a season.

I was up early this morning and I called a man I respect, the Chaplain of a State Prison. I asked him two questions. How many prisoners are in the state of California? And if they were all unleashed for five months, what would happen to the state of California? He told me that just in the state penitentiaries, there are 200,000 inmates. If you add the Federal penitentiaries and Juvenile Halls, you would probably double that. So that would be 400,000 to 500,000. He said if you add all of America, you are looking at approx. 3 million. That is just in this country. He went on to say that if we just unleashed one prison it would change a whole community drastically. Now if every prison was opened in the state of California and 500,000 men could do anything they wanted for five months, what do you think would happen? It would be a terrible thing. There would be murders and the crime rate would soar, because most of the people in the prisons are not kind people. And if they had the opportunity to do what they wanted, it would be terrible destruction. If you multiply these thousands of times, this is what we are looking at, when Lucifer has the opportunity to let his fallen angels out of the pit of hell.

Lucifer was a famous figure. In Ezekiel 28:15, it says he was the perfect one. No one was created any better than him. He was in the presence of the Father. The Bible says he is full of wisdom and that he was beautiful. He was an angel of light. When he made the decision to be like God, God cast him down. Now look at the power of this created being. He took one third of heaven with him! The Bible says that in Revelation chapter

12:4. **Jude verse 6,** *"And the angels which kept not their first estate, but left their own habitation, he hath reserved in everlasting chains under darkness unto the judgement of the great day."* God allows this created being to come out for a time and create havoc on this planet. I can't comprehend that.

You may wonder how the devil could ever get to the point with that kind of persuasion when you are in the presence of God. Why would any one want to go with SATAN, when someone like him is so persuasive and manipulative?

Example: Imagine if Josh decided to go to the mall and stand on a box in a polka-dot T-shirt and tell everyone that he is from Planet Q, and he knows what is going to happen in the future. He begins to spill out things that sound very interesting and very inticing. Probably in a few weeks, he could have men following him. It is just the way of man. Guys would be showing up in purple polka dot T-shirts and say they too were from Planet Q.

So the greatest created being persuaded them to come and follow him. The Bible says that he fell. He is so mad and in a fit of rage that we can't comprehend the attitude that Lucifer is in when he comes down to unchain some of these locusts. Think about it. He has failed to overthrow God. He has failed to overthrow man. He has failed to overthrow the prophets, the priest. He has failed at Calvary and the Resurrection. He failed in the early church. And he is failing in your life. Even though you may be harassed and tempted, he is failing. *"Greater is He that is in you than he that is in the world."(Speaking of Christ here)* That is where the devil is at, in the world!

We have the Savior today to lead us through. A question I get asked me from time to time; "can I be filled with a demon?" In other words, can I be demonically possessed as a believer? No! If you are a believer today, you can't be demonically possessed. You can have harassment and oppression and you can be buffeted. You cannot be possessed. You will have trials all your life. But if you have Christ in you, you are greater than this devil. A Christian cannot be possessed by a demon. What we are talking about here are creatures who are under the control of the wicked one.

1 John 5:19, *"And we know that we are of God, and the whole world lieth in wickedness."*

This dungeon that he goes to is called the abyss. There are many synonyms in the Bible for "hell:" Hades, Sheol, the Furnace, where the worm dies not, Gehena, Lake of Fire, deep Abyss, and Fire & Brimstone. This is a place of torment where demons dwell and Lucifer comes and he has the key to the bottomless pit and he will unleash them.

"And he opened the bottomless pit; and there arose a smoke out of the pit, as the smoke of a great furnace; and the sun and air were darkened by reason of the smoke of the pit. And there came out of the smoke locusts upon the earth: and unto them was given power, as the scorpions of the earth have power. And it was commanded them that they should not hurt the grass of the earth, neither any green thing, neither any tree; but only those men which have not the seal of God in their foreheads."

Remember the 144,000 are preaching, and the locusts can't harm them. And if anyone comes to Christ during that time, they have the seal of God and there is no harming those people. The church is already gone. But there is going to be torment because of these demonic creatures.

Let's say there are one hundred million that come out of the pit. Did you know the same hundred million in eternity in the past were lovely and pure as they were in the fellowship of the Father. They made a choice to follow this angel of light and now they are in eternal punishment and torment. And all of these cliché's that you hear today about wanting to go to hell because 'that is where my buddies are'. I will tell you how bad hell is. What does the Bible say? Does it say that the demons just want to stay in the pit to have a 'party'? No, they are out of there. They are out of there so quick, they hate it there. In Luke 8 Jesus confronts some of the demons there. They begged not to go there before their time because they didn't want to go there yet. They hate hell! When Satan comes to unleash them, they are out of there so fast. They have broken fellowship, broken future, broken plans, and they will forever be in torment.

"And to them it was given that they should not kill them, but that they should be tormented five month: and their torment was as the torment of the scorpion, when he striketh a man. And in those days shall man seek death, and shall not find it; and shall desire to die, and death shall flee from them."

Man will be stung by these creatures. It will be so bad they will wish to die. But the Bible says they will not die. They will just be tormented. I can't imagine that. For five months they will be repeatedly stung. They will probably jump in the ocean or off buildings because they want to die, but they can't. That is true torment for five months.

I find this interesting. Even though John tries to describe them, he says they are like locusts. But the reason they are not locusts is because they don't go after vegetation. They go after flesh. They are not locusts. The Bible says in Proverbs that locusts do not have a king. The Bible says that these locusts have a king. It is Lucifer. They are going around to sting and sting some more. This is the demonic activity from the pit of hell!

"And the shapes of the locusts were like unto horses prepared for battle; and on their heads were as it were crowns like gold, and their faces were faces of men. And they had hair as the hair of women, and their teeth were was the teeth of lions."

It says they have a man's face. A man's face is the index of the soul. You look at the people on 'wanted' posters. Their face is the index of their soul. You can't judge their age. They look in wretched woe. It is because sin has made them that way. These locusts that come on the scene, they will have wretched looking faces. That is an index of the evil that is from within. And they are going to attack people and sting them.

They have hair like a women. They only thing I can understand from that is that they are perhaps seductive and attract people and then sting them. They have teeth like a lion. They are going to sink their teeth in. When lion's teeth sink in, what happens? There is no escaping. So now they have got them.

"And they had breastplates, as it were breastplates of iron; and the sound of their wings was as the sound of chariots of many horses running to battle. And they had tails like unto scorpions, and there were stings in their tails: and their power was to hurt men five months."

They will be completely insensitive to the suffering of the people they sting. The more they shriek, the more they yell, the more they sting. That is a demon for you. They could not care less about the soul of men.

They will have wings. There will be no place that men will be able to hide or escape.

Why is it that people say today that there are no demons? Maybe people want to make it a myth so that it will go away. If you go back to the 1600's and walk the streets of London and if you really listened, you would hear a lot of coughing. There were hundreds of thousands of people dying from the Bubonic plague. And they thought the culprit was 'fresh air'. They thought they were getting sick because there was too much fresh air. So they went in their homes and sealed up the chimneys and let the smoke come in thinking that would take care of it. But the problem was bacteria. They went the wrong direction and killed thousands of people.

When it gets down to this time, men will turn their backs and say it isn't that big of a deal and say that there are not demons and they will get stung and bit. It is real and it will happen.

"One woe is past; and, behold, there come two woes more hereafter. And the sixth angel sounded, and I heard a voice from the four horns of the golden altar which is before God, Saying to the sixth angel which had the trumpet, Loose the four angels which are bound in the great river Euphrates."

What we have here is another prison block about ready to be opened. Make this one the 'death row' one if you please. You think the first demonic angels and their activity is bad, but all they did was torment. But when this angel sounds, now there is death. Here they were tormented for five months and they couldn't die. But now when the sixth trumpet sounds to the four angels by the great river Euphrates, now we are talking about death. More death than anywhere else in the book of Revelation. This is like the apex, the crowning of God allowing Satan to do his thing. In Revelation 6 it said that one-fourth of the planet was slaughtered. Here we see that one-third of mankind is killed. If you add the fractions, one-half of the planet will be dead because of the activity here in the ninth chapter. Three billion people dead. I can't even fathom that.

"And the number of the army of the horsemen were two hundred thousand thousand: and I heard the number of them."

John says he is not making any mistake here. He **heard** the number. It is two hundred million and that is the number when they will come on the scene and they will kill a third of the planet. Why the River Euphrates? Why not the Amozon? Why not Dry Creek? Why not the Mississippi? Remember that Revelation is the cycle, the finish of the circle of truth. Things that began in Genesis will end in Revelation. Things that begin in the Holy Land will end in the Holy Land. That is what is talked about here. This army will destroy a third of humanity. But think about this, sin started at the Euphrates River, the Garden of Eden. Misery started at the Euphrates River. The tower of Babel was at the Euphrates River. The first murder was here. Everything bad that started, started here. All the major bad world powers started at the Euphrates River. Roman, Medo-Persian, Babylon, Greece. Maybe these four demonic angels that were in control of those world powers now are unleashed here and they allow them to run rampant again and enter these horsemen and they slaughter a third of the planet. It started here and it will end here.

I don't want you to be confused. This is not Armageddon (Ezekiel 38 and 39). I think it is in line with the two hundred million here. When we get to the battle of Armageddon, we will have specifics of kings from the east. There is no mention of those kings here. I think this is a demonic-controlled army. The reason I think it is Ezekial 38 and 39 is because when these people are slaughtered here, it says it will take 7 months to bury them and to burn their implements of warfare. It says it will be a continual stench to their nose. That will happen when you have this many people die. If you have two billion people lying around, it will stink on the planet. In the battle of Armageddon, I do not think there will be that many. There could be, but it is a different battle.

This is bad. But there is something that jumps out of here to me. Every time one of these trumpets blew, there was destruction. That is sad. Then it gets down here to where all this demonic activity is happening and that is sad. And then the horsemen come and all these people are dead because of it, that is sad. But do you know what is just as tragic? Verses 20 and 21.

"And the rest of the men which were not killed by these plagues yet repented not of the works of their hands, that they should not worship devils, and idols of gold, and silver, and brass, and stone, and of wood: which neither can see, nor hear, nor walk; Neither repented they of their murders, nor of their sorceries, nor of their fornication, nor of their thefts."

That is very tragic. You have 144,000 evangelists preaching the gospel of the kingdom and people dying for Christ during this terrible time. Men will be witnessing the judgment, and the hand of God, and the Bible says in verse 20 that those who were not killed did not repent. It is a lesson for us today that needs to sink down into our hearts as we share the Gospel. If men do not accept the love of God now, they will not accept a God of judgement then. The Bible proves that. If a man can not accept the love and the gift of God's Son now, he will never accept a God of judgement then. That is what the Bible says. They are going to turn against God and they will not repent. So he will not be done with them. A little later on he has His Vials. He is going to pour out on these people that reject him and his son. We can't comprehend that. If you are sitting there reading this and you say, "Well, I am going to wait until I see some of these things happening, then I am going to get with it." No, you won't. The Bible says that you will be sent a very strong delusion that you will believe a lie. Accept the God of grace and love now.

In a way we see that today, God sending a judgement of AIDS. Does man repent? No, he just keeps doing it and seeing if he can get around it with 'safe sex'. Does it change with pornography? No, he just keeps doing it. You can talk about drugs and their consequences and man just does not change. In the face of God he just says, no, no, no. God will bring judgement upon all that sin in a climatic way and that will be it.

God loves us so much that He sent His Son. But if we reject Him, He will be a God of judgement. His wrath is as strong as His love. That is very serious.

Another lesson that is kind of a background for this chapter is Calvary, the devil's Waterloo. He really got beat up there didn't he? And for 2000 years he has been hounding all of us because he knows enough of the Bible to know what is going to happen. That tells me today that you are not going to be without a battle in your life. Take the comfort to know the challenge. Therefore the Bible says to take up the whole armor of God that you may be able to withstand anything, any dart, anything that he throws our way. *"Greater is He that is in you than he that is in the world."* That makes me want to take my Bible every single day and just draw on it and draw on it and draw on it and allow it to come into my life and heart. Then I can always keep my focus on Him. I can know that I am here

196

because of Him and to glorify Him. And no matter how I get buffeted, it is all about Him.

Now we can say, *"We shall fear no evil... for thine is the kingdom and power forever. Amen."*

THE SUN IS STILL SHINING
Revelation 10

"And I saw another mighty angel come down from heaven, clothed with a cloud: and a rainbow was upon his head, and his face was as it were the sun, and his feet as pillars of fire:

And he had in his hand a little book open: and he set his right foot upon the sea, and his left foot on the earth, And cried with a loud voice, as when a lion roareth: and when he had cried, seven thunders uttered their voices. And when the seven thunders had uttered their voices, I was about to write: and I heard a voice from heaven saying unto me, Seal up those things which the seven thunders uttered, and write them not. And the angel which I saw stand upon the sea and upon the earth lifted up his hand to heaven, And swear by him that liveth for ever and ever, who created heaven, and the things that therein are, and the earth, and the things that therein are, and the sea, and the things which are therein, that there should be time no longer: But in the days of the voice of the seventh angel, when he shall begin to sound, the mystery of God should be finished, as he hath declared to his servants the prophets. And the voice which I heard from heaven spake unto me again, and said, Go and take the little book which is open in the hand of the angel which standeth upon the sea and upon the earth. And I went to the angel and said unto him, give me the little book. And he said unto me, take it and eat it up; and it shall make thy belly bitter, but it shall be in thy mouth sweet as honey. And I took the little book out of the angel's hand, and ate it up; and it was in my mouth sweet as honey: and as soon as I had eaten it, my belly was bitter. And he said unto me, Thou must prophesy again before many peoples, and nations, and tongues, and kings."

The reason I title this The Sun Is Still Shining, is because it is like a parenthetical pause that God knew that we need to sort of 'get a breath of fresh air'. As I look through the book of Revelation, I see it happening three times. In the seventh chapter there was a parenthetical pause, and in Revelation 10 we will see the same thing. All of the sudden we are not looking down on what is happening on the planet. God is just reminding us that the sun is still shining through.

You could break this chapter up into two basic ways: turn your eyes upon Jesus and look back at the apostle John. In my meditations as I study Revelation, I get so excited to get into the millennial reign and thoughts on heaven. I can't wait until chapter 22 when we sit down by the River of Life and we see the great things that will be a part of our eternity. And we say, even so, Come Lord Jesus. There are still hard times to come first. And yet God is still there.

"And I saw another mighty angel come down from heaven, clothed with a cloud: and a rainbow was upon his head, and his face was as it were the sun, and his feet as pillars of fire:

And he had in his hand a little book open: and he set his right foot upon the sea, and his left foot on the earth, And cried with a loud voice, as when a lion roareth: and when he had cried, seven thunders uttered their voices. And when the seven thunders had uttered their voices, I was about to write: and I heard a voice from heaven saying unto me, Seal up those things which the seven thunders uttered, and write them not."

.

I will share with you who I think this angel is. It is all over the course of commentaries that this angel is the Archangel Gabriel and some are convinced that it is a new angel that does not have a name. I would like to submit to you that this is the reincarnate Christ. This is none other than Jesus himself. I believe my reason is based in the Bible. The reason is, as you look at the description of this angel, to me it seems like the angel of Jehovah, Jesus Christ. And here He is and He comes down here and one of the first things that describes Him is He is wearing a cloud. If you look in the Bible, just about everywhere you see the mention of a cloud, there is God or Jesus Christ there in the transfiguration, Exodus 13 as they moved in the wilderness, there was God moving in a cloud. So you see this angel here wearing a cloud. In Psalms it says that He makes the clouds His chariot. This angel makes the clouds his chariot.

It also says that He is crowned with a rainbow. Again, as you look through the Bible as you see the depiction of the rainbow, even the ones surrounding the throne, it comes when Christ is there. It is a complete circle of the fulfillment of that rainbow.

Then it says that his face is shining as the sun. Again, go back in scripture and look at the pictures of where Christ is present. Look at where Paul was struck down on his way to Damascus. He is struck down by a great bright shining light. Who was it? It was Jesus Christ. Just like here where his face is shining as the sun.

Malachi 4:2 "He is as the sun of righteousness." In Revelation 1 when John tries to describe him there it says, "His head is full of white, his face is bright as the sun." I believe that this individual standing here in Revelation 10 is none other than Jesus Christ.

Then it says that His feet are as fire. Jump back to Revelation 1:15 and it talks about his feet as flames of fire.

He is standing there with his power. His face is so bright that you probably can't look at it. His feet are as flames of fire, and He is standing there with power and authority and He has a book in His hand that is open. Back in chapter 5, who was worthy to take this book out of the hand of God the Father? Who was worthy to not only take the book, but to open the book and open the seals? If it is still in the hand of this angel, then it must be Jesus Christ.

What is he doing here? The book is open. In essence I believe he is saying something like this to John. He says, "**The seals are off. They have all been opened, the trumpets have nearly all blown. We have one more to blow which will open the vial judgements. We are right in the midst of something that has never been witnessed before, the last 3 ½ years, the last 1260 days. But John, I want you to notice something here. The sun is still shining through and I am still in control.**"

Sometimes there seems to be so much demonic activity and so much evil going on in the world out there, people start to think that the 'bad guys' are winning. Revelation 10 says NO! God is in control! I am still here. It is all right my people. I have it all in control.

Here he is crying with a loud voice. I have wondered about that loud voice. I believe we will be there and maybe witness Revelation 10 when He cries with this loud voice. Here is Christ standing on the earth and the seas and He is crying with a loud voice. In Proverbs the Bible says that the King will cry with a loud voice as a roaring lion. The Bible says in another place that the Lion will roar out of Judah. This is a picture of Jesus saying, "Don't worry, I am still here and I am still in control. It will happen the exact way I have planned it and it is still yet to come."

Something that I thought was strange happens here. This thundering. I looked everywhere and I do not believe you are going to find the answer to this. But as Christ cries with a loud voice like a lion and it says, when He had cried, a seven-gun salute takes place. The Bible says that seven thunders uttered their voices. And when they had uttered their voices, John is right there with his pen and he is just about ready to write it down, and what happens? And then he is told that he is not to write them down. That was puzzling to me. This apocalypse occurs this total revelation of Jesus Christ of what is happening in Revelation. He has opened up the seals. He has opened up the trumpets, and he will open up the vials and he will show us what they are. Then all of the sudden here in the middle of the book there is a seven gun salute and these thunderings go out, and God says, "Don't write it!"

I started imagining what is could be. And it is interesting as I read the commentaries that they started trying to imagine what these thunderings were too. We do not know. John is the only one here that knows. He is ready to write it down and God says not to do it. I would like to suggest that perhaps the reason why he wasn't allowed to write it was this. The Bible says in Psalms 29, *"The God of heaven thundereth."* When God speaks and God thunders, man should listen.

There may be a chance here that these seven thunderings are not coming from God. As Jesus speaks with a loud voice and cries out, what happens? All of the sudden seven thunders utter their voices. Maybe just maybe these seven thunderings are the response of all the evil when Christ is speaking.

The response is so blasphemous and so horrible of a reaction that Jesus says He doesn't want any of it written down. That might be it. But I do know this. You can search all through the Bible and try to figure out what the seven thunderings are, but you are going to have to come back to Deut. 29:29, *"The secret things belong to God, but the things that are revealed, they belong to us."* There are times in life when we experience things and the secret things belong to God. You have to leave it there. That is why I do not know. We can give our opinions on the seven thunderings but for some reason it was important that Jesus told John not to write it down.

Another thought I had was that it might be names and dates and places specifically of everything that was to be involved here and He says He doesn't want to have it written down. There is a purpose why he said it. I do not know what the seven thunders are.

"And swear by him that liveth for ever and ever, who created heaven, and the things that therein are, and the earth, and the things that therein are, and the sea, and the things which are therein, that there should be time no longer:"

You might ask, how could this be Jesus? I looked up the word 'swear'. I think it is still Jesus and I base this on **Hebrews 6,** *"For when God made promise to Abraham, because he could swear by no greater, he swear by himself and said, 'surely blessing I will bless thee, and multiplying I will multiply thee."*

In that essence, that swearing is not bad, if God wants to swear, and God did. Jesus in Revelation 10 is saying that this is it. There will not be any more delay. The long-suffering of God has come to an end. This is it. The judgements that are going to be coming now, they are going to be unleashed, there is no more time for delaying. And all the scoffers and all the people who say, "Oh, where is the promise of His coming?" "oh, since the fathers fell asleep it has never changed, he is never coming back, it will not happen!" Jesus says, "No longer! No more delay! This mystery is finished." And I believe that is what He is saying here. He raises his hands to the stars and he swears like God did in Hebrews chapter 6. No more delay, judgement will be completed forever.

"But in the days of the voice of the seventh angel, when he shall begin to sound, the mystery of God should be finished, as he hath declared to his servants the prophets. And the voice which I heard from heaven

spake unto me again, and said, Go and take the little book which is open in the hand of the angel which standeth upon the sea and upon the earth."

Your eyes are on Christ and He has everything in control. There won't be any delay, I am still here. Now I want you to look at John for a moment. Turn your eyes on John and listen to the commandment I give John. What does he mean when he says, *"the mystery of God is finished?"* I think this mystery is that this evil that God has allowed for centuries on this planet, this evil, this mystery… "How could God allow Satan to do this?" And, "How could the angels fall?" and, "How could men be so degenerate in their minds?" He is saying that all of this is over now. Satan is not in charge and it will all change when I come back. I have to confess that in some areas of life I feel like Habakkuk, and I wonder why God doesn't do something.

He looks to John here to play a part. He asks him to do something very strange. He asks him to take this little book which is open in the hand of Jesus. He went over to Jesus and asked if he could have this little book. And Jesus tells him to take it and eat it. Jesus explains that when he eats this book, it will taste sweet in his mouth; but when it goes to his stomach, it will be very bitter. So here you have a picture of Christ in His power and authority. He has the book and John walks over and takes the book and puts it in his mouth and it tastes good. But as it goes down into his stomach it gets very bitter. What is he saying here when he talks about this book being eaten? Did you know that in Ezekiel 3, this prophet takes this book and takes it in and it tastes good, but it gets down into his stomach and it is terrible?

So what does he mean? I believe as he takes this open book, it is no different than taking this Word of God as a lesson in our own life. This is a book of love and grace. If you read this book, it will be like sweetness to your soul. But as you take this book and permeate your life with it and as you share it with other people, there is a bitterness that goes with that. You know that when you stand for the cause of Christ, there will be rejection. There will be bitterness that will overwhelm your life from time to time. He tells his disciples this in the upper room, *You will have intense persecution, but greater is he that is in you than he that is in the world."* And when you have the love of Christ in your life, it is like sweetness. People can't take that away; but as you begin to share that sweetness, so often you will have bitterness. Have you ever experienced that in your life? As you pray for a loved one, you may experience a bitterness that hurts.

"And I took the little book out of the angel's hand, and ate it up; and it was in my mouth sweet as honey: and as soon as I had eaten it, my belly was bitter. And he said unto me, Thou must prophesy again before many peoples, and nations, and tongues, and kings."

When you share this book, something is going to happen in your life. It hasn't changed for thousands of years, has it?

On a very private note, when you teach through the book of Revelation this is what happens to you. I love the book of Revelation. You teach about hell sometimes and make a study on demons or some of these dark passages in the Bible, and there is a very real uncomfortable feeling that goes on in your spirit. I believe that happened when John took this book and ate it and then went out and preached it and became an elder in Ephesus and died an old age. And then you read 1 John, 2 John, and 3 John and it is a different story than the 'Son of Thunder' at that point. John was doing everything he could to talk to the children, the young ones and doing everything he could to share the sweetness of the gospel. And yet there is a heaviness in his spirit. He wants John to take this book and tell exactly what it is and do not skip over anything. It is sad to say that too often in the last stages of the history of mankind, it is beginning to get that way. Everybody just wants to hear about honey, every one just wants to hear about the love of God but no one wants to be warned! No one wants to talk about judgement or the hail that will come upon those who reject him. That is the stain on the steeple of churches. "We will pick this and pick that, pick that, don't make people uncomfortable…" You have to take it all. It is all there. Yes, it is fun to talk about honey, but it is awfully hard to talk about conviction and judgement that makes us uncomfortable.

But when John took the book, He didn't tell him to eat pages three and four and then chuck a couple of those others that have mustard and then maybe eat some of these other ones here. He wanted him to eat the whole book. I love to read and study the Bible, but when I go out and live it and practice it and share it, sometimes I do not feel so comfortable.

The other night I read the "F" Encyclopedia on the "French Revolution". I read about France and the French Revolution. I found there are many similarities between what John was experiencing here, the sweetness and the bitterness. To some people the French Revolution was the worst of times, but for some it was the best of times. For some it was the winter of total despair, and for some it was the spring of eternal hope. And that is where we are in Revelation. You have both sides.

There are some people who will never change and never repent, and they will fight God up to the day of the Battle of Armageddon. Some will wait and join the battle of Gog and Magog when Satan is loosed for a season. They will still reject Him. But God still has it all in control and the message of grace is clear through the Revelation. The final wrath is getting ready to come, but with that wrath is a spring of hope that we can't even imagine.

What does this chapter look like in my life? One, be content in the fact that you do not know everything. The secret things belong to God. There is contentment that comes with giving it all over to the Lord. Two, keep proclaiming the Word of God. It is both a blessing and a burden. Not everyone will receive it. Let the Holy Spirit do the teaching. Three, suppose that you knew that Jesus Christ was coming back tomorrow morning at 6:00. In what way would that be sweet and in what way would that be bitter. I answered that for myself. If I knew beyond a shadow of a doubt that I would hear that trumpet sound and I knew He was coming… there would be sweetness there unimaginable and there would be a heavy burden. That is one of the reasons that chapter 10 is here. But with all the sweetness and blessing and burden, remember He is still in control. He loves us so much that He can't wait to come and receive us home. I know one thing, He is Coming AGAIN!!!!

REVELATION 11

God's Two Witnesses

"And there was given me a reed like unto a rod: and the angel stood, saying, Rise, and measure the temple of God, and the alter, and them that worship therein. But the court which is without the temple leave out, and measure it not; for it is given unto the Gentiles: and the holy city shall they tread underfoot forty and two months. And I will give power unto my two witnesses, and they shall prophesy a thousand two hundred and threescore days, clothed in sackcloth. These are the two olive trees, and the two candlesticks standing before the God of the earth. And if any man will hurt them, fire proceedeth out of their mouth, and devoureth their enemies: and if any man will hurt them, he must in this manner be killed. These have power to shut heaven, that it rain not in the days of their prophecy: and have power over waters to turn them to blood, and to smite the earth with all plagues, as often as they will. And when they shall have finished their testimony, the beast that ascendeth out of the bottomless pit shall make war against them, and shall overcome them, and kill them. And their dead bodies shall lie in the street of the great city, which spiritually is called Sodom and Egypt, where also our Lord was crucified. And they of the people and kindreds and tongues and nations shall see their dead bodies three days and a half, and shall not suffer their dead bodies to be put in graves. And they that dwell upon the earth shall rejoice over them, and make merry, and shall send gifts to one another; because these two prophets tormented them that dwelt on the earth. And after three days and an half the Spirit of life from God entered into them, and they stood on their feet; and great fear fell upon them which saw them. And they heard a great voice from heaven saying unto them, Come up hither. And they ascended up to heaven in a cloud; and

their enemies beheld them. And the same hour was there a great earthquake, and the tenth part of the city fell, and in the earthquake were slain of men seven thousand: and the remnant were affrighted, and gave glory to the God of heaven. The second woe is past; and, behold, the third woe cometh quickly. And the seventh angel sounded; and there were great voices in heaven, saying, The kingdoms of this world are become the kingdoms of our Lord, and of his Christ; and he shall reign for ever and ever. And the four and twenty elders, which sat before God on their seats, fell upon their faces, and worshipped God, Saying, We give thee thanks, O Lord God Almighty, which art, and was, and art to come; because thou has taken to thee thy great power, and has reigned. And the nations were angry, and thy wrath is come, and the time of the dead, that they should be judged, and that thou shouldest give reward unto thy servants the prophets, and to the saints, and them that fear thy name, small and great; and shouldest destroy them which destroy the earth. And the temple of God was opened in heaven, and there was seen in his temple the ark of his testament: and there were lightnings, and voices, and thunderings, and an earthquake, and great hail."

Revelation 11 is considered the most difficult chapter to talk about in the book of Revelation. You will notice when people get to a subject in the Bible and they shy away from it, it is because there is too much controversy in it. The reason is, some people will take all of this portion of scripture as symbolic, some people will take and spiritualize it, and then some will take it literally.

As I began to study the book, it was my interpretation and understanding, to study the whole book in a literal sense. So there are three things I want to make clear as we look at this chapter. ***One***, this is about the Jews, for the Jews, and this is a Zionist movement. The church has been raptured in chapter 4 so this is not about the church. We are going to get a glimpse of the church here today, but this is not about the church. ***Two***, this is a prophetic statement. This temple where the witnesses are at is not currently there. It needs to be built. ***Three***, it is literal. There are two men who are witnesses for God. There is a literal Jerusalem. Here it is called Sodom and Egypt. There are two witnesses. There is a literal earthquake. There are literally seven thousand men of renown being slain. And there is a literal rejoicing in heaven.

Just as Jesus Christ would come to the town of Bethlehem, born of a virgin, literally walked on this planet, I say that everything in Revelation would be the same. There are some symbols, but this is a literal interpretation as we look at the 11th chapter.

God never leaves Himself, this planet or people, without a witness. I find this very fascinating. You could do a whole study on that alone. You will see it back in Noah's time. There was Noah and Enoch. They were God's witnesses. You see it in the dark days of Israel for a thousand years or so. They had Elijah and Elisha. There was Joshua and Caleb. There was Moses and Aaron, Peter and John, Paul and Silas, Titus and Timothy. He sends the seventy disciples out two by two. You see the two witnesses here in the tribulation period. God always is breaking it down to two witnesses. The Word of God says, *"by the mouth of two or three, every word shall be established."* There is something about a witness that is very precious.

"And there was given me a reed like unto a rod: and the angel stood, saying, Rise, and measure the temple of God, and the alter, and them that worship therein. But the court which is without the temple leave out, and measure it not; for it is given unto the Gentiles: and the holy city shall they tread underfoot forty and two months."

Jerusalem shall be trodden down by the Gentiles. This will be a literal 1,260 days, 3 ½ years, 42 months. We have seen some of the catastrophic things that have gone on with the sealed judgements and the trumpet judgments. Now as this one blows we will see the vial judgements down here…

Whenever he talks about taking a rod or measuring instrument in Scripture, there is judgement. (That is the connotation there). He is saying, John I want you to measure this because there is going to be a time of judgment on Israel, judgement on Jerusalem. John takes the rod and begins to measure this. I do not believe the temple has been built yet. You can go over there today and there is no temple. There hasn't been a temple since the last one was destroyed in Herod's day. There are five major temples in the Bible and you can follow that in the Word. It is rather easy to follow that. There was Solomon's Temple which was destroyed by Nebuchadnezzar. There was Zerubbable's Temple, after 70 years in the captivity of Babylon, they went back and built that temple, and it was destroyed and desecrated by Antiochus Epiphanes. Herod's Temple was during Christ's time, and it was destroyed in AD 70 by the Romans. And there has not been a temple for over 2,000 years. Yet, there is going to be a temple rebuilt in the tribulation. If you go to Jerusalem today, you can go down to what they call the Temple Institute. It is behind locked doors, another locked door, and then a locked room. It is a very private tour, and you can go on it if you pay enough money. But it is incredible what is in the Temple Institute. A man comes out and speaks in hushed tones. He has gold vials and bowls and artifacts that they are making now for the Temple. What Temple? This temple will be built previous to this tribulation period or during this tribulation period. When the Jews sign a covenant with the Anti-Christ, who will come out of the European nations, he will promise them that no one will hurt them any longer. They are coming back into their homeland and the first thing they are going to do, and they are already discussing it, is to build the temple.

In the Temple Institute, they are already collecting the artifacts and making the clothes for the priest. (the ephods). It is amazing. Millions and millions of dollars are in this room. The Jews are sending gold from all over the world and they are melting it down and making their artifacts for the Temple Institute. There is a structure (made to scale) made out of big Legos, that will be like the one built in the future. It is constructed like Solomon's Temple, and it is a beautiful display. They will build somewhere near the Temple Mount. Now we know that there will be conflict if they try, because of all that is going on over there. But somehow it will fit there.This temple will be the temple that the two witnesses are going to be preaching at in the future.

So we have a temple that is going to be measured and it is going to be the tribulation temple and then that will be destroyed too. When it is built, it will be constructed somewhere in the middle of the week. We call that the Abomination of Desolation. That is when the Anti-Christ steps in and he says he was just fooling everyone, the Jews are out of here and he will set himself up as "God." He will desecrate the temple. Just about like Antiochus Epiphanes at that other temple. He came in and slaughtered pigs and offered sacrifices in a mockery of God. The Anti-Christ will come in and say that He is "God" now and the wrath that God begins to unveil will take place here.

Satan has access to heaven right now. When you do something wrong, what happens? He is the accuser of the brethren. Somewhere, somehow when Christ is seated at the right hand of the Father, he is accusing us.

When Satan is cast out heaven, he has no access to heaven at that point. He comes down and pours his judgement and wrath out and tries to do even more evil. You think it has been bad here, it will get even worse. That is why we look at Revelation chapter 11 as being a parenthesis or parenthetical chapter. It is a pause or catch your breath chapter.

"And I will give power unto my two witnesses, and they shall prophesy a thousand two hundred and threescore days, clothed in sackcloth. These are the two olive trees, and the two candlesticks standing before the God of the earth."

Why are the messengers called 'olive trees' and why are they called 'candlesticks'. Simply this: These two messengers are going to be fueled by the Holy Spirit of God. Their faces are going to shine as bright lights in the communities like candlesticks. So he is saying that when these two witnesses come on the scene they are going to be fueled by the Holy Spirit, and they are going to be shining in the community.

Who are the messengers? I would never get dogmatic about this, but I will share with you who I believe the two messengers are: **Elijah and Moses**. Enoch could also fit the picture because both Elijah and Enoch were translated and they never died. But I think it is Moses and Elijah, from the aspect of what they are doing as the messengers. They are doing the same miracles that they were doing the first time. Think about what Elijah did. He stopped the rain for 3 ½ years. What does he do during the tribulation? He stops and causes a drought for 3 ½ years. Who was on the Mount of Transfiguration in Matthew 17? It was **Moses and Elijah**. Why would we say Moses? Moses body has never been found. What is the big deal about that? I do not know for sure, but it is a pretty big deal because in Jude verse 9, it says that Michael the archangel was arguing with the devil and disputing that they wanted the body of Moses. Why? I don't know. But somehow God has always hid or taken the body of Moses somewhere else. I think he will resurrect it here as a witness with Elijah and they will join together as two powerful "Billy Grahams" witnesses, messengers, during the tribulation.

This is the exciting part about it. Men are going to hate these people. They are going to hate them so much that they are going to be household names just as Saddam Hussein is today. You can't find a place on the planet today (probably) who has not heard of Saddam. You will not find a household during the tribulation period that has not heard of Moses and Elijah. They will be on the network, on TV and everything else that comes down the pike because they are going to be preaching the gospel and the message of repentance and talking about Jehovah God. No one will be able to do anything about it! The Bible says that they can not be destroyed.

"And if any man will hurt them, fire proceedeth out of their mouth, and devoureth their enemies: and if any man will hurt them, he must in this manner be killed."

Can you imagine? They will walk anywhere they want, getting any crowd they want. These witnesses can preach the Word of God and no one can hinder it. Satan will have his two Witnesses at this time and Satan's two Witnesses will be the ones who will end up killing these two Witnesses. The Anti-Christ and the False Prophet-they are the copycats. They will come on the scene with powers of persuasion telling people not to listen to the message of these "Jesus Freaks". They will be out there trying to counteract everything. So God knew in His sovereignty that He had to send these two men to get the message out. I believe that one of the fruits of their messages is the 144,000 who become ministers themselves. They will most definitely be opposed.

"These have power to shut heaven, that it rain not in the days of their prophecy: and have power over waters to turn them to blood, and to smite the earth with all plagues, as often as they will."

This is just like Moses did. However Satan always has his two counterfeits. What happened when the two witnesses (Aaron & Moses) in Egypt were doing their miracles? Who were Satan's counter parts to them? It was Janese and Jambrese. They were trying to do the same thing. And there is only one distinct difference between the two-the 'bad guys' can never give life to an individual. There will be a counterfeit from the Devil at the end where he tries to resurrect the Anti-Christ. But it will be a false miracle or an illusion.

Look at the miracle of the Messengers. They preach with power to a hostile audience but with them they have three weapons of mass destruction. Everywhere they go they have these three weapons of mass destruction. They do not have patriot missiles, they do not have sand missiles, they are not nuclear, they are not atom bombs, but they are found in Revelation 11:5-6. It is death, drought and disease. They will take these three and cause terrible things to be inflicted upon nature and people, that some men will repent and come to the Savior.

"And when they shall have finished their testimony, the beast that ascendeth out of the bottomless pit shall make war against them, and shall overcome them, and kill them. And their dead bodies shall lie in the street of the great city, which spiritually is called Sodom and Egypt, where also our Lord was crucified."

Notice, when they had *finished*, God is still in control here. It is not before they finished their testimony. And why would we say *Sodom and Egypt* means *Jerusalem*? In this sense; when it gets this bad, at this time during the tribulation period. The great city Jerusalem may be called Sodom and Egypt for this reason; Sodom is always talking about unhealthy wicked devices, and Egypt is always a place of terrible vanities. If you combine these two then you have the great city of vice and vanity with the power of all kinds of evil and violence.

"And they of the people and kindreds and tongues and nations shall see their dead bodies three days and a half, and shall not suffer their dead bodies to be put in graves."

This verse could not have been believed at all in the 1800's. Why? How do you kill somebody and lay them in the street in Jerusalem, and have every nation, every kindred, every tongue see the bodies? We are living in a secular society that will see these men laying there destroyed. I have a big imagination, but as I read this verse, I could just see CNN and NBC and all these people out there with daily reports. Then they leave the bodies in the streets, which is wrong to the Jews who always bury a body the same day. And here you have these bodies lying in the streets and being laughed at!

I believe they will start special tours and busloads to come in here with cameras on them, and millions are watching them… But then notice what happens! In the death of the Messengers you have a new Christmas Holiday. It will get so bad here with people hating Christ that I believe that holidays like Christmas won't be recognized any longer. But they come along and kill people who stand for Christ and now we have a new holiday! Isn't that what it says here?

"And they that dwell upon the earth shall rejoice over them, and make merry, and shall send gifts to one another; because these two prophets tormented them that dwelt on the earth."

Because of the death of God's prophets in the streets they are out buying gifts for each other and celebrating everywhere on the planet. It is a shame! It will happen because that is what the Bible says. They will celebrate in this way because the prophets tormented them with their speech and because of the 'weapons' they brought with them. I can just see the society and the Anti-Christ, the ones who killed them being ecstatic with joy. It will be broadcasted on the news and there they are looking at the bodies in the streets. Again, this is my imagination, but can you see a Dan Rathers standing there in the streets. "We are now bringing you an update from the streets of Jerusalem, Ben Yehuda Street. We are looking at these two false prophets. They called themselves Moses and Elijah, but here they are folks. It is day 2 ½." Then he comes back on the next day. "It has been 3 days and here they are… but something is happening … we bring you an update." And then the bodies begin to RISE AGAIN!

"And after three days and an half the Spirit of life from God entered into them, and they stood on their feet; and great fear fell upon them which saw them. And they heard a great voice from heaven saying unto them, Come up hither. And they ascended up to heaven in a cloud; and their enemies beheld them."

Fear came upon them who were watching. God will resurrect these two Witnesses bodies. They are taken home to the Father. This causes quite an upheaval in this city. *"Come up hither."* We saw this in chapter 4 where God raptured the Church and we see it here. This is where some people believe the rapture will be (mid-trib), which is somewhat understandable in this verse. Moses and Elijah being a representation of the Church and they say, *"come up hither."* And we will see it later, where some people believe it is the rapture. (post-trib). One thing we know is, there will be a rapture and Christ is definitely coming again.

"And they ascended up to heaven in a cloud;" If you look at the Greek terminology, this was written in the Greek text, it says *the cloud* instead of *a cloud*. The understanding is that they were caught up to be with Christ who is "the Cloud".

"And the same hour was there a great earthquake, and the tenth part of the city fell, and in the earthquake were slain of men seven thousand:"

This is a little confusing here. The Bible does not mention things unless there is a specific reason. You don't throw in the number 7,000 for any good reason. God knew in eternity past that when He wrote Revelation 11, He would mention 7,000 men dying. Again, if you go back to the original text and look at the translation there, it says there, *"men of renown – 7,000."* I went back to look at the harmony of scripture. I found in Jude verse 19 where it says, *"those of men of advantage."* The same thing will happen here. More than 7,000 died, but it mentions the popular people. Maybe there were many Kings and Rulers in Jerusalem because of these men lying on the streets. It says that 7,000 men of renown will be slain. It is a literal earthquake and it will take place.

It breaks into a completely different subject here. I am surprised that it did not break into a new chapter, but it goes on in chapter 11.

A peak preview of the coming Messiah. *"The second woe is past; and, behold, the third woe cometh quickly. And the seventh angel sounded; and there were great voices in heaven, saying, The kingdoms of this world are become the kingdoms of our Lord, and of his Christ; and he shall reign for ever and ever."*

Who borrowed that phrase and wrote a famous song? Handel in *The Messiah*. Handel pulled this verse out of Revelation 11 and wrote a famous song.

"And the four and twenty elders, which sat before God on their seats, fell upon their faces, and worshipped God, Saying, We give thee thanks, O Lord God Almighty, which art, and was, and art to come; because thou has taken to thee thy great power, and has reigned."

This is a preview. God knows that there are so many things that we have witnessed and He is just telling John to remember what is going to happen down here. Remember God is still in control. The sovereignty of God is already settled. We win at the end. And He is telling John that regardless the judgments that we have seen on this earth, do not forget that there is still jubilation in heaven! Don't forget it! He wants us to know that while there is rage on earth, there is rejoicing in heaven. Every time you have witnessed cursing on earth, there is also worship and praise in heaven. "Remember this, My Sovereignty is not to be questioned." The Almighty is in control! Even with everything you have witnessed, the seals, the trumpets, the witnesses, and the vials that are happening on the planet. There is rejoicing, worship, praise and honor going on in heaven. He didn't want John to forget that so He gave him a quick preview of what is going to happen.

"And the nations were angry, and thy wrath is come, and the time of the dead, that they should be judged, and that thou shouldest give reward unto thy servants the prophets, and to the saints, and them that fear thy name, small and great; and shouldest destroy them which destroy the earth."

I had an interesting study on this verse. This can be very confusing to a lot of people. Some say this verse shouldn't be here because how can you have a thousand years happen in one verse? You see when it talks about the judgement of the evil dead and in the same verse it talks about the reward of the saints. When we were raptured, we went to the judgement seat of Christ and we had rewards. This same verse is talking about the judgement of the dead, when they come back at the great White Throne Judgment. How can you have a thousand years in one verse?

If you look through Scripture and see the harmony, God does this all the time. **Isaiah 61:2,** *(this is a prophetic statement of Christ)* *"The Spirit of the Lord is upon me; because the Lord hath anointed me to preach good tidings unto the meek; he hath sent me to bind up the broken-hearted, to proclaim liberty to the captives, and the opening of the prison to them that are bound; To proclaim the acceptable year of the Lord, and the day of vengeance of our God; to comfort all that mourn;"*

This is talking about 2,000 years. Because the acceptable day of the Lord is when Christ came by incarnation and He came and lived for 33 years. That is the acceptable day of the Lord. But the day of vengeance is right here. That is two thousand years difference.

How can Christ stand there and put 2,000 years in one verse? I will tell you how he does it. If you go to Luke 4, He went into the city of Nazareth one day and He stood up, opened the Word of God to Isaiah and notice what he read, "I have come to preach the acceptable year of the Lord." And then He closed the book and sat down because He knew that there would be

2,000 years before he could say the rest at the end of the tribulation. That is the way the Lord works. He said it was all we needed to know now. " I am here, but my vengeance will come later" That is 2,000 years in one verse.

"And the temple of God was opened in heaven, and there was seen in his temple the ark of his testament: and there were lightnings, and voices, and thunderings, and an earthquake, and great hail."

What is he saying here? When God begins to open things, He is just revealing more of his promise and faithfulness. He has taken this temple of God in heaven and shown that His standard of righteousness has always been true. "My promises have always been fulfilled and my righteousness has always been available to everyone. You have access to the throne, and to the temple and to the ark through me." This is the Lord speaking. I would like to put it like this. This is real power being married to truth. The world today sees power without truth and they are flabbergasted. Wow! "Look at that bomb go off! Look at what it did! Look at the power unleashed there!" And they are impressed.

But if you take power and marry it with the truth of God, then that is very fascinating. That is what He is doing. He is taking the truth and promises of everything He has said and He is marrying it with His power and promises. And at the same time there is the miracle of a new birth of anyone who comes to Christ. The promises and the power of God with truth are a miracle that can not be topped! That is impressive. But it took this world, where they are at here, to reject that.

God said it is open now. He opens the door of heaven in Revelation 4. He opens the seals in Revelation 6. He opens the abyss and lets the demonic warfare come out in Revelation 9. He opens the temple here in Revelation 11. And He will open the door again and come back, from the north in Revelation 20. That is the faithfulness of God.

What kind of application would you come up with for yourself in 2009? I want us to think about a couple things.

Catastrophic things that happen in our lives are not done for punishment, but they can open our eyes. I am not necessarily saying to see more of Him. But let me use an example.

Something catastrophic could happen to Jason, my son-in-law this week. People know Jason loves the Lord and is a born-again believer. People watch Jason's life and because of his reaction and his love for the Lord, everything still looks the same. But catastrophic events can change other human hearts when they watch the witness and the testimony of people who love Christ.

What will happen here is humans will die as martyrs for Christ. They are not going to recant their faith and they will be beheaded if they don't accept the mark of the beast. Then they will be burnt at the stake and that will bring others to the Lord. Satan thinks he is having his way, but it doesn't go his way at all! Satan got his teeth kicked in at Calvary and he is furious! The more persecution, there will be more and more come to Calvary!

Catastrophic events can happen in our lives, but maybe it is not always a bad thing.

Final thought. The tension that we are experiencing in our communities right now and still having a hope for tomorrow is really big. Everyone has tension in their life. And every born again believer has confidence and hope that they are going home someday. But somehow we have to bring that together, the balance of this great expectation of going home and still be a participant in this life. We have to put that together. I have to keep my hope alive and yet the responsibility of being a vicar, a witness, and my faithfulness to Christ must remain real. We are not in a compound living alone behind a fence! We are living for Christ now in a troubled world! **And yes He is Coming Again….**

REVELATION 12

Satan's Schemes Unmasked

"And there appeared a great wonder in heaven; a woman clothed with the sun, and the moon under her feet, and upon her head a crown of twelve stars: And she being with child cried, travailing in birth, and pained to be delivered. And there appeared another wonder in heaven; and behold a great red dragon, having seven heads and ten horns, and seven crowns upon his heads. And his tail drew the third part of the stars of heaven, and did cast them to the earth: and the dragon stood before the woman which was ready to be delivered, for to devour her child as soon as it was born. And she brought forth a man child, who was to rule all nations with a rod of iron: and her child was caught up unto God, and to his throne. And the woman fled into the wilderness, where she had a place prepared of God, that they should feed her there a thousand two hundred and three-score days. And there was a war in heaven: Michael and his angels fought against the dragon; and the dragon fought and his angels, And prevailed not; neither was their place found any more in heaven. And the great dragon was cast out, that old serpent, called the Devil, and Satan, which deceiveth the whole world: He was cast out into the earth, and his angels were cast out with him. And I heard a loud voice saying in heaven, Now is come salvation, and strength, and the kingdom of our God, and the power of his Christ: For the accuser of our brethren is cast down, which accused them before our God day and night. And they overcame him by the blood of the Lamb, and by the word of their testimony; and they loved not their lives unto the death. Therefore rejoice, ye heavens, and ye

that dwell in them. Woe to the inhabitants of the earth and of the sea! For the Devil is come down unto you, having great wrath, because he knoweth that he hath but a short time. And when the dragon saw that he was cast unto the earth, he persecuted the woman, which brought forth the man-child. And to the woman were given two wings of a great eagle, that she might fly into the wilderness, into her place, where she is nourished for a time, and times, and half a time, from the face of the serpent. And the serpent cast out of his mouth water as a flood after the woman, that he might cause her to be carried away of the flood. And the earth helped the woman, and the earth opened her mouth, and swallowed up the flood, which the dragon cast out of his mouth. And the dragon was wroth with the woman, and went to make war with the remnant of her seed, which keep the commandments of God, and have the testimony of Jesus Christ."

There is a war going on right now that involves six and a half billion people. It is a war that Satan is trying to win in every heart on the planet today! Galatians 6 says, *"the flesh lusteth against the spirit and the spirit against the flesh"* and that is a tremendous battle.

We will be looking at a war here in Revelation 12 that we will witness from the balconies of heaven. It will be called the War in Heaven. An easy outline here in Revelation chapter 12 is: **the Woman, the War, and the Woe.**

Here in the middle of the week we are looking at chapters 12 and 13. There is a pause as we look at Satan's schemes being unmasked by heaven itself.

That is why this unmasking or revealing of Revelation is very clear if you walk through it. But Satan does everything he can to hide it because it shows his final demise. He loses. He not only lost at the cross, but now he loses because his sentencing is being exposed. He does not like that. Make no mistake about it, these verses call him the Dragon, the Serpent, Satan, and the Devil. When he is cast out here in this conflict in heaven, you think this is bad, but it gets worse!

God's glorious plans have been revealed in the book of Revelation. But now God's unmasking of Satan and what He has been up to all of these 6000 years are now being exposed to us. He is now being shown for what he really is.

There is a scarlet thread of redemption that starts in Genesis 3 and goes all the way to the Revelation. It is a trace of God's shed blood that goes all the way through time. You can also see a diabolical black line of Satan and all of his deviousness. He has tried for 6000 years to destroy the lives of men and woman.

One, he wants to eradicate all people who remind him of God-the irritation of anything or anybody who reminds him of God. Why does he hate the Jew? It reminds him of that chosen seed. Why does he hate Christians today? Because they talk about glorifying God. The bottom line is that we are in a spiritual battle. We have a Christian president who is saying things that the world does not want to hear. Above and beyond the conflict with Iraq, they do not want to hear about good morals or faith or praying to God or praying for the troops. We see the distancing of the European Common Market as they are starting to pull away from America.

Look at the world in light of Ezekiel 38. It is all lining up. It is all during the time of Israel going back to her homeland. Thirteen million Jews are in the world today. Six and a half million are now back home. Are they going back in belief? No, God is pulling them back in unbelief. Hopefully through the preaching of the 144,000 and the two witnesses, they may come to the foot of the cross. There will be tremendous pressure and persecution. The Devil thinks he is winning but he is not. That is why he is getting more frustrated in a fury that will be unleashed.

Two, he wants to destroy all of God's plans. Does Satan know the Bible this morning? Yes he does. Just as much as we study the book of Revelation, he sees that. He does not want anyone to know anything about that. He knows what the Old Testament books have said about him. He wants to destroy everything he can. He has tried destroying the Bible, but it is God's chosen Word and will never be destroyed.

Three, he has a great desire to be adored by the whole world. He wants to be worshiped like God. It will come close as we look at the Antichrist. He will move through these three and a half years, the mark of the Beast, the Satanic Trinity, and it says that the whole world will wonder after the beast. We think we are strong; but without the shed blood and the power of the Holy Spirit in us, we are nothing. Do not try to take on the Devil. Michael the archangel could not do it. It has to be the Lord God who does it. We can't match that kind of diabolical sin.

221

This chapter reveals how this great tyrant is brought on stage to show his purposes and that one ruling passion that he has. The one ruling passion that the Devil has is to destroy God's seed and the remnant of his seed, Israel, and any person who makes a claim for the Messiah. That is his ruling passion.

"And there appeared a great wonder in heaven; a woman clothed with the sun, and the moon under her feet, and upon her head a crown of twelve stars: And she being with child cried, travailing in birth, and pained to be delivered."

Genesis 37 is the only scripture in 1189 chapters that has any correspondence with this verse. Genesis 37 talks about the eleven people bowing down, Joseph being number twelve. These are the twelve stars, this is the sun and the moon, and this is the nation of Israel. This is where God's chosen remnant came from. This is the royal line. This is what makes the red dragon mad. It is the nation of Israel.

Some people will come along and say that this woman who is with child in verse 2 is really Mary. It is not Mary. Mary does not fit anything else in this chapter. Some say it is Mother Theresa. No. Some say that it is the church, and no, it can't be the church. The church didn't give birth to Jesus. Jesus gave birth to the church. Jesus had already come and died and rose again. Then the church came at Pentecost because of the power of the Spirit. This is the woman called the nation of Israel. This is what this great conflict is going to be about.

"And there appeared another wonder in heaven; and behold a great red dragon, having seven heads and ten horns, and seven crowns upon his heads. And his tail drew the third part of the stars of heaven, and did cast them to the earth:"

This is describing all of his earthly power of all the things that he is doing as the prince and power of the air and the things that he is trying to maneuver on this earth.

Jesus says one place in Matthew, "I saw Satan as stars from heaven and he drew a third part of the angels with him." This is the power of this created being. In this sense he is the greatest created being that God has even created. The Bible says he is even higher than the archangels. He was the cherub that covereth. (Revelation 13) He was the angel of light. This created being is mighty. But God is Almighty!

Satan says in Ezekiel and Isaiah, *"'I am going to ascend and be like the most high and people are going to bow down to me,' and a third of the angels went with him."* How many? I do not know. But it is a sad commentary that he took a third of the angels with him.

"and the dragon stood before the woman which was ready to be delivered, for to devour her child as soon as it was born."

We know that happened, don't we? We know what took place in Herod's time. The Devil was doing everything he could when Mary gave birth to devour the child, but God's protection and His sovereign grace never allowed that to happen. Herod tried to kill every male child in the community. Jesus went to Egypt.

This child was the promised seed that started in Genesis 3, and this was the ringing theme of all the prophets. If you would go back to those days, every young woman knew that the Messiah would come from the Jews, and they wanted to be this woman. The Devil knew this and he was going to do everything he could to stop it.

"And she brought forth a man child, who was to rule all nations with a rod of iron: and her child was caught up unto God, and to his throne."

This is a prophetic utterance of what He will do during the millennial reign for 75 days. He is caught up to the throne. Call it the resurrection, call it the ascension, he is caught up to the throne. Where is He today? He is seated at the right hand of God, the throne in heaven. Jesus came out of this nation of Israel.

"And the woman fled into the wilderness, where she had a place prepared of God, that they should feed her there a thousand two hundred and three-score days."

Somehow God will make a preparation. This is bad, but it will even get worse. God will make a preparation somehow, and some say it might be "Petra" or the term "eagle." Yet you are really stretching it to say America will be involved. Somehow God will make a way to preserve this remnant even toward these last days. I think that significantly the 144,000 are a part of those who are saved.

This woman is Israel. There has always been a conflict with the woman. The great hatred of this universe is the hatred of the Devil toward the Jew and God's children. Doesn't the Bible say that we are children of Abraham by faith? Yes, and when anyone who comes to Christ by faith, it is the great hatred of the demonic forces in this universe. Genesis 3:15, *"I will put enmity between you and the woman."* This is the same woman who we are talking about, *between your seed and her seed.* Satan moves in to kill Abel. But God raises up Seth to carry the seed.

He does not stop there. You can pick hundreds of things out of the Bible and I just picked one of them. Satan has sowed wickedness on this planet doing everything he could to destroy this seed by way of the flood. The Bible says, *"Noah found grace in the eyes of the Lord."* Eight were saved and the remnant made it through. Satan is mad.

He comes back at it another way. He causes Esau to say, "I will kill my brother Jacob." And if he would have did that, he could have stopped that flow. But God intervenes and saves Jacob and now we have the 12 sons.

Satan is really upset now so he moves into Pharaoh to slaughter all the males. He has a dream and understands that he has to get rid of these people. Harrod had all the Hebrew males slaughtered, but God saved Moses. God is always there with His grace and protection.

The age of all the kings, specifically Jehoram, he slew the royal seed. He thought he had them all gone, but all of the sudden Jehosheba took this little baby that was about six weeks old and hides him in a bedroom and saves him for six years. He was the only one left in the royal line. God's protection comes out and Joash is saved. The Devil just keeps trying and trying and trying.

Then in Esther, Haman tried to destroy all the Hebrew people. Haman's plot was foiled because of Esther and he went to the gallows.

Then you see Satan moving in to Herod to kill all the male children. Jesus goes down to Egypt and he is saved. Then Satan moves in to tempt Jesus three times and he says, "Now I have victory! I have Him where I want Him. I have Him at the cross." Then Jesus goes to the cross and that was really Satan's undoing. And when that third day came, no longer was there a party, but Satan and his demons really went to battle. He moves from the physical body of trying to destroy Jesus to trying to destroy the Body of Christ. And for the last 2000 years, he has been going about as a lion, trying to kill and destroy!

It is a fascinating study to look at the book of Acts. There are ten waves of persecution like tumbleweed rolling through that book trying to destroy God's people, doing everything he can to disrupt the Body of Christ. And the more persecution he brings to the church, then more people get saved. It is because God is Almighty.

Look at the Inquisition. It almost makes your stomach upset. There were degrees from the Holy See, from the papel system in Rome. Fifty million Christians died during the Inquisition.

You can look at Hitler and all the people going after the Jews. But Satan is still at war and he hates you and he is roaming like a roaring lion, the Bible says. The underlying theme of anti-Semitism has it's root in the mind of Satan. He will do everything he can to destroy this woman and the remnant. You and I would be included in that remnant because by faith we are saved through Jesus Christ our Lord. That is the hatred of this universe.

How does this really happen and is it happening today? It is happening today. Notice the slow erosion of sin. We will use the Jews, because this is who Satan is after, and you too.

First look at the history of the Jews. What does he do first? He laughs at them and gets people going in that direction. Then in that slow erosion he starts to condemn them. Then he does everything he can to silence them. Then he will move on into persecuting them. Then he will make a prison for them that he might bring them in to kill them. It has been the same for centuries. You can take that same thing and match it to the life of Christ. You can take the same thing and apply it to missionaries on the planet today who are standing for the cause of Christ. You can see it in the media today.

Where are we in this scheme now —as far as Christians are concerned? In the funny papers we are being laughed at. Some are being condemned for our intolerance. People are trying to silence Christians because we do not tolerate sin. Christians in this world are being persecuted, imprisoned, and some are being killed. I read somewhere recently that in Indonesia 10,000 to 12,000 Christians have died in the last decade.

Look at your life. Do you have a problem here with any relationship? You laugh at them, you condemn them, you try to silence them, you persecute them when you can or try to detour away from them? You may not kill them with a sword; but if you have murder in your heart, you just accomplished the slow erosion of sin, the same thing that Satan uses. It can happen in a human heart. Satan is the cause for all the suffering we see.

"And there was a war in heaven:"

" Michael and his angels fought against the dragon; and the dragon fought and his angels, And prevailed not; neither was their place found any more in heaven. And the great dragon was cast out, that old serpent, called the Devil, and Satan, which deceiveth the whole world: He was cast out into the earth, and his angels were cast out with him."

This is Satan's last gasp to take over God's kingdom. I do not know why God allowed it to go on until now. But we want to make this clear! Satan lost as the cross. He was judged at the cross. But now the sentencing of this diabolical created being has started. He was judged at the cross, make no mistake about that. And we have power through the resurrection. But we wonder, why is Satan still around doing all of this? He was judged at the cross but the sentencing continues with this war in heaven. The Bible says here in Revelation 12 that he is cast out of heaven in a great battle and now he is back on the planet. The final sentencing will be later in Revelation where he is thrown into the lake of fire. As we get toward the end of this great tribulation, it continues to get worse, because Satan knows he is just about there. He knows what the Bible says about 1260 days. Once this tribulation starts and he is cast down, there is a fury that is unmatched. That is why I do not believe that we are here. Regardless of whether we are or not, we are still in the Lord.

Why is there are war in heaven? This may sound a little strange, but that is where sin originated. Sin started in heaven because Lucifer was there. In the mind and heart of Satan through pride he said he would be like the Most High God. That is where sin began. That is why God said there must be a war in heaven because in that sense Satan still has access to the throne. The proof is in Job **1:9,** *"Now there was a day when the sons of God came to present themselves before the Lord, and Satan came also among them. And the Lord said unto Satan, 'whence comest thou?' Then Satan answered the Lord, and said, 'From going to and fro in the earth, and from walking up and down in it."* Satan has access to the throne.

I do not want to frighten you, but you will sin this week. It may be a sin of omission or commission but you will sin this week. And when you do, he is there somewhere pointing out everything you did, trying to accuse. He is an accuser of the brethren. Jesus is there. He is our advocate, our intercessor. He is our defense attorney and He is saying, "They are covered by my blood." There has been an ongoing onslaught of the Devil trying to accuse and accuse and accuse. When he is cast out of heaven, verse 10 says there is a hallelujah chorus that begins again.

Why is there a battle? Because he has to be cast out of heaven and cast to the earth. God will show that Satan will be taken out completely! He is the prince and the power of the air. How strong is he? (Daniel 10) Daniel is eating his sandwich by the River Hiddekel. He is depressed because he has been praying for three weeks, twenty-one days and there was no change. Then all of the sudden he gets a tap on the shoulder and this angel of the Lord came to him. And this angel told Daniel that they knew when he started this prayer twenty-one days ago. But on the way to Daniel they were hindered by the demonic forces. And there was a wrestling going on in the spiritual dimension, and now they had finally made it. That is how powerful he really is. We should pray without ceasing, fighting against the spiritual world. It may be months or even years, but keep praying. There is tremendous power in prayer but there is a battle in that dimension that we can't even comprehend. God has His angels and He will deliver us.

Someday we will see the total failure of Satan's entire demonic forces cast out of heaven at the middle of the week. It is over! And then look what happens in verse 10.

"And I heard a loud voice saying in heaven, Now is come salvation, and strength, and the kingdom of our God, and the power of his Christ: For the accuser of our brethren is cast down, which accused them before our God day and night. And they overcame him by the blood of the Lamb, and by the word of their testimony; and they loved not their lives unto the death."

What brings you victory in your life? It is the blood of Jesus Christ and the word of your testimony as you stand for the truth. The blood makes you safe, the Word of God makes you certain and you use that in your prayer life. This is how they overcame them.

"Therefore rejoice, ye heavens, and ye that dwell in them."

These are the Christians who stood and died for Christ. (Read the Foxe's Book of Martyrs) They are people who stood in the flames and never denied their Savior.

If someone came to you like they did to the girl at Columbine and told you to recant your faith, what would you do? Would you try to make a deal with them?

The Hallelujah party in heaven is really a song of the martyrs. It is a song we will be witnessing. It is an exciting time for them. They have seen this "created being" accusing all these years, and they see people dying and coming into the throne room. And then all of the sudden he is cast out...

"Woe to the inhabitants of the earth and of the sea! For the Devil is come down unto you, having great wrath, because he knoweth that he hath but a short time."

In other words, now he is very angry. He's cast down into the earth and he gets up off the earth, shakes himself off and he is full of fury, choking with hatred. He is going to do everything he possibly can now to go after God's people. He will not just go after the Jews, but he will go after all of God's people. That is how mad he is.

"And when the dragon saw that he was cast unto the earth, he persecuted the woman which brought forth the man child."

God is bringing back the Jews in unbelief that He might work on them and give them an opportunity to come to him through the preaching of the gospel. Satan will unleash his fury all the more.

"And to the woman were given two wings of a great eagle, that she might fly into the wilderness, into her place, where she is nourished for a time, and times, and half a time, from the face of the serpent."

Somehow they will go off into the wilderness just like in Exodus 15, and God has His hand of them for 3 ½ years. Intense persecution for the Jews and God's remnant and He still makes a way for them. There are many interpretations here, but somehow God nourishes them. There is a protection there and God cares for them.

"And the serpent cast out of his mouth water as a flood after the woman, that he might cause her to be carried away of the flood."

There are many interpretations for this verse as well. It will be an onslaught of trauma! It might be something like this: "Woe to the inhabitants of the earth". There will be an aggravated assault of the Devil, there will be anti-Semitism like never before, there will be force from the Devil and an aggressiveness to harm. In the midst of all of that, the Bible says there will be divine protection. Satan is trying to kill and destroy, but the Lord still has a His protection covering them. You have that protection today too if you are in Him. *"Greater is He that is in you than He that is in the world."* Satan may be the prince and power of the air and he may take the whole world who will follow after him, but greater is He that is in you because of the blood of Christ and the word of your testimony.

He is furious here because he can't touch the man-child. If he can't touch the man-child, he will try to touch the Jews and the saints of God.

God has a plan for His people. *"I will bless them that bless you and curse them which curse you."* Look at every major world power that went down the dumps and look at what they were doing to the Jews.

"And the earth helped the woman, and the earth opened her mouth, and swallowed up the flood which the dragon cast out of his mouth. And the dragon was wroth with the woman, and went to make war with the remnant of her seed, which keep the commandments of God, and have the testimony of Jesus Christ."

This could be the 144,000 or the two Witnesses, or those who stand for the cause of Christ. This can be the children of Abraham by faith, which is you and I. He will go against anyone who loves God and Jesus Christ.

As you think about the significance of this war, what is the conclusion?

One man praying can move a lot of angels in heaven. I believe these people who are saved in the tribulation period are on their knees and they are calling out to God and God answers that prayer.

Do not quit praying. God and his angels are doing everything they can to come to you.

Satan is mighty but God is Almighty. Do not despair. If you are keeping the Word of God today and things are not going right, don't despair, because you are on the winning side and someday you will be with Him. I look at the Foxe's Book of Martyrs and I can't imagine what they have gone through, but they are on the winning side.

Paul says, **"Whether I live or whether I die, I am in Him."** Keep that hope alive. We may go through conflict, but keep the hope alive because He is alive in our hearts.

Every morning in Africa in the Serengeti Desert when the gazelle wakes up, it is running. If the gazelle can't out-run the fastest lion, it is dead meat. Every morning in Africa, when the lion wakes up, it has to run faster than the slowest gazelle, or it will starve to death. In other words, every morning in Africa, everything that is waking up is off and running. It should be no different from you and I. When you get up in the morning, you need to put on the full armor of God because there is a roaring lion out there that will do everything he can to hinder you, to trip you up and throw fiery darts at you. We need to put on the full armor of God and stand, yet then run with confidence that He is with us. That is the life we are in. That is why the Christian life is exciting because we are on the winning team.

He loves us so much. He knows how much we need, when we need it, where we need it and how we need. He will deliver us from the crafty evil one.

Donald Barnhouse was very good at illustrating truth. Donald says in one of his books that there was a man who owned a beautiful estate with wonderful trees, flowing fountains and rivers everywhere. Everybody in the community loved him except for one evil man who hated him. He was enemy of the owner of the estate. He did everything he could to destroy the owner. He was always after the owner of the estate. Then word came to this enemy that the owner had three huge trees right in the middle of his estate that he was very proud of. The owner would walk around these trees… so the enemy thought that when he was away for a few days, he would go in and destroy the trees. So that is what he did. He went in and started cutting them down. But when he was in the middle of cutting down the last one, he saw the owner of the estate coming back. He went to work harder and finally the last tree began to fall over. As it went over, one of the branches pinned him to the earth. And it pinned him right through the stomach and he knew that he was just about gone. There was blood everywhere. He was just about to die when the estate owner came over. In his last gasp the enemy said, "I destroyed your trees, the things you liked the best, so take that!" And then the owner of the estate smiled and said, "No, you failed for nothing, because I was getting ready to come back and take these trees out and build a bigger mansion and to clear my estate and build a better one. You failed. In your bitterness and in your hatred, you will die with the same." And the enemy died.

Satan has tried to do everything he can to hinder the plans and purposes of God. There are hundreds of millions of people who have died in the onslaught of this evil one. This egotistical being believes he might have a chance here on earth to take care of God, but in the end he will be impaled with the righteousness of God. He will be cast into utter darkness, the lake of fire, and God will build a new mansion, a new heaven and a new earth.

REVELATION 13: 1-10

Satanic Superman

"And I stood upon the sand of the sea, and saw a beast rise up out of the sea, having seven heads and ten horns, and upon his horns ten crowns, and upon his heads the name of blasphemy. And the beast which I saw was like unto a leopard, and his feet were as the feet of a bear, and his mouth as the mouth of a lion: and the dragon gave him his power, and his seat, and great authority. And I saw one of his heads as it were wounded to death; and his deadly wound was healed: and all the world wondered after the beast. And they worshipped the dragon which gave power unto the beast: and they worshipped the beast, saying, Who is like unto the beast? Who is able to make war with him? And there was given unto him a mouth speaking great things and blasphemies; and power was given unto him to continue forty and two months. And he opened his mouth in blasphemy against God, to blaspheme his name, and his tabernacle, and them that dwell in heaven. And it was given unto him to make war with the saints, and to overcome them: and power was given him over all kindreds, and tongues, and nations.

And all that dwell upon the earth shall worship him, whose names are not written in the book of life of the Lamb slain from the foundation of the world."

From the beginning of time, men have always dreamed of ruling the planet. If you go back to 1500 B.C. to the time of the Pharaohs, the Pharaohs wanted to control everyone and everything. 900 years ago King Nebuchadnezzar was the same way. He wanted to rule the planet. He builds statues of himself. One was even in gold. He wanted people to adore him and worship him as god. Then there was Hitler, Mussolini, Stalin, and people like Hussein. Men have always wanted to rule the planet. This is just a 'dress rehearsal' for the individual we are going to see here in Revelation 13. In a sense, this man will rule this entire globe we know as planet earth.

The Bible is very clear that this is a literal man because it uses a personal pronoun when it talks about his head wound. In John 5:43, Jesus Christ himself says, *"I came in my Father's name and you receive me not, but another shall come in his own name and you will follow after him."*

This is more than just an evil empire that we are seeing here. This is a beast, an individual, a man born on this planet of a woman. He will be Satan incarnate.

Some of the major religions have a prophecy outlook of an evil ruler in the end times. The Islamic faith, in their Koran declares that there is a wicked ruler who will come on the scene in the last days. His name is the 12th IMAN. He is an individual who will scare everyone into serving him. He also has a gigantic eyeball in the middle of his forehead. This is actually in their writings.

Judaism talks about a ruler to come named "Armilus", who will come in the last days when King David the Messiah will overtake him.

Christianity believes in Revelation 13 and the rising of the beast or the Antichrist.

"And I stood upon the sand of the sea, and saw a beast rise up out of the sea, having seven heads and ten horns, and upon his horns ten crowns, and upon his heads the name of blasphemy."

As we have previously said, we need to consider the entire Word of God as we study Revelation. Especially, when you take the books of the Old Testament and put them along side this book, (Revelation) for comparison. You will see this same quotation in Daniel 7 regarding this beast. What is the meaning of the seven heads, ten horns, and the ten crowns? As we look at the lineage of the rising of the beast, this Antichrist, he is a real man. This is talking about the control he will have in the end of times.

What are the seven heads? There have been six major world powers from the beginning of time. They are Egypt, Assyria, Babylon, Medio-Persia, Greece and Rome. There is one more yet to come, it is the revised Roman Empire. The European Union, which was the Common Market, was ratified in 1957 after they had already been established in 1948. They went to Brussels, Belgium and signed a new treaty called the Treaty of Rome. It would be my understanding as we think about the world events today that this rising of the beast will be this revived Roman Empire, this seventh head. Out of this seventh head there will be ten kings. The European Union has 15 nations now but there might be only 10 in the next decade. There will be only 10 at one time because the Bible says that.

We know what is happening in the situation in Iran and Iraq today. Germany and France are against England right now. And anything can happen. They started with five, it went to seven, it went to eleven, and then back to ten, it went to twelve, and there are fifteen today. There is a lot of juggling in the European Union right now.

But with the rising of the beast reviving the last Roman Empire, the eastern nations there, he will come out and rule them. Daniel says that one little horn will come out, that is the Antichrist and he will take over the ten kings and rule them.

The beast's parentage is of the Devil. He will do everything to mimic God to prove that he is the Messiah. But his parentage is from Satan. Have you heard the expression, "like father like son"? Just as much as you have seen Christ you have seen the Father in heaven. Likewise, if you have seen the beast you have seen the Devil. They will do everything they can to copy. Satan, the Antichrist, and the False Prophet.

The origin – Christ came from heaven. The Antichrist comes from the abyss or the pit of hell.

The nature – Christ is the good shepherd. The Antichrist is the foolish shepherd, the one who lies all the time.

The Dynasty – Christ is exalted on high. The Antichrist will be cast into hell.

The goal – Christ came to do His Father's will. (John 19) The Antichrist's goal is to do his own will. (Ezekiel "I will be like the Most High)

The purpose – Christ came to seek and to save that which was lost. The Antichrist will destroy men's souls. He will kill, steal, and destroy.

The Authority – Christ comes in His Father's name. (John 17) The Antichrist comes in his own name. (11 Thes. 2)

The Attitude – Christ humbled Himself, took the form of a servant, and became obedient to that. (Philippians 2) The Antichrist will do everything he can to exalt himself to be like God.

The Fruit – Christ is the true vine. (John 15) But the vine of the earth, Antichrist, is fleshly and sinful.

The Response of Men – Christ was despised and rejected of men. The Antichrist will be admired and the whole world will wander after him.

The Truth – Jesus said, *"I am the way, the truth and the life."* The Antichrist is the father of lies, the Devil.

These are the contrasting descriptions of the man we will be talking about in this chapter.

Who is he? Is he living today? I do not know, but he is a real man, and he will be Satan incarnate. He will be like his father. If you see the Antichrist, you will see Satan. When the rising of the beast comes on the scene you will be able to look at his lineage. Daniel 7:2 has the same description as we see here in Revelation 13. He will be like a leopard. He will not be able to hide his spots. A leopard is wild and ferocious and it has a desire to kill. The same thing is true with the feet of a lion. It will rend and tear, it is raging and tearing. He will come on the scene and be a great orator and good-looking, but the motive of his heart is devilish and demonic to the point of doing everything he can to disrupt everyone and get the focus off of God and on himself. I do not think we can comprehend a man like that. There have been men who came on the world scene and become very popular. In his own day and in his own time Hitler was popular. In his own day Alexander the Great was very popular. Some other men have come on the scene and been very popular, but nothing like the answers and works that this man will express!

Since the days of Darwin, men have said we come from beasts. They will have the opportunity to worship one some day. He is a beast from the pit of hell. He will be just like a Caesar. He will be all for republic and democracy, but in time he will control the empire. He will have the power and authority to control everything and anything in his path to the point that men will be deceived. They will enjoy being deceived, because they will get the answers from 'the great one'.

How far are we from seeing someone like that? I don't know. Maybe it is not too far away. Isn't the world looking for answers today?

Just a few short years ago, the European Union met in Brussels, Belgium. The Prime Minister of Belgium said these words, "To the member body of the European Union: "All methods of world government and world peace are failing today. We need a man of exceptional intelligence and ability to rule and lead this world. If he comes I guarantee you the world will follow." This was said by the Prime Minister just a few years ago. If a man of importance is standing up and saying that, there are a lot of other people thinking about it.

Jesus Christ came on the scene and stood on the Mount of Temptation one day with the Devil. The Devil said he wanted to promise Jesus some things. The Devil said he would give Jesus the world and the people in it and whatever else he wanted if he would bow down. There will be a man come on the scene some day that will do those three things, for control of the world, for control of the planet, for control of men's hearts. This man will be the Antichrist.

Why will he be so popular? *"And I saw one of his heads as it were wounded to death; and his deadly wound was healed: and all the world wondered after the beast."*

What would cause someone to wander after the beast if he had a deadly head wound? It says that he comes back to life. We do not know for sure if that is a lie or a deceit. But it does say he has a deadly head wound. If he is going to try to copy Christ, then he will probably do it here. I can imagine he will do it for about three days. He has done everything from the beginning of time to mimic Jesus. He is the greatest copycat of all time. He is the greatest mimic of all time. If you think about every cult that has ever been started, they will never start without error. A cult can only be started with truth. Then a bunch of error jumps piggyback and just crushes it. That is how cults start. Whatever religion you look at, they all have some truth in there so that people will listen. Then they just crush it. This is what the Antichrist will do. He will be the biggest mimic of all time. Christ comes on the scene in Matthew chapter 9 and he does miracles, signs and wonders. The minute the Antichrist comes on the scene in Revelation chapter 6, it says he will do miracles, signs and wonders. He will come like Satan with all power, signs, and lying wonders. He is a mimic. People will see all of these signs and wonders and believe that there has to be some truth to it. "He has to be a great man to be able to do that, so let's follow him."

Look at this. Christ comes and the Word says He is God. (John 10:36) *"You say that I am the Son of God and I am."* Satan claims to be God, exults himself, and tries to copy everything Jesus did.

Christ says in Ezekiel 37:26, *"I will make an everlasting covenant of peace with you Israel."* Satan says in Daniel 9:27, *"I will confirm a covenant of peace with you for one week."* This is the guarantee of the Antichrist. He will come on the scene and promise Israel seven years of peace.

He causes men to worship God, Revelation 1:6, *"Dominion and power forever and ever."*

Satan comes on the scene and causes men to worship Satan or the Antichrist. *"And all the world will wander after him."*

Revelation 14:1. Remember how the 144,000 and the two witnesses were sealed on their foreheads. Satan, in Revelation 13:16-17 says unless you have the mark of the beast on your forehead or right hand you will die.

We are married to a virtuous bridegroom. We are the bride and Jesus is the bridegroom. The Devil comes along in the 17th chapter and marries a vile prostitute full of fornication.

Christ sits on the throne in Revelation 3:21. Antichrist comes and sits on the throne and takes over the throne, which is called the Abomination of Desolation. He desecrates the temple and says, "I am God."

Everything the Antichrist is doing is to mimic our Messiah so that people will follow after him, the false one.

Jesus rides in on a white horse in Revelation 19, and you will be with him if you are a believer. "Christ shall come with 10,000 of his saints." The Devil comes in on a white horse to save in Revelation 6:2 and it is a false security because of the riding of the other horses after that.

There are going to be Christians here and the ones who die for Christ will see this man and know that this is not right. But once a man receives the mark of the beast, I believe they will be strongly delusional. That is a warning to everyone to come to the Savior today.

Maybe a scene like this could happen in the near future:

"The President of the nations was shot today. (I came up with the name Judas Hitler) Judas Hitler was pronounced dead upon arrival at Rome's International Hospital. He was shot in the head in the presence of all ten kings and billions who were watching TV. The loss of this man cannot be measured. No man has ever done more to solve the problems of this planet than this man, our god. The tragedy that is now surrounding this planet is unmeasured… and yada yada yada…"

And three days later he stirs and is revived somehow. Do you think they will follow him then? The whole world will wander after him. Once that happens, this world will march to what we call 'the ruling of the beast'.

"And they worshipped the dragon which gave power unto the beast: and they worshipped the beast, saying, Who is like unto the beast? Who is able to make war with him? And there was given unto him a mouth speaking great things and blasphemies; and power was given unto him to continue forty and two months."

The answer to these two rhetorical questions is an obvious answer: no one. There is no one who is like this beast. There is no one who will come on the scene and try to make war against the beast. He will be number one on the planet. They will support him and do everything they can to follow after him. This will be the shape of this planet that is so desperate at this point. They will follow him, they will implement his policies, they will do whatever he says, and they will think that he is invincible. In my opinion, he will do everything he can to the point of even changing the calendar. Anything that has a hint of God he will do away with. If it means changing the time, he will change it. He does not want a calendar that has AD and BC. He will do everything he can to get people's attention off of Christ, Jews, or Christians and get their attention on him. That is the attitude of Satan himself in this incarnate creature, the Antichrist. And people with worship him, he will rule over the nations.

The nations involved today in the European Union are: Austria, Belgium, Denmark, Finland, France, Germany, Greece, Iceland, Italy, Lexonburg, Netherlands, Portugal, Spain, Sweden and the United Kingdom.

In the 60's, it was a sensational thing to talk about the European Common Market (now it is the European Union) and how it would be popular. People would laugh and scoff at that. They said there was no way there would be anyone to come along as great as America or to be as popular as America or as strong as America. Then they would really laugh and they would say that the Bible says there will be one political system, one military system and one economic system, and one currency, and everyone would laugh. In the year 2002 the Euro dollar was printed and those nations use the Euro dollar today. They are not going to go back to their own currency. We are witnessing one of the greatest signs coming on the scenes right now, this confederate working of nations in Europe. In 1947 and 1948, five major things happened to get the ball rolling to where we are today. We are living in the last pages of the final chapter of God's prophetic desire for his planet.

On May 18, 1948 Israel became a nation. The Bible says in the last days he will pull his people back to the nation of Israel, even in unbelief. He is doing it. 1948 there was the ratification of the European Union or the Common Market. 1948 was the beginning of the World Council of Churches. 1948 was the beginning of the World Monetary Fund. These things are not a coincidence. *"Until this generation passes away, the Son of Man may come."* You can debate the meaning of generation, but it is my understanding that it means 100 years. He is coming again. The rapture is very near. Things that are happening today are in direct line with what is being prophetically spoken about in Scripture.

The rising and ruling of this beast is right around the corner. He will come on the scene and solve the world's greatest problems. What is one of the world's greatest problems today? Maybe it is the Middle East conflict. Well, this man will come on the scene and solve it. How is he going to do that? I believe Scripture gives us a hint in this sense, who is this man? I do not think we can put a name on him, but we can trace his lineage. Daniel 11 says, *"He foresook the faith of his fathers."* This is speaking about a Jew so he may have Jewish lineage, which will give him a great advantage if he is going to make a peace treaty with the Jews. If *he forsook the faith of his fathers* means that he will probably be born a Jew and probably come up out of the European Union, so maybe he is alive today somewhere in Europe. I don't know. But there is no better man to come on the scene to make a covenant with the Jews than a Jew himself. He will come on the scene and somehow solve this and make a peace treaty with the Jews, which is a joke because it will only last for 3 ½ years. Then He will say, "I am god, worship me." This will cause a multitude of problems.

So begins the career of the Anti-Christ. He will appear in the later days following the rapture of the Church, II Thess. *Tthen that wicked one shall be revealed after the catching and the calling out of God's saints."* He will be the epitome of all Gentile world powers. All people will wander after the beast. They will make a choice to follow him.

In Daniel it says that one little horn will come up out of the ten and he will control them. He will gain economic and political and militant control of the entire world. The Bible says, "through his policies he shall cause crafts to prosper, he shall also magnify himself and by peace he will destroy many." (Daniel 8) He will gain power by promising world peace. He will not have any intention of fulfilling that promise. What we witness on a small scale today in Sadaam's regime, this man will do it on a world wide scale.

His personal intelligence, persuasiveness, and power will deceive all nations. The Bible says in Daniel, *"He will have a fierce countenance and speak in harsh sentences."* And people will accept it. He will sign a peace treaty to guarantee Israel's protection, Daniel 9:27. He will break that promise in the middle of the week and then demand to be worshipped as god. He becomes a fierce, demonic adversary of Israel and he will persecute the Jew. Daniel 8 says he will destroy the holy people of God. And he will receive his own power and authority from Satan himself in Daniel 8.

When this man comes on the scene he will be full of Satan himself. I can't imagine as I think of a little baby being born and becoming this man. Maybe he is born and maybe he is a teenager today. But Satan will enter him and he will have a gigantic leap forward in visible popularity.

"And he opened his mouth in blasphemy against God, to blaspheme his name, and his tabernacle, and them that dwell in heaven. And it was given unto him to make war with the saints, and to overcome them; (this is talking about the saints here) *and power was given him over all kindreds, and tongues, and nations. And all that dwell upon the*

earth shall worship him, whose names are not written in the book of life of the Lamb slain from the foundation of the world."

God will allow this man to stand on a world scene and exalt himself as 'God' and blaspheme and curse God's name before billions. He will not be able to harm us because we will be with the Lord in heaven. But he can harm the saints that choose to follow Christ who are on the earth. His blasphemy will not be subtle. He will do it openly in an outrageous manner. It will be done in such a monstrous way.

But he will have a leash on him, and he will only be on this leash for 3 ½ more years. God allows him to blaspheme Him for 1260 days, 42 months, 3 ½ years. He will do everything he can against the people of God. The Bible says he will kill two-thirds of the Jews. He will annihilate anyone who is in his way. The Bible says in Zechariah 14 that he will conquer Jerusalem. He will walk into the temple and say, "I am god, worship me!" What do you think will go through the Jews mind at that point? I believe many will come to know the Messiah at that point. He will not destroy their faith. He will destroy their lives.

He can't destroy your faith today if you love God. He can destroy your life. Satan may be hounding you like he did to Job, but he can't destroy your faith. He can take your life and destroy your circumstances he is the prince and power of this world.

I John talks about this man. He is the fulfillment of that. Anti- Christ, he is opposed to God and he is the beast against Christ.

I am not looking for the Antichrist. I am looking for Christ. This thought came to me over and over as I studied this chapter. I probably spent more time in prayer than anything. I do not like to study about this man. He is in the book of Revelation, but I am not looking for him. I am looking for HIM that I might flee the wrath to come. I am not looking for the undertaker, which is what he is. I am looking for the upper-taker, which is what my Savior is. I am not looking for a sign. I do not need a sign. But Jesus said that He is allowing us to see these signs; because when they come to pass, we should look up because He is almost here. I am looking for my Savior and the sound of His trumpet. This is encouraging to me.

Revelation 13: 5 and 7, *"It was given unto him."* These words are encouraging in this sense. Satan doesn't have it together. He does not have enough power because the Bible says it was given unto you by some body else to be able to do these things. Satan, you are on God's leash, you are on a choke hold and you are straining for all you can to get all the souls you can. The Bible says it was *given* unto you. This is comforting.

This man is a mighty beast, but our God is Almighty. God is in control. He knows exactly where Satan is at right now. He knows where the seat of Satan is right now and He knows men's hearts. He has this Antichrist on a leash.

My granddaughter got very sick three weeks ago. We got more and more concerned as things didn't work and the doctors couldn't find what was wrong. When things didn't change and got worse, we got more concerned. A week ago at the Children's Hospital in Madera, the doctors came in to look at her and they said, 'We have a treatment available for her and we believe this is what it will take to give her hope." Now the question that can go through a parent's mind, it went through mine, "Will it do any good?" "You say you have a medicine, a treatment, but we have been through so much already. Will it do any good?" The answer is "No, not until she takes it."

If I would have a message for anyone who does not know Christ today, "Does He do any good?" You will never know until you taste Him and take Him into your heart! The Bible says in Hebrews to consider Him. The Bible says in Psalms to *Taste and see that the Lord is good."* The Bible says, *"Come unto Me all you who are weak and heavy laden and I will give you rest."* You will never know until you receive Him. The imminent return of Christ is near. He is Christ and it makes a difference where we spend eternity. It is far greater than the physical body, it is Him.

Present Christ to the world that others may consider Him at least. You do not know when you are going to die.

(Story about Jesus Valasques being shot on Crows Landing last night)

That is how fast life is. If you do not consider Him now, do not think that you will 'get around to it' someday. Today is the day of salvation! There is no safety like being in the arms of the Savior.

Someday these events will unfold on planet earth. Someday the Antichrist and the False Prophet and the Beast will all go back to where they belong in the abyss. But someday you and I have an opportunity to be with the Heavenly Trinity throughout the ages!

REVELATION 13:11-18

The False Prophet/ Beast From the Earth

"And I beheld another beast coming up out of the earth; and he had two horns like a lamb, and he spake as a dragon. And he exerciseth all the power of the first beast before him, and causeth the earth and them, which dwell therein to worship the first beast, whose deadly wound was healed. And he doeth great wonders, so that he maketh fire come down from heaven on the earth in the sight of men, And deceiveth them that dwell on the earth by the means of these miracles which he had power to do in the sight of the beast; saying to them that dwell on the earth, that they should make an image to the beast, which had the wound by a sword, and did live. And he had power to give like unto the image of the beast, that the image of the beast should both speak, and cause that as many as would not worship the image of the beast should be killed. And he causeth all, both small and great, rich and poor, free and bond, to receive the mark in their right hand, or in their foreheads: And that no man might buy or sell, save he that had the mark, or the name of the beast, or the number of his name. Here is wisdom. Let him that hath understanding count the number of the beast: for it is the number of a man; and his number is six hundred three score and six."

We are in the middle of the week in the tribulation period. We have covered in these chapters 3 ½ years and we will have another 3 ½ years to go. God has introduced the False Prophet and the Antichrist at this juncture. Even though the Antichrist was introduced at the reading of these seals, I think he is also introducing these two men at this juncture to show that this hellish trinity is going to do everything they can to bring death and destruction! Revelation is often dark and catastrophic, and there are evil things being experienced. But as you get nearer the end, at the return of Christ, he will intervene and we will see the Marriage Supper of the Lamb.

We once had a picture in our home of the Marriage Supper of the Lamb with a table spread out into infinity with place settings. I loved that picture. I used to try and picture where Jesus and I would sit at that table, when I was little a little boy.

The Holy Trinity is God the Father, God the Son and God the Holy Spirit. The hellish trinity is Satan the Dragon, Antichrist the Beast, and the False Prophet. In Revelation 19:20, *"the beast was taken with him and the False Prophet."* **It is a man.**

The ultimate deception in the days we are living in is strictly involving a worldwide worship of the Antichrist. That will be one of the big features of the *End Times.* But with this Antichrist there is going to be another man who is the False Prophet, and these two will be working hand in hand.

Now if I was the False Prophet, I think I would want to be getting my Bible out because I know what happens to him. They will be cast into the lake of fire. The Antichrist will even turn on the False Prophet. He will say that he is god and he will set himself up there. In a way, the False Prophet will become insignificant. Even though the False Prophet is telling people to worship him, he is kind of a part of it. But then when the Antichrist takes over, which will be the *Abomination of Desolation* as the Bible calls it, things will really turn sour.

When the False Prophet and the Antichrist come on the scene, they will probably be everywhere together. You will see in the Bible many times where he is supporting him. He will be the Christ of all the cults. He will be the Mohamed of the Islamic faith. He will be the Buddha of Buddhism. Whatever it is, he will be "IT". Man is incurably religious. He will bring all the religion into something that everyone will say, "Hey, that sounds pretty good." And they will wander after this beast, and the False Prophet will be a large part of that. These two men will be the perfect counterfeits. We are living in a nation of counterfeits. Our government alone spends billions of dollars every year to try to stave off counterfeit products, money and all likes of things. When this man comes on the scene, it is all about deception and counterfeit.

Jesus Christ came on the scene and was hailed as the Prince of Peace. The Antichrist will come on the scene and be hailed as the prince of all humankind. *Jesus Christ* rides in as the King of the Jews. This man will ride in as the king of the earth. *Jesus Christ* is worshiped by millions. Antichrist will be worshiped by billions. Everything that the Antichrist is doing will be to copycat what the Holy Trinity has already done.

What is a false prophet? There are three characteristics that you will find in the Bible of a false prophet. They are greedy, caught up with fornication and adultery and they love to lie to the point of wanting you to worship any kind of an idol. Every time you look into the Old Testament or the New Testament, you will see one of these characteristics. A false prophet deceives. So many times in the Bible Christ tells us to be aware because there will be false prophets come on the scene.

How do we know if someone is a false prophet? If they deny the deity, if they deny the trinity, if they deny the blood atonement, and if they deny that the blood of Jesus Christ avails for anything, then they are a false prophet. For example: Joseph Smith is a false prophet.

But let God be the judge of an individual. I am just telling you what the Bible says in 1 John 1. This is a study of a false prophet. We will see the characteristics in this man in Revelation.

Why is there a false prophet? Satan needs to try to do what Jesus Christ did. He needs to have a trinity. The Father of Lies in John 8:44, the Antichrist and this world religious leader that has revelation from somewhere, but he does not. His revelation is that he will take everyone he can to hell with him.

"And I beheld another(Greek meaning: "of the same kind") *beast coming up out of the earth* (he does not have any heavenly origin like he claims)*; and he had two horns like a lamb, and he spake as a dragon."*

That does not sound like a pretty picture of a lamb. A lamb is meek, soft and very easy to be around. But you get next to this 'lamb' and he is speaking like a dragon. What does the Bible mean here? This man will come and look so right and say things so good, and he will sound so logical, but what is coming out of his mouth is lies and deception. One of the first things he will tell people is to follow the Antichrist. We are going to see a welding of church and state like this continent has never seen before. That is the only way it will work for them. The Antichrist will be in charge of all the military and political ruling, and now this man who will be in charge of the religious section, and they will weld them together and this will be his appearance. He is a man. You can't spiritualize this fellow. In the Bible it says that he will be cast into the lake of fire. He is not only a person, but he is also a man who comes on the scene and has center stage and he knows it. He will be born of an earthly mother. He will be well educated. He will be a great orator. He will be able sway masses of people with his language and it will sound so good that people will believe that it is right.

This man will come on the scene and carve out a path of unbelievable deception to the point that many people who want to believe in the Bible and its teaching will even change and decide to follow after this new teaching. It will be very tragic. In Galatians 1:8 the Bible says, *"If any man preach any other gospel let him be accursed."* The Bible is very plain and very basic. Jesus Christ died according to the Scriptures. He was buried according to the scriptures. He rose again according to the Scriptures. That is the Gospel. Any man who comes along and teaches any other gospel is cursed and people will be swept away with that.

I like to think that when the Anti-Christ comes on the scene, not only will he have control of the planet in the sense that people fear him, but he will have the media and televisions enabling him to portray himself in a light that will make it hard for people to go against him or contradict him. You will see this in the last verse as well. He will be very deceptive in his looks and appearance.

"And he exerciseth all the power of the first beast before him, and causeth the earth and them which dwell therein to worship the first beast, whose deadly wound was healed. And he doeth great wonders, so that he maketh fire come down from heaven on the earth in the sight of men, And deceiveth them that dwell on the earth by the means of these miracles which he had power to do in the sight of the beast; saying to them that dwell on the earth, that they should make an image to the beast, which had the wound by a sword, and did live."

Think for a moment about this dynamic appeal and attraction that this man has when he comes.

You can take a basket of bad eggs and you can have a very clever arrangement of the bad eggs but you will never get a good omelet out of it. On the scene will come two individuals who are 'bad eggs'. And they can say what they want but nothing good will come of these two individuals. They will be controlled with a diabolical sense of satanic presence. I think that a person who comes to the Lord during the tribulation period will be frightened to look into their eyes. It would be shuttering to us to even think about. People will be dying as martyrs for Christ; because when they look at these men, they know that what they are is bad.

When you think about the dynamic appeal of this man, you will see that he will rise out of this earth and he will be born of a woman. He will control the religious affairs. He will love church. He isn't going to tell people not to go to church. He is going to encourage people to go to church and become involved, but it will be his kind of church. Satan will motivate him. (verse 11) He will promote the worship of this beast. He will stand at revivals and say, "Listen, this is what God wants. I have had a revelation. I am a prophet of God. This man here is the Messiah. This is the man we need to worship." And he will promote the worship of the beast to the point that there will be a 'false resurrection' that takes place.

The Bible also says that he will perform signs and wonders. II Thessalonians says in the last days there will be men on the scene and they will do "lying wonders" and signs and they will call down fire from heaven. Do you know why they will call down fire from heaven? Because they know that is what happened with the real prophets in the Old Testament. Elijah called fire down from heaven. The two witnesses that we have studied earlier in Revelation called down fire from heaven. God brought fire down from heaven. So this false prophet will bring fire down from heaven. They will say that he is the 'real deal' if he can bring fire down from heaven and it is all false! It is no different from Jannes and Jambres duplicating almost every miracle of Moses. But they were false. Proof: Moses' snake ate up their snakes.

He will deceive the world. He will empower the image of the beast. He will kill all of those who refuse to worship the beast. He will control the economic commerce. He will control the 'mark of the beast' during that time.

Do you know what the satanic motto is today? This is what it says, "**Do what you will and you shall be the whole of all law and living.**" Bottom-line, "you are your own God". Do whatever you want to do and do whatever feels good because you are your own God. This is okay because you are fulfilling your own law and you are really living. That is the kind of thing that will come down the pike when this false prophet takes over.

Remember when I said that he will encourage people to go to church? But it will be more of a 'ritual' church with strange things that he has complete control over. There will be big revivals in big church settings in big cities possibly. But the revivals will be different. You won't hear about the cross, but you will hear about activities of loving one another. People will love these kind of revivals. Sin is all relative anyway… grow a flower and have peace and every one will be cool with that. People will believe they have a good church going. He will encourage 'togetherness' with the emphasis on activity and not worship.

The Bible says the world will wander after him. He is a counterfeit to the core. Every miracle and sign that Jesus Christ did on the earth was followed by a message to gain a hearing for the gospel of Christ. When this man comes on the scene it will not be any different. He will show a miracle followed by a message from the Antichrist. Man will be deceived. The Bible says that God will send a strong delusion that men will believe a lie.

We are not talking about neat little 'abracadabra' magic tricks. We are talking about a full-fledged wonders and signs that will convince people. It is hard to imagine but he will do them.

"And he had power to give like unto the image of the beast, that the image of the beast should both speak, and cause that as many as would not worship the image of the beast should be killed."

God has not given the devil power to bring anyone back to life. So this will be some kind of fake trickery. Whatever it is he will somehow empower this beast to come back to life and people will be awed. They will believe he is the 'real thing' because of this and they will follow after him. But they will look at this false resurrection and the battle lines will be drawn in this sense. Man will either accept the Antichrist at this point or they die. Revelation 20 says *'beheaded'*. It will be a time of slaughter across the planet because there will be men who will not bow down to the beast.

The mark or *charagma*, which is Greek for mark, will be for all men. The Bible says the mark of the beast is 666. What is this mark?

"And he causeth all, both small and great, rich and poor, free and bond, to receive the mark in their right hand, or in their foreheads: And that no man might buy or sell, save he that had the mark, or the name of the beast, or the number of his name. Here is wisdom. Let him that hath understanding count the number of the beast: for it is the number of a man; and his number is six hundred three score and six."

This is one of the most graphic, specific, fascinating, unusual verses in the New Testament. There have been more gallons of ink written about this verse because people are trying to figure out who is the beast. They have calculated all kinds of numbers and come up with every thing from Nero to Domitian to Hitler to Stalin and even the Kennedy. You can just about run numbers however you want to make this fit even for you!

The Lord is saying here, "I want you to sit up and pay attention here. This is wisdom,. If you are living during that time you will have to have this understanding that this man will have this number." I do not know how the number will be put on the forehead or hand, but it will be there. If you walk into a store and want to buy something, you will not be able to without the mark. If you want to sign a multi-billion dollar deal in a company to buy somebody out, you will not be able to without the mark. Anyone who buys or sells will have the Mark of the Beast. Men have spent countless hours to find out who this is, and I did too, but no one will know until that time comes. He is telling us to aware.

Isn't this logical? I can't think of anything more logical today than to have a mark to buy and sell. "Prophetic events cast their shadows before them." You can go to any store today and 'swipe your card. "That means you are cashless. It is a credit card but that means that someday you will not need a credit card. Someday man will not need cash. Someday man will walk into a store and swipe his hand and, if the number is there, he will be allowed to buy or sell. It is logical. It does not even sound evil. Someday it will happen and it is being tested in some cities today.

You can really get carried away trying to figure out the numbers 666.

Here is something that is interesting to show you how people get involved in this number. Thirty-six times in the book of Revelation is the mention of *beast*. (That includes Satan, Antichrist, and False Prophet). Take the numbers 1 – 36 and put them all down in a row and add them, it comes out 666. Well, that is interesting. What does it mean? It doesn't mean anything. Does it really settle anything? No. But the number of man is 6. If you are in the Lord today, that is not your number. The Bible is very specific about numbers and they do mean something. It will hold all the way from Genesis to Revelation.

The first one is unity. Everywhere you see number *one* in the Bible it means 'unity'. That is what Ephesians is talking about, "one body, one spirit, one hope, one Lord, one faith, one baptism, one God."

Every time you see the number *two* in the Bible it is about 'union'. There is a union in marriage. There is a union of the two natures. There are the two natures in Christ, the two witnesses, and the testimony of two as they would go out to share Christ.

Three is a number of divinity. It is holy, a trinity. There is the trinity of man, the body, soul and spirit. There are the three great feasts in the Bible, the Passover, the Pentecost, and the Tabernacle. And every time you see Holy, Holy, Holy speaking about God the Father it is written three times. It is divinity. Isaiah 57, *"For thus saith the high and lofty one who inhabited eternity whose name is holy… holy, holy, holy."* He dwells in a high and holy place.

The world is number four. Everywhere in the Bible where there is *four*, it is *world*. Four seasons. There are four points of the compass: east, west, north, south. There are four elements: earth, air, fire and water. There are four divisions of humanity: tongues, kindred, people, and nations.

Number *five* is a number of *divisions*. Five wise, five foolish. Five thousand sat on the hillside fed with five loaves and they divided amongst themselves. David collected five stones. The five digits of your hands and feet. It is all about division.

Then man comes along in a number six. Created on the sixth day. We are to work six of seven days. The kingdom of this age is to last for 6,000 years.

A Hebrew could only be a slave for six years before he was freed. You could only work your ground for six years before you let it lay fallow. The great man of the Bible, Goliath, was six cubits high, he had six pieces of armor and they weighed six hundred shekels. The tower of Nebuchadnezzer was sixty cubits high.

Seven is perfection. Seven is used more than any number in the Bible. Seven days, seven years, seven trumpets, seven feast, seven churches and we have seen that it is God's completion, it is perfection. When He is in the picture, it is about perfection. He brings seven of these vial judgments. It is all perfect judgment. Seven Churches, perfection.

The number *eight* is about *new order*. The order of new things. He rose on the eighth day, new creation. Circumcision came on the eighth day. The eight day is a new order. We have six thousand years of recorded history. I believe the Lord will come any time. We have one more thousand years of the millennium, then the eighth one is with Him, in anew order. Forever!

Ten is *worldly completion*. The sum of the world is four plus man, which is six, which equals ten. In Daniel there are ten toes and ten horns referring to the Antichrist. The one that is confusing is the Ten Commandments. How do you put that in with worldly completion? I read Hebrews chapter 9 this morning and at the end of reading it, it hit me; "And this earthly tabernacle that they had in the wilderness is called 'a worldly tabernacle'". The Ten Commandments were housed in a worldly tabernacle. In that chapter it says He is going to take these and write them on the inward part of our hearts. We will be a spiritual man and the inner man will be fed so that is a worldly completion.

Twelve is an *eternal perfection*. There are twelve tribes, twelve apostles, twelve stars, twelve gates, twelve manner of fruits. All of these are about eternal perfection. We will see that in Revelation 21 and 22.

The number forty is easy to understand. Every where you see forty in the Bible it is about *probation*. Forty days and forty nights it rained. Moses was in the dessert for forty years in the "penalty box". The Israelites wandered in the wilderness for forty years. Jesus had forty days after the resurrection before He went back to the Father. Jesus was tempted for forty days by the Devil.

Let's go back to number six. That is the number of man. Six means "not quite there." You are not complete. Six six six is the trumpet shout "you are not there at all yet." And when this man comes on the scene saying that he wants the number 666 to be on man, it is not complete. The Bible says you will die in your sins if you receive the mark. The only way we will go to heaven is if we become a seven. Today, if you are in Christ, you are a seven. The Bible says, "Your life is hid with Christ in God." And if your life is hid with Christ in God, how did that happen? The Bible says in Colossians 3, "by the faith of the operation of God." He did it. He gave you a new heart. You receive a new heart by faith believing and you become a seven. We can look at ourselves in an "earth suit" of six. I am still trapped in this body wearing this tent around, but someday I will lay this tent down and the seven is going to go home with the Lord. I can't wait! I will never go home if I am a 666. I will only go home if I have the perfection of a seven.

Have you ever experienced a moment when some one starts to talk or starts to sing and then they stop? Does it bug you? "Silent night holy...." "Do Re Mi Fa So La...." Say it! "Night!" "Ti Do". If someone is playing a musical instrument and they never finish it, they just keep starting over at the beginning, that is frustrating! It bugs me because I want to hear it completed. We are all walking around a six. Until we are in Him, we will never be complete.

There are a lot of people enjoying life, but until you are in Him, you will never enjoy the abundant life. Do you know what the abundant life means? It means I can have more trials, tribulations and heartaches, and yet I survive, because I have an inner peace because I know I am a seven and I am in Him.

If you have a trial in your life today, you can have peace because you are in Him and you are a seven. You can cry at night on your pillow and be concerned about things; but if you are a seven, then maybe these trials are not so big of a deal. I do not think I could have survived even five of the things that the apostle Paul went through; but he was a seven and so he understood that and he picked up and went on. He said he despaired of his own life. He didn't feel like living any more, but he was a seven.

How do you apply Revelation 13 to your life today?

Do not believe just because people do miracles and great things that they are from God. We are living in a day when we see these things coming to past. Try the spirits.

We need to have a sensitive awareness in our lives, wherever we are at. Discern religion, economics, material things, and be aware that none of these things pull you away from living and following Jesus Christ. You may think that you are so strong, but the Bible says "without me you can do nothing." Do not be pulled away by deception. When you wake up in the morning, is Jesus the first thing you desire?

Pray that God gives you the patience and gives you the faithfulness that you can be able to face tough times. OTIC –Occupy Till I Come. We are living in deceiving times, but it will get worse.

In Washington DC you can go to the Treasury Building where all the money is printed. There are hundreds of dollars being printed in sheets and you can walk through and see it through thick glass windows. There is a question that is asked often by someone on the tour every single time. It is one of the most frequently asked questions of the tour guide: "What is the best way to avoid a counterfeit?" "How do you know it is not counterfeit?" **Just know the marks of a true bill**. That is all you have to know.

The Bible says in Revelation that you do not have to know the depths of Satan. Just follow the true One. Just as long as we are following Him, He has given us the promise that He will perform a work in us until He comes. That is a simple promise for all of us. When we follow the true one, Jesus Christ, then we are going home with HIM!!!!!

Two Hundred Miles of Mud and Blood

"And I looked, and, lo, a Lamb stood on the mount Sion, and with him an hundred forty and four thousand, having His Father's name written in their foreheads. And I heard a voice from heaven, as the voice of many waters, and as the voice of a great thunder: and I heard the voice of Harper's harping with their harps:

And they sung as it were a new song before the throne, and before the four beasts, and the elders: and no man could learn that song but the hundred and forty and four thousand, which were redeemed from the earth. These are they which were not defiled with women; for they are virgins. These are they which follow the Lamb whithersoever he goeth. These were redeemed from among men, being the firstfruits unto God and to the Lamb. And in their mouth was found no guile: for they are without fault before the throne of God.

And I saw another angel fly in the midst of heaven, having the everlasting gospel to preach unto them that dwell on the earth, and to every nation, and kindred, and tongue, and people, Saying with a loud voice, Fear God, and give glory to Him; for the hour of his judgement is come: and worship Him that made heaven, and earth, and the sea, and the fountains of waters. And there followed another angel, saying, Babylon is fallen, is fallen, that great city because she made all nations drink of the wine of the wrath of her fornication.

And the third angel followed them saying with a loud voice, If any man worship the beast and his image, and receive his mark in his forehead, or in his hand, The same shall drink of the wine of the wrath of God, which is poured out without mixture into the cup of his indignation; and he shall be tormented with fire and brimstone in the presence of the holy angels, and in the presence of the Lamb:

And the smoke of their torment ascendeth up for ever and ever: and they have no rest day or night, who worship the beast and his image, and whosoever receiveth the mark of his name. Here is the patience of the saints: here are they that keep the commandments of God, and the faith of Jesus. And I heard a voice from heaven saying unto me, Write, Blessed are the dead which die in the Lord from henceforth: Yea, saith the Spirit, that they may rest from their labors; and their works do follow them.

And I looked, and behold a white cloud, and upon the cloud one sat like unto the Son of Man, having on his head a golden crown, and in his hand a sharp sickle. And another angel came out of the temple, crying with a loud voice to him that sat on the cloud, Thrust in thy sickle, and reap: for the time is come for thee to reap; for the harvest of the earth is ripe. And he that sat on the cloud thrust his sickle on the earth; and the earth was reaped.

And another angel came out of the temple which is in heaven, he also having a sharp sickle. And another angel came out from the altar, which had power over fire; and cried with a loud cry to him that had the sharp sickle, saying, Thrust in thy sharp sickle, and gather the clusters of the vine of the earth; for her grapes are fully ripe.

And the angel thrust in his sickle into the earth, and gathered the vine of the earth, and cast it into the great winepress of the wrath of God. And the winepress was trodden without the city, and blood came out of the winepress, even unto the horse bridles, by the space of a thousand and six hundred furlongs."

Two hundred miles of mud and blood. (verse 20)

At this point in the drama we will see angels flying through the heavens here, giving announcements and also pouring out more wraths. As we look at these angels, remember that the other chapters were overwhelming; but now as Satan makes his final play for the soul of man, we will see it get even more intense. Through it all we will see the mercy and grace of God. The book of Revelations seems to be sorrow, death, and problems-but there is always a song and people being saved. That is the joy of the book of Revelation, the unveiling of Jesus Christ and what He does as man is ruined by sin. God will come back and reclaim His planet.

"And I looked, and, lo, a Lamb stood on the mount Zion, and with him an hundred forty and four thousand, having His Father's name written in their foreheads."

Who was the Lamb and why are they mentioning this about Mount Zion? What we have here is a picture of the 144,000 and it is just like we have a parenthetical pause here again. The 144,000 preach through the tribulation period; but now we are going to be caught up, and God is going to give us a picture of what takes place when they have accomplished their purposes in preaching the gospel. A special group of preachers is standing before Christ.

And I heard a voice from heaven, as the voice of many waters,"

Who is this? In Revelation 1:15 Christ was that voice of many waters.

And as the voice of a great thunder: and I heard the voice of Harper's harping with their harps:

And they sung as it were a new song before the throne, and before the four beasts, and the elders:"

We have a picture here of the 144,000 before Christ and the throne. He gives them a 'reward ceremony' for what they have done and will do on the earth, these 144,000 sealed messengers of the gospel of Christ. Here they are standing before the Lamb. It is a picture of what will take place in the millennium. Not only in Hosea, but also in Psalm 2, *"The Lord shall sit in heaven and have them in derision."* Men will be trying to take over and they will not be able to. God steps into the picture to set up a millennial kingdom. I believe that to be literal.

Listen to the words of Psalm 48:1-3, *"Great is the Lord and His name is greatly to be praised in the city of our God, the mountain of His holiness. Beautiful for situation, the joy of the Lord is Mount Zion, the city of the great King."*

Psalm 132:13 *"For the Lord hath chosen Zion, He hath described it for His habitation."*

Isaiah 2 supports Mount Zion being Christ's chosen place where He will rule and reign for a thousand years. It's better than any book. *"It shall come to past in the last days that the mountain of the Lord's house shall be established in the top of the mountains and all the nations shall flow into it. And He shall teach of His ways and we will walk in His paths, for out of Zion will go the word of God."*

"These are they which were not defiled with women; for they are virgins."

They are not married or polluted with things of the world, they are spiritually in tune with Christ.

"These are they which follow the Lamb whithersoever he goeth. These were redeemed from among men, being the firstfruits unto God (the firstfruits from the tribulation) *and to the Lamb. And in their mouth was found no guile: for they are without fault before the throne of God."*

It does not take too much understanding to figure out who these people are. Revelation 7 talks about them. They are not the church, or the Jehovah Witnesses, or some special cult that comes on the scene, but they are the twelve tribes chosen by God to preach the gospel during the tribulation period.

Why would Christ call them virgins? He calls His bride "virgin" in 2 Corinthians 11, "chaste virgins". In other words they are set apart for Him. The 144,000 are set apart for God to preach the word of God. They are without fault before the throne. Can you imagine a worldwide revival where you have 144,000 men preaching the word and they cannot be harmed or killed or stopped and everywhere they go one thing is on their mind? Preach the Word! They are so devoted and focused. We will have that view as we are seated around the throne. The 144,000 are an army of militant believers marching unscathed to proclaim the gospel of Christ.

The lesson I get from these men would be this: Do I have that kind of absolute devotion? Paul said that whether I live or whether I die, it is gain. Wherever we go we need to remain devoted to the cause of Christ.

Day and night the 144,000 will be hounded by the Gestapo of the Antichrist and the False Prophet, doing everything they can to hinder the message. But it will not work.

The devil is having his final play here. It is so bad that it would appear that not very many people would come to Christ. Not so! In fact, from the day of Pentecost until now God only knows the number of people who have been saved. It has been 2,000 years. But I would like to suggest to you this morning that there are only 22,000 missionaries in the world right now. I do not know how many of them are actually legitimate, but can you imagine 144,000 "Apostle Paul's" and then the two witnesses come to preach the Word? I suggest that there will be just as many people saved during the tribulation as there have been from Pentecost until now. Because when you think about the same wording in the book of Revelation, not only after the rapture in chapter 4 when it says, *"a great multitude that no man can number,"* then it comes along and talks about the tribulation saints in the same language. All the people who do not accept the mark of the beast and listen to the preaching of the 144,000 and the two witnesses and then come to Christ may die a martyr for Him. I believe there will be countless millions who die for Him and stand for Him. So the Revelation is dark and gloomy in some ways but it is exciting because people come to know Christ!

The Devil thought he had victory at Calvary. He never had victory. It opened up a whole new door. That is why he has hounded people from Pentecost on, but people just keep coming to the Lord. I find that very thrilling.

"And I saw another angel fly in the midst of heaven, having the everlasting gospel to preach unto them that dwell on the earth, and to every nation, and kindred, and tongue, and people, Saying with a loud voice, Fear God, and give glory to Him; for the hour of his judgement is come: and worship Him that made heaven, and earth, and the sea, and the fountains of waters."

As you look at these verses, it becomes very interesting in this sense. Here you have an angel preaching the gospel. What is the gospel? Christ came, died for us, and was buried, and rose again according to the Scriptures. That is the gospel. It is very simple. Here is an angel coming in the midst of heaven giving this everlasting gospel, and he will preach this on the earth.

It is like the last opportunity to repent. Why does he mix this other verse in here and say to worship Him who made heaven, earth, the sea, and the fountains of water? I believe it will get so bad here that all men will believe evolution is right and this angel will come and preach the gospel and cry, "Worship your Creator." He wants people to understand that this God is the Creator. He must be a Creator before He can be a Savior. And he brings them all the way back to the basics. This God of creation is the same God who will save your soul.

The witnesses came to share the gospel and the 144,000 came to preach the gospel. It does not say that this angel is sealed, but somehow it says it is in the midst of heaven. Somehow he will be in the midst of heaven proclaiming this gospel. Men will hear it and they will have another opportunity to accept it. It is the grace of God during these troublesome times to give recognition that people will have an opportunity to accept Him. The gospel saves us and gets our priorities straight. Life is not about us. Life is about Him. Life is about serving Him and loving Him and living for Him and looking for His return. That is what real living is about.

John 10 says *"I come that you might have life and that you might have it more abundantly."*

It is not about us any more. It is not about my dreams, my desires, my wants, and my needs being fulfilled. It is about pleasing Him. He says he wants them to *"Fear God"*. The Greek meaning there is *"to stand in awe."* We stand in awe of this God. He is the one who created and saves and He is the one who lives in us.

"And there followed another angel, saying, Babylon is fallen, is fallen, that great city because she made all nations drink of the wine of the wrath of her fornication."

This is the only verse mentioning that Babylon is fallen. We will talk about this in more detail when we study Revelation 17 and 18. This is a preview of this angel flying through heaven and seeing this great economic collapse, military collapse, and religious collapse. The False Prophet and the Antichrist will all be a part of Babylon being fallen.

We have mentioned this before, but we will say it again. Any time something is mentioned in the Bible for the first time, it must hold continuity and harmony all the way through the Bible. A great example is blood. Genesis

3 – *shed blood* there which means death substitute. Death gave life and it was somebody else outside of themselves. Here you have the continuity of blood all the way through the Bible, all the way to the cross, and all the way to our salvation. The same is with Babylon. Babylon is mentioned for the first time in Genesis 11. Everything about Babylon is all about man trying to rise up and be a god. So everything about Babylon is evil and wicked and bad, and it ends up this way in Revelation. The circle is completed.

This angel comes along and says that Babylon is fallen, is fallen. It is an echo of Isaiah 21:9 when it says Babylon is fallen, is fallen. Every thing the devil did to try to renew in the hearts of man the desire to worship him and follow him will all collapse. This is a little "video" we get from this angel of the satanic system of that city.

"And the third angel followed them saying with a loud voice, If any man worship the beast and his image, and receive his mark in his forehead, or in his hand, The same shall drink of the wine of the wrath of God, which is poured out without mixture into the cup of his indignation; and he shall be tormented with fire and brimstone in the presence of the holy angels, and in the presence of the Lamb: And the smoke of their torment ascendeth up for ever and ever: and they have no rest day or night, who worship the beast and his image, and whosoever receiveth the mark of his name."

This is about as clear as you can get. If you receive the mark of the beast during this tribulation period, that means *hell forever* for the individual who accepts it. There is no turning back at that point. There will be no repentance. But if you do not receive the mark, then you will be dying as a martyr for Christ and forever be in His presence.

This angel comes here with a final warning against the mark of the beast and worship of the beast or there will be eternal damnation.

I sat in my chair as I studied and thought about this for awhile. I remember something my grandpa told me when I first became a pastor. He said that no one preaches on **hell** anymore. So I started checking that out and my grandpa was right. The Devil is so subtle in his ways of taking people away from this 'no more torment' and 'God is so loving that He only wants you to believe that He is a God of love and there will never be punishment.' I read a statistic concerning hell in a Christian book in my library brought on by a Christian man named George Beck of Northwestern University

–which is amazing. This is a survey he did. He went and canvassed thousands of churches and this is what he came up with. 96% of all the ministers of small congregation churches do not believe in a hell. 95% of all Episcopalian ministers do not believe or preach about hell. 82% of all Methodist ministers do not believe in a literal hell. 85% of all Presbyterian ministers do not believe in a literal hell. 30% of all Lutheran ministers today do not believe in a literal hell. 40% of all Baptist ministers today do not believe in a literal hell. So people are not being warned about it and it is not that big of a deal to them an more.

Christ said more about hell than He did about heaven, and I believe it was a way of warning. If you are going to talk about an everlasting time of being with the Father in His presence, there is also a judgement of everlasting hell. That is why people today do not talk about it, because they do not believe it. They do not believe in a literal torment or judgement forever. Jesus warned and warned and warned that those who reject Him would stand in eternal punishment.

"Here is the patience of the saints: here are they that keep the commandments of God, and the faith of Jesus. And I heard a voice from heaven saying unto me, Write, Blessed are the dead which die in the Lord from henceforth: Yea, saith the Spirit, that they may rest from their labors; and their works do follow them."

These are Christians who are saved as martyrs who die for the cause of Christ during the tribulation period. They are saved by the preaching of the 144,000. They are saved by the preaching of the two Witnesses. They are saved by the preaching of the warning of this angel who gives the final gospel message. These people will die in the Lord, because they are willing to stand for Him, that they may rest from their labors and their works and follow Him.

"And I looked, and behold a white cloud, and upon the cloud one sat like unto the Son of Man, having on his head a golden crown, and in his hand a sharp sickle."

I want to pause here and look at this. Here is a picture again of Jesus Christ. Because John is looking and he is looking at this white cloud and on the white cloud there was someone seated and it says it was like the Son of Man with a golden crown on His head. This is the royal diadem crown. The only one who wears this is Christ.

A sickle has a handle. There is a curve on it, a sharp blade like a razor blade. In the olden days they would cut their wheat and their vines with something like this and then they would gather them in. Here is Christ seated on the white cloud with a sickle in His hand for the purpose to make division. If you look in Matthew 13 and read about the wheat and the tares and the separating of the grapes there, this is a picture of Christ. This is the last time in the Bible that He is mentioned as the Son of Man. He comes as the Son of Man to bring harvest. From here on out in the book of Revelation, He will be King of Kings and Lord of Lords! This is the dividing of the wheat and the tares. The vision of these angels is different from the first three in that sense. They will be a part of this division. They are from the temple. They have a sharp sickle, and they have firepower to bring judgement. Christ is leading them. I believe we will witness this and see this division in the last days.

"And another angel came out of the temple, crying with a loud voice to him that sat on the cloud, Thrust in thy sickle, and reap: for the time is come for thee to reap; for the harvest of the earth is ripe. And he that sat on the cloud thrust his sickle on the earth; and the earth was reaped."

The Greek meaning of "the earth was reaped" is rapidity or rapid. This is a very fast, rapid harvest of separating the wheat and the tares. In that sense, I believe you can put these angels together.

"And another angel came out of the temple which is in heaven, he also having a sharp sickle. And another angel came out from the altar, which had power over fire; and cried with a loud cry to him that had the sharp sickle, saying, Thrust in thy sharp sickle, and gather the clusters of the vine of the earth; for her grapes are fully ripe. And the angel thrust in his sickle into the earth, and gathered the vine of the earth, and cast it into the great winepress of the wrath of God."

Read Joel 3 – a prophetic utterance of Joel from the Lord.

This is a preview of what is to come in the next part of Revelation. These angels are flying through heaven and they will show how God will intervene and cut them all down. This is an actual record. This battle will be so bad. Ezekiel 37 says it will take seven years just to burn the implements of their weapons. Two hundred miles of mud and blood.

=*"And the winepress was trodden without the city, and blood came out of the winepress, even unto the horse bridles, by the space of a thousand and six hundred furlongs."*

Can you grasp that? Can your mind wrap around that and make any sense of that? Is this symbolic or spiritual or literal? Again, I like to take the book of Revelation literally, although at times he will refer to symbols. How is this literal?

If you look in Josephus, he is a very good historian. He says in A.D. 70, when Titus came in and destroyed Jerusalem, the slaughter was so great that the city streets were actually running with blood. Over a million people died during that slaughter. There were pockets in that city that were actually two and three feet deep in blood. So in that sense I like to think that when you have two hundred million people slaughtered from the valley of Megedo clear down to Bersheba when God intervenes, there may be pockets up to the horses bridle or four feet.

Some commentaries say that this is just a matter of blood being splattered that high. Whatever it is, there will be a sea of human blood so traumatic that it will be the final battle where God brings judgement upon humanity.

Why does the Bible even mention this? This may send chills up your spine. We know we win in the end. This shows the mind and the love of God to me in this sense. Notice that they mention that the blood came from the winepress and the winepress was trodden without the city. Jesus was crucified without the city. God brought judgement upon His Son for the sins of all of humanity. He will come again. And all who reject Him, He will take their blood without the city. That is why it is mentioned. They took the life of Christ without the city and He shed His blood voluntarily that all of us might have life. This whole gospel will be preached until that final battle. Those who do not accept the One who shed His blood without the city, their blood will be shed without the city. That is the message! And if we do not wake up to that and realize that we are living near these times, maybe we are missing the conclusion of the matter.

Check your pulse and ask your heart "Are you in the group of people today who love Christ and are fully devoted to Him? Or are you in the group of people who are rejecting Him?" Check your pulse and find out where you are at because we are nearing the end of time. Be honest with yourself. Are you in Him or out of Him?

We need to be focused on worshipping and praising God because He is the Creator. We must keep that message clear to those who we share the gospel with. It is astounding that professors as well as the sea of humanity today say that evolution is right. No, it is not right, because we were created by God. Keep that message clear. He is our redeemer, but He is also the Creator. Do not allow the system of humanity to change your mind.

The building that we are living in is on fire. We are living in a time when the building is on fire. Warn people that they do not have to die in the building in their sin. It is better to share the Word of God and be ridiculed than to allow someone to die in their sins in a burning building.

Let God judge the sinner and the sin. You share the Word and tell them about the good things of Christ and tell them what the Bible says, but let God judge the sinner. God always has His people coming to Him. And someday we will have that great opportunity to live and rule with Him the King of Kings and Lord of Lords!

Seven Angels, Seven Plagues:
Earth at its Worst

1And I saw another sign in heaven, great and marvelous, seven angels having the seven last plagues; for in them is filled up the wrath of God.

2And I saw as it were a sea of glass mingled with fire: and them that had gotten the victory over the beast, and over his image, and over his mark, and over the number of his name, stand on the sea of glass, having the harps of God.

3And they sing the song of Moses the servant of God, and the song of the Lamb, saying, Great and marvelous are thy works, Lord God Almighty; just and true are thy ways, thou King of saints.

4Who shall not fear thee, O Lord, and glorify thy name? for thou only art holy: for all nations shall come and worship before thee; for thy judgments are made manifest.

5And after that I looked, and, behold, the temple of the tabernacle of the testimony in heaven was opened:

6And the seven angels came out of the temple, having the seven plagues, clothed in pure and white linen, and having their breasts girded with golden girdles.

7And one of the four beasts gave unto the seven angels seven golden vials full of the wrath of God, who liveth for ever and ever.

8And the temple was filled with smoke from the glory of God, and from his power; and no man was able to enter into the temple, till the seven plagues of the seven angels were fulfilled.

1And I heard a great voice out of the temple saying to the seven angels, Go your ways, and pour out the vials of the wrath of God upon the earth.

2And the first went, and poured out his vial upon the earth; and there fell a noisome and grievous sore upon the men which had the mark of the beast, and upon them which worshipped his image.

3And the second angel poured out his vial upon the sea; and it became as the blood of a dead man: and every living soul died in the sea.

4And the third angel poured out his vial upon the rivers and fountains of waters; and they became blood.

5And I heard the angel of the waters say, Thou art righteous, O Lord, which art, and wast, and shalt be, because thou hast judged thus.

6For they have shed the blood of saints and prophets, and thou hast given them blood to drink; for they are worthy.

7And I heard another out of the altar say, Even so, Lord God Almighty, true and righteous are thy judgments.

8And the fourth angel poured out his vial upon the sun; and power was given unto him to scorch men with fire.

9And men were scorched with great heat, and blasphemed the name of God, which hath power over these plagues: and they repented not to give him glory.

10And the fifth angel poured out his vial upon the seat of the beast; and his kingdom was full of darkness; and they gnawed their tongues for pain,

11And blasphemed the God of heaven because of their pains and their sores, and repented not of their deeds.

12And the sixth angel poured out his vial upon the great river Euphrates; and the water thereof was dried up, that the way of the kings of the east might be prepared.

13And I saw three unclean spirits like frogs come out of the mouth of the dragon, and out of the mouth of the beast, and out of the mouth of the false prophet.

14For they are the spirits of devils, working miracles, which go forth unto the kings of the earth and of the whole world, to gather them to the battle of that great day of God Almighty.

15Behold, I come as a thief. Blessed is he that watcheth, and keepeth his garments, lest he walk naked, and they see his shame.

16And he gathered them together into a place called in the Hebrew tongue Armageddon.

17And the seventh angel poured out his vial into the air; and there came a great voice out of the temple of heaven, from the throne, saying, It is done.

18And there were voices, and thunders, and lightnings; and there was a great earthquake, such as was not since men were upon the earth, so mighty an earthquake, and so great.

19And the great city was divided into three parts, and the cities of the nations fell: and great Babylon came in remembrance before God, to give unto her the cup of the wine of the fierceness of his wrath.

20And every island fled away, and the mountains were not found.

21And there fell upon men a great hail out of heaven, every stone about the weight of a talent: and men blasphemed God because of the plague of the hail; for the plague thereof was exceeding great.

Earth at its worst! Revelation is broken into three symbols: Seals, Trumpets and Vials. We are studying the vials in this passage, the fury of God's wrath at its very worst. Chapter 15 is a preparation chapter for chapter 16. Chapter 16 covers the seven plagues. I like the way the Holy Spirit works through the Apostle John. John is writing this in Revelation, and there are times he gets very excited. He is excited about hearing the songs of Moses and the Lamb! He loves to see these people on the harps, the tribulation saints; and we the church, having already been caught up. There are also times where he has written about the seals, the trumpets, the war in heaven, the satanic trinity, and the vials. John is human so I think he is very exhausted when he writes these words. Before the trumpets, before the seals, and before the vials, it seems like God pauses. We have chapter 15, where he pauses, and we get to go up and look around for a little bit in heaven. Then we have this catastrophic judgment that is starting to come on. This is the final judgement that we will see in the book of Revelation. We will see the seven dooms of Babylon.

1. And I saw another sign in heaven, great and marvelous, seven angels having the seven last plagues; for in them is filled up the wrath of God.

This is the picture that John sees. There are seven angels standing here with a vial near the temple of God, in the holiest of holies, and they have in them the wrath of God. These are seven special angels which will be unleashed by the cherubim later on in chapter 16. They are standing here just waiting. What they are holding in their hands and in their bowls or vials is something so terrible that it doesn't sound fair. Here they are, standing there filled up with the wrath of God and then he says:

2. And I saw as it were a sea of glass mingled with fire: and them that had gotten the victory over the beast, and over his image, and over his mark, and over the number of his name, stand on the sea of glass, having the harps of God.

3. And they sing the song of Moses the servant of God, and the song of the Lamb, saying, Great and marvelous are thy works, Lord God Almighty; just and true are thy ways, thou King of saints.

4. Who shall not fear thee, O Lord, and glorify thy name? for thou only art holy: for all nations shall come and worship before thee; for thy judgments are made manifest.

This is the song of the tribulation saints and of those who have been delivered. It is a direct parallel of Exodus chapter 15. Revelation 15 is a parallel to Exodus 15. In Exodus they were being lead out of Egypt. They came out of the bondage of Egypt. They were delivered and they stood on that side of the sea singing the song of Moses. Here in Revelation as they stand on this side of the sea of God's deliverance from this tribulation period, the tribulation saints are singing the song of the Lamb. A redeemed and chosen people, thanking the Lord for redemption, deliverance, and salvation from wrath! A deliverance, not only from the wrath of the False Prophet and the Antichrist, but also delivered to be in God's presence. This is what is flowing out of their hearts.

Would you agree with me that we live in a music-driven era? The number one language in the world today is music. When written in a right way, it can reach out and touch lives and change people. If it is done in a wrong way, or whatever you want to call it,(rock, metal, rap), it can actually change the emotions and lives of a human. Wherever you are on this planet, music can reach you. We live in a music-driven era. When these people are delivered out of this tribulation, the first thing that comes out of their hearts is praise to the Lamb. John is witnessing this. He says that all the nations will come and worship before Thee for Thy judgments are made manifest.

5. And after that I looked, and, behold, the temple of the tabernacle of the testimony in heaven was opened:

6. And the seven angels came out of the temple, having the seven plagues, clothed in pure and white linen, and having their breasts girded with golden girdles.

7. And one of the four beasts gave unto the seven angels seven golden vials full of the wrath of God, who liveth forever and ever.

8. And the temple was filled with smoke from the glory of God, and from his power; and no man was able to enter into the temple, till the seven plagues of the seven angels were fulfilled.

What is he saying? For some reason in this time period, God has barred any entrance into the holiest of holies. He pours out this rapid fire "Uzie –like" machine gun judgement on the planet. We are not talking about one little bowl being poured, and then He waits for forty five years and another bowl will be poured. In rapid fire sequence we will see in Revelation 16 He pours it out. He pours it out, and He pours it out , and it gets worse and worse and worse. Then God comes. This will all be just as literal as it was in Pharaoh's time. We are seeing the same kind of plagues here on a worldwide scale. Blood, darkness, boils, heat-it is all the same. Just as God gave them deliverance in Egypt, now the tribulation saints stand on this side of that sea of glass and they thank the Lord with a song of the Lamb.

I would love to have been standing there with John as he witnessed this scene! Just watching the angels with their harps, and singing with joy radiating on their faces. Then John turns around and sees these angels getting ready to walk out in the midst of this temple. I think these angels know that what they are holding in their hands is so terrible that you can't describe it. We will try to describe it, but we won't even come close. What they have in these vials is so terrible and at the same time they are so right. God's justice, so terrible yet so right.

I do not understand why God would bar the holiest of holies. But the time has come for the final storm to break on planet earth. So we walk into Revelation chapter 16.

1. And I heard a great voice out of the temple saying to the seven angels, Go your ways, and pour out the vials of the wrath of God upon the earth.

2. And the first went, and poured out his vial upon the earth; and there fell a noisome and grievous sore upon the men which had the mark of the beast, and upon them which worshipped his image.

This is a seven-year period. We are to the time of the seven vial judgements. The last of the vial judgements will be the battle of Armageddon. What is taking place here in chapter 16 is earth's worst nightmare. The information of chapter 16 should cause all men to examine their hearts. What we are going to read here will take place.

"and there fell a noisome and grievous sore" I looked at that in the Hebrew text and it is the same as the boil that fell upon the Egyptians in the plague in Exodus. This boil is a wound that is malignant. It oozed and it was so painful that men would scream out. God touches them first because they received the mark and their rejection of God will be a boil. It will not go away. It will be so sore that it will be a plague that will cover all the inward parts of their body. Something that they see on the outward will just be a manifestation of inward corruption of their heart for God. I can't imagine anything like this.

As Jesus was looking at the Pharisees in Matthew 23, He said , "You may look good on the outside but you are nothing but a bunch of white sepulchres. You are dead men's bones on the inside. You are corrupt. "The people who break out in these boils were part of the world church. They thought that they were right but they were WRONG. And God pours out this vial like a fulfillment of Old Testament prophecy. In Deut. 28, he calls it a curse, an itch, a boil, a scab and a curse to those who refuse Him. This will happen to a wretched people!

There will be people who have not accepted the mark and they will not receive a boil. This is a very specific judgement upon those who have the mark of the beast. It is a direct parallel to Exodus.

3. And the second angel poured out his vial upon the sea; and it became as the blood of a dead man: and every living soul died in the sea.

Think about that one for awhile. God unleashes this vial and all of the salt water turns to blood. You think what happened back there at the seal judgements and the trumpet judgements was pretty bad. I would wonder if, down here in the last of the seven-year period, the majority of the food supply is coming from the ocean and the fish. Then God comes and pours out this blood upon the sea and it says that everything dies. Now you have a gooey stagnation of death and stench.

It is hard to picture. To think that all the salt water and fish will be affected. Again it is like Exodus chapter 7 in Moses' time where all the water was turned to blood and all the fish died in the Nile River and surrounding streams. Here on a worldwide scale God will pour out His wrath as the blood of a dead man and every living soul dies in the sea. That sounds bad and it is. How can this really happen? I don't know, but the Lord made it happen in the Old Testament times and now He will make it happen on a large scale as a supernatural act of God. But it will happen.

4. And the third angel poured out his vial upon the rivers and fountains of waters; and they became blood.

5And I heard the angel of the waters say, Thou art righteous, O Lord, which art, and wast, and shalt be, because thou hast judged thus.

6For they have shed the blood of saints and prophets, and thou hast given them blood to drink; for they are worthy.

7And I heard another out of the altar say, Even so, Lord God Almighty, true and righteous are thy judgments.

I love verse seven because one of the first things that comes to our minds when we read this is, "God, you are not fair." It is one thing to have boils and another thing to ruin the food supply for the people on the planet, but now you come along and all the fresh water and everything has blood. The running water from a faucet is bloody. The main water systems through cities have blood and the shower is blood instead of water. That doesn't sound fair. But look at verse seven. True and righteous are Your judgements.

That is the answer to all the questions we may have. The Bible is very clear in Habakkuk 2:20 *"But the Lord is in His holy temple: let all the earth keep silence before Him."*

It does not matter what man's opinion is at this time. God is bringing judgement to those who refuse to come and worship Him. It is fair. It is the way it will happen. Can you imagine the hysteria after the first three vials?

8And the fourth angel poured out his vial upon the sun; and power was given unto him to scorch men with fire.

9And men were scorched with great heat, and blasphemed the name of God, which hath power over these plagues: and they repented not to give him glory.

This is a verse that saddens the heart. God pours out His wrath on men and what do they do? They do not repent. They just keep blaspheming Him and they repent not of their evil deeds and they do not get it. This shows how evil men have become and it shows the righteous judgement of God.

Have you ever had sunburn before? God allows men to be scorched in a supernatural way with this intense heat. Luke 21 talks about the signs in the sun and moon and stars. This is one of the signs. God will allow the sun to become seven times hotter and people will get scorched. So not only is there famine and boils but also they are being scorched now. Isaiah 24:6 says , *"Therefore, hath the curse devoured the earth, and they that dwell therein are desolate: therefore the inhabitants of the earth are burned, and few men left."*

Malachi 4:1 *"For behold the day cometh that shall burn as an oven and all the proud, yea, and all that do wickedly, shall be stubble: and the day that cometh shall burn them up, saith the Lord of hosts, that is shall leave them neither root nor branch."* They will be burnt worse than sunburn, they will be scorched. This is a prophecy that is fulfilled in Isaiah, Luke and Malachi.

Their response is to blaspheme the Lord. That is tragic.

10. And the fifth angel poured out his vial upon the seat of the beast; and his kingdom was full of darkness; and they gnawed their tongues for pain,

11. And blasphemed the God of heaven because of their pains and their sores, and repented not of their deeds.

This is another picture of God putting the pressure of His punishment upon man. Instead of turning to Him, they blaspheme Him. This has got to be very exhausting and frustrating for John. "People wake up!"

This darkness is on the seat of Satan. Wherever Satan has his kingdom at that time, in the center of Jerusalem or Babylon, and he has all his dignitaries surrounding and God brings a darkness, that is now a direct hit upon the throne of the beast. How bad is this darkness? A darkness so bad that it is the same as it was in the plague of Egypt. It says that they felt the darkness. It will be so bad that it will be painful.

Scientist say that you can go down to Carlsbad Caverns and if everyone is out of the cave and you go down there without a lamp for ten days, you will lose your mind because of the darkness. You can't see or feel anything and it becomes oppressive and man just goes wild. That used to be one of the Chinese tortures. Void of sound and full of darkness, man goes crazy. I know. I have been to the bottom of Moaning Caves and it didn't take me ten days to go "different." It only took three hours!

It says this darkness will come to the point that it will be felt. But it says that they repented not of their deeds.

12. And the sixth angel poured out his vial upon the great river Euphrates; and the water thereof was dried up, that the way of the kings of the east might be prepared.

13. And I saw three unclean spirits like frogs come out of the mouth of the dragon, and out of the mouth of the beast, and out of the mouth of the false prophet.

This is demonic activity under the control of Satan, coming out of these three men, the Satanic Trinity. They are the spirits of devils and they will go out and work miracles with all these kings. They will talk them into coming together that they might go down to the valley of Jezebel, Armageddon, Megiddo, and they will fight the beast and take on the armies of God. That is ludicrous. We know this because we read about it, but somehow these men will be so convinced that they will fall for that.

I would call this a preparation plague for Armageddon. The River Euphrates is the main river in that region. It is 1,800 miles long and thirty to eighty feet wide as it winds through there. But just as God dried up the Jordan

River and the Dead Sea, God will dry up the Euphrates River so that the armies of the North and East will come down and meet in the valley of Armageddon for the great and final battle. Demons will be causing these kings to assemble because they believe they have come to a point in time that they can take on God. They will attempt to take Him on. That is a sad commentary of how strong the demonic activity is in the planet today.

15Behold, I come as a thief. Blessed is he that watcheth, and keepeth his garments, lest he walk naked, and they see his shame.

He is telling people that even in the time of judgment, He will show His mercy to those who do not listen to the evil spirit of the demons. In the midst of God's judgment, there will be a time of mercy. He is saying here that there will be a time of mercy.

This is not the church. God doesn't come to the church as a thief in the night. The Bible makes that very clear **in 1 Thes. 4, "We are not in darkness that that day should overtake us as a thief."** We can see the signs of the time and we know the imminent return of Christ is near. It will not be a surprise to us. But during the tribulation period, He will come as a thief. In the Olivet Discourse in Matthew 24, Jesus warns that it will be like a thief, talking about this time period here.

This is a very comforting verse. He warns them to make sure that they are watching for Him. "You may die as a martyr; but as long as you are looking for me and remaining focused on me, I will come and you will be all right. You will not be ashamed."

16And he gathered them together into a place called in the Hebrew tongue Armageddon.

If you have been to Israel, you can look out over that plain of maybe sixty or seventy miles long and twenty miles wide. It is a beautiful valley. This is where the armies will come out of the Euphrates River to meet in the valley of Jezreel or Jehosaphat or as some would call it "Megadu". This is the valley were God's people will come back with Christ and change things forever.

17And the seventh angel poured out his vial into the air; and there came a great voice out of the temple of heaven, from the throne, saying, It is done.

This may be my favorite verse. It is not because I like this vial and the earthquake that happens with it but, I just love the words, "**It is done.**" Why do I like that verse? Remember when Christ was hanging on the cross in John 19 and right before he gives up the Ghost He says, "It is done." Same words. I find that so exciting. When all the wrath of man's sin was poured upon our Savior on the cross of Calvary, He took on the wickedness of our sins voluntarily and He said, "It is finished!" He met all of God's wrath and He said, "It is done." Here we have all the wrath of God being poured out on mankind at the end of the age and He says, "It is done." It is over. "My Son took the wrath for all of you and now I am pouring out my wrath upon this planet and it is over." When He says, "It is done," He means it just like He meant it on the cross.

18And there were voices, and thunders, and lightnings; and there was a great earthquake, such as was not since men were upon the earth, so mighty an earthquake, and so great.

19And the great city was divided into three parts, and the cities of the nations fell: and great Babylon came in remembrance before God, to give unto her the cup of the wine of the fierceness of his wrath.

In Genesis it says that God in this terrible time of wrath as He was pouring out the flood says, "God remembered Noah and He saved him." Now here in the cycle of completion in Revelation, God remembers Babylon and He destroys it. This terrible earthquake comes as never seen before.

20And every island fled away, and the mountains were not found.

21And there fell upon men a great hail out of heaven, every stone about the weight of a talent: and men blasphemed God because of the plague of the hail; for the plague thereof was exceeding great.

The stone was about the weight of a talent, in other words, 120 lb. Barbells are flying out of heaven, smashing people into the earth. This is the final fury and judgement of God because of the plague of the hail, for the plague thereof was exceedingly great.

Zechariah 14:1-

"Behold, the day of the Lord cometh, and thy spoil shall be divided in the midst of thee. For I will gather all the nations against Jerusalem to battle; and the city shall be taken, and the houses rifled, and the

women ravished; and half of the city shall go forth into captivity, and the residue of the people shall not be cut off from the city. Then shall the Lord God go forth and fight against those nations, as when he fought in the days of battle. And his feet shall stand in that day upon the mount of Olives, which is before Jerusalem on the east, and the mount of Olives shall cleave in the midst thereof toward the east and toward the west, and there shall be a very great valley; and half of the mountain shall be removed toward the north, and half of it toward the south. And ye shall flee to the valley of the mountains; for the valley of the mountains shall reach unto Azal: yea, ye shall flee, like in the earthquake in the days of Uzziah King of Judah: and the Lord my God shall come, and all the saints with thee. And it shall come to pass in that day that the light shall not be clear, nor dark. But it shall be one day which shall be known to the Lord, not day, nor night: but it shall come to pass, that at the evening time it shall be light. And it shall be in that day, that the living waters shall go out from Jerusalem; half of them towards the former sea, and half of them toward the hinder sea: in summer and in winter shall it be. And the Lord shall be King over all the earth: in that day there shall be one Lord, and His name alone."

This is the end. This is when Christ comes back at the intervention at the battle of Armageddon. He will come to earth with ten thousand of His saints, you and I with Him, to the battle of Armageddon. This will set up the thousand-year reign with Christ.

We will look at forty different scriptures as we look at the millennial reign, and what we will experience. Whether we rule and reign from heaven or from earth, I believe it is a literal thousand years and everything here can be taken literally.

Now for the application of Revelation 16 for your life today. I would like to suggest a few here for all of us. We are living in a very exciting time, but I would like to encourage you to continue to admire God's creation. Why do we say that? Because someday it will all be over. Every ocean and mountain and valley that we can see today, the Bible says it will all melt with a fervent heat. We will have a new heaven and a new earth, but what we are witnessing today will melt away. Enjoy His creation; and as you enjoy the creation, remember that it is not eternal. What is eternal is what you have in you with Him. Do not get so focused on this earth that you want to live here forever. It is not eternal. Creation is not eternal but redemption is.

Do not waste your time trying to set dates and places. People will look at the end of times and the book of Revelation differently, but just remember that He is Coming! Do not let that promise be taken away from you. Sometimes we will get to focused on how it will happen, but the important thing is that He is coming again! Be ready for that coming!

As you share the Word of God remember that you will be rejected a lot. We see here in this chapter that some men will never repent. Do what you can with your ministry and your gifts, but do not let it get you down when people reject you. Some people will never repent.

If you have a batting average of 300, you can make any major team in America. Three out of Ten? Yes. You may not have even one percent as you share the Word of God, but that one is worth it.

Make sure that you abide in the Word of God and in worship and prayer. The Bible says in James, *"Be patient for the coming of the Lord draweth nigh."* Do not be ashamed at His coming. Do not live horizontally, but live vertically. Make sure you are abiding in Him. Look for Him all the time.

II **Thessalonians 1:2** *"May the name of our Lord Jesus Christ always be glorified in you."*

Revelation 17

The End of all World Religions

1And there came one of the seven angels which had the seven vials, and talked with me, saying unto me, Come hither; I will shew unto thee the judgment of the great whore that sitteth upon many waters:

2With whom the kings of the earth have committed fornication, and the inhabitants of the earth have been made drunk with the wine of her fornication.

3So he carried me away in the spirit into the wilderness: and I saw a woman sit upon a scarlet colored beast, full of names of blasphemy, having seven heads and ten horns.

4And the woman was arrayed in purple and scarlet color, and decked with gold and precious stones and pearls, having a golden cup in her hand full of abominations and filthiness of her fornication:

5And upon her forehead was a name written, MYSTERY, BABYLON THE GREAT, THE MOTHER OF HARLOTS AND ABOMINATIONS OF THE EARTH.

6And I saw the woman drunken with the blood of the saints, and with the blood of the martyrs of Jesus: and when I saw her, I wondered with great admiration.

7And the angel said unto me, Wherefore didst thou marvel? I will tell thee the mystery of the woman, and of the beast that carrieth her, which hath the seven heads and ten horns.

8The beast that thou sawest was, and is not; and shall ascend out of the bottomless pit, and go into perdition: and they that dwell on the earth shall wonder, whose names were not written in the book of life from the foundation of the world, when they behold the beast that was, and is not, and yet is.

9And here is the mind which hath wisdom. The seven heads are seven mountains, on which the woman sitteth.

10And there are seven kings: five are fallen, and one is, and the other is not yet come; and when he cometh, he must continue a short space.

11And the beast that was, and is not, even he is the eighth, and is of the seven, and goeth into perdition.

12And the ten horns which thou sawest are ten kings, which have received no kingdom as yet; but receive power as kings one hour with the beast.

13These have one mind, and shall give their power and strength unto the beast.

14These shall make war with the Lamb, and the Lamb shall overcome them: for he is Lord of lords, and King of kings: and they that are with him are called, and chosen, and faithful.

15And he saith unto me, The waters which thou sawest, where the whore sitteth, are peoples, and multitudes, and nations, and tongues.

16And the ten horns which thou sawest upon the beast, these shall hate the whore, and shall make her desolate and naked, and shall eat her flesh, and burn her with fire.

17For God hath put in their hearts to fulfil his will, and to agree, and give their kingdom unto the beast, until the words of God shall be fulfilled.

18And the woman which thou sawest is that great city, which reigneth over the kings of the earth.

This will be the end of all World Religions. I do not mean to demean any specific religions here. But this is how I understand the Bible, and I will try to back it up with Scripture. I do not mean to say that all people in all other religions are not saved. I do not mean that at all, but what I do mean is that the system that is portrayed in the Catholic Church for instance is rotten to the core. Does that mean that you can be saved in the Catholic Church? Yes, you can. But it also means that if you are a Catholic, or a Mormon, or Muslim, and you are a Christian, then I have confidence that the Holy Spirit in time will lead you to truth. And I doubt that you would remain there. As I mention some religions, I want to be clear to say that I am not condemning the people. We are condemning by the authority of Scripture, a system of religion.

Religion will be destroyed here in Revelation 17. This is a tough study because I have close friends who are involved in some of these religions and they are great people. Yet as you look at this Scripture here, it becomes very uncomfortable as you see the truth.

Babylon. The background of Babylon, a religious system in the end times, will have its concentration in Rome. I want you to have this understanding because this is a passage of Scripture that is vehementantly argued about. People want to stay completely away from the 17th chapter of Revelation because you offend people. It is my understanding as we look at Babylon here that we are looking at this city of Rome. This will be the concentration where the False Prophet and the Beast will have the religious system. It is not the city of Babylon that has been destroyed. They may attempt to resurrect it again; but when we talk about the mystery Babylon, we are talking about Rome.

Some might think I am just speculating about this. But I am not, and I will let the Apostle Peter answer that question. How do you know that this mystery Babylon is Rome? I Peter 5:15 "The church that is at Babylon we salute you." What could he mean? There was no church in Babylon. The early Christians all looked at Rome as being Babylon. Peter was writing from Rome when he wrote this to the Christians. He is sitting in Rome writing I Peter, and he says the church that is at Babylon/Rome, we salute you.

The Apostle John on the Isle of Patmos, when he thought about Babylon, it was equal to the system there at Rome. This city controlled all the known empires at that time. Rome was the evil concentration of world religion. Two thousand years later we can say, "here we go again," because it is going to happen again. It's the same kind of persecution that was back there in John's time coming out of the false system of Rome. In the End Times we will see the same things happen.

This is a false religious system by way of Babylon. In Genesis chapter 10, this false system started with a man called Nimrod. I believe he was the great grandson of Noah. Nimrod was the one who built Babel and Babylon and Ninnevah. Nimrod married a women named Semiramis and they had a child named Tammuz. This is documented in Myths and Ledgends, and it is also in the Bible. If you look in culture in Assyria it was "Astarte", in Egypt called "Isis" and in Greece called, "Aphrodites" and in Rome it was called, "Venus". Nimrod's wife was the first High Priest of Idolatry. She started the whole thing and Nimrod was right in there with her. They helped to encourage Baal worship at the tower of Babel. Nimrod's wife gave birth to a son Tummuz and the trouble begins.

There is a scarlet thread of redemption that starts in Genesis 3:15. This thread is Christ, and He goes all the way through the Bible to Revelation. Also in Genesis 3 and 10 there is a scarlet thread of the serpent (the snake) that will go all the way to Revelation 17. This is the way that it begins. There is a legend that says that Tammuz was killed by a wild boar, but forty days later his parents said that he was miraculously resurrected. And they started this legend that their son was resurrected. People became so caught up in the legend that all false religion can be traced back to Babel and Babylon today.

One of the greatest religious systems on the planet today, which is Catholicism, has its roots here in Genesis. That started the cultic worship of mother/child and so you look back at those religious systems in Assyria. This is all a mimic. Then come Mary and Jesus. What started at Babylon will encourage this worship from a wrong perspective. There is still the mother/child worship today of Mary and Christ. All of these represent the false religions of a mother/child worship. There is no place in the Word of God where there is a worship of the female deity. The false religions of the world today encourage this. The religion of the mother/child spread quickly. What are the characteristics of this mother/child worship? It is not only in Catholicism. It is in some other religious cults. It is the wafer that is offered for the love of the mother. It is the forty days of lent, the weeping for a Tammuz. You may think I am speculating again but I am not.

Ezekiel 8 "And he said unto me, turn thee again, you shall see greater abominations than even these that they are doing, then he brought me to the doors of the gates of the Lord's house, which was towards the north, and behold there sat the women there weeping for Tamm."

This cultic worship that started in Babylon had already crept into the Jewish life. The women who were caught up in Baal worship were weeping in the 40 days of lent for Tammuz.

Jeremiah 44 "Then all the men which knew they had wives that burnt incense to other Gods, and all the women that stood by with a great multitude, even those that dwelt in Egypt, they answered Jeremiah"(they are trying to argue here) And he says, You are offering incense to the Queen of Heaven, the Mother Child and you are worshipping this Tammuz and you are burning incense and pouring out drink offerings to her and making wafers to worship here, why?"

And then Jeremiah answered and said, *"The Lord God could no longer bear this because of the evil of your doings and because of the abominations that you have committed and therefore your land will be desolate, a curse, without inhabitance to this day because you have burned incense and sinned to the Lord God because you were worshipping this Mother/ Child and even a Tammuz."*

These are the characteristics. Then the Ishtar celebration started and that is where you come up with Easter eggs. The Ishtar eggs were when they had them as a celebration. They would all get together and do their eggs. And then the virgins were sacrificed, and from what I understand it was at the request directly from leadership. I do not know the history of some of these churches. But it is not speculation. That was just two verses I picked out that mention Tammuz. The Mother/Child worship is an abomination to the Father. The Mother/Child worship that originated in Babylon is not dormant. Satan has had this mimic system, this false religious system, all the way through time until today. The trail of the snake is that they went from Babylon to Pergamos. Revelation 2 says that is where the seat of Satan is. They went from Pergamos to Rome by the way of the Tristians, who were lead by Julius Caesar (the first emperor of Rome). Then the succession there was when Rome fell, the Carmelite Monks kept it alive and they said that all the lead- maxims, and all the popes from then on, were the vicars of Christ. These people encouraged the Mother/Child relationship and it has never ended. So you are saying that the Catholic Church is a false religion? I am saying that this is the foundation. In the last days this apostate Christianity or false religion is not only included in this, but the ecumenical movement will go back to ride on this beast and it is false.

My grandfather received a letter from Rome when I was young, encouraging our church to join the mother church. It was our understanding that these letters were being sent everywhere. But there is a constant pressure of a worldwide religion. We are in the way. That is why there will be a rapture up to heaven, because we are in the way here. Man wants religion. Man does not care about a relationship, because he wants religion. And when the saints are taken out of the picture, there will be a mad dash to religion again. Man has an incurable disease that is a desire to worship something. When we are caught up to Christ they will run pell melll to this False Prophet and the religious system. This is the background which brings us to Revelation 17.

1And there came one of the seven angels which had the seven vials, and talked with me, saying unto me, Come hither; I will shew unto thee the judgment of the great whore that sitteth upon many waters:

This is very clear, bold language. He uses the Greek word *porna* and it is also where we get our word "pornography" from. Why does he call it this a great whore? Because this whore who is sitting on the beast is a false religious system, and it is committing spiritual fornication. It is wrong. You can trace this harlot or prostitute throughout Scripture and the connotation is always against God.

Isaiah 1:21 *"See, Jerusalem, how you were once faithful, that you have become a prostitute."*

Isaiah 23:15 *"And it shall come to pass in that day, that Tyre shall be forgotten seventy years, according to the days of one king: after the end of seventy years shall Tyre sing as an harlot."*

Jeremiah 13:27 *"I am keenly aware of all your adultery and lust and your abominable idol worship."*

Hosea 1:2 *"Go ahead and marry then a prostitute. This will illustrate the way that my people have been untrue to me openly committing adultery against the Lord by worshipping other gods."*

Are there people today that worship other gods? Yes. There are people today who worship this mother/child relationship and they actually pray to a mother. I am going to read one of the most popular Catholic prayers today:

"Oh Mother of Perpetual Help… in thy hands I place my eternal salvation, and to thee do I entrust all of my soul… For if thou protect me, dear Mother, I fear nothing; not from my sins, because thou wilt obtain for me the pardon for them; nor from the devils, because thou art more powerful than all hell together; nor even from Jesus, my Judge himself, because by one prayer from thee, He will be appeased. But one thing I fear; that in the hour of temptation, I may neglect to call on thee and thus perish miserably. Obtain for me, then, and pardon of my sins…"

No, No, No….we do not pray to a mother. We pray to God the Father through Jesus Christ, and He is the only pardon for our sins! This borders on cult worship.

Who is the woman on the many waters? It is the apostate system, which will be concentrated in Rome, in the End Times.

3So he carried me away in the spirit into the wilderness: and I saw a woman sit upon a scarlet colored beast, full of names of blasphemy, having seven heads and ten horns.

4And the woman was arrayed in purple and scarlet color, and decked with gold and precious stones and pearls, having a golden cup in her hand full of abominations and filthiness of her fornication:

5And upon her forehead was a name written, MYSTERY, BABYLON THE GREAT, THE MOTHER OF HARLOTS AND ABOMINATIONS OF THE EARTH.

Daniel talks about the abominations that come out of this cup. Now there are a lot of professing Christians today, people who profess to be Christians, and are not. There are wealthy religious systems who believe they are Christian. I have a friend in the Mormon Church who told me that they are proud of the wealth of their church. The Catholic Church is worth over 200 billion dollars today and that is a conservative estimate.

If you go down to Keto, Equator you will find a main Catholic church that is decorated with solid gold, yet the people are literally begging and starving out on the streets. This is a picture of a system that is so far from Christianity as far as Christ is concerned. John was astounded as he wrote this and as he saw this vision. Salvation is for sale today in professing Christianity.

Even during the days of lent, forty days, it is a different price. But if you commit murder, steal, commit fornication or adultery, there is a price tag that you pay to the church and it is forgiven. Regardless of what you do you are forgiven. Millions of dollars are made during lent for the sale of salvation. That is an abomination and filthiness in the sight of God. Men do not want to say wrong things about this system anymore because we have to show tolerance. I am sorry, do not defame the name of Christ with selling salvation. The Bible says that we are saved by grace through faith. You do not pay for it, and it is a free gift.

6And I saw the woman drunken with the blood of the saints and with the blood of the martyrs of Jesus: and when I saw her, I wondered with great admiration.

This can not be talking about ancient Babylon. There were no martyrs of Jesus in ancient Babylon. This can only be a prophetic statement of something in the future. Why does he make the difference between the two? It is because of the blood of the saints were the things that were taken in the name of this false religious system, which would be like the Inquisition and the blood of the martyrs of those who are dying for Christ. This religious system is killing people even during the tribulation. Here we go again. It is starting to happen again.

I read this statistic. In 1950 to 1960, there was an average of 7,000 to 10,000 people killed a year in the name of Christianity. In 1998 to the year 2000 there have been 300,000 people being slaughtered for Jesus. We do not see it in this country, but there are places all over the world suffering for Christ today and it will get worse.

This false religious system will do everything they can to get these people out of the way so that they can have their religion. Twenty million people were killed during the Inquisition. Religious people were killing Christians. In just Spain alone there were 300,000 people burned during a weekend at a stake because they would not recant their faith in Jesus. People were being called heretics because they would not come to the Mother Church.

7And the angel said unto me, Wherefore didst thou marvel? I will tell thee the mystery of the woman, and of the beast that carrieth her, which hath the seven heads and ten horns.

8The beast that thou sawest was, and is not; and shall ascend out of the bottomless pit, and go into perdition: and they that dwell on the earth shall wonder, whose names were not written in the book of life from the foundation of the world, when they behold the beast that was, and is not, and yet is.

This is the mystery of the woman and the beast that carried her. This is the false religious system, the false prophet, riding on top of the political realm, which is the Antichrist, and they are married. Didn't that start with Constantine being married with Rome, and the church and the state came together and they got married. That is why the Inquisition came and the Popes had enough power to kill anyone they wanted. 1195 AD the pope said that there is no one who has more power than all of the Popes. They claimed to rule over kings and countries. It is a false religious system. You can add any system that branches out of that together-Islamic faith, Mormonism, and many more. It is all false.

We have a riddle here as well. What does it mean? *The beast that was, and is not and yet is.* I believe that is a picture of John looking at the Antichrist. He *was* there during the first 3 ½ years, he *was not*, he was wounded through a mortal wound, and then somehow through a false resurrection he *yet is.* So he was, is not, and yet is.

Who are the seven heads? The Bible says that the seven heads are seven mountains on which the woman is seated. What city today is known for the seven hills? Rome. If you study Geography you will know that Aventine, Caelian, Capitoline, Esquiline, Palatine, Quirinal, and Viminal are these seven mountains where Rome is. This is where the Vatican is today. This false system's dominant factor is going to be in this city again. Peter says, "I am writing from Babylon or Rome." So how much more proof do you want?

Then it says she will have control over the kings and the nations. I find it interesting that there is only one religious system in the world today that has ambassadors that do not have a country. The Vatican is a separate entity. We send an ambassador from the United States to the Vatican and they send "something" to the United States, and all the countries do the same. In that sense it shows that there is an enormous power base there.

10And there are seven kings: five are fallen, and one is, and the other is not yet come; and when he cometh, he must continue a short space.

11And the beast that was, and is not, even he is the eighth, and is of the seven, and goeth into perdition.

This sounds like a riddle but it is not. There are two ways you can look at it. I lean a little more in this direction, that the seven heads are the seven kings, and five of them are already fallen. When John was writing this he was on the Isle of Patmos and he would look at these five kings that had already fallen: Julius Caesar, Tiberius, Caligula, Claudius, and Nero. One is Domitian in the day that John wrote this letter. One is to come and that is the Antichrist.

Another way to look at it is something I have mentioned before. The five world powers, Egypt, Babylon, Greece, Media-Persia, Assyria, and Rome, and Rome to come, which would be the revived Roman Empire. Either way it is an evil way.

12And the ten horns which thou sawest are ten kings, which have received no kingdom as yet; but receive power as kings one hour with the beast.

This is saying that when the Antichrist comes on the scene to rule over the European Common Market, the United Nations, he will be the ruler of all the World in that sense. So John is watching this woman, the harlot who is a false religious system, on the back of the beast, which is the Antichrist, and there are these heads. It shows where she is from and where they are at. When the beast comes to power there will be ten nations that he will be in control of. This will really be the "World Power Center."

I read the other day that on one of the paper Euro dollars, there is a picture of a woman riding a beast. I want to see it before I say for sure that that is right, but I find it very interesting if it is correct. It is interesting that people used to say there would never be a Euro dollar or a one world currency, but it is already there.

13These have one mind, and shall give their power and strength unto the beast.

14These shall make war with the Lamb, and the Lamb shall overcome them: for he is Lord of lords, and King of kings: and they that are with him are called, and chosen, and faithful.

They have one purpose and that is to worship Satan and to give power to the beast. They will follow whatever he says. This is in direct opposition to what the Apostle Paul said, *"This one thing I do, I press toward the mark and for the cause of the high calling of God in Christ Jesus!"* Not in some false religious system. He says, "I want to know more about Him and the power of His resurrection, not mother/child worship."

15And he saith unto me, The waters which thou sawest, where the whore sitteth, are peoples, and multitudes, and nations, and tongues.

16And the ten horns which thou sawest upon the beast, these shall hate the whore, and shall make her desolate and naked, and shall eat her flesh, and burn her with fire.

This world religious system is here today. The Antichrist and his ten kings will hate this prostitute. And all of a sudden they will eat her flesh and burn her with fire. In other words, in the last half of the tribulation period the Antichrist will turn on the False Prophet and the religious system. He will not need him anymore because he will claim to be god. He will rend her, and tear her, and kill her. Everything changes doesn't it? They will see for the first time that this is mother/child worship, and all this religion that they thought was right, will be wrong. Yes, it will happen. Verse 17 shows that God still has everything in control.

17For God hath put in their hearts to fulfil his will, and to agree, and give their kingdom unto the beast, until the words of God shall be fulfilled.

18And the woman which thou sawest is that great city, which reigneth over the kings of the earth.

Man wants his religion. Man is not really very interested in a relationship with Christ because with that there is accountability. Man wants religion because he likes to do things in an outward show, that he can prove that he is better than everyone else. That gives him some sort of satisfaction. It is all idolatry and spiritual fornication.

Let's look at some application for us today:

Beware of the seductive power of the world and religion. Things may look fair, but it is probably going to be foul when it is done in man's name. Physical things can be an abomination to God. Do not be seduced by the power of the world and the seductive power of religion. Christianity is a relationship with Christ. As you enter into that relationship with Christ and you look at His Word, He will direct you, lead you, comfort you, and give you exactly what you need for the moment. You do not need something out here to hold onto. You do not need a statue or something to help pay for your sins. You go to HIM!

Be prepared to face persecution in all kinds of unexpected avenues. Do you think you have it bad now? We all may see worse things in the days and years ahead. I think things are tightening up. In the 60s and 70s, it was popular to be a Christian. Everybody was a Christian. It is not popular to stand on the Word of God today. If you do not know that, then go spend a year in Indonesia. You probably won't make it back. I believe the persecution will become more intense as time goes on.

Rejoice that your name is written in heaven. The false religions on the planet today have no clue if they are saved or not. You can talk to Muslim's, you can talk to Catholics, or you can talk with Mormons. They have no clue if they are saved or not. I do not want anything to do with that kind of a religion. There is proof of this. There was a man who went to Spain and on the outskirts of Madrid. He interviewed 2,000 people. Two people out of 2,000 knew that they were saved. 1,998 had no clue what the Gospel was. They were astonished. It so unnerved this man that he is spending his time now with this as his mission field, to go to the people who are caught up in religion. These people think that if you pay enough or live a little bit better, then God may accept you or He may not. It is all in the balances. Would you like to live under that pressure or horror? I find it interesting that the highest suicide rate today is in Catholicism and Mormonism. Why is that? Because religion is oppressive. A relationship is awesome. When you understand your relationship with Him, then it is your reasonable service to live for Him.

Philippians says, *"Work out this salvation that you do have in this cup."* Work it out, be thankful for it, and be glad that your name is written in heaven. When you wake up you do not have to be worried about whether you are saved or not. Anything that takes that peace away from you is wrong.

I John 5 says "That I may *know*." That I may know, know, know, not guess. That I may know.

Faithfully follow Christ even when evil attacks. We get hounded with life and we have weaknesses in our lives. We get opposition and yet we still need to follow Christ faithfully. We do not follow after carnal things to do this. Paul in Corinthians says not to follow after carnal things but we take faith, prayer, Bible reading, love, Christ, and the Holy Spirit to faithfully follow Him. I do not need to go out and buy absolution and hang three more crosses around my neck and put some things on my car and then I feel back in shape. That is not faithfully following after Christ. We need to live for Him moment by moment as God guides your spirit. When there is wrong, we confess our sins. He is the one who is faithful and just, not a perpetual mother.

Christ is coming soon and His reign will be forever and ever. There is a hint of this in this chapter. It was mindful to me to remember that the best is yet to come. I have enjoyed my life in Christ. It has been fascinating. There are burdens with the blessings but when I know that the best is yet to come, it is overwhelming! But it gives me an incentive to keep pressing on. The best is yet to come!

Columbus came back from discovering America and sailed back into the quiet harbor in Spain. He could hardly get it out, and he just kept saying, "Oh it is so much better!" "It is so much better!" It got everyone excited because they too wanted to go see this New World that is so much better. Well, the best is yet to come. "**There is a land of pure delight where saints and mortals reign.**" That is where we are going. We have confidence in Him that He will carry us and take us to Himself someday!

17For God hath put in their hearts to fulfil his will, and to agree, and give their kingdom unto the beast, until the words of God shall be fulfilled.

18And the woman which thou sawest is that great city, which reigneth over the kings of the earth.

Revelation 18

Babylon is Fallen, is Fallen

1And after these things I saw another angel come down from heaven, having great power; and the earth was lightened with his glory.

2And he cried mightily with a strong voice, saying, Babylon the great is fallen, is fallen, and is become the habitation of devils, and the hold of every foul spirit, and a cage of every unclean and hateful bird.

3For all nations have drunk of the wine of the wrath of her fornication, and the kings of the earth have committed fornication with her, and the merchants of the earth are waxed rich through the abundance of her delicacies.

4And I heard another voice from heaven, saying, Come out of her, my people, that ye be not partakers of her sins, and that ye receive not of her plagues.

5For her sins have reached unto heaven, and God hath remembered her iniquities.

6Reward her even as she rewarded you, and double unto her double according to her works: in the cup which she hath filled fill to her double.

7How much she hath glorified herself, and lived deliciously, so much torment and sorrow give her: for she saith in her heart, I sit a queen, and am no widow, and shall see no sorrow.

8Therefore shall her plagues come in one day, death, and mourning, and famine; and she shall be utterly burned with fire: for strong is the Lord God who judgeth her.

9And the kings of the earth, who have committed fornication and lived deliciously with her, shall bewail her, and lament for her, when they shall see the smoke of her burning,

10Standing afar off for the fear of her torment, saying, Alas, alas that great city Babylon, that mighty city! for in one hour is thy judgment come.

11And the merchants of the earth shall weep and mourn over her; for no man buyeth their merchandise any more:

12The merchandise of gold, and silver, and precious stones, and of pearls, and fine linen, and purple, and silk, and scarlet, and all thyine wood, and all manner vessels of ivory, and all manner vessels of most precious wood, and of brass, and iron, and marble,

13And cinnamon, and odours, and ointments, and frankincense, and wine, and oil, and fine flour, and wheat, and beasts, and sheep, and horses, and chariots, and slaves, and souls of men.

14And the fruits that thy soul lusted after are departed from thee, and all things which were dainty and goodly are departed from thee, and thou shalt find them no more at all.

15The merchants of these things, which were made rich by her, shall stand afar off for the fear of her torment, weeping and wailing,

16And saying, Alas, alas that great city, that was clothed in fine linen, and purple, and scarlet, and decked with gold, and precious stones, and pearls!

17For in one hour so great riches is come to nought. And every shipmaster, and all the company in ships, and sailors, and as many as trade by sea, stood afar off,

18And cried when they saw the smoke of her burning, saying, What city is like unto this great city!

19And they cast dust on their heads, and cried, weeping and wailing, saying, Alas, alas that great city, wherein were made rich all that had ships in the sea by reason of her costliness! for in one hour is she made desolate.

20Rejoice over her, thou heaven, and ye holy apostles and prophets; for God hath avenged you on her.

21And a mighty angel took up a stone like a great millstone, and cast it into the sea, saying, Thus with violence shall that great city Babylon be thrown down, and shall be found no more at all.

22And the voice of harpers, and musicians, and of pipers, and trumpeters, shall be heard no more at all in thee; and no craftsman, of whatsoever craft he be, shall be found any more in thee; and the sound of a millstone shall be heard no more at all in thee;

23And the light of a candle shall shine no more at all in thee; and the voice of the bridegroom and of the bride shall be heard no more at all in thee: for thy merchants were the great men of the earth; for by thy sorceries were all nations deceived.

24And in her was found the blood of prophets, and of saints, and of all that were slain upon the earth.

Babylon is fallen, is fallen. This is not the angel stuttering. God's angels do not stutter. The reason he says it this way is because in verse two it says:

1And after these things I saw another angel come down from heaven, having great power; and the earth was lightened with his glory.

2And he cried mightily with a strong voice, saying, Babylon the great is fallen, is fallen, and is become the habitation of devils, and the hold of every foul spirit, and a cage of every unclean and hateful bird.

In other words, that is the collapse of the religious system. This is the collapse of the government. This is the collapse of the Antichrist and his political military. Everything comes crashing down. We understand that this whole world functions on money. If everything would collapse in one hour, then everything would collapse with it. That is what will happen here in the destruction of Babylon. In this chapter we will be finished with

Babylon, the seven dooms of Babylon, for it is finally come to an end. It is over!

We could rightfully say that the Bible is about Christ. The two major cities in this book are Babylon and Jerusalem. There are 260 verses in the Bible that mention Babylon. Everything about Babylon is bad. Jerusalem is good. This Bible will end in the New Jerusalem. Everything about Jerusalem is good. It is the tale of two cities. In 1859 Charles Dickens wrote the book the Tale of Two Cities. The book starts like this, "It was the best of times, it was the worst of times, it was the age of man's wisdom and the age of foolishness, it was the epic of belief and the epic of unbelief, it was the season of light, it was the season of darkness, it was the spring of hope and the winter of total despair. We had everything before us and we had nothing before us. We were all going up to heaven yet we were all going the other way." Charles Dickens could have paraphrased in his own words the tale of two cities. He was not writing about Babylon and Jerusalem but this is the tale of two cities. In this chapter we will see the destruction of Babylon.

The highway to hell and the people who lead the pack are people who are full of pride. Everything about Babylon is about pride and arrogance.

7How much she hath glorified herself, and lived deliciously, so much torment and sorrow give her: for she saith in her heart, I sit a queen, and am no widow, and shall see no sorrow.

"I sit as a queen." In other words, I am the mistress of the whole world. The Antichrist is in control of everything. He says he is on top of it all and he says that he is not a widow. He is not alone because all the kings are his lovers. Ever body on this planet will wander after this beast. He goes on with arrogance and pride, "I will never mourn." In other words, everything will turn out right and nothing is wrong with him.

Isaiah 47 *"For thou hast trusted in thy wickedness, you have said 'none seeth me', thy wisdom and thy knowledge, it perverts thee, thou hast said in thy heart there is no one like me. Therefore shall evil come upon thee and thou shalt not know from hence it riseth, and mischief shall come upon thee and thou shalt not be able to put it off and desolation shall come upon thee suddenly and you will not know it is happening."*

Isaiah is talking about Babylon. The Bible says that Babylon will be destroyed in a day or an hour. God is in control. **Proverbs 16:18 "Pride goeth before destruction and a haughty spirit before a fall."** This is the arrogance of the Antichrist and the people in the end times government and religion. God will blow the whistle and it will be over and Babylon will be destroyed.

Is it a system or a city? It does not really make any difference. Maybe Babylon is Rome, or maybe it will be rebuilt; but based on what we read in Isaiah, we know that it will never be inhabited. I know one thing, that for 1,700 years it has been a heap of sand there. For some reason God has allowed Iraq to be opened up to the world. It is like a can opener has come over and pried everything back. The entire world wants to come in there and get everything back together-United Nations, France, Germany and the United States. We do not know what will happen there, but we do know one thing. This system, whether it is a city or a government city, will be destroyed. It is going to be destroyed. It will be the destruction of humanism, it will be the destruction of the world system, and it will be the collapse of everything that we know of today that seems normal.

Some people have asked me recently about where the United States is in all of this. It is a good question that I have considered for a long time. My answer is that I do not know. But I want to suggest these three chapters for you to read and study. These passages are in Isaiah 18 and Jeremiah 50 & 51. That sure seems like the United States. It is like the prophet could be writing about the United States as you read those chapters. In a sense, we will be included in this. We will be a part of this Babylonian government and we will be supporting it as a nation.

Why is the judgement brought?

2And he cried mightily with a strong voice, saying, Babylon the great is fallen, is fallen, and is become the habitation of devils, and the hold of every foul spirit, and a cage of every unclean and hateful bird.

In the parables in Matthew 13, the birds are used as demons. The birds that come in the tree are not good. These demonic spirits will be lodging in the kingdom of the Antichrist.

3For all nations have drunk of the wine of the wrath of her fornication, and the kings of the earth have committed fornication with her, and

the merchants of the earth are waxed rich through the abundance of her delicacies.

Why is judgement brought? Judgement is brought because of her sin and iniquities. It is like the Lord shows them that when Babylon was first built, they tried brick by brick to build a tower and it did not work. So God says, "I will take all their sins for the last 6,000 years brick by brick, and I will make them all collapse because of their sin and iniquity." Babylon will be destroyed because of her iniquity. And her sins have piled up higher and higher, and she has become a home for demons.

4And I heard another voice from heaven, saying, Come out of her, my people, that ye be not partakers of her sins, and that ye receive not of her plagues.

Why would John write this? This is what you could call primary and secondary application. Primary application to those who are living, is to not be a part of that system, not to accept the Mark of the Beast, and to get away from Babylon. Secondary application is that he is looking down with a telescope at you and I today. Do not be a part of the Babylonian system, materialism, humanism, or any part of it. Be separated to God, because if you are not, then you will collapse with this Empire. It will be judged. This is an ungodly world full of wickedness. In James it says to "weep and howl you rich men." He is not talking specifically to those who have large bank accounts. He is talking about people who are only trusting in riches. Weep because it will all collapse with you. This will be happening in the last days with Babylon. If you do not have time for God, then God will not have any time for you and He will bring judgement.

Babylon represents everything opposite from God. From Genesis 10 unto today, everything about Babylon is in opposition to God. God says "no more."

5For her sins have reached unto heaven, and God hath remembered her iniquities.

6Reward her even as she rewarded you, and double unto her double according to her works: in the cup which she hath filled fill to her double.

7How much she hath glorified herself, and lived deliciously, so much torment and sorrow give her: for she saith in her heart, I sit a queen, and am no widow, and shall see no sorrow.

8Therefore shall her plagues come in one day, death, and mourning, and famine; and she shall be utterly burned with fire: for strong is the Lord God who judgeth her.

Some people believe this is talking about New York City and the Twin Towers collapsing in one hour. New York City may play a part of the Babylonian system at the end of times, but this is not specifically talking about New York City here.

She will be judged for her infidelity. All the way down through time, they have always looked at life from an earthly perspective. It is always about what *I* want to do. It is *my* way, it is the pride of what *I* have accomplished. In Daniel chapter 4, Nebuchadnezzar said "nothing is like my Babylon." Nothing is like Babylon and that is why God will bring judgement. The Antichrist will say the exact same thing, "Is this not a great kingdom that I have built? I am god now." At this point the dooms of Babylon begin to start. It will be devoid of life, burned with fire, it will be destroyed in one hour. People will be fearful to enter it. Riches are brought to nothing and violently they are overthrown, and all activity in the Antichrist's kingdom ceases to exist.

Christ Jesus will intervene and place His feet upon the Mount of Olives. There will be a great earthquake and everything will be over for the Antichrist and his kingdom. It is all over.

9And the kings of the earth, who have committed fornication and lived deliciously with her, shall bewail her, and lament for her, when they shall see the smoke of her burning,

10Standing afar off for the fear of her torment, saying, Alas, alas that great city Babylon, that mighty city! for in one hour is thy judgment come.

11And the merchants of the earth shall weep and mourn over her; for no man buyeth their merchandise any more:

12The merchandise of gold, and silver, and precious stones, and of pearls, and fine linen, and purple, and silk, and scarlet, and all thyine wood, and all manner vessels of ivory, and all manner vessels of most precious wood, and of brass, and iron, and marble,

13And cinnamon, and odours, and ointments, and frankincense, and wine, and oil, and fine flour, and wheat, and beasts, and sheep, and horses, and chariots, and slaves, and souls of men.

14And the fruits that thy soul lusted after are departed from thee, and all things which were dainty and goodly are departed from thee, and thou shalt find them no more at all.

I could only find one thing that is a necessity. This is what this Empire and final government has become. Everything is about show. Everything is about money and impressing someone. Everything in their life is about merchandise for higher and downing somebody else. Everything is about oppression. It says even to the point that they will be selling people. That is truly amazing. They will be selling the slaves and souls of men.

Think about the slave markets during the Roman times and the Civil War days. Babylon will be judged because of her inhuman ways and her treatment of humanity. Why would it talk about slaves here? Because when you do not believe there is a God, then the soul and body of a man is just a commodity. If you think you came out of a frog or something or you were a part of a monkey, then you are not really worth anything anyway, so why not be sold. This is the type of an atmosphere that is here. No one will care about life or people. If you could go back to the last days during the Babylonian times it is just like 'yellow pages'. The 'yellow pages' of Babylon is like a direct parallel of Ezekiel 27, full of jewelry of gold and silver and stones. Everyone will be into the fine linen, the clothing stores, the fancy wood and ivory, the furniture stores, decorating stores of marble, perfumes of cinnamon and spices, the fancy foods, animal stores, the slave markets, and the bodies and souls of men. Everything here will come crashing down in one hour.

During the Stock Market Crash in the 20s, I was not living yet. But I do remember black Monday in October in the 70's when they had a 500-point drop in the Market, and it scared everyone. But if you would have all the financial markets collapse in one hour across this planet, everything would come to a screeching halt. Obviously God is in control, but God who is in control is the one who pushes this over the edge by way of judgement. God brings judgement on the jewelry store, and the clothing store. He brings judgment on all of this because that is what they are focused on. They do not care about Him.

In one place He says that when man has wealth, he tends to forget God. The whole system of the Antichrist is not about Jesus Christ. So God says, "No more!" And Babylon will fall and judgement will come.

Think about the reaction of these people. You can laugh, but it is not laughable. If you think about everyone in the world here as it comes crashing down, do you think there will be anarchy? Yes there will be. I believe this whole planet will be so mad that they will turn on the Antichrist and they will go the valley of Armageddon just to fight God or anyone, because everything they knew as god is not there any more. They will be furious.

Let's imagine that the financial markets of America collapse next week and everything comes to a halt. Then all of the sudden all the doors are locked at Save Marts and all stores. Do you think there would be a traffic jam from the Bay Area to the Valley? Why would they want to come to the valley? Because people will do anything to eat. People will go anywhere to find food. And in a larger way, the same thing will happen here right before the battle of Armageddon. The whole planet will be furious.

14 and thou shalt find them no more at all.

21 Babylon be thrown down, and shall be found no more at all.

22 And the voice of harpers, and musicians, and of pipers, and trumpeters, shall be heard no more at all in thee; and no craftsman, of whatsoever craft he be, shall be found any more in thee; and the sound of a millstone shall be heard no more at all in thee;

23 and the voice of the bridegroom and of the bride shall be heard no more at all in thee:

Six times as a reminder, as an echo, God brings judgment. Then He says six times that none of this will be found any more and it vanishes forever. The delights of this evil system are now over! It is finished! No more at all in thee! Everything that was trusted in on the planet is over before your eyes. It is a wonderful description to me of the judgement of God. He takes away everything that man has trusted in and it has all come to collapse. Now it is over!

<u>Notice the reactions.</u>

9And the kings of the earth, who have committed fornication and lived deliciously with her, shall bewail her, and lament for her, when they shall see the smoke of her burning,

10Standing afar off for the fear of her torment, saying, Alas, alas that great city Babylon, that mighty city! for in one hour is thy judgment come.

11And the merchants of the earth shall weep and mourn over her; for no man buyeth their merchandise any more:

17For in one hour so great riches is come to nought. And every shipmaster, and all the company in ships, and sailors, and as many as trade by sea, stood afar off,

18And cried when they saw the smoke of her burning, saying, What city is like unto this great city!

They are weeping, they are not repenting. They are furious and so God will lead them into this valley for one final battle. That is a very sad picture of humanity. It is very troubling. It shows that man makes a decision. The Bible says that man is in the valley of decision. We all make decisions. The decisions you make today and in this life are decisions of where you spend eternity.

It is the same for all these millions or billions of people left here. The kings are mourning because everything they depended on is gone. The merchants are crying because the millions are gone. It is over for all the great seaports of the world. The boats stop here. Think about all the great harbors in Tokyo, San Francisco, Los Angeles, and London. Iit is over and the anchors are dropped and there is nothing else happening.

You can see in Isaiah, Jeremiah, Daniel, and Ezekiel, that everything about prophesy is all brought to a head in Revelation 18. There is chapter after chapter of warning to Babylon. It says in Isaiah 13 that Babylon is fallen, is fallen. Everything comes to a halt in Revelation 18 and all prophesies are fulfilled.

Meanwhile back in heaven with the Lord we are there with Christ.

20Rejoice over her, thou heaven, and ye holy apostles and prophets; for God hath avenged you on her.

All the prayers that have been prayed through the ages are being answered here. Be grateful because our Lord has brought judgement. In Habakkuk it says, "How long O Lord are you going to wait?" David says in the Psalms, "How long O Lord are you going to bring judgement." God takes all of these prayers to a vocal point and He says to rejoice because He has brought judgement. This system is all over now and Satan will be chained.

21And a mighty angel took up a stone like a great millstone, and cast it into the sea, saying, Thus with violence shall that great city Babylon be thrown down, and shall be found no more at all.

In the Old Testament there is this millstone. For some reason God is going to take this millstone and slam it down into the sea and say, "Thus with violence shall that great city Babylon be thrown down, and shall be found no more at all." He says, "You want to see destruction? Then I will show you destruction. I will take this and throw it so hard that you won't even be able to find it any more. It will be total destruction. Judgement!"

4And I heard another voice from heaven, saying, Come out of her, my people, that ye be not partakers of her sins, and that ye receive not of her plagues.

I like to think that there are some, even in the last hour, like the thief of the cross, who cry out to God when they began to see the collapse. I trust that there are.

This verse is for us today. We are called and chosen. If you are separated unto God, then do not go back into Babylonian things. If you go back to the early church, what were they doing? The Bible says in Acts 5:42 that they were doing everything they could to preach and teach Jesus Christ crucified. The result of that was that it turned the whole world upside down. So here we are in 2010. We have the same Word of God and the same Holy Spirit within us. Are we turning the world upside down?

Notice the change, and the strength, and how subtle this system works. I can read my Bible for a half-hour a day and then I set it aside. Now I can spend the rest of my waking hours doing things I enjoy: my work, my family, my projects. There is nothing wrong with these; but if all of my focus is now about me and my things, then I have completely flip-flopped from the early church. You see, they could never get enough of Him. Then why is it in the day and age that we live in that I can never get enough of all of this "stuff?" We are inflicted a little. Can you honestly answer right now that you cannot get enough of the Bible? Or can you not get enough of everything out there? Money is not sin, it is the focus on it and my desire for it. The challenge to us is to make sure that we can't get enough of the Word. Paul said in Philippians, "This one thing I do. I press towards the mark and for the prize." Does that mean he gave up on his job? No. He still made tents and did the work of the church. But his focus was on Him.

We are living at the end of time. We need to spend time with Christ and our life needs to be about Him; because if it is all about this, then it will all go up in smoke.

Here is an easy equation. I want to invest my life, my faith, and my trust in things that last. Jewelry and clothing stores aren't going to last. Furniture stores are going to burn up. The food stores are not going to last. The animal stores aren't going to last and the slave markets aren't going to last. What is going to last? You and the Bible. I suggest that you invest in Him and each other and to those of the household of faith. That is how you lay up treasures in heaven. If I am so caught up in myself and my 401k, then it won't last. When I become older in life, will I have any disappointment that I didn't spend more time on eternal things? Make a conscience choice when you wake up in the morning that life is about Him and loving others. It makes all the difference.

Everything we see in life today is temporary.

Determine in your own heart the ways that you are too close in alliance with the Babylonian culture of the world today: the religious system, the government, or whatever it is. You know your own heart what you struggle with.

This may not come; but if it does, be willing to pay the price of martyrdom if you are persecuted in any way. I do not think we will go through the tribulation period. Maybe your persecution in America is affluence. It may be something else. We are not free from persecution. But maybe it will come to martyrdom. There are people physically dying today for the cause of Christ. Be willing to pay the price for Christ.

Rejoice that God is in control because someday Babylon will be judged.

This is the tale of two cities, Babylon and Jerusalem.

There is the story of a man who made a choice. Martin Luther King lived in the 17th century and he made a statement that shocked people. "Men, I have decided to leave the city because I am coming out of the *system*." That not only meant the Vatican, but it also meant the Roman Catholicism.

We may have things we struggle with today, but this same Holy Spirit is still alive today. Just because we are Christians doesn't mean we won't be confronted with temptations. He is still alive. Martin Luther also wrote, *"I stand convicted by the Bible and scripture alone because my spirit is captive by His Word and then I can do nothing else."*

I do not want to compromise with this world system. My focus is Jesus Christ and Him crucified. The key is that we keep Him first; because when the final curtain falls on this planet, there will only be one city that remains, and that is the city that you want to go into, the New Jerusalem.

REVELATION 19:1-10
Wedding Bells in Heaven

1 And after these things I heard a great voice of much people in heaven, saying, Alleluia; Salvation, and glory, and honor, and power, unto the Lord our God:

2 For true and righteous are his judgments: for he hath judged the great whore, which did corrupt the earth with her fornication, and hath avenged the blood of his servants at her hand.

3 And again they said, Alleluia And her smoke rose up for ever and ever.

4 And the four and twenty elders and the four beasts fell down and worshipped God that sat on the throne, saying, Amen; Alleluia.

5 And a voice came out of the throne, saying, Praise our God, all ye his servants, and ye that fear him, both small and great.

6 And I heard as it were the voice of a great multitude, and as the voice of many waters, and as the voice of mighty thunderings, saying, Alleluia: for the Lord God omnipotent reigneth.

7 Let us be glad and rejoice, and give honor to him: for the marriage of the Lamb is come, and his wife hath made herself ready.

8 And to her was granted that she should be arrayed in fine linen, clean and white: for the fine linen is the righteousness of saints.

9 And he saith unto me, Write, Blessed are they which are called unto the marriage supper of the Lamb. And he saith unto me, These are the true sayings of God.

10 And I fell at his feet to worship him. And he said unto me, See thou do it not: I am thy fellowservant, and of thy brethren that have the testimony of Jesus: worship God: for the testimony of Jesus is the spirit of prophecy.

Wedding Bells in Heaven!

We are now making a transition from gloom to glory. We have been talking about catastrophic, mournful, gloomy, and raging wars going on in the book of Revelation. Now we are going to switch from **gloom to glory**. Even though there will be a war in chapter 19, it really is just about Christ coming back again, and that is glory!

We see the four and twenty elders mentioned again because they are the bride and bridegroom.

Fredrick Handle wrote the *Messiah* in the 18th century. In the *Messiah*, one of the crescendos that he has towards the end is what we call the Hallelujah Chorus. When you hear that, it is impossible not to be caught up into that climatic ending when they are singing, Alleluia, Alleluia! And here in chapter 19, we have for the only time in the book of Revelation and the only time in the New Testament, that the word *Alleluia* shows up. It shows up four times in this chapter. You will find it nowhere else in the New Testament and only twenty-two times in the Old Testament. I believe the Holy Spirit is saving this great word for the language of all men to praise Jehovah for this time when we finally come face to face with Christ and we say Alleluia, Alleluia, Alleluia Amen! There are only two words in all the 150 nations on this planet that every kindred, every nation, every tribe, and every tongue understand it, and the two words are Alleluia, Amen!

There is the story of the black man who spoke a different language. He was on a cruise ship and he bumped into a white man on his walk one morning. He had a Bible in his hand and the black man had a Bible in his hand as they passed each other. The white man began to say something, but they didn't speak the same language. The black man tried to say something. Yet neither of them could understand each other. Then the white man said, "*Alleluia!*" And the black man said, "*Amen!*"

1 And after these things I heard a great voice of much people in heaven, saying, Alleluia; Salvation, and glory, and honor, and power, unto the Lord our God:

2 For true and righteous are his judgments: for he hath judged the great whore, which did corrupt the earth with her fornication, and hath avenged the blood of his servants at her hand.

3 And again they said, Alleluia And her smoke rose up for ever and ever.

4 And the four and twenty elders and the four beasts fell down and worshipped God that sat on the throne, saying, Amen; Alleluia.

5 And a voice came out of the throne, saying, Praise our God, all ye his servants, and ye that fear him, both small and great.

6 And I heard as it were the voice of a great multitude, and as the voice of many waters, and as the voice of mighty thunderings, saying, Alleluia: for the Lord God omnipotent reigneth.

Verses 1-6 reveal the praise that belong to God alone. It would be my understanding that these special words *Alleluia, Alleluia* are saved for this great moment when Christ comes to receive us home. We respond that way. Notice that three groups of people are responding with this kind of praise. The great multitude, the four and twenty elders, and the bondservants.

Who are they? The great multitude are the tribulation saints who died as martyrs during that terrible seven years. Those who did not receive the mark died for Christ and they are here now saying "Alleluia, Salvation, Glory, Honor, and Power!"

The Church who were raptured in Revelation chapter 4, the four and twenty elders who are seated there, the entire body of Christ are saying, "Alleluia," because of the redemption that they received. The bondservants were the Old Testament saints, the prophets, the priests, and the kings. They too are saying, "Alleluia! For the Lord God omnipotent reigneth". Praise ye Jehovah.

I believe there are seven major descriptions of you and I in the Word of God in relationship with our Savior.

1) The sheep and the Shepherd. John 10
2) The Vine and the branches. John 15
3) The Cornerstone and the building stone. Ephesians 2
4) The High Priest and the kingdom of priests. I Peter 2
5) The Head and the body. Ephesians
6) The Last Adam and the new creations. Romans 5
7) The bride and the Bridegroom. Revelation 19

Do you see what has happened here from the beginning of Revelation? All the focus of the world and it is doing its thing with the Antichrist and the False Prophet. They are funneling down to the final climatic end. You have the body of Christ, the Church, the tribulation saints, and now we are going on and we are coming to our end, but it is glory! It is not gloom, it is praise. It is not hardship and death forever. They are meeting here in Revelation 19. The two great scenes of this book are ready to unfold. It is a wedding, it is a war, and it is a division forever. After this chapter, the choices you make and the decision you make will make the difference of where you spend the rest of your eternity.

I woke early this morning and I thought about that. I remembered that song that says, "Where will you be a million years from now? Will you be happy or will you be singing while ages roll throughout all of eternity. I ask the question, where are you going to be?"

Revelation 19 says that if you are not at the wedding that will go on into the millennium, then you will be somewhere waiting for the great White Throne Judgment. You do not want to be at the great White Throne Judgment. You want to be at the wedding. When I think of the awesome opportunity that Christ has given to us through faith alone, and because of the marvelous grace of God that we can go to be a part of this praise and Alleluia chorus, it is amazing! It is amazing what praise does!

What does praise do for you? I have an inclination to dwell on problems. Where does that get me? Absolutely nowhere. So does that mean I should forget about problems? No, I should still meet the problems and solve them. But if I would dwell more on praise, then it would enable to me deal with problems easier.

Those who died martyrs for Christ and those who are suffering right now for the cause of Christ, every single one of them is singing, "Alleluia Amen!"

What is this praise about? It says in verse one that it is salvation, glory, honor, and power unto the Lord our God.

When is the last time that you personally have praised the Lord for your salvation? When is the last time that you have praised God for the glory that the Holy Spirit can reveal through your earthly vessel? When is the last time you have thought about honor and glory for Him? We have an inclination to think about the man, but God says He created us for one reason. We are created to give Him praise and honor and glory.

II Corinthians 4:6, *"To give the light of the knowledge of the glory of God in the face of His son Jesus Christ."* That is why we are here. We are here to give glory to God. That is why everyone in the world was created, to have fellowship with the Father and praise Him. But if it is all about 'self' then we are going in the wrong direction and we will miss the wonder and glory we can have with Him.

As we stand before the Bridegroom, we will be singing to the top of our lungs saying, "Alleluia," because of the salvation, the severity, the sovereignty, and the supremacy of our God. It will roll on and roll on and roll on throughout eternity.

Stories about the Trip I just took to Uganda.

They had an amazing time of praise and worship. It is tiring because of the energy they spend in their praise time! They are not just putting it on. They are singing with their eyes closed to the top of their lungs to the Lord. It was a glimpse of something like we will see in eternity with hundreds of millions of people with the same attitude giving praise and worship to the King.

7 Let us be glad and rejoice, and give honor to him: for the marriage of the Lamb is come, and his wife hath made herself ready.

8 And to her was granted that she should be arrayed in fine linen, clean and white: for the fine linen is the righteousness of saints.

This is a description of the bride. I believe the church, which is the greatest asset on the earth today, is the most precious object to our Savior Jesus. You can talk about galaxies and many amazing things on this planet; but when it comes down to it, the most precious thing to our Savior is His bride the church.

One of the girls (on my trip to Uganda) was leading worship one morning. Then she began to pray. I love to hear them pray in other countries. We all pray to the same God, but everyone prays a little different. This girl kept on saying "Oh precious King of Glory!" over and over in her prayer. It was thrilling! For the rest of the day I wanted to think about my King of Glory! Her prayer made me want to praise the Lord. Here is a member of the body of Christ looking for the Bridegroom!

The Bible says the bride is not only ready, but she is robed. And not only is the bride robed, but she is rejoicing. That is a beautiful picture of the bride of Christ. Then the Bridegroom comes!

What are the beauty treatments that are involved as the bride gets ready for an earthly wedding? I have no clue. But there are many things that go into a woman getting ready for her wedding. There is something so beautiful about a bride coming out to her groom at her wedding. All the focus and attention is on the bride. We have it all mixed up. But in Asian customs and in this picture here in Revelation that is not how it happens. The focus will not be on us, but it is on the Bridegroom.

Here we have the beauty treatments that have prepared us for this wedding.

1) **Redemption.** (Romans 3) When He clothes us (Isaiah 61) He cleanses us with His righteousness. That is redemption. You will not get any cleaner in preparation for a spiritual wedding than having redemption through the blood of Jesus at Calvary. Since I have lived for 59 years, I have taken 23,500 showers! It didn't help clean my heart at all. The only thing that ever cleansed me, and has me ready for this special wedding to come is the cleansing of the blood of Christ on Calvary. That redemption is what got me ready for this wedding. That is called *Imputed Righteousness.* (Romans 4:5) All of this righteousness was imputed unto me when I placed my faith in Him.

2) **Rapture.** I believe the Rapture has gotten us ready for the wedding. Revelation chapter 4 says we are caught up. Thessalonians says we shall all be changed in the moment in the twinkling of an eye. When that trumpet sounds, we will go to the judgement seat of Christ, ushered into the wedding, and then we will have the marriage feast.

3) **Rewards dressing treatment**. It says the *righteousness of the saints.* This is talking about the deeds done in the body on planet earth. Your

imputed righteousness, which is redemption, is a free gift, salvation. But imparted righteousness when there is a divine inflow producing human overflow that wants you to live a good life for Him. That is the fine linen, the righteousness of the saints. That is why He says not to be ashamed at His coming. There are people who will be saved by fire that will not have a lot to offer Him. He will take care of all of that. But we think in human terms. He wants us to follow Him and live for Him because someday there will be a reward. And when we are on our honeymoon for a thousand years and you rule and reign with Him, you will not have to be ashamed.

I had someone ask me one time about what good work they could do. The greatest work is **belief.** Followed with that is a list of works in Romans 12 and Titus 2 and I Timothy 3. You could get a whole list from the Bible of good deeds to do.

In my parents home when I was young there was a picture of the marriage supper table and you can see it go on into infinity. I used to look at that picture and wonder. But someday it will happen and we will be with Him and He will receive us.

I did a little side study of a Jewish wedding. There are three major things that go on in a Jewish wedding: 1.There is a day when the bridegroom will come to the house to take the young woman to his house. 2.There is a seven-day period where there is a supper prepared for the bride & bridegroom.

3. There is a seven-day feast following the supper.

Think how this is going to happen to us. We are in an engagement period right now. The Bible says that in Ephesians. In I Peter 2 it says, "I have never met Him, but by an eye of faith I can see Him. I know He is coming again." He is my bridegroom. When He comes, then He will take me to His house. John 14, "In my Father's house are many mansions... I am going to prepare a place for you and I will come again..." That will happen via the rapture. Then after the wedding, which I believe will take place during the tribulation period, there will be a supper and a feast that was go on for a thousand years. Remember a thousand years is one day and one day is as a thousand years.

The dowry has already been paid for. You are His and you are chosen.

9 And he saith unto me, Write, Blessed are they which are called unto the marriage supper of the Lamb. And he saith unto me, These are the true sayings of God.

There will be guests there. A bride is not a guest at a wedding. A bride is a chosen individual by the bridegroom and is not a guest. We are the bride of Christ and we are going to a wedding with our bridegroom, and there will be guests there. Saints of all the ages, tribulation saints, Old Testament saints. Does that mean in eternity we are going to be different? No. But during this moment in time, there is a difference. But on into eternity, the new heaven and new earth, we will all be together with Him. For some reason, as much as God chose Israel, Christ has chosen you, the church, and He will come to take us home. Someday we will be with Him.

10   And I fell at his feet to worship him. And he said unto me, See thou do it not: I am thy fellowservant, and of thy brethren that have the testimony of Jesus: worship God: for the testimony of Jesus is the spirit of prophecy.

"And I fell at his feet to worship him." This is John.

One of the most stressful things about a wedding is that everyone wants it to go right. If you are involved in a wedding you want it to be perfect. But at this one we see John so caught up with the excitement of all of this that he turns to the nearest angel he can find and bows down to worship him. Now that is a big blunder. You do not worship angels. Our praise and worship should be directed to God. *"For the testimony of Jesus is the spirit of prophecy."* In John 4:24 it says we are going to worship Him in spirit and in truth.

My first inclination is to worship me. I get self-centered instead of thinking first about Him. This is what happened to John here.

There are so many times when we fall down in life and worship the wrong things. Priority should be on Him. We need to worship God first. I like the song that says, "Turn your eyes upon Jesus and look full into His wonderful face. And the things of this world will grow strangely dim, in the light of His glory and grace." Turn your eyes upon Jesus.

As I looked at these ten verses, I found something very exciting. Not one word is mentioned about the inanimate objects of a wedding. Nothing is mentioned about what is on the table. Nothing is said about what is in the background behind the people standing there. It is all about Him. It is all about worshiping Him. It is all about the Bridegroom. I believe when we get there it will be the same thing for us because we will be awed when we see the believers from all the ages. We will be awed when we see glory and heaven and the singing. But when we see HIM!!! I can't put it into words what will be expressed when we say our Alleluias!

My wife and I often get invitations in the mail and they all have RSVP on them. It is a French phrase meaning "Respond if you would please". There has been a loving invitation from the cross of Calvary for 2000 years. You take any of Christ's words that He said on the cross, and it is a loving invitation that has gone out to everyone. "Come unto me!" That is what Christ is saying for these 2000 years. "Come unto me!" He is asking for a response. He is saying that you do not have to dress up or live better. "Just come to me and let me live a life in you. I can change you and that others may respond to the RSVP in a right way."

If you concentrate on the problems in your life, you will miss out on what it is like to praise Him. You know what I am talking about. If the majority of my life is concentrated on trouble, I will miss out on the praise. If that is happening in your life, stop. You can open the Word of God and praise Him. Just thank Him for His salvation, honor, praise, and glory.

Prepare for His coming. That will be characterized in your life by living with biblical principles and standards. The Word of God says to love your neighbor as yourself. The Bible says to let the peace of God rule in your hearts. Let the peace of God flow in your hearts. Romans 12. Let your life be characterized by a biblical life and prepare yourself for a wedding.

Can you answer these questions in Elisha Hoffman's song? You have to answer it. If you do not answer it, then you have answered it. "Have you been to Jesus for the cleansing power? Are you washed in the blood of the Lamb? Are you fully trusting in His grace this hour? Are you washed in the blood of the Lamb? Are you walking daily by the Savior's side? Are you washed in the blood of the Lamb? Do you rest each moment in the crucified? Are you washed in the blood of the Lamb?"

There is only one individual who can answer that and that is you.

Every opportunity we have to reign with Him is right there. How far away is salvation? About nine inches, from the head to the heart. You know what your response is. You want to be at that feast. If you respond in faith, believing on Christ Jesus at the foot of the cross, then you will be washed in the blood of the Lamb.

Revelation 19:11-21

The Second Coming of Jesus Christ

11And I saw heaven opened, and behold a white horse; and he that sat upon him was called Faithful and True, and in righteousness he doth judge and make war.

12His eyes were as a flame of fire, and on his head were many crowns; and he had a name written, that no man knew, but he himself.

13And he was clothed with a vesture dipped in blood: and his name is called The Word of God.

14And the armies which were in heaven followed him upon white horses, clothed in fine linen, white and clean.

15And out of his mouth goeth a sharp sword, that with it he should smite the nations: and he shall rule them with a rod of iron: and he treadeth the winepress of the fierceness and wrath of Almighty God.

16And he hath on his vesture and on his thigh a name written, KING OF KINGS, AND LORD OF LORDS.

17And I saw an angel standing in the sun; and he cried with a loud voice, saying to all the fowls that fly in the midst of heaven, Come and gather yourselves together unto the supper of the great God;

18That ye may eat the flesh of kings, and the flesh of captains, and the flesh of mighty men, and the flesh of horses, and of them that sit on them, and the flesh of all men, both free and bond, both small and great.

19And I saw the beast, and the kings of the earth, and their armies, gathered together to make war against him that sat on the horse, and against his army.

20And the beast was taken, and with him the false prophet that wrought miracles before him, with which he deceived them that had received the mark of the beast, and them that worshipped his image. These both were cast alive into a lake of fire burning with brimstone.

21And the remnant were slain with the sword of him that sat upon the horse, which sword proceeded out of his mouth: and all the fowls were filled with their flesh.

Isaiah 63:1-4

"Who is this that cometh from Edom, with dyed garments from Bozrah? This that is glorious in his apparel, travelling in the greatness of his strength? I that speak in righteousness, mighty to save. Wherefore art thou red in thine apparel, and thy garments like him that treadeth in the winefat? I have trodden the winepress alone; and of the people there was none with me: for I will tread them in mine anger, and trample them in my fury; and their blood shall be sprinkled upon my garments, and I will stain all my raiment. For the day of vengeance is in mine heart, and the year of my redeemed is come."

The Second Coming of Jesus Christ! This is the most thrilling event in all of human history! There is nothing comparable on earth to what it will be like to witness the return of Jesus Christ. It is the most thrilling event that will ever take place on this planet. One of the most dramatic passages in the Bible is in Revelation 19 when He comes again! Today I would like to make a distinction between the two phases of His Second Coming.

The Second Coming takes place immediately after the tribulation. (Matthew 24) There are all kinds of things that will occur in the sun, moon, and the stars. Heaven will open and all eyes will see Him when He comes at the Second Coming. Christ will be followed by the armies of heaven including you, Old Testament saints, and the tribulation saints. Christ will come in power and great glory. Christ will stand at the Mount of Olives. The Beast and his armies will confront Christ at the Second Coming. Unbelievers will mourn because they are not ready and Christ will cast the Beast and the False Prophet into the lake of fire. There is nothing that will ever equal the Second Coming of Jesus Christ. Why do we say that? Because all the dreams and all the hopes and all the desires that have ever been in the breast of anyone who truly loves God will finally be realized when He comes again! It will be the most dramatic scene that will ever be witnessed.

I had a terrible disease when I was twelve years old. It was a strange disease. It most definitely had a cure, but it was horrible in this sense. It only took place at 8:00 a.m. on a Sunday morning. All of the sudden, I was deathly sick on these Sunday mornings. It happened when everyone was getting ready for church. One Sunday morning when my mom came in to take my temperature it read 108 degrees! I got a little worried that she might call the ambulance. When you have a temperature of 108 degrees you are ready for the funeral home. Oh I was moaning and groaning. Now it was 108 degrees, because I rubbed the thing at the end of the thermometer between my fingers as hard as I could! I tried it last night and it still works!!! So I did get to stay home that first Sunday. Then the next Sunday when it cropped up again, at the awful degrees of 105, I think my parents were wise to it. But there was something else fascinating about this disease. It only lasted about three hours max! All of the sudden when everyone came home from church, I was ready to play, and I was ready to eat.

Now when Sunday comes, I get up early! I look forward to a Bible study before church. Then I look forward to going to church to hear the Word of God preached. I look forward to the fellowship with believers, and it has been that way for many years now. What changed? What took Peter, a man that lied, cursed and denied Christ, to the point that he was crucified for Christ? What changed in his life? What took the Apostle Paul, a man who cursed Christ and slaughtered Christians, to the point where he turned the world upside down with the gospel of Christ? What changed in his life? Why did the early Christians turn the world upside down? There is one answer. In that answer is a mix of what we are studying here in Revelation.

When a man is born again in the Spirit of God, it doesn't relieve him of his troubles. But it does place within him a spirit and a hope and a dream of a desire to see Him who saved Him. When I came to the foot of the cross in August of 1967, everything changed in my life. There has been one thing that has been an incentive for me in my walk with Christ and one thing that has changed so that I do not rub a thermometer anymore. It is that I know that He is coming again!

I do not care where I am. There is something about the knowledge within me that my Savior is coming again that radically changes my life. He is coming again.

I would have loved to have been there with John as he wrote this down. I counted about six times that you can see that he knows that he is witnessing something that he hasn't seen yet. He says six times "I saw, I saw, I saw, I saw, I saw, I saw." John is excited and I am excited with him.

11And I saw heaven opened, and behold a white horse; and he that sat upon him was called Faithful and True, and in righteousness he doth judge and make war.

Did you know that the triumphal return of Jesus Christ in this book gives us many snapshots of who our Savior really is. We will see Him coming in a cloud of great glory and we will be with Him.

And I saw heaven opened. To me, this makes the separation of this Second Coming and the rapture. Two times in the book of Revelation, one in chapter 4 *I saw heaven open*, and now finally again here in Revelation 19. Heaven is opened again, but he is not asking John to come up any more. He is asking to let Jesus out that he might come with Him to the earth.

Here are some of the snapshots:

1) **We see His character**. It says He is faithful and true. If you are worried about your salvation and the direction of your life, just think about his truthfulness and faithfulness. It tells me that I not only have His divine protection but I have security in Christ. (Romans 8). It doesn't matter what is out there. When the Faithful and True says, *"I have you in my hand"* that is divine protection and security for your life.

2) **It is a picture of His commission**. Why is He coming back to the planet? He is coming back to judge and wage war on those who rejected Him. Think about that, a Savior who is full of compassion and yet the same Savior who is willing to wage war.

3)   It is also a picture of His clarity. It says that He comes with eyes like a flame of fire.

12   His eyes were as a flame of fire, and on his head were many crowns; and he had a name written, that no man knew, but he himself. He knows what every heart is thinking, who is judged and who is not judged. It is a flame of righteous judgement.

4)   He comes with a secret name that no man knows.

5)   He comes and His clothing is dipped in blood. What does that mean? That is not the blood of your redemption (Isaiah 63). That is the blood of an Almighty God bringing judgement upon those who rejected His salvation. That is the picture of His clothing.

6)   He is called the Word of God. What is His command? He says He is coming to rule with a rod of iron. I suggest that it will only last about 75 days and then every one will be in shape for a thousand years. It will only take that long for Him to come and set up His kingdom. People will get the message.

7)   His celebration, King of Kings and Lord of Lords.

I get a lot of questions about the book of Revelation, and I want to mention here that this is my "view" of the book of Revelation.

I believe there are two phases of His one coming. What do I mean by that? I mean that He comes for us, the Church, and we are caught up via the rapture.

Titus 2:13 *"Looking for the blessed hope and glorious appearing of the great God and Savior Jesus Christ who gave Himself for us that He might redeem us and purify unto Himself a peculiar, zealous people doing zealous works."*

He separates the blessed hope, which is caught up in the moment of a twinkling of an eye, and the glorious appearing when every eye shall see Him. To me, that is two phases of His one coming.

This makes sense in that Christ comes in the air for His own, and here Christ comes with his own back to the planet in Revelation 19. Christians are taken from Father's house and resurrected saints never see Father's house. When Christ comes again the Bible says in Daniel that the resurrected Old

Testament saints are resurrected with the tribulation saints here. They will go to Father's house some day but we are in Father's house when we are raptured or when we die. There is no judgement on this earth at the place of the rapture. Christ will judge during the tribulation period all the inhabitants of the earth. The church is caught up to heaven. In the Second Coming, Christ comes to set up His kingdom on the earth immediately. To me the imminent return could happen right now. (Thessalonians) When that happens we will be changed in the moment of a twinkling of an eye and we will be caught up to be with Him forever. But in Revelation it can't occur for seven years. The Bible is very clear about 84 months, 1260 days, 1260 days and now He comes.

No signs are necessary for the rapture of the church. But the Bible says in Luke 21, **"Look up and lift up your heads for your redemption draws nigh."**

As I get closer to San Francisco, I see signs so I know I am getting closer. We are living in the last days and I think we are seeing signs for this return. Matthew 24 says that signs will be happening in the last days. No signs are necessary for us, but we have the privilege of seeing these things. But there will be many physical signs before His Second Coming. This is a time of joy for believers only. It is a time for mourning during the tribulation period. The Bible says that we are taken before the day of wrath, the tribulation, and then the Second Coming is immediately following the tribulation of those days.

This is my personal conclusion as I think about rapture and tribulation and the Second Coming of Christ. The Lord promised in Revelation 10 when He said, "I will keep you from that hour of evil or tribulation." Thessalonians says, "He will deliver us from the wrath to come." If I say that He can't come today and I will have to go through the seven years of tribulation, then I have taken away the "imminent return of Christ. I have said that He can't come until this happens. I Thes. 5:9, "He has not appointed us to wrath but to salvation and deliverance." That is the rapture. The church is absent in the text. I know that can be debated but there is no mention of the church from chapter 4 to Revelation 19 here at the Second Coming. That is my understanding and to me this fits with the Old Testament and New Testament.

"And he had a name written, that no man knew, but he himself."

How do you take that? The Bible says in Acts that you can't be saved by any name except for Jesus. So why would He say that He has a name written on Him that no man knew but He Himself? One way to look at this would simply be that no one has ever fully comprehended Him. I thought about that again and I read something by Vance H. "The name of Jesus will change your life. But you can call out on that name all of your life and you will never fully comprehend Him. For 2,000 years man has never fully comprehended the depth and the sovereignty and the love of Jesus. Only He really knows Himself." And Vance goes on to say, "You not only can't fully comprehend Him but you will never equal Him." You will never equal the name of Jesus. The Bible says in Hebrews that he was without sin. No one in the world is without sin and no one can equal Him. No one can escape Him. Men will try it by wine, pills, powders, drugs, procedures, and whatever. Men will try to escape Him for a season, but the Bible says that every knee shall bow and every tongue shall confess that Jesus is Lord.

You can't exclude Him. People will try to run to other nations and try to get to a place where they can exclude Him. The Bible says, every nation, every kindred, every tongue, every tribe, he will be everywhere. So if we understand that you can't equal our God, you can't comprehend Him and you can't escape Him, and you can't exclude Him, then there is one thing left-you can enjoy Him. One of the greatest enjoyments is when you come to the foot of the cross and you know beyond a shadow of a doubt that you can cry *Abba* Father. You can enjoy Him. We can't comprehend it but someday He will come back. We will rule and reign with Him for 1,000 years and we will enjoy every moment, and we will not even be in heaven yet. Can you imagine the majesty and the ministry of the name of Jesus?

13And he was clothed with vesture dipped in blood: and his name is called *The Word of God*.

14And the armies which were in heaven followed him upon white horses, clothed in fine linen, white and clean.

It is my understanding that the armies that followed him upon white horses is the church. It says that He will come with 10,000 of His saints. I believe that the resurrected Old Testament saints and the resurrected tribulation saints that died during the tribulation will all come back with Him somehow.

15And out of his mouth goeth a sharp sword, that with

it he should smite the nations: and he shall rule them with a rod of iron: and he treadeth the winepress of the fierceness and wrath of Almighty God.

When this Word of God comes out of heaven and He is dipped in blood and He comes with His armies, and this Word of God gets ready to speak, here you have the complete full expression of the mind and the heart and the will of God the Father. Everything in eternity past in the plan of God is now finding its complete fulfillment as this individual on this white horse gets ready to ride back to the planet. The full expression of the mind, the will, and the heart of our Savior is evident.

16And he hath on his vesture and on his thigh a name written, KING OF KINGS, AND LORD OF LORDS.

If you go back thousands of years ago to Nebuchadnezzar, he is running to Daniel with the terrible dreams. Daniel starts to tell him his dreams, and then finally Nebuchadnezzar falls down before Daniel. He says, "Is this not the God of your God. Is this not the Lord or the King of your Kings?" And Daniel says, "Yes it really is." And when he comes back in Revelation, we will see the King of Kings and the Lord of Lords. He alone is now in complete control.

17And I saw an angel standing in the sun; and he cried with a loud voice, saying to all the fowls that fly in the midst of heaven, Come and gather yourselves together unto the supper of the great God;

Why is this disturbing to me? It is disturbing to me in this sense. Because everyone who does not come to Christ when they have the opportunity will experience this supper. The Bible says that there are multitudes in the valley of decision. Seventy thousand people come to Christ every week. Satan is making his final play and God through His Holy Spirit is wooing people to the cross. But if you do not make a decision, you will experience this supper. You who have named the name of Christ are going to experience the supper that has already been talked about in Revelation, the marriage supper of the lamb. If you are not at the marriage supper of the Lamb, then you will be here at the supper of the great God where the birds come.

18That ye may eat the flesh of kings, and the flesh of captains, and the flesh of mighty men, and the flesh of horses, and of them that sit on them, and the flesh of all men, both free and bond, both small and great.

19And I saw the beast, and the kings of the earth, and their armies, gathered together to make war against him that sat on the horse, and against his army.

20And the beast was taken, and with him the false prophet that wrought miracles before him, with which he deceived them that had received the mark of the beast, and them that worshipped his image. These both were cast alive into a lake of fire burning with brimstone.

21And the remnant were slain with the sword of him that sat upon the horse, which sword proceeded out of his mouth: and all the fowls were filled with their flesh.

I used to receive the Jerusalem Report. (This may sound sensational) Some time ago in an article I read this: There are migrating patterns of birds that come out of Europe and Asia at a certain time of the year. I forget when it was, but there are millions that migrate. And this is such a problem for Israel. They are in the line of this funnel that comes down from Europe and Asia as they migrate to Africa. There are warnings from control towers for pilots who fly in Israeli airspace at this time of year, to be wary of these birds. I let my mind wander. If you wonder if there will be enough birds here to eat the flesh, then that may happen in this sense. God has them there ready to eat supper. It will happen in His time and His way.

The collapse of the empire in verses 17 – 21 is like a deck of cards collapsing. It will all come down at once. This is the final battle of Armageddon. This will be such a slaughter of humanity and beasts. After the birds have had their fill and they have gorged themselves and left, the Bible says in Ezekiel 39 that then there will be seven months of time just to bury the dead. There will be so many dead in this valley.

I wonder what will be going through the mind of the Antichrist at this time. He knows that his hour is about over. He knows the Word of God and what it says. He knows what the last chapter says and that he is doomed. But for some egotistical reason, he says he is going to take Him on. What do you think the last speech of the Antichrist will be? Somehow he has connections with everyone on the planet. He has deceived them in all of these areas. I would like to tell you what I think he may say. They are gathering all the armies of the earth to battle and somehow via satellite he may say something like this:

"Gentlemen of the earth, we are at war and we have been at war one with another for seven years. The time has now come for us to unite with a common cause. The things that unite us now are far more important than the things that divided us through this catastrophe of seven years. It is no longer a question of which of us will rule the world. I am in control now. It is now a question of common survival. The time has come for us to take a final council against this man called "The Lord" and against His anointed. He has put himself in our power. He has dared to appear now on our planet. The last time He came, we crucified Him. This time we shall cast His bonds asunder and we will cast His cords away from us forever. We will finally be free. We have tried uniting for peace, but that has not proved a very durable bond for us. Now let us unite for war. Let us deal with this invasion of our planet once and for all. Let us deal with this invasion of these white robed religious freaks, these psalm-singers. Let us show them how real men freed of all religion can fight. Let's hurl our defiance in their teeth. Time and again I have given you proof of my might, of my supernatural powers. You will now follow me. And that dread lord of darkness who we serve and we love has defied these Heavenly Hosts for countless ages and centuries. He is more than a match for them. Come to me and let us rid the world of its atmosphere forever of these unwanted, weak chanters of hymns."

I am sorry, but if that is his final words, then that is a lot of words. He may make a speech like that someday but it is just the same old story. Down through the ages it has been nations and men against the Savior.

15And out of his mouth goeth a sharp sword, that with it he should smite the nations: and he shall rule them with a rod of iron: and he treadeth the winepress of the fierceness and wrath of Almighty God.

I love this verse. *Out of His mouth goeth a sharp sword.* Do you know what I think will happen here? I think He will just say one word, but I do not know what it will be. We are all with Him, the armies of heaven. We do not need patriot missiles. We do not need machine guns and Uzis. We are just with him. He will come with the defiance of this two hundred million man army and they are all shaking their fists at the heavens. And Christ comes and He just speaks one word.

Zephaniah 1, *"The great day of the Lord is near, it is near and it hasteth greatly, even the voice of the day of the Lord and men shall cry bitterly, that will be a day of wrath, a day of trouble, a day of distress, a day of waste, a day of desolation, a day of darkness, a day of clouds, a day of thick darkness, a day of the trumpet that will alarm all the cities. And I will bring distress upon all men and they shall walk like blind men because they have sinned against the Lord and their blood shall be poured out on all the dust and their flesh shall be as dung. And I shall deliver them in the day of the Lord's wrath but the whole land shall be devoured by the fire of his jealousy for he shall make a speedy riddance of all of them that dwell in His land."*

One word. I love the way that the Scripture is in harmony with all of that. What happened in Genesis chapter 1? He spoke, maybe one word, and everything that you see today He spoke into existence. The Bible says in Colossians 1:16 that all things were created by Him. He spoke it. He was walking through the streets of Jerusalem one day and all of the sudden He sees a fig tree. He spoke one word and the thing withered. He was walking by the Sea of Galilee and He sees a legend of demons. He spoke one word and they all fled.

And here He comes in the power of great glory with the armies of heaven and he speaks one word and the armies of men are forever annihilated. It is over with one word. The Bible says that they will beat their swords into plowshares and their spears into pruning hooks. The tanks will become tractors and you can go on and on from there. I like to let my mind wander. Go one hundred years into the millennium. A schoolboy is on his way to school and Christ is ruling and reigning,. The schoolboy asks his teacher, "What is a missile?" And she says, "I am not really sure. There is not really such a thing existing." And drugs and all these things will not be in their vocabulary any longer. This is what is getting ready to take place when He comes.

We talk about heaven and hell being real and they are. You take a man like the False Prophet and the Antichrist and the Bible says that they will be slain and cast into the lake of fire for a thousand years. Heaven is real and it is for eternity. Hell is real and it is for eternity.

By way of encouragement, he is coming again, He is coming on a white horse and He will speak a word and it will take care of the armies of the earth. He is coming again and we will be with Him.

I would like to suggest some things. Just as much as you have the confidence that you will have eternal life, you also should have the same amount of confidence when He says *I will come again* in John 14. Believe it, He is coming again.

It should always encourage us to remember Him at the Lord's Table. Communion should be an exciting time for us. The Bible says in John 13, *This do in remembrance of me*, because He is coming again. *"I want you to proclaim the Lord's death until I come again."* (Corinthians)

Commit yourselves to a life of ministry. Everyone who is saved is a minister, *"You are ministers of the reconciliation."* When you are saved, then you have the opportunity to share the blessed hope with others. That is the ministry of reconciliation. But beyond that you have a ministry. Timothy says to *"make full proof of your ministry."* He charges you before Jesus Christ and at His appearing. He is saying that he charges Timothy to make full proof of his ministry. You should know what your ministry is. What does the Word say about your ministry? If you have the Word of God in you, then you can share it with others. And you can reprove and you can exhort and you can endure affliction and you can suffer for the cause of Christ. This is a ministry.

There are people laying in hospitals and rest homes and they are ministering to people. How? Because of the attitude of their life, they know that they have the Savior in them. When people are around them, they are cheered up. That is ministry. The Bible says not to be ashamed at His coming. Be involved in a ministry and that will bring fulfillment in your life.

Do not neglect the body of Christ. I do not know how many times it says that in the Word of God, but it comes to a conclusion in Hebrews where it says, "Let us not forsake the assembly of ourselves together." Not forsaking. This is a challenge for everyone. Do what you can to be with other believers.

When I know that he is coming again and I have the confidence that we will be with Him and I know that the rapture will be any time, the enormity of that should challenge us to join the task of our lives and our vision together. If someone asked you what your vision was, what would you tell him or her? If you are away from the Word of God, then you won't have a vision anymore. But if you want to join your excitement of the Lord and your vision with your task, then realize the enormity that He is coming again, because everything will come in sync at that point.

Everyone has expectations. I have all kinds of expectations in life. But sometimes what I experience is far removed from my expectations. How do I bring them closer together? But what brings them together is when we never fail to neglect Him. When you get so busy in your life, then your view of Him dims and it affects everything you do. My expectations begin to distance God from my experiences. What is that? I have neglected Him.

You will never get away from problems; but if you never neglect Him, you will have peace in your life.

In Luke 10: 41-42, He says, "Martha, Martha Martha… Mary chose the only thing that is needful."

When I think about the Second Coming of Jesus Christ, the only thing that is needful in my life is this: It is complete unashamed dependence on my Savior every moment of every day. If I get away from that, then I have a dim view of the future.

Military history gives us lessons by Fredrick the Great. He sent a note and it said, "General, I am sending you sixty thousand men for you to go against the enemy with." This got the general excited. The men started rolling in and the General had his men start to count them. They only came up with fifty thousand just a few days before the battle. The General was upset and sent a courier back to Fredrick the Great and said, "I counted only 50,000 men and you said 60,000. You are 10,000 short. What is the deal?" Fredrick the Great sent a note back immediately and it said, "General, there was no mistake. I counted you for 10,000 men." And they went to the battle and they won. This is the question I have for you today: You know you are in Him and you know He is coming. What do you count Him for?

You have battles you are facing in your life and you say you can't handle everything. What do you count Him for? *"Greater is He that is in you than*

He that is in the world." We will face obstacles in our lives, but He is coming again! And we can count Him far more than 10,000 people.

I read a story on a missionary in Africa. They found this in on his wall in his hut after he died. To me, this is a man that cared about Christ far more than 10,000 men. This is what he wrote:

"I am a part of the fellowship of the unashamed. I have Holy Spirit power. Oh, the dye has been cast in my life. I have stepped over the line. The decision has forever been made. I am a disciple of His. I won't look back. I won't let up, I won't slow down, I won't back away until He comes. My past is redeemed and my present makes sense and my future is really secure. I have finished and done with low living, sight walking, small planning, smooth knees, colorless dreams, tame little visions, mundane talking, chintzy giving, and dwarf goals. I no longer need preeminence. I no longer need prosperity. I no longer need position. I no longer need promotions or popularity. I do not have to be right or first or top dog or recognized, or praised or regarded or rewarded. I now live by His presence. I lean on His faith. I love by patience, I live by prayer, and I labor by His power. My face is set, my gate is fast, my goal is heaven, my road is narrow, my way is rough. My companions are few, but my guide is reliable. My mission is clear. I can't be bought, compromised, detoured, lured away, turned back, deluded, or delayed. I will not flinch in the face of sacrifice. I will not hesitate in the presence of adversity. I will not negotiate at the table of the enemy. I will not ponder at the pool of popularity or meander in the maze of mediocrity. I don't give up, shut-up, let up or burn up until I have preached up, prayed up, paid up, stored up, and stayed up for the cause of my Christ and His glorious return. I am a disciple of Jesus, and I must go until He comes and give until I drop and preach until everyone knows Him. When He does come to get His own, He will have no problem recognizing me at all because my colors will be clear, because I am His and He is coming for me."

Revelation 20:1-10

The 1000 Year Reign

1And I saw an angel come down from heaven, having the key of the bottomless pit and a great chain in his hand.

2And he laid hold on the dragon, that old serpent, which is the Devil, and Satan, and bound him a thousand years,

3And cast him into the bottomless pit, and shut him up, and set a seal upon him, that he should deceive the nations no more, till the thousand years should be fulfilled: and after that he must be loosed a little season.

4And I saw thrones, and they sat upon them, and judgment was given unto them: and I saw the souls of them that were beheaded for the witness of Jesus, and for the word of God, and which had not worshipped the beast, neither his image, neither had received his mark upon their foreheads, or in their hands; and they lived and reigned with Christ a thousand years.

5But the rest of the dead lived not again until the thousand years were finished. This is the first resurrection.

6Blessed and holy is he that hath part in the first resurrection: on such the second death hath no power, but they shall be priests of God and of Christ, and shall reign with him a thousand years.

7And when the thousand years are expired, Satan shall be loosed out of his prison,

8And shall go out to deceive the nations which are in the four quarters of the earth, Gog, and Magog, to gather them together to battle: the number of whom is as the sand of the sea.

9And they went up on the breadth of the earth, and compassed the camp of the saints about, and the beloved city: and fire came down from God out of heaven, and devoured them.

10And the devil that deceived them was cast into the lake of fire and brimstone, where the beast and the false prophet are, and shall be tormented day and night for ever and ever.

This chapter is probably the most controversial chapter in the book of Revelation. You might wonder how this chapter could be controversial, so I will mention it in a brief way. Why? It is just the different ways people interpret Bible prophecy. There are people who look at the entire book of Revelation a lot differently than I do because they look at it allegorically or spiritualize it all. I look at the book with a literal view. We will be looking at the 1000 year reign as a literal interpretation. As we look at this chapter I will break it up three ways. We will look at:

1. The removal of Satan.

2. The reign of Christ with you and I.

3. The revolt of humanity.

Why would anyone want to revolt after having the opportunity to live during Christ's reign? There is an answer.

At the very heart of all Bible prophecy is a simple phrase of four words that Jesus Christ says about twelve hours before His death. He said, *"I will come again."*

That is the heart of all Bible prophecy. That is the background of everything we have witnessed and talked about in the book of Revelation. *"I will come again."* For the past 6000, years man has yearned and prayed and longed and dreamed for Utopia. He has never received it. Apart from Christ and salvation in Him, man has floundered and sees nothing but war, rebellion, hardship and death. Man has never had satisfaction in his soul. It will change here for 1000 years.

My imagination really goes wild but can you imagine 1000 years with Jesus? Can you imagine Utopia on this planet?

Here are three ways people look at the Millennium.

1. PRE-MILLENNIALISTS. I am a pre-millennialist. "Pre" means Christ is coming before the millennium. I am pre-tribulation. That means that I believe the imminent return of Christ could be now. There is nothing that has to happen before Christ blows the trumpet and we are caught up to be with Him. The rapture chapter is in Revelation 4 where we are caught up to be with Christ at the marriage supper of the Lamb. Then we come back here pre-millennial. The Bible says that every eye shall see Him and we will come back to rule and reign with Him for 1000 years. That is a pre-melliniast. Then there will be the resurrection of the unjust and the great white throne judgement and then the new heaven and the new earth. Christ is coming back before the millennium.

2. POST-MILLENNISTS. It isn't very popular any more. Very few people are post-millennialist. A post-millennialist believes that Christ will come back some day but He will come back after the 1000 year reign and then we go to heaven. The post-millennialist started this in the early church, they believed there would be a reign but that the body of Christ would make the world a better place to live. Then after it was past 1000 years and World War I and World War II took place, that view point became unpopular.

3. THE A-MILLENNISTS. "A" means no millennium. And "A" millennialist believes that all the blessings that God promised Israel will now be transferred to the Church, the body of Christ. So there will not be a literal kingdom that was promised to Abraham and David. They say that the kingdom is within you. The Lamb is lying down with the Lion inside of you and there is peace and joy in your heart now. An A-melliniast says there is no significance in what we are witnessing today with the rebirth of the nation of Israel. That is the way they look at it.

I find this song interesting, Isaac Watts' Joy to the World. We sing this song at Christmas but it wasn't written for Christmas. He wrote it for the Millennium. He wrote it to talk about the Second Coming of Christ and what He would do when He comes back to rule and reign.

"Joy to the world the Lord has come,
let earth receive her King,
let every heart prepare Him room
and heaven and nature sing.

Joy to the world the Savior reigns
Let men their songs employ,
While fields and floods
Rock, hills and planes
Repeat the sounding Joy!

No more let sin and sorrow grow
Nor thorns infest the ground.
He comes to make His blessings flow
Far as the curse is found.

He rules the world with truth and grace,
And makes the nation prove
The glories of His righteousness
And the wonders of His love."

Isaac Watts wrote this song as He thought about the Millennial reign of Christ.

1 And I saw an angel come down from heaven, having the key of the bottomless pit and a great chain in his hand.

I looked up *"a great chain"* and most of the commentaries didn't have any comments on it. But it was obviously a chain of authority.

2And he laid hold on the dragon, that old serpent, which is the Devil, and Satan, and bound him a thousand year.,

The Lord is having John write this down by the way of the Holy Spirit and He is saying, "I do not want you to make a mistake here of who we are talking about, who we are sending to the abyss. We are talking about the serpent, the dragon, the Devil also known as Satan." Twelve times in the book of Revelation he is called the dragon. He is an old slimy serpent. Fifty-three times in the Bible the Holy Spirit uses the word Satan. The word Devil is all through the Scripture too. He will bound this creation for 1000 years. He will not have any influence for 1000 years.

3And cast him into the bottomless pit, and shut him up, and set a seal upon him, that he should deceive the nations no more, till the thousand years should be fulfilled: and after that he must be loosed a little season.

Some people believe he is annihilated here, but it says in verse three that he will be loosed for a little season, so he will not be annihilated. Then later in this chapter he will go back down there and live forever and ever. And every one who goes with him will be in the same circumstance forever and ever. The removal of Satan, that is amazing.

If you look back through the centuries, every time a king would set up his kingdom, the first thing he wanted to do was to kill the people who didn't agree with him and completely remove rebellion. So when Christ comes back with us for a 1000 years the first thing He does is He removes rebellion. Who is the height of all rebellion? The dragon, the serpent, the devil.

4And I saw thrones, and they sat upon them, and judgment was given unto them: and I saw the souls of them that were beheaded for the witness of Jesus, and for the word of God, and which had not worshipped the beast, neither his image, neither had received his mark upon their foreheads, or in their hands; and they lived and reigned with Christ a thousand years.

If you had the opportunity to jump into this vision with John, I will tell you what you would see. You would see you. The Bible says in Corinthians 6:2 *"Do you know that the saints will someday judge the world?"* So someday you will rule and reign with Him and be in a position of judgement with Old Testament saints, with the disciples. The Bible is clear about that in Revelation 3:21 *"I give you authority to judge all nations."* He told the disciples one time, *"you will sit on twelve thrones judging."* In Daniel 7:27 He says, *"the ruling and the judgement of the saints."* So this is you and I.

5But the rest of the dead lived not again until the thousand years were finished. This is the first resurrection.

I will try to put this very simply. If the trumpet would sound right now, that is the rapture of the Church. The Bible says in Thessalonians that we will be caught up… and so shall we ever live with the Lord. If He comes right now, you will be with Him and you will stay with Him. But what about the spiritually dead? They are down here. When Jesus Christ comes back with 10,000 of His saints, this first resurrection is all of the tribulation saints and Old Testament saints. So you see the body of Christ, the Old Testament saints and the tribulation saints, those who were beheaded. But there is still one more class of people and the Bible says they are dead and will not be resurrected until now. All of those who did not believe in Christ as their Savior will remain dead until the end of the millennium.

6Blessed and holy is he that hath part in the first resurrection: on such the second death hath no power, but they shall be priests of God and of Christ, and shall reign with him a thousand years.

The first resurrection is the resurrection of all righteous, Old Testament saints and tribulation saints. This says that death and hell were cast into the lake of fire. This is the second death. Those who are apart from Christ have no power.

Let's look at the features of the 1,000 year reign. The proof of the 1,000 year reign is in the Old Testament. They were looking for the coming kingdom. For two thousand years we have been looking for it and praying for it. "Thy Kingdom come."

We will look at about ten features of the 1000 year reign. It is incredible to look through the Old Testament. Obviously if you just look at this chapter, you will not get any features of the millennial reign; but that is why I think if you use the Old Testament Scriptures in harmony, you will see this 1,000 year reign. The solid proof to me of the 1000 year reign is the Old Testament. Consider Isaiah 11 and Isaiah 6 and 9. Isaiah 2:4 says, "Peace." Can you imagine living on planet earth with total peace? The last 5,600 years of recorded history, there has been over 20,000 peace treaties broken, 4,000,750,000 people have died in battles, and there have been 14,500 wars. It has never ended for about 6,000 years. And it says here that they will beat their swords into plowshares and their spears into pruning hooks and their tanks into tractors. There will be a time of complete peace. In Isaiah 2:4 it says, *"They shall learn war no more."*

If you are born during the Millennium, you will never see or witness, or even know what they are talking about when they talk about war. It will not be in their vocabulary. There will be no conflict. Why does the Bible say that He will rule with a rod of iron? It would be my understanding from Daniel in chapter 7 or 9 that there is a seventy-five day period. It is my opinion that the first 75 days when Christ comes back to set up His millennial reign, it says that He will rule with a rod of iron. There will be swift punishment to those who do not recognize His authority and I believe it will take seventy-five days to set up His kingdom reign. After that it will be nothing but peace. If you think about that, it is pretty awesome.

Then you think about holiness. In Ezekiel 26:24-31, it is saying that everything will be set apart for Him. You will be clean. Everything will be clean. Everything will be holy. Everything will be right and everything will be set apart. The King, the land, the people, and the cities are all holy. Everything will be set apart for Him. There will not be disappointing billboards along the streets. You will not see bars or restaurants. You will not see any of that. It is one thing to think about peace and another to think about an entire planet set apart to holiness. Wouldn't that excite you? Just think about a whole planet set aside for His glory.

In Isaiah 12:6 it says, "cry out and shout for joy." Can you imagine seeing joy everywhere you go? Joy at the airports, joy at the supermarkets, joy at the malls... but I see nothing but suffering at those places, but it will be joy-filled.

Isaiah 42:1-8 says that with righteousness He will judge. The Lord will not make any mistakes. There will not be people coming to Him with questions that He will have to think about. He will have swift, right judgement. Sometimes we do not think Christ is fair, but He is right and perfect in His judgement.

Isaiah 41:20 *"People shall see, know and consider and understand."* There will be an opportunity for increased knowledge here. Think about it. If you take away the stress of wrong in your life and the stress of sin and the temptation of the Devil, there would be an increase in knowledge that is unparalleled, and in the teaching of His ministry as well. I believe it will be an exciting time just to see that unparalleled ministry of the Holy Spirit. Can you imagine all the four letter vocabulary words that will not be in the language? Here are a few that I came up with; fear, jail, drug, pain, hate, rape, dope, … all of these things will not be here.

What we are going to witness during the 1000-year reign of Christ will be like what Adam and Eve were witnessing in the garden. I believe even geographically we will go back to that kind of a hot house. We will be on a planet that has perfected everything. It will not be tainted at all with sin. And if Adam and Eve hadn't sinned, they would have gone right into the kingdom. They would have witnessed what we are talking about here, perfect everything. Perfect sickness – not. Isaiah 33:24 says, *"The inhabitants shall not say 'I am sick.'"* We see sickness everywhere today but there will be no sickness there. He will take it away. In one place the Bible says, *"The tongue shall speak plain."* The Bible also says that we will all speak the same language. He says, *"I will bind the broken hearted and strengthen them that are sick."* No blind, no dumb, no lame, and no stuttering.

The Bible says in **Isaiah 65:25 "The lion and the lamb will lay down together, they will not hurt or destroy."** The only curse that is not lifted during the millennial reign from what I understand is that snake will still slither. He will not harm anyone, but he will not walk upright. There will not be any thistles or thorns.

During the Millennium, everyone will have their own 'zoo' in this sense: when that curse is lifted for a season on the animal kingdom, the lion will lie down with the lamb, the wolf with the lamb. Animals might be in your back yard. We will enjoy them how God wanted us to. It will be an exciting time to see God's creation and enjoy it! Can you imagine a zoo like that. I believe the environment will be similar to pre-flood. In a perfect environment, hot house effect, the sun is seven times hotter and the moon is seven times as bright. The Bible says in Isaiah that there will be a circle that covers the earth, a strange atmosphere, and so things will grow better. It is my understanding that things and creatures will thrive differently and better. We may even have dinosaurs.

Look at Isaiah 66:17-23. There will be a perfect King. This is talking about a King that has given his people an opportunity to always worship Him. Can you imagine a King on this planet who every one worships? And He will do everything right. That will be comfort to anyone who is living here, perfect kingship. I believe we will have a fully industrialized economy. It says that the plowman will overtake the reaper. There will be tractors sold and they will not be able to keep up with the reaping. It will be an exciting time. No ghettos, no homeless, and no welfare. No drunks or drugs, no immorality, and you can just keep going down the list to see that everything is perfect.

Join prosperity with that. I had a little bit of fun with this one. When you take sin away from this planet and you allow someone to come in and rule and reign right with proper stewardship, (obviously Him), we will witness something that we can't imagine. He says, "It has not entered into our hearts or our minds of what He has planned." Think about prosperity. When I think of prosperity I think of millions and billions. But that is not prosperity. The Bible says in Isaiah that the desert shall blossom as a rose, the parched places will become like pools. They will all build their own houses and plant their own vineyards and the people shall possess all things." It has been said that the planet today, with a partial curse, and add all the natural resources, then it is worth about 2.5 decimillion. That is a lot. (million, billion, quadrillion, quintillion, sextillion, septillion, octillion, novillion, decillion) If you would divide that by 4 billion people then everyone would be worth hundreds of billions. That is quite a bit of things; but we will not be thinking about that, because our focus is going to be on Him and our enjoyment will be Him! But there will be prosperity unimaginable.

Isaiah 30:26 "the moon will be as bright as the sun and the sun will be seven times hotter." Somehow the circle of the earth will be different.

What about church worship or synagogue worship? What will the Lord do here? He will be ruling and reigning and we will be with Him. But what about the people born during the millennium? I believe "kingdom kids" need to go to church. Why would they need to go to church when everything is perfect? For this reason. We still have the same Bible and everyone born during the millennial reign and everyone living during the millennial reign that comes out of the tribulation period may need to know that some day this thousand year reign will be over because the Bible says it will end someday. What happens when the Devil is loosed for a season? I believe there is a need in the 1000 years to recognize that you need to be born again. This is the same King who is our leader. Our King is the one who died at the cross and someday you will have to make the choice for Him.

This brings us to the question, why a millennium? Why does the have to be a millennium? There is an answer and it is found with the kingdom kids. During the millennium there will be a reward. Matthew 16 "When the Son of Man comes in His glory He will reward man according to his works." Not for your salvation, but for your works. He also says that there will be a millennium to answer your prayers. There is also a millennium because he is going to redeem creation. This planet is groaning and travailing and waiting for redemption. Even the plants, mountains and ocean are waiting. He will come and make it right for a season. There needs to be a millennium because He made a covenant with Abraham. There is a divine covenant in II Samuel with David, "He will sit on the throne." There will be a millennium for the Jews and they will witness it.

Here is the key to all of what we have mentioned. Every child born in the Millennium will have to make a decision for Christ or against Him when He allows the chain to be loosed for a season. God is proving a final point, regardless of creation, regardless of your environment, regardless of your circumstances, regardless of your heredity. If a man is apart from the grace of God, he will spend eternity in Hell. "Unless you choose my Son, you will never be in heaven with me"

He has been doing that for 6,000 years. In every dispensation down through time God has given man a responsibility. Man has failed and God has brought judgement. This is the seventh. He is saying that, "You better see my point by here. This perfect, and you who are born here are without excuse. You have perfect peace, you have perfect holiness, you have perfect joy, and you are not sick. You have perfect kingship. There is not one excuse you can give me for not worshipping me."

7And when the thousand years are expired, Satan shall be loosed out of his prison,

8And shall go out to deceive the nations which are in the four quarters of the earth, Gog, and Magog, to gather them together to battle: the number of whom is as the sand of the sea.

9And they went up on the breadth of the earth, and compassed the camp of the saints about, and the beloved city: and fire came down from God out of heaven, and devoured them.

10And the devil that deceived them was cast into the lake of fire and brimstone, where the beast and the false prophet are, and shall be tormented day and night for ever and ever.

When the Devil is loosed for a season at the end of this 1000 years of perfection, this will be the opportunity for those who are born in the Millennium to be saved and choose Christ. Many will follow this Devil and that shows the basic nature of man is sin.

The Devil finally meets his end at this last battle of Gog and Magog. He lost at the cross, He lost at Armageddon, and He lost at Gog and Magog. He will eternally experience the Lake of Fire.

In high school I was in FFA. (Future Farmers of America) I remember a boy in our class. We will call him Bruce. He was a good friend of mine. Bruce and I had a lot in common, we were the little short guys of the class, and so we were teased a lot. It was fine with me, but it wasn't fine with Bruce. I will never forget one day in Ag class, some boys started pushing and shoving Bruce around. This had been going on for quite a few months in this Ag class. I was fortunate because they never picked on me. I do not know why, but they kept picking on him more and more. They were really cursing and mocking him. Then they threw him up on a table. Bruce was getting beat up severely! I could just tell that he was going to snap and he did. Little Bruce came off of that table and he said **"No more!"** And he came off of the table with his fists flying and he took on all of these bullies and he wailed away! It was amazing because the teacher came in and saved these bullies from really getting hurt. He completely snapped. From that day on, He was never bothered again. In fact some of the bullies were "in fear" of him after that day!

But in a far far greater way, some day, after thousands of years of this "bullying" by the Devil, the Devil will be stopped! The Bible says he is hounding us and there is a war going on in our minds right now. The flesh is against the spirit, the spirit against the flesh. Paul says sometimes I do not even know how to react rightly. He says, ***"There are things that I want to do that I do not do and things I should do I don't, oh wretched man!"*** What makes him a wretched man? It is the Devil and the hounding and he has been doing this for thousands of years and finally God says "No more!"

CHRIST said, *"It is finished"* at the cross. And he is saying it again here in Revelation 20:9-10. No more Devil! No more bully! Yes, the Devil got his teeth kicked in at Calvary, plus a whole lot more! And from now on through all of eternity those who chose Him will know nothing but what we spoke about in this chapter. I have always looked at the Millennium as a honeymoon. We have been married to Christ and He is going to take us on a 1000 year honeymoon, and then we are going to go to heaven to be with the Father. I can't wait.

SO…..LET'S……

1) **Stay on the alert.** The Devil will do everything he can to deceive, distort, hinder, and trick us. You know what I am talking about if you have a relationship with Him. You read your Bible, you pray, and you worship, but you know you are hounded. Do everything you can in the power of the Holy Spirit to stay alert. In James, the Holy Spirit says, "Be patient brethren for the coming of the Lord draws nigh." In II Peter He says, "The Devil is like a roaring lion." And in another place it says, "He is an angel of light." He will not leave you alone. Do not ever think that you will become so perfect that you have it made; because if you get to that point, then he's got you again.

2) **Pray for those who are facing martyrdom.** We are living in a country today where there are not many people being martyred in Modesto. But that is not true for the planet. There are people being martyred all over the world. Pray for those who are standing for Christ. Be aware of what other Christians are experiencing; because the more time we spend praying for others, it just flushes more of 'self' out. We need to be getting rid of selfishness.

3) **Prepare your testimony, or your ministry of Jesus Christ.** Make sure you have an answer or a testimony of Jesus Christ when some one asks. You can share it with your life and your reactions. The older you get, (like me); the greatest ministry is our reactions and not necessarily our actions. How does Gordon react to this problem or that problem? The young ones are watching and they need to see Christ in us.

4) **Be confident.** When you experience tragedies and loss and pain, be confident because you are qualified to live during the 1000 years because of what you did for Him. Be confident in that! Don't take a back seat. Christians should not be embarrassed or ashamed. We

should be confident that we are in Him. We are qualified to go with Him, live with Him, and continue with Him. Be confident and love one another. Do not be too ashamed to pray with each other and love each other. If you have something bothering you in your life, call someone. We need each other. The Bible says to lift up the hands that hang down. It does not matter what you are facing when you are in Him. I desperately need the body of Christ.

The key is that we are in Him!

REVELATION 20:11-15
The Great White Throne Judgment

11 And I saw a great white throne, and him that sat on it, from whose face the earth and the heaven fled away; and there was found no place for them.

12 And I saw the dead, small and great, stand before God; and the books were opened: and another book was opened, which is the book of life: and the dead were judged out of those things which were written in the books, according to their works.

13 And the sea gave up the dead which were in it; and death and hell delivered up the dead which were in them: and they were judged every man according to their works.

14 And death and hell were cast into the lake of fire. This is the second death.

15   And whosoever was not found written in the book of life was cast into the lake of fire.

It is all over folks! As far as humanity is concerned, it is all over. At the end of this chapter we see the day that this planet is finally annihilated.

It was a dark and stormy night in 1975 when I received a call from a Pepsi Cola plant in Stockton. I had sent my partner Mike to wash some trucks there. Our code number was WEH84 and he had forgotten it. He went ahead, went into the Pepsi Cola plant, and started washing the trucks without punching in the security numbers! Almost immediately the place was surrounded with cop cars. I received a call from Mike as he tried to explain to me on the phone what had happened. There were dozens of cops surrounding him so he was very frightened. I jumped into my Monte Carlo and I quickly drove towards Stockton. At French Camp Road, four miles from the Pepsi Plant, I saw red lights behind me so I pulled over. It was raining and very windy as I pulled over for the patrol to come in behind my car. I did a very foolish thing in that frantic moment. I jumped out of my Monte Carlo and ran back and jumped into the passenger side of the police car! It was a big mistake, and I will never forget the Highway Patrol officer as he yelled, **"What are you doing?"** I said, "Sir, I have a real problem!" He said, "You do have a problem young man! You do not jump into any patrol car!" I said, "Sir, can I quickly explain?" He said yes, I could. When I explained the situation, he seemed to soften a little. Then he told me that he would follow me to the Plant. I think he really wanted to find out if I was telling the truth. On the way to the Pepsi Plant, I was really hoping that Mike was still surrounded with cop cars! Well, when we arrived at the plant he was still surrounded. But what I remember is talking to the Highway Patrolman afterwards. I thought that I had done a good deed, going 110 miles per hour to get a man out of trouble. I didn't think I deserved a ticket, but the law says otherwise! I deserved a long written violation that night; but after such excitement, and an even longer lecture, the patrol officer let me go. But I will tell you this, this is not a picture of what it will be like at the Great White Throne Judgment someday!

When men stand before the Great White Throne Judgement it will not matter what an individual says. You can stand there and say that you have done many many good deeds. You can say that you have lived right and helped people. But you will hear these words, "Depart from me you who work iniquity!"

At the Great White Throne Judgment, there will be a judge but no jury. There will be a prosecutor but no defense. There will be a sentence but there will never be an appeal. There will be a sentence handed down that will be more than a month or a year. It will be for eternity.

But if you are in Christ this morning, you have no fear of this judgement. If you have not placed your faith in Christ, then you will stand here someday. Iit is my prayer that you come to Christ and put your confidence in Him.

It has been said that there are three red-letter dates in the history of man. The first is Genesis chapter one, when God created everything. Red-letter date number two is at the cross of Calvary. (John 19) There Christ gave His life voluntarily that we may have an opportunity for salvation. And then you come to this time, Revelation 20, when the planet and humanity cease to exist as far as what we know of it today. It is the Great White Throne Judgment. No more history, no more time for man. This is where we are at today. Everything that we have studied in Revelation and all 6,000 years of recorded history end here. Time will be no more when this judgement takes place.

You are probably familiar with a courtroom. You have either been to one or read about one. We all understand there are judges, attorneys, juries, witnesses, and judgement being handed out. But it will be completely different here. It has been said that there has probably been seventy billion people created since the beginning of time. It is hard to come up with a number because it is hard to get a number of pre-flood people. If the earth was populated then there may have been billions for that 1000 or so years. Only God knows how many people are saved. But when God calls the dead and they stand before the throne try to picture fifty or sixty billion or more. It is a sea of humanity there at the Great White Throne Judgment. They have been called to the final judgment and when He calls them there, they will all show up. They will come out of the grave and they will be there at this moment of time.

I do not want to confuse you with both of the judgments. I do not believe that the Judgment Seat of Christ and the Great White Throne Judgment are together. If you put them together, then here is what you are doing. The saved and the unsaved show up, and one of the things that come to mind is that God has a scale out here. If you have good things, then it will weigh it down, but if you have done bad things, then if it tips a little bit more on the bad side you are out the door. Then someone else who has a little more good deeds goes out the other door. And back and forth and back and forth. According to Scripture, that is not the way that it is.

Because of the salvation of your soul, you are judged at His appearing. We talked about that in Revelation 4, the rapture chapter. If the trumpet would sound today, (February 11, 2010), and you are in Christ the Bible says in the moment of a twinkling of an eye you will be caught up. (1 Corinthians 15) You will appear at the Judgment Seat because you are a

Christian. The only ones who will appear at the Judgment Seat are the Christians. The only ones who will appear at the Great White Throne Judgment are the unsaved and they are 1007 years apart at least. The Bible says in Romans 14:10, *"We shall all stand before the judgement seat of Christ."* It is talking to believers. In 2 Corinthians 5:10, *"For we must all appear before the judgement seat of Christ to receive for the deeds done in the body."* That is in complete harmony with 1 Corinthians 3. As a believer we will stand there someday and everything we have done in our life we will have judged-but not for your salvation. If you are a Christian today and you have never really followed the Lord or been sincere about wanting to live for Him, you will stand there someday, ashamed at His coming. But you will still be saved! Because the righteousness that is found in you is because of His blood, it is because of what He did! That is what the Bible says. The bad works will be burned, but you are saved as by fire.

The Bible says the Judgment Seat is called the resurrection unto life. Acts 10:42, *"the quick and the dead."* Titus 2:13, *"looking for His blessed hope and the glorious appearing."* That will be done here at the Great White Throne Judgment. You have two judgements and they are separated by 1007 years. They are not the same. Titus 3:5 "Not by works of your righteousness but by His mercy," He saved you. So as you stand at the Judgment Seat of Christ and you are found in His blood, then you will be in heaven with Him. But if you stand here at the Great White Throne Judgment, then you are going in one direction. All the evidence is against you and you will go to Hell.

I want to spend time looking at these things:

Location of the judgment?
Who are the people surrounding the throne?
What is the intent of the Great White Throne?
The punishment, what is it like?

11   Earth and the heaven fled away; and there was found no place for them. And I saw a great white throne, and him that sat on it, from whose face the earth...

This tells us that there is a Great White Throne but no heaven and no earth. So where is it? We do not know. When it says in 2 Peter that the elements shall melt with a fervent heat and the heavens are destroyed and the whole earth is consumed by fire. We are at the end of the Millennium, the end of the battle of Gog and Magog. Al former things are passed away and all of the sudden God tells the dead to rise up and they are before the throne. The saved are with Him somewhere. The new heaven and the new earth will not be established until the next two chapters. So where is the Great White Throne? It is just out there. The unsaved can't reach out to grab or hold onto anything. They are just there for their sentencing. To me it sounds very frightening, just out there between heaven and earth. A Great White Throne, a picture of sovereignty, purity, majesty and all of these people are before it.

As I read this passage I thought that if I was not in the Lord today, then I would be extremely frightened. There is no recourse now for them, every opportunity will be over.

Who is this individual on the throne?

12 And I saw the dead, small and great, stand before God; and the books were opened: and another book was opened, which is the book of life: and the dead were judged out of those things which were written in the books, according to their works.

Many people say this is God, and yes He is. But I would like to suggest with the harmony of Scripture that the individual on the throne is Jesus Christ. The Bible says in John 5:22, *"God hath committed all judgement to His Son."* "I have committed all judgment to my son." In Acts 10:42, *"Jesus Christ is the judge of both the quick and the dead."* The Judgement Seat of Christ and the Great White Throne-He is the judge of both of those. The Bible says in 2 Timothy 4:1, *"Jesus Christ shall judge the quick and the dead at His appearing and at the kingdom."* There is a separation there. Who is the judge? It is Jesus Christ. John 10:20, *"The Father and I are always one."* So we have God/Jesus Christ seated on the throne.

I was reminded of Psalm 139. You can run, you can hide, you can go to the depth of the ocean or the top of the mountains, but you can't flee from the presence of God. Some day when He says to rise forth, then billions of people will stand before Him.

What about the purpose or the intent?

13   *And the sea gave up the dead which were in it; and death and hell delivered up the dead which were in them: and they were judged every man according to their works.*

When it says twice dead it means dead physically and dead spiritually. We are looking at people who come out of the dead physically; and then they denied Christ, and so they are dead spiritually. I find it interesting when it says they come up out of the sea. All the people that are under the ocean are finally, after thousands of years, standing before the Father. The first resurrection is when the trumpet sounds, the second resurrection is here. All the twice dead rise.

What is the purpose of the Great White Throne Judgement? This is not going to be a place to determine whether you are good enough. When I think about the purpose that God has for the Great White Throne Judgment, it comes back to His Son and salvation. There is no one on the planet that will ever go to Hell because they are a murderer. There is no one on the planet that will go to Hell because they took too many drugs. There is no one on the planet that will ever go to Hell because they beat their wife or their husband or their children. There is no one on the planet that will ever go to Hell because they cursed and swore. There is no one on the planet that will ever go to Hell because they were a witch or because they were wicked or because they were in cults. You do not go to hell because of that! Men go to Hell because there is no righteousness found in them! Every soul that is at the Great White Throne Judgement is there because of the evidence against them. He will share their works, but the bottom line is that there is no righteousness found in them. Likewise the only reason that anyone ever goes to heaven is not because you did more good deeds, but it is because righteousness was found in you! That separates the dead from the living. It is about what is done in response to Jesus Christ!

If the trumpet sounds today and you go up then you will go up because righteousness is found in you because you placed your faith in Christ. If you find yourself at the Great White Throne Judgement someday, it is not because you are so wicked. It is because no righteousness is found in you.

The Bible is very clear. *"For by grace you are saved through faith, not of yourselves, not of works."* Titus 3:5 says it is not by your works of righteousness that you are saved but according to His mercy and lovingkindness that we have the opportunity to be with Him.

The books are opened and man is presented with the evidence and the bottom line is a Christ-rejecting soul.

I find it interesting that He talks about a book of life and then all of these books. I suggest that possibly five books will be opened at this judgment. This is not something I just drew out of my imagination but you will find that He mentions this in the Bible. I think there is a reason for Him mentioning these books here at the Great White Throne.

The Bible will be open at the Great White Throne Judgment. The Bible says that the Word shall judge you in that day. The Bible says in John 12:48 that the Word will judge us. The Bible is going to be open.

In Matthew 12:36, "**Every idle word** man shall give an account in the day of judgement." All of this evidence will come out, but you will not go to Hell because of an idle word. You will go to Hell because no righteousness is in you. I believe that God is showing this so that you can see that if you would have had Christ then that idle word could have been forgiven. So He says the book of words will be opened at the Great White Throne.

The book of conscience. Romans 2:15, "The law that is written in their hearts and their conscience will always bear them witness." Some day in eternity in billions of years from now, man will still have a memory and a conscience of the opportunity that they could have come to Him. That reminder will be torture throughout eternity. God will open this and show them that they are without excuse, because they knew that there was a God and then they rejected Him.

The book of secret things will be opened. Romans 2:16 "God shall judge all the secrets of man through Jesus Christ." Someday the things that are done in the secret of men's hearts will be exposed.

I suggest that there will be a book opened of all **public words and works.** The Bible says in 2 Corinthians 11:15 "Your end shall be according to your works and your words." Your actions portray what is in your heart and everything that comes out of the fountain of man's heart will be revealed. "As a man thinketh in his heart so shall he be." The evidence will be at the Great White Throne.

Then there is the **Book of Life.** I ask you this question, "Are you confident today that your name is in the Book of Life?" Five times in God's Word He talks about the Book of Life. It is referred to as the Lamb's Book of Life. There is an obvious question that comes when we talk about this Book of Life. Can a Christian's name be blotted out of the Book of Life? Let's look at it this way. When a child is conceived and there is life in the womb, that is an individual who will never cease to exist throughout eternity. That is life. I believe when that life is first conceived then that name is written in the Book of Life. What blots an individual's name out of the Book of Life is when they are given an opportunity to know Him and come to Him and if there is a Christ-rejecting soul saying "I want no part of that" then their name will be blotted out of the Book of Life. Those who receive the Mark of the Beast are blotted out of the Book of Life. There was still opportunity for those who where still living, but they chose the way of the Antichrist and their names were blotted out of the book of life. Psalm 69:28 "let them be blotted out of the book of the living." Those who refuse God will be blotted out of the Book of the Living. Every human being is written in the Book of Life. But if you reject the wooing of the Spirit then your name is blotted out of the Book ofL.

Consider the Book of Life.

1) It is not the absence of enough good works that dooms a person. It is the absence of your name in the Book of Life. If your name is not written in the Book of Life it is because you have rejected the righteousness of Christ.
2) It is not a matter of too many bad works. That has nothing to do with it. There have been all kinds of bad people through the ages who have turned to Calvary. So it is not too many bad works.
3) All names that are not there will be cast into the Lake of Fire. As God opens this Book of Life at the judgement you can see the evidence handed out. If He looks for your name and it is not there and there is no righteousness found in you then you will hear "depart from me."
4) The entries of all names are finalized long before the Great White Throne Judgement. You are either in Him or you are not. Every opportunity in life that we have today is our opportunity. But when you die physically, then there is no other chance at that moment. You do not stand there and plead with the judge. All the evidence is

against you and it all comes back to Jesus Christ and what you have done with Him.

Think about some of the bad things you have heard in your life. Like when somebody shares something with you and your whole metabolism changes. You just feel terrible or you are totally embarrassed. I want you to imagine the people who will stand before the Great White Throne and hearing these words, Matthew 25:31-46, "Depart from me you cursed, unto everlasting fire that was prepared for the devil and his angels." That is very final. That tells us that Hell was never prepared for humanity. God did not want any of His creation to go to Hell. It never says that in the Bible. The Bible says that Hell was prepared for the Devil and his angels. But if you want to follow the Devil then you will end up there some day in that same rebellion. Jesus pleaded and warned, He cared and shared, He loved. He said at least three words about hell, when He was on the earth, to every word about heaven. Warning "please, please, please!" There will be a Great White Throne Judgement someday.

In the Old Testament in the scarlet thread of redemption all the way to Calvary the echoing of the words come in Deuteronomy. "I have set before you life and death, blessing and cursing, therefore chose life that you many live." And it goes on to say, "Therefore choose life that both you and your seed can live." What an opportunity we have as parents and grandparents to transfer the truth of God's Word that our children have an opportunity for salvation and that others that I know might have an opportunity for salvation. He gave us the choice. Chose life.

Why is it that He separated the two judgements? Here is an author's opinion and I like it. I believe God separated the two judgements because I do not believe that as believers in Christ we could handle witnessing the Great White Throne Judgement. Why do I say that? Let us think about it.

There you stand as a believer in Christ and He says that righteousness is found in you and then your son or your daughter is next. Would you like the thought of standing there and witnessing your son or your daughter or your spouse standing before God and hearing that there is no righteousness found in them? "Depart from me you who work iniquity!" And then as they are walking away they turn back and look at you and say something like this, "Daddy! Mother! Why didn't you tell me that this moment would come?" Could you handle that? Or a neighbor down the street... "You lived by me for thirty years, why didn't you share with me? Look where I am going!" I do not think we could handle it.

The Bible says that every one of us will give an account of himself before the Lord.

I challenge you today to do what you can with your children or the people that you know. Do what you can to tell them that their house is on fire. They have to get out! It is very simple!

My parents took us to hear many evangelists over the years as I was growing up. There are men presenting the gospel everywhere today. We hear it in churches, the gospel being presented. I remember going into Denny's one time as a child and standing before Billy Graham and Cliff Barows and getting our hymnbooks signed. We thought that was amazing. So every time I had an opportunity to hear Billy Graham then I was going to be there to listen. Everything He has said over the years has meant a lot to me. I will tell you one thing that he always did in a very basic way. He never let a revival go by without bringing the simplicity of the gospel. Faith in Jesus Christ. Repent of your sins. Turn to the Father. Celebrate your belief. Live for Christ daily. Recognize that you must die daily to sin. It is a free gift. If you ever get away from the freeness of salvation, then you got away from it. Get back. Salvation is a gift from God. When we reach out in faith believing and we receive that gift from the Father, then righteousness is found in us at that moment. **Isaiah 61, "You are clothed in white garments at that moment."** Yes you are not without sin and you have problems in your life; but when the trumpet sounds, you will be found in Him!

In the Revolutionary War there was an atheist soldier by the name of Ethan Allen. One day Ethan Allen found out that his fourteen year-old daughter had an incurable disease and would die within a week. In those days, they didn't have the medicine we have today. So here is Ethan Allen who has a daughter who is going to die within the week and she wants to talk with her daddy alone. And as the story goes, he walks into the house one day in the last week of her life and she says, "Daddy, I want to talk to you." So Ethan Allen sat down next to his dying daughter and she said, "Daddy, all my life Mommy has told me about Jesus. And since I was a baby, Mommy told me about how Jesus came to save us from our sins and He died on the hill of Calvary for our sins. And if I trust and believe in that then I will go to heaven. And Daddy I've always loved you, but I have heard you reject Jesus. All my life you have told me that what Mommy tells me is not true. Daddy, I wanted you to come to me today to ask you this; who do you want me to believe?" The story goes on to say that Ethan Allen got off of his chair and got on his knees and put his arms around his little girl and he said, "You believe your Mommy!" And today Ethan Allen is waiting for the first resurrection with a fourteen year-old daughter who will be there too.

The beauty of all of this is in the words of Jesus. "He that hears my words and believes on Him that sent me, you will have everlasting life, and you will not come into judgement but you will be passed from death into life!"

What is your passing going to be like?

REVELATION 21-22

Home Sweet Home

<u>Revelation 21</u>

1 And I saw a new heaven and a new earth: for the first heaven and the first earth were passed away; and there was no more sea.

2 And I John saw the holy city, new Jerusalem, coming down from God out of heaven, prepared as a bride adorned for her husband.

3 And I heard a great voice out of heaven saying, Behold, the tabernacle of God is with men, and he will dwell with them, and they shall be his people, and God himself shall be with them, and be their God.

4 And God shall wipe away all tears from their eyes; and there shall be no more death, neither sorrow, nor crying, neither shall there be any more pain: for the former things are passed away.

5 And he that sat upon the throne said, Behold, I make all things new. And he said unto me, Write: for these words are true and faithful.

6 And he said unto me, It is done. I am Alpha and Omega, the beginning and the end. I will give unto him that is athirst of the fountain of the water of life freely.

7 He that overcometh shall inherit all things; and I will be his God, and he shall be my son.

8 But the fearful, and unbelieving, and the abominable, and murderers, and whoremongers, and sorcerers, and idolaters, and all liars, shall have their part in the lake which burneth with fire and brimstone: which is the second death.

9 And there came unto me one of the seven angels which had the seven vials full of the seven last plagues, and talked with me, saying, Come hither, I will shew thee the bride, the Lamb's wife.

10 And he carried me away in the spirit to a great and high mountain, and shewed me that great city, the holy Jerusalem, descending out of heaven from God,

11 Having the glory of God: and her light was like unto a stone most precious, even like a jasper stone, clear as crystal;

12 And had a wall great and high, and had twelve gates, and at the gates twelve angels, and names written thereon, which are the names of the twelve tribes of the children of Israel:

13 On the east three gates; on the north three gates; on the south three gates; and on the west three gates.

14 And the wall of the city had twelve foundations, and in them the names of the twelve apostles of the Lamb.

15 And he that talked with me had a golden reed to measure the city, and the gates thereof, and the wall thereof.

16 And the city lieth foursquare, and the length is as large as the breadth: and he measured the city with the reed, twelve thousand furlongs. The length and the breadth and the height of it are equal.

17 And he measured the wall thereof, an hundred and forty and four cubits, according to the measure of a man, that is, of the angel.

18 And the building of the wall of it was of jasper: and the city was pure gold, like unto clear glass.

19 And the foundations of the wall of the city were garnished with all manner of precious stones. The first foundation was jasper; the second, sapphire; the third, a chalcedony; the fourth, an emerald;

20 The fifth, sardonyx; the sixth, sardius; the seventh, chrysolyte; the eighth, beryl; the ninth, a topaz; the tenth, a chrysoprasus; the eleventh, a jacinth; the twelfth, an amethyst.

21 And the twelve gates were twelve pearls: every several gate was of one pearl: and the street of the city was pure gold, as it were transparent glass.

22 And I saw no temple therein: for the Lord God Almighty and the Lamb are the temple of it.

23 And the city had no need of the sun, neither of the moon, to shine in it: for the glory of God did lighten it, and the Lamb is the light thereof.

24 And the nations of them which are saved shall walk in the light of it: and the kings of the earth do bring their glory and honour into it.

25 And the gates of it shall not be shut at all by day: for there shall be no night there.

26 And they shall bring the glory and honour of the nations into it.

27 And there shall in no wise enter into it any thing that defileth, neither whatsoever worketh abomination, or maketh a lie: but they which are written in the Lamb's book of life.

Revelation 22

1 And he shewed me a pure river of water of life, clear as crystal, proceeding out of the throne of God and of the Lamb.

2 In the midst of the street of it, and on either side of the river, was there the tree of life, which bare twelve manner of fruits, and yielded her fruit every month: and the leaves of the tree were for the healing of the nations.

3 And there shall be no more curse: but the throne of God and of the Lamb shall be in it; and his servants shall serve him:

4 And they shall see his face; and his name shall be in their foreheads.

5 And there shall be no night there; and they need no candle, neither light of the sun; for the Lord God giveth them light: and they shall reign for ever and ever.

6 And he said unto me, These sayings are faithful and true: and the Lord God of the holy prophets sent his angel to shew unto his servants the things which must shortly be done.

7 Behold, I come quickly: blessed is he that keepeth the sayings of the prophecy of this book.

8 And I John saw these things, and heard them. And when I had heard and seen, I fell down to worship before the feet of the angel which shewed me these things.

9 Then saith he unto me, See thou do it not: for I am thy fellowservant, and of thy brethren the prophets, and of them which keep the sayings of this book: worship God.

10 And he saith unto me, Seal not the sayings of the prophecy of this book: for the time is at hand.

11 He that is unjust, let him be unjust still: and he which is filthy, let him be filthy still: and he that is righteous, let him be righteous still: and he that is holy, let him be holy still.

12 And, behold, I come quickly; and my reward is with me, to give every man according as his work shall be.

13 I am Alpha and Omega, the beginning and the end, the first and the last.

14 Blessed are they that do his commandments, that they may have right to the tree of life, and may enter in through the gates into the city.

15 For without are dogs, and sorcerers, and whoremongers, and murderers, and idolaters, and whosoever loveth and maketh a lie.

16 I Jesus have sent mine angel to testify unto you these things in the churches. I am the root and the offspring of David, and the bright and morning star.

17 And the Spirit and the bride say, Come. And let him that heareth say, Come. And let him that is athirst come. And whosoever will, let him take the water of life freely.

18 For I testify unto every man that heareth the words of the prophecy of this book, If any man shall add unto these things, God shall add unto him the plagues that are written in this book:

19 And if any man shall take away from the words of the book of this prophecy, God shall take away his part out of the book of life, and out of the holy city, and from the things which are written in this book.

20 He which testifieth these things saith, Surely I come quickly. Amen. Even so, come, Lord Jesus.

21 The grace of our Lord Jesus Christ be with you all. Amen.

As these chapters were being read to me, I had my eyes closed. I was actually feeling the frustration that John must have felt when he was there witnessing everything in heaven and trying to put into man's words. I have to confess that after studying the book of Revelation for two years the frustrating thing is this, how do you talk about heaven? There is a verse in Corinthians that kept coming to me over and over again, *"eye hath not seen nor ear heard, nor has it entered into the heart of man the things that God has prepared for those who love Him."*

Home Sweet Home! I am so glad that I am a child of God. I know where I am going! It is incomprehensible!

A true story was recently shared with me that I want to share with you. A little twelve-year-old girl was blind from birth. Her mother was always with her since she was small always explaining everything to her. Whether they were in town or in the mountains or along the beach, her mother would try to explain what everything looked like. One day she had the opportunity to go under the surgeon's knife in a corrective surgery. When she came out of recovery, for the first time in her life she could see! She could see her mother's face and everything. When she first got the chance to walk outside, she came back in almost immediately and exclaimed, "Mother! Why didn't you tell me it was so wonderful?!"

Someday we will be walking the streets of gold and we will see the Apostle John and we are going to say, "John! Why didn't you tell us how wonderful it really is?!" And he will have the same kind of an answer that this mother had, "I tried."

There are over fourteen thousand words in the English language and more than that in the Greek, but all John could use to describe it was words. If you read Ezekiel you will see that he tries to express what heaven looks like. Isaiah tried it. You can read Revelation 21 and 22. You can re-read it and memorize it, but all you are going to be able to imagine is what you see here (in your imagination). Heaven is as great as Yosemite. Heaven is as great as Carmel. All you can do though is try to say it in human terms. John is seated here on an island, and he is looking up into the heavens, and what he sees, he tries to write it down. To say the least, how frustrating to put that kind of a picture into words!

Take this test. Imagine that there is a big white button in front of you. Here is the quiz; If you want to go to Heaven right now, push the white button. If you had that opportunity, knowing that you would escape death, if you pushed the white button, would you push it? And you would go immediately to Heaven. No death, just go immediately to Heaven. If you had that opportunity, would you push the white button? Would you really push it? THINK!

This test was taken in a church one time. The pastor told them that they had one hour to think about it. Then at the end of the hour they had the opportunity to push the white button. In just one hour, 30% of the people didn't push the button. Why? You see, the first thing that came to their mind was, "Well if I had the opportunity to go to Heaven right now, I would push the button, because I want to go to heaven." We all want to go to Heaven. But when they began to think about it, some of the younger ones said they want to go to Heaven **but not right now**… The reason was that people look at life and it is real, but Heaven seems so unreal.

I got up early this morning and I was going to try to draw the New Jerusalem. In conversation with my lovely companion, as I began to share with her on a scratch pad of what I thought maybe it looked like. "Oh my goodness! I do not want to live there!" It looks claustrophobic. It looks like I would be trapped inside. That is the way it is because we can't put it into human terms. So I didn't draw it. I have it in my mind but even then it hasn't entered into our hearts and our minds.

When I was young my grandparents would always let me ask questions. My brothers and I would ask grandpa and grandma anything that would come to our minds. And as I looked at Revelation 21 and 22, I decided to keep it that basic. As I studied different books on Revelation, these questions came up in these books. I am going to try to answer some of these questions. The questions will be like these: Where is heaven? What is heaven like? What will my body be like when I get there? What will we be doing when we get to heaven? Where does it talk about these questions in the Bible? Does it even say anything about what we will be doing in the Bible?

One thing I think we should understand as we begin as a biblical truth. Everything, everything that is really of importance is in heaven. Everything that is of any importance at all is in heaven! God, Jesus the Lamb, the Holy Spirit, the Saints, the Angels, your inheritance, your eternal home, and everything of importance is in heaven.

Where is it? Heaven is up. You might not think that sounds very profound, but that is what the Bible says. Anytime you see heaven being discussed in the Bible it is always *up*. Paul was stoned to death in the city of Lystra because he says in Corinthians, "I was caught up into paradise." And he goes on to say that when he arrived there he saw things and he heard things that he couldn't even put into human terms. Paul was frustrated with that. Paul was caught *up* into heaven. The Bible says in Acts 1:11 (two angels talking to the disciples that day) "Men, why are you gazing *up* into heaven? This same Jesus that was caught *up* into heaven will come back again." Revelation 4:1 (rapture chapter) "He called John *up* into heaven to witness the things that were going to come to pass." Heaven is *up*. 1 Thes. 4:17 "There will be a day when the trumpet sounds and we shall be caught up to be with Him." We are trapped in this known universe that we have. The Voyager has gone out seven hundred million miles now. The Hubble Telescope is out there taking pictures of galaxies that are two trillion light years away. Heaven is up and out there and it is so big and so vast and it is so "**out there.**" The Bible says in Jeremiah 23:24 "God says, I will fill all of heaven." Hell is always down. Separation is the key. Hell and Heaven are always separate.

What is heaven going to be like? In verse three it says that God will dwell with us. The minute some people read that, it is good enough for them. God is going to be with us and then in verse five it says that all things

367

will be new. Can you imagine what it will be like in glory with all things *new*? All former things are passed away. The Bible says in 2 Peter that all of that will melt with a fervent heat and all former things are passed away and all things are new. A new city, a new earth, a new Jerusalem, and new bodies.

I get excited when I sing songs about Heaven and think about strolling the streets and everything is new. But there is one thing that I will not be doing in Heaven as I stroll down the streets. No one will ask me how I'm doing. Everything in Heaven will be perfection. How much time do we spend on this planet talking about our problems, our pains, and our frustrations? We spend a lot of time doing that. Paul says, *"Set your affections on things above, not on things on the earth."* Why? Because our lives are hid with Christ in God. When we set our minds on eternal things it will actually change our attitude while we are still here on earth.

The Bible says that this is going to be in Heaven – roads and rivers, gardens and gates, walls of diamonds, streets of gold, fountains, singing and activities, banquets and food, fellowship, sights and sounds, light and thrones, homes and mansions, angels and saints, a city and an earth, harps and trumpets, symbols and songs and you can go on and on. All of these things in perfection.

Daniel 7:10 "We know how many are going to be around the throne because it tells us how many, 110 million just in a choir around the throne. There will be ten thousand times ten thousand and thousands of thousands. The calculator says that is 110 million, so there will be a minimum of that. I will be there and I actually might have a good voice. You may be able to pick up a harp and play it. If you want to play it for 5 trillion years, then go for it. It will be a time of immeasurable joy.

Let's look at the city through John's eyes. It says John was taken to this high mountain and John looked at the city. The Bible says that he got a measuring rod out and he measured it at fifteen hundred miles by fifteen hundred miles by fifteen hundred miles by fifteen hundred miles. If you would walk around it, it would be 6,000 miles and it is also 1,500 miles high. I like to think that the inside of the city is open. When you get into chapter 22, I believe you are walking into the city. There might be hundreds of miles of fountains and hanging gardens inside the city itself.

The space shuttle only went 200 miles up, yet this city will be 1,500 miles up. Look at it this way. If it goes up two miles and then it staggers another two miles and then another two miles clear up to 1,500 miles then you could have 250 billion miles of roadways all paved with gold. If God has 10 to 20 billion mansions there (and we do not know the number), but everyone could have hundreds of thousands of acres just for a lawn for your mansion. We can't even imagine it. It is fun to think about it, but we do not comprehend. That is just the city itself. It doesn't say much about the earth. I think in terms of the planet, but it may be something so much bigger than our sun right now/ We do not know. But I do know one thing and that is that it will be perfect.

As I began to walk through Revelation inside the city, I wondered what I would see. I began to look for the throne. And as we walk down through the center of the city, we see these fountains and the river of life and the tree of life on either side. And guess what? No church. The Bible says in **Revelation 21:3, 3 *"And I heard a great voice out of heaven saying, Behold, the tabernacle of God is with men, and he will dwell with them, and they shall be his people, and God himself shall be with them, and be their God."***

There is no need for a church or light or electricity any longer, because He is the light. But as we walk closer we see the tree and the throne.

4   And God shall wipe away all tears from their eyes; and there shall be no more death, neither sorrow, nor crying, neither shall there be any more pain: for the former things are passed away.

These are all things we have experienced in life that are negative to us. We do not like pain, mourning, or sorrow, so he says that when we get to this city there will not be any of this anymore. So what are we going to do and what are we going to be like?

1 John 3, *"We know that when He shall appear we shall be like Him."*

The Bible says that we will have new bodies in heaven. In a way that we can't comprehend there will be uninterrupted joy forever. Can you imagine that? Not for a moment, not for a year, not for 10 billion years, but all joy and all perfection forever more! As I get older, I think in terms of aches and pains in my body. There will be no more of that. I believe there will be the same personalities, but we will be in a glorified body enjoying perfection in a wonderful environment forever! It makes it precious to think about all the saints that have gone on before us who we will recognize. But what about Him? Immeasurable joy when we get there. *"If any man be in Christ he is a new creature." "We are partakers of a divine nature."* When we get there, it is in full perfection.

When you walk into that eternal city and you stand in the presence of God, there will be six of these *no mores*. There will be no more prayer. There is no need for prayer. What would you pray about? There is no need to pray for anyone. There will be no more repentance because you will have nothing to repent of. There will be no more witnessing, because everyone there is born again. There will be no more confession of sin, because there is no sin. There will be no more preaching. You will not listen to a preacher anymore because there is no need for preaching. There will be a ministry and you will be a kingdom of priests sharing the word somehow. There will be no more pain or suffering. It is all over with. But there will be something to replace all of these things. And there will be things to replace it.

There will be pleasure forever more. Psalm 16:11 *"In thy presence is pleasure forever more."* When I think of the activities that I am involved with here on earth and remember the things that give me great pleasure, I try to magnify that when I get there. There will be comfort and joy that we can't comprehend. Can you imagine not having even one split second of discomfort? That is amazing. There are pockets of time in our humanity when we are way up here. Everything is going good and we feel good and our circumstances are right and we are just up here. But there are also times in our lives that we are way down here. Things are not going right in our circumstances and it is not good. But in Heaven it will be perfection. Not one split second of interrupted joy. Wow!

Then I thought about love. Love is probably the greatest gift given to man through Jesus Christ. Love. We love each other, the body of Christ, even in spite of our different personalities. But when we get there, we will really understand what love is all about. Here it is sloppy-agape, but there it is perfection-agape. We will see maximum love personified not only in Him, but we will have that with our Savior.

When the Bible says that it has not even entered our minds what heaven will be like then we need to leave it there. But God gives us minds to imagine and think about positive things so I will mention this. We are not going to be in heaven sitting on a bench for trillions of years mumbling praises. That is not heaven. Sometimes people get this thinking that heaven will just be singing forever. But when we get to heaven we may want to sing forever.

Our God placed Adam and Eve in paradise to do what? To dress it and to keep and to enjoy it. Somehow in God's plans for heaven and eternity, there will be activity. There will be things to do. He will have many activities for us to enjoy. We do not know what it will be like, but there will be activity. I believe there will be productivity. We will be able to do things with our hands and minds and the Scripture and fellowship. It will be a time of enjoyment. You can ask Apostle Paul questions and eat all kinds of fruits by the tree of life and discuss the Scripture for ten thousand years. Then if you realized that you were going to meet someone you could just walk through walls… it doesn't matter.

God created us to praise Him and to glorify Him. He knows that for he rest of eternity, we will never cease to exist. He knows that the greatest joy we can experience is found in Him and whatever activity that involves. I get so excited as I study this. This doesn't even scratch the surface and the Lord is saying, "Amen". Just be patient, you will be there someday.

As you walk into chapter 22, it gets real serious.

1 And he showed me a pure river of water of life, clear as crystal, proceeding out of the throne of God and of the Lamb.

2 In the midst of the street of it, and on either side of the river, was there the tree of life, which bare twelve manner of fruits, and yielded her fruit every month: and the leaves of the tree were for the healing of the nations.

3   And there shall be no more curse: but the throne of God and of the Lamb shall be in it; and his servants shall serve him:

One dominant character in Heaven is God the Father, God the Son and God the Spirit. The central theme of the Bible is Jesus Christ and Him crucified Revelation 22:9 says "They will worship God." John was so quick to fall down, that he started to worship an angel. The angel had to tell him not to do that, but to worship Him. When we get there it will be about

Him. He says, "I fell down, I saw and I worshipped." This is a snapshot possibly of our first day in heaven. We will fall down to worship Him.

Then what about now? All I can say is this. When we really see and we really understand who He is, and what He has done for us, we will be in an attitude of falling down and worshiping Him now. People who are not humble and couldn't care less and think they are on their own path making it alone, that is not worship. When we recognize that there is nothing of ourselves and that without Him we can do nothing, then we can get to an attitude of worship. That is what John was doing as he walked into heaven.

4 And they shall see his face; and his name shall be in their foreheads.

5 And there shall be no night there; and they need no candle, neither light of the sun; for the Lord God giveth them light: and they shall reign for ever and ever.

6 And he said unto me, These sayings are faithful and true: and the Lord God of the holy prophets sent his angel to shew unto his servants the things which must shortly be done.

7   Behold, I come quickly: blessed is he that keepeth the sayings of the prophecy of this book.

You mean to say that this same Jesus who started before Genesis is speaking at the end of the book? These are Christ's words, "Behold I come quickly." He is telling John to get this right, He wants everyone who reads this book to know that there are only two destinations. There are not seven, but there are only two. When Jesus comes, there are only two things that you could hear. If you are in Christ today and He comes, then you will hear, "Come! Well done thou good and faithful servant. Come into my beloved." But if you are not in Him today then you will hear this word, "Depart! Depart into everlasting darkness." He wants us to listen. What a way to start this book. What a way to end a book. When everything in this book is about Him, what a way to start it. From the Genesis to the Revelation you hear those two words.

Genesis 7:1 "Come into the ark that you might be saved."

Revelation 22 "Come because I am coming quickly."

This is the final invitation to humanity. Isn't this really a summary of the entire gospel? In verse seventeen it says, "And the Spirit and the Bride say come and let him that heareth say come and let him that is thirsty say come and whosoever will let him take of the water of life freely." That is the Gospel. What is it saying here? It is saying that if you are thirsty and you are needy and your life is parched and dry and there is no hope forever, then you have to come to Christ! It is free! Salvation is a free gift. Whosoever will, no one is excluded. It doesn't matter who you are because, "Whosoever will take of the water of life freely." There are no restrictions whatsoever. Its starts in paradise and ends in paradise. I find that so fascinating. Genesis started in paradise in the cool of the evening. There are about 3 gardens in-between the Garden of Eden and this one and everyone has to do with Him. He was there in the Garden of Eden with Adam and Eve. Then He went to the Garden of Gethsemane and He prayed the prayer and He suffered for you and me. And then the Bible says in John, in the place that He was crucified there was a garden and that is the Garden Tomb. He was resurrected the third day. The Bible says that if you believe what took place in each of these Garden's, you will then experience the Garden in Paradise! Our God goes by way of "The Gardens."

Why is He saying this? Not only because of this tribulation period, but all the history of man, God's global purposes for humanity are just about over. When the final trump sounds then it is over at that point. There will not be someone running along the boat trying to get into the ark. They will hear, "Depart from me."

The greatest work we will ever do is to believe on Him. The Bible says that the greatest gift that was ever given was His Son Jesus. You will never match that gift. *"For God so loved the world that He gave His only Son."* And if you believe that, then you will have life. The greatest decision ever made was made by a man who was living with pigs. There he was eating with the pigs and then all of the sudden he remembered his father's house. In Luke 15 he says, *"I will arise and go home."* The greatest decision you have every made, if you have made it, is to go home by way of the cross. *"I will arise and go to Father's house."* "Come home!"

John 14 *"In my Father's house are many mansions, if it were not so I would have told you, I go to prepare a way for you and if I go to prepare a way for you then I will come and receive you unto myself that where I am there you may be also."* He prepared a way through the cross that you may someday go to the mansion. That is the greatest promise you or I have ever had. That gives us the hope that we have within us today.

The greatest opportunity for the soul of man is decision time. Amos says there are multitudes in the valley of decision. There are people trying to decide what is right and what is wrong but they just need to come to Christ. *"Today is the day of Salvation."*

If you have never heard the Gospel, this is the gospel. The good news is that God loved us. The Gospel is that Christ came, He lived, and He died for our sins. He was buried and rose again according to the Scriptures. If we believe that truth, and place our faith in the provision that He has made at Calvary, the Bible says that by **faith** we can have **a new life**. That is salvation.

There are two things that I would like to leave with you as we come to the end of Revelation:

1. If you are on the road to glory and you know it, then do not be content to go there alone! If you know you are saved and you are confident that you are in Christ and you know you are on the road to glory, then don't be content to go there alone. Show someone else the way to Jesus, so that they too can settle forever, Eternity in their hearts!

2. If you have no interest in Heaven, then you have a very serious earthly problem. If you have no interest whatsoever in Heaven and it hasn't crossed your mind to push the white button, then you have a real earthly problem. Christ said. "Come unto me, all of you that are weak and heavy burdened.....I will give you rest!!" It is free! You need to come to the foot of the cross and open up your heart. Then place your faith, where Christ places your sins, (on the cross) and be on the road to "HOME SWEET HOME." Because if you die outside of Him, what then?

When all the great planets and plants of our cities
Have turned our their last finished work
When our merchants have made their last bargain
And dismissed the last tired clerk
When our banks have raked in the last dollar
And have paid out the last dividend
When the judge of the earth says
"closed for the night" and he asks for the balance,

what then?
When the choir has sang its last anthem
And the preacher has said his last prayer
When the people have heard their last sermon
And the sound has died out in the air
When the Bible lies closed on the pulpit
And the pews are all empty of men
When each one stands facing his record
And the great book is opened,
What then?
When the actors have played their last drama
And the mimic has made his last fun
When the movies have flashed the last picture
And the billboard displayed its last run
When the crowds seeking pleasure have vanished
And have gone into darkness again
And the world that rejected its Savior
Is asked for a reason why,
What then?
When the bugles last call sinks in silence
And the long marching columns stand still
When the captain has given his last orders
And they have captured the last fort and last hill
When the flag has been hauled down from the masthead
And the wounded of field have checked in
When the trumpet of all ages has sounded
And we stand before Him,
What then?
John 20:31 "These things are written that you might believe and that believing you might have life through His name!"

Breinigsville, PA USA
17 June 2010
240041BV00001B/3/P